Saints & Society

The Two Worlds of Western

Saints & Society

Christendom, 1000 - 1700

Donald Weinstein and Rudolph M. Bell

The University of Chicago Press
Chicago and London

The University of Chicago Press, Chicago 60637
The University of Chicago Press, Ltd., London

Library of Congress Cataloging in Publication Data

Weinstein, Donald, 1926–
    Saints and society.

    Includes index.
    1. Christian saints—Cult—Europe.   I. Bell, Rudolph M.
II. Title.
BX4659.E85W44   235'.2   82-7972
ISBN 0-226-89055-4 (cloth)   AACR2
ISBN 0-226-89056-2 (paper)

To Traian Stoianovich
and Warren I. Susman—
splendid historians,
dear friends

Contents

Illustrations

Acknowledgments

Friends, colleagues, wives, students, and some who were initially strangers helped us in making this book with their encouragement, cheerful labor, and strenuous criticism. We learned from all of them, and we thank them.

Donna D'Eugenio Galer and Francesco Parise assisted us in setting up the initial project in a graduate seminar at Rutgers. The American Philosophical Society and the Rutgers University Research Council gave us money for research trips abroad. In Rome, Father John O'Malley, S.J., helped us gain permission to consult the special canonization archives of the Archivio Segreto Vaticano. Père Yvon Baudouin, O.M.I., was a gracious guide in the archives of the S. Congregatio per le Cause dei Santi. In Florence Ivaldo Baglioni was generous as always in sharing with us his masterly knowledge of the Biblioteca Nazionale Centrale. John Lenaghan in Florence and Joyce Salisbury in Madrid came to our rescue by locating several "impossible to find" works.

We are also grateful to the staffs of the Biblioteca Apostolica Vaticana, the library of the Pontificia Universitas Gregoriana, the Biblioteca Riccardiana, Saint Bonaventure University Library, the Free Library of Philadelphia, Saint Vincent College and Archabbey Libraries, the library of the Union Theological Seminary, the Widener Library, the Folger Shakespeare Library, the University of Illinois Library, Rutgers University Library, the University of Arizona Library, and the Speer Library of the Princeton Theological Seminary.

Analysis of our data was made possible through the resources of the computer centers of Rutgers University and the University of Arizona. Willis Lamb generously provided indispensable technical help in preparing the manuscript.

The following people read and criticized drafts at various stages: Edward Barnhart, Marvin Becker, Laura Bell, Maureen Babula, Paul Clemens (to whom a special word of thanks for various emergency missions), Traian Stoianovich, and Warren I. Susman.

Beverly J. Parker took the major responsibility for finding and selecting our illustrations, with timely assists from Fabio Bisogni, Donald Garfield, and Padre Mario Milani. Marilyn Bradian heroically typed and retyped the manuscript, with help from Dorothy Donnelly, Nikki Matz, Maudi Mazza, and Dawn Polter.

Finally, a word about the nature of our collaboration in this study and the resulting book. We came to the idea of the enterprise during a conversation that included saints and historical quantification. Since then our collaboration has been extremely close, so that, apart from the resolution of certain technical problems where we brought our very different specialties into play, we would ourselves find it impossible to separate our respective contributions. In the actual writing of the book we did not divide separate parts between us but conceived, wrote, and rewrote every sentence jointly. Our final acknowledgment, therefore, is to each other: we immensely enjoyed working together; it cemented an already good friendship.

Introduction
The Historian and the Hagiographer

Our theme is the two worlds of sainthood, those rival republics of temporal becoming and spiritual being between which saints moved as dual citizens. Our subjects are the men and women and children from the eleventh to the seventeenth century who sought spiritual perfection, came to be venerated as holy, and received some degree of recognition as saints among Christians. The questions we ask concern the perceived actions and the social and religious contexts of these holy people. Who were they? How did they come to pursue spiritual perfection? How did their fathers, mothers, husbands, and wives deal with them when they began to respond to inner voices, private visions, and holy evangelists? What did saints do that captured the attention, and ultimately the affection, of the faithful? How did communities—monasteries, towns, guilds, princely courts—respond to a holy person in their midst, and what did they hope to obtain in return for their veneration and their prayers?

Questions about saints and their societies have been asked and answered before, occasionally by admiring companions and hagiographers, more frequently and systematically by modern biographers and historians who have collected, sifted, and analyzed the surviving vitae and other documents of the hagiographic record. In a way, modern investigations of the history of sainthood take up again the medieval division between the Nominalists and the Realists, between those who sought truth in individual cases and those who held that particulars have only an imperfect share of the reality that lies in the collective whole.[1] Not surprisingly, in the study of saints the Nominalists have dominated the field. To go no further back than the seventeenth century, when modern hagiographic scholarship

1

began with Jean Bolland's launching of the *Acta Sanctorum*, and continuing well into the present century with the critical studies of the great Bollandist Hippolyte Delehaye, the study of sainthood has been primarily the study of the lives—or more accurately, of the vitae—of individual saints.[2] And when scholars have allowed themselves to look beyond the documents to the underlying reality, when they have passed from text to context, they usually have taken very small steps. The complexities of hagiographic sources and the problems of their interpretation dictated that inferences be very conservative, that generalizations be kept to a minimum, and that saints' lives be dealt with one at a time. The continuing vitality of this approach is demonstrated by such recent triumphs of hagiographical scholarship as Charles W. Jones's study of the legend of Saint Nicholas, in which the author reveals in a masterly way "the macrocosmic imagination through observation of a microcosmic image."[3]

The macrocosmic approach, on the other hand, or what we have called hagiographic Realism, is a relatively late trend with few such successes to its credit. An early, unsung exception is John Mecklin's remarkable book *The Passing of the Saint*, which presents a composite picture of the saint as a type that mirrored the changing values of European society from early Christianity to modern times.[4] Mecklin was writing sociology in the grand style of Max Weber, and his ideal saintly type was as much a philosophical meditation as an empirical construct. Like Weber himself, he has had few imitators, with most Realists preferring a more "scientific" approach.

An innovator in this respect was Ludwig Hertling, a medievalist who pioneered in constructing a typology of saintly virtues in the Middle Ages by studying hagiographic vitae.[5] Another was the sociologist Ptirim A. Sorokin, whose study of altruistic love and creative genius was partly based on Catholic saints.[6] Sorokin was interested in the saint as a social type, and he constructed a composite picture of the saintly personality by taking what he called a "statistical consensus" based on a list of 3,090 saints for whom he compiled such information as sex, nationality, race, "occupational or economic composition," routes to saintliness, and age at death. Aside from the historical problems he incurred by applying modern categories and value judgments to this two-thousand-year roster, Sorokin removed himself still further from his subjects by relying for his information on Butler's *Lives of the Saints*, a popular compendium of sketches culled mainly from the *Acta Sanctorum* and retold and edited for an English-speaking audience.[7]

Another pioneering macrocosmic study is the 1955 article by Katherine and Charles George.[8] The Georges were interested in the social status of saints, a rather more historical, if not more objective, question than Sorokin's search for the secret of saintly creative genius, and they made some useful observations about the relation between spiritual and social elites. Unfortunately they repeated Sorokin's mistake of gathering their information from Butler's *Lives,* and they adopted an overly simple social classification of nobility, middle class, and proletarian; but with Sorokin they pointed the way to more refined studies of the same type such as Michael Goodich's 1972 doctoral dissertation, "The Dimensions of Thirteenth Century Sainthood," an examination of the behavior patterns of more than five hundred saints based on familiarity with the earliest sources and using rather more sophisticated techniques of quantification.[9]

Not that a macrocosmic approach demands statistical procedures. Counting has been minimal in the work of some of the most successful of the hagiographical Realists, who have preferred to go about their business in the more usual impressionistic way; but indispensable have been their critical reading of their textual sources, their specialized knowledge of the period, and their careful framing of questions that reasonably admit of credible answers. Models of this kind are Frantisek Graus's study of Merovingian saints in relation to their society, Joseph-Claude Poulin's study of the Carolingian ideal of sanctity, and Simone Roisin's investigation of changing ideals of sainthood as revealed in thirteenth-century Cistercian hagiography.[10] A more restricted example is Romeo De Maio's study of the heroic ideal in Counter Reformation canonizations.[11]

Still, as Pierre Delooz has pointed out, a sociology of sainthood has yet to be written. Delooz himself laid out some of the problems and requirements of such a work, not underestimating its difficulties, but at the same time suggesting the rich possibilities it offers for understanding three civilizations—Hellenic, Byzantine, and Western—for studying the collective mentalities of societies, and for exploring the connections between sociology, theology, and religion.[12] His method would combine the traditional philological skills of the hagiographical scholar and the scientific techniques of the modern quantifier and, while he does not say so, would undoubtedly require the combined efforts of a research *équipe,* for only a team of specialists working in many countries and over a long period of time could be expected to mount such an enterprise.

Our aim is relatively more modest, being limited to a sample of the saints of Western Christendom over a period of about seven hundred years, though some may find this too an excessively ambitious undertaking. We enlist with the latter-day Realists: sainthood, not individual saints, is our primary emphasis. We begin, of course, with specific saints, but we deal with them as components of a collectivity, the parameters of which we are seeking to understand. The period of our study, 1000 to 1700, commences as the church of Rome was beginning to fulfill its claims as the spiritual and ecclesiastical center of Latin Christendom, a process highlighted by the late-eleventh-century papacy of Gregory VII and completed at the turn of the thirteenth century by Innocent III, who extended papal power in Europe even into the temporal sphere. It includes the difficult years of the Babylonian Captivity, when the papal court was in Avignon, of the Great Schism, when there were two, then three, rival popes, the era of Hussite heresy, Conciliarism, and, at the very end of the fifteenth century, the confrontation between the worldly Borgia pope, Alexander VI, and the apocalyptic Dominican preacher Girolamo Savonarola. Our study continues through the era of the Catholic Reformation and Counter Reformation, when the church rallied against Protestantism and began to establish its modern contours.

During this period the cult of saints flourished as a major expression of Catholic doctrine and of popular piety. Connections between sainthood and hierarchy were many. As early as the eleventh century the papacy attempted to bring the process of official recognition of saints under its control, but not for another six hundred years was that control firmly established. This was an era when canonization was used by the prelacy to reward its outstanding members as well as to give permanent recognition to the heathen kings and queens who brought their subjects into the Christian fold. Sainthood was also a powerful medium for teaching religious values: monastic reformers projected the renewed ideals of Benedict of Norcia and sanctioned such radical versions of the apostolic life as those pursued by Francis of Assisi and Dominic de Guzmàn.

Saints were not, however, merely complacent supporters of papal policy, nor did the ideals of sainthood entirely reflect the mentality of clerical elites. In the fourteenth and fifteenth centuries especially, when church leadership faltered, saints' cults gave expression to innovative forms of piety that served the needs of lay people. Later, in the sixteenth and seventeenth centuries, the Reformation papacy was well served by the militant Catholicism of such holy people as Ignatius Loyola, Francis Xavier, Teresa of Avila, Philip Neri, and many others; but saints responded to religious impulses that did not wait upon official initiative or direction. Apart from its role in the history of the official church, the pursuit of holiness was a search for forms of individual religious expression that were yet deeply bound up with piety as defined by society and culture.

Throughout our study we will use the term "piety" to mean the many manifestations of religious feeling and behavior that, it seems to us, revolve around two impulses. The first of these is the need for purity, for a feeling of spiritual perfection, which comes from separating oneself from material and carnal thoughts and acts—what William James described as "the cleansing of existence from brutal and sensual elements." The second component of piety is the feeling of reverence, the emotions of love, awe, and fear that believers direct toward divinity and its attributes. Saints were those who were recognized as having experienced so much reverence and achieved such a degree of purity that they had transcended the sinfulness of ordinary existence. Thus they took their places among the heavenly host and themselves became objects of reverence to the rest of the faithful, acting as intercessors for divine favor on behalf of those among whom they once had lived. Through their love of God, saints had achieved this superior state; now their love for God's creatures moved them to use their merit on behalf of human need.

Though piety was ideally a selfless quest for purity and a powerful feeling of reverence for divinity, most Christians were inclined to expect some material benefit in exchange for fasts, pilgrimages, and prayers. Saintly piety was active, world-denying, God-seeking. Ordinary piety was more likely to be passive and favor-seeking, the majority of the faithful blurring the goals of purification and reverence with those of petition and covenant. Besides, Christian piety could be exercised vicariously, through the agency of priests with special sacramental powers and saints who had achieved a degree of spiritual perfection. Our concern is not to make judgments about the quality of Christian piety by distinguishing beween some notion of authentic faith and superstitious or magical practice, but to examine the actual beliefs and practices of professed Christians in the long period covered by our study. When we speak of "popular" piety we refer to the more or less spontaneous, at least partially autonomous, religious ideas and impulses of men and women who were neither sophisticated doctrinalists nor members of the upper echelon of the clerical hierarchy. The distinction between clergy and lay people was not so neat in the Middle Ages as we moderns might suppose. The former contained many whose religious understanding and behavior were scarcely more sophisticated or authoritative than those of the latter. Especially with regard to the recognition of new saints, the veneration of holy men and women even during their lifetimes by the people of a given locale usually transcended any formal division between clergy and laity. Still, the division itself has a history, a point to which we will return presently.

The cult of saints illustrates perfectly how piety embraced the pursuit of spiritual perfection, the feeling of reverence, and the expectation of divine help in this world. We will show that the common conception linked all three and held that God bestowed supernatural power upon those who had achieved a high spiritual state. But the chasm between the saint's quest for an otherworldly perfection and the crowd's thirst for this-worldly miracles was bridged only imperfectly by medieval dialectic. Venerated for their holiness but invoked for their power, saints stood as a reproach to the wonder-seeking crowd even as they served its humble needs. This paradox of the two spheres of sainthood is one of the themes that runs through our study.

We study saints in order to understand piety; we study piety in order to understand society, for it is one of our basic premises that the pursuit as well as the perception of holiness mirrored social values and concerns. We see piety neither as an abstraction nor as an autonomous category of human experience. In this we take our stand with the sociologists of religion who build upon and modify Emile Durkheim's work to treat religion as a social product. Notwithstanding Rudolf Otto's contention that the idea of the holy is a fundamental category of human experience, and William James's observation that there is a "certain composite photograph of universal saintliness, the same in all religions," we maintain that, historically, such universality found expression in concrete situations and that these varied with the social context. Consequently, we study sainthood not only for what it reveals about religious feelings and ideas but also for what it can tell us about European society from the High Middle Ages to the early modern period.

Obviously sainthood is not a complete index of piety, much less of society in general. Our observations can only be partial as well as incomplete, but they may help to illuminate certain issues that have been all too little understood, ranging from medieval attitudes toward children to adolescent rebellion to marital tension. The study of sainthood also sheds light on the great differences between official church doctrine and the popular canons that influenced religious belief and practice no less for being unspoken, even unconscious. Yet we stop short of Mecklin's contention that "sainthood is a rationalization of human experience," for this, it seems to us, gives too little consideration both to the individuality of the saints and to the universality of religious need. The ground between the two poles of individuality and universality is social and historical, and this is the ground upon which we have built our study.

The very definition of sainthood, however, raises questions about using saints' lives to shed light upon broader social issues and collective mentalities. One question we have had to ask ourselves concerns typicality. Since saints were exemplars of extraordinary holiness, believed to have achieved immunity from the ordinary human frailties and ascendancy over the various temptations of the flesh—since, in short, the spiritually perfect were considered a class apart—how can we make inferences about the generality of believers or about "ordinary" lives from the evidence of hagiography? This question is not peculiar to the study of saints; everyone who tries to make connections between great individuals and their historical milieus soon must ask how and in what respects their subjects are representative. To be sure, with saints the special supernatural dimension complicates the question of typicality or representativeness, but the components of the problem remain essentially the same: What can we learn about Dante's Florentine world from his life and thought? What can we learn from the life of St. Francis about Assisi during his time?

Our answer is that it depends very much on the kinds of information we are looking for and the kinds of inferences we are trying to make. In the first place, there are the questions of social milieu, of class, family, education, and the social mores that accompany these institutions. It seems not very dangerous to assume that not even St. Francis was unique in these respects, that he shared the material and social experiences of his compatriots and his class. And, indeed, the stories of his life, particularly those that originated among his companions and contemporaries, shed a good deal of light on the burgher world of Assisi. The problem here is twofold: first, to determine whether the information reflects the world of the saint and his contemporaries or the experience of a much later biographer; second, to distinguish between those details that are intended to establish the saint's relation to the supernatural community of all saints and that belong, therefore, to hagiography *tout court*, and those that connect the saint to the natural order, to family, peers, class, and the broader society, and therefore belong to history. This differs in every case, and so there is no simple rule of procedure that will apply universally. We have tried to exploit the vitae and other material for clues about the social and cultural environments of our subjects without forgetting that we are dealing with a very special kind of subject. In every case we have been careful to note the proximity of the source to the saint's own time, and in the Appendix on Sources the reader will find a case-by-case indication of the quality and dating of extant documentation.

In the second place, there are questions regarding the saint as a religious exemplar, hero, or leader. Obviously, saints were unlike most of their contemporaries in the degree and quality of their religious dedication and zeal, and in some cases also in the originality of their forms of piety. In this sense they were unrepresentative, and it would be dangerous to assume that their own religiousness might be generalized to the larger population, or even to the social and religious groups to which they belonged. But there is more than one way representativeness may be understood. It may, for instance, have been inherent in the stimulus rather than in the response. Saints who were highly atypical in their choices of religious vocation may yet have been quite typical in the moral or spiritual situation that inspired those vocations. Leadership implies a following, and followers assemble around a leader, or a cult figure, because they perceive that they will thereby satisfy certain needs—needs, to be sure, that the leader may have made explicit for the first time.

One way we can make the saint's very atypicality work for us here is by applying a kind of structural analysis. For example, St. Francis's spiritual goals were fashioned as an explicit counter to the besetting sins of his class and place. His embrace of Lady Poverty, while deriving from the ancient evangelical tradition of the *vita apostolica*, was his timely solution to the anxieties generated by such worldly Assisians as the merchant Ser Bernardone, Francis's father. It seems reasonable to assume that many thirteenth-century Italians, and soon others, came to see Francis as the embodiment of those virtues that they were able to honor only in the breach. They themselves sought profit but conceded that poverty was a higher goal. They pursued worldly honors but acknowledged that humility was more pleasing to God. They gave priority to the needs of themselves and their families but recognized that Christ commanded them to put their fellow creatures first. Our premise here is that a society's heroes reflect, through antithesis and projection, its real condition and its longings.[13]

Granting that saints are, in these respects, representatives of their social milieus, can we assume that the information about them contained in the hagiographic texts is trustworthy? The great Bollandist Delehaye has put us on our guard against confusing saints with their legends. Hagiographers wrote to inspire their readers, to honor their saint, and to make a case for canonization by demonstrating that the venerable person was a member of the supernatural community of saints. Hagiographers were, as Delehaye said, poets, not historians or biographers. How can we tell whether the figure who emerges from their pages was a real historical person rather than a creation of legend, myth, and propaganda?

This is a far more serious problem for the saints of the first millennium than for those of the period of our study, when critical standards were beginning to change and interest in collecting and conveying biographical information began to manifest itself. Between the eleventh and the seventeenth centuries hagiographical material ranges from the traditional legend and miracle tale to sophisticated biographies rich in detail and delineation of personality, with the preponderance somewhere between these two extremes. But the problem remains: facts are relatively few and tend to be subordinated to myth; therefore they are to be treated with skepticism. Whenever possible we have tried to cross-check our information, and we have tried not to claim a greater degree of historical accuracy than the vitae are able to provide.

Above all, it is necessary to discriminate between different sorts of purported facts—to decide which are likely to have been embroidered, invented, or borrowed from stories of other saints—and this requires that we keep in mind the hagiographer's purposes. For example, as the Georges pointed out, there was a strong temptation to elevate the social status of saints. This was particularly true in the earlier medieval centuries, when society's prejudices ran in favor of nobility. For this reason, as well as because medieval class distinctions were extraordinarily complicated, we have tried to exercise restraint in dealing with information about a saint's social origins. The simple designation of class, such as "noble" or "peasant," is less valuable than more extensive descriptions of the material circumstances of the saint's background. At the same time, we have been grateful for any information we have been able to glean from the vitae about such matters as the number of brothers and sisters a holy person had, on the ground that this kind of information was not crucial to the main purposes of the hagiographer and therefore was unlikely to have been invented or distorted (and for the same reason, unfortunately, was too often omitted altogether.) Where it was possible to find accurate biographical detail we have done so; facts such as where and when the holy person was born, specifics relevant to social class, whether there were brothers and sisters, whether and how the saint was educated, and when the saint died make up the social patterns and provide the setting for the struggles and triumphs that allow us to portray a historical life. We also tried to verify the saint's worldly activities, such as service to kings or popes, peacemaking, preaching, missionary activity, charitable work, and the like.

Such public actions, however, never constituted the entire life of a saint. A great part of most hagiographic vitae consists of observations and assertions that are not subject to empirical verification. Saintliness was gauged in the judgments of beholders and devotees who were at various degrees of remove from the saint, and they were inevitably subjective. We can document that a saint was perceived to be humble, or chaste, or heroically penitent; within limits we can even determine the importance of a particular virtue in the reputation of a saint; but it is the *perception* we are documenting, the *reputation* we are gauging, more than the actual fact of the saint's acts of humility or charity. This is the case whether a saint was a real historical personage with a verifiable holy life, or a person for whom a reputation for sanctity was somehow constructed, or a purely mythical figure, such as we now know St. Christopher to have been. As Delooz summed it up so well, "the reputation of sanctity is the collective mental representation of someone as a saint, whether based on a knowledge of facts that have *really* happened, or whether based on facts that have been at least in part *constructed* if not entirely imagined. But in truth, all saints, more or less, appear to be constructed in the sense that being necessarily saints in consequence of a reputation created by others and a role that others expect of them, they are remodelled to correspond to collective mental representations."

By clarifying this distinction between the saint as historical person and as construct, the creation of other people's perceptions and expectations, Delooz launched the critical study of the sociology of canonization. But a crucial question remains: Who are those "other people" whose perceptions we are attempting to gauge? Can a study of changing ideas of sanctity lead to valid inferences about some aspects of society as well as about changing modes of popular piety? At the heart of the matter lies the circumstance that our sources are predominantly clerical: most hagiographers were clerics, to some degree removed from the rest of society by occupation and training. A majority of *these* were regular clergy, monks and friars still further distinguishable from the rest by their ascetic vocation. How representative were they of the society at large? Can we say that their religious views reflect the views of the laity who made up the bulk of the population, or that their social experience matched that of men and women living "in the world"? To ask these questions is to acknowledge that our sources, and therefore our findings, are subject to certain limitations of perspective and perception, the degree of limitation being exactly the degree to which clerical hagiographers constituted a separate subculture.

But what was that degree? The most obvious social demarcations were those of education and sexual status: clerics were literate and celibate, lay people were neither. But any medievalist knows that these supposedly stark differences were far from general or absolute; degrees of education and chastity were many among the clergy, as they were among the laity. Not all clerics were sexually pure, nor were all laity innocent of letters. Some religious enthusiasts who never took clerical orders practiced celibacy, while Latin as well as vernacular education was far more widespread (and increasing) among the knightly as well as the merchant class in the twelfth and thirteenth centuries than we used to think. As Ralph V. Turner recently put it, the use of the term *clericus* was "maddeningly imprecise."[14]

To be sure, the term is less precise for regular than for secular clergy. Those set apart by contemporary usage as "the Religious" because they sought spiritual perfection in taking vows of poverty, chastity, and obedience were a recognizable group with an ethos all their own, and this should be reflected in their writings. Again, however, it is not clear what we may assume about them. Where do we place the mendicant clergy in this scheme? Friars were Religious; they were members of regular orders who had taken the triple vows and presumably would share the ascetic outlook of cloistered monks. But they lived in the world if not of it, among the laity whose spiritual welfare they were dedicated to serving. Even among the monastic clergy, presuppositions about a common clerical outlook are difficult to sustain. What do we make of the many members of the Benedictine order, Augustinian canons, and others who were lawyers, university professors, royal and princely counselors, and feudal landlords? Surely they had at least as much in common with the experiences and outlook of lay professionals and aristocrats as with those of their more retiring brethren.

The problem of establishing the boundaries between clerical and lay cultures is further compounded by social class. It is a truism of medieval sociology that while the clergy constituted a single juridical order or estate, it did not constitute a single social class. Bishops, abbots, and other high dignitaries belonged to the aristocracy and were likely to be "wellborn"; simple village priests usually came from the local peasantry; the rest of the regular and secular clergy were distributed along the intermediate rungs of the social ladder. The range of differences in experience and outlook as well as in the sense of identification with the laity must have been considerable.

The foregoing is not meant to explain away the clerical bias of our sources, only to suggest some cautions against an overly schematic formulation of the problem. Distinctions between religious attitudes of clergy and laity have been emphasized lately in numerous studies of the medieval emergence of lay piety, the efforts of lay men and women to find avenues of more direct spiritual experience than were afforded them in the clerically dominated structures of official Christianity and to formulate a religion in the world that served their special needs. We believe this has been a salutary tendency, and we support it in the course of our study, but it is important not to exaggerate the differences between medieval clerical and lay religious experience. Much of late medieval and Renaissance lay piety called upon clerical models of belief and practice, and to a considerable extent it was conceived and carried on under the guidance of the clergy. The extent to which autonomous structures of lay religious expression emerged varied considerably in different regions and times, as Lionel Rothkrug's recent studies of popular religion and shrines in pre-Reformation Germany suggest.[15] In what ways lay notions of sanctity differed from clerical ideas is not at all clear, mainly because we have so few lay sources, but it seems reasonable to assume that whatever the differences may have been they consisted not so much in lay *ideas* about sanctity, where the laity was dependent upon clerical instruction, as in the lay *use* of sanctity—in other words, in the laity's emphasis upon the practical benefits of cultic veneration. Even here, moreover, differences could not have been uniformly great when we consider that clerics were so often responsible for promoting the popular cult of a particular saint not only by writing a vita but also by publicizing the relics and the shrine itself.

If medieval clerical and lay religious perceptions about saints were so intertwined that it is difficult and sometimes misguided to try to separate them, the situation ought to be clearer for the Counter Reformation. In the history of clerical-lay relations the mid-sixteenth century was a watershed. Jean Delumeau writes that the seminaries of the Counter Reformation "engineered what amounted to an 'ecclesial revolution.'"[16] The Council of Trent etched the distinction between cleric and lay in a series of awesome decrees that affirmed transubstantiation, the objective power of the sacraments, the sacrificial character of the Mass, the equal authority of ecclesiastical tradition alongside scriptural revelation, and many other matters. By such means as catechetical formulas, renewed emphasis upon preaching, and indexes of forbidden books, Mother Church sought to form and control the minds of her sons and daughters. Confraternities, since the thirteenth century the primary agency of lay spirituality, were brought firmly under clerical supervision, as were most other forms of popular religious devotion. As James Obelkevich puts it: "the relatively open situation passed . . . as the Reformation and Counter Reformation gathered force. The militant clergy of both faiths sought to impose on the masses what was essentially an elite pattern of religion, inaugurating an era of one-way religious pressure from the top down—and equally an era of increasing resistance and partial conformity from below." The same writer recognizes, however, that the divergence between clerical and popular religions was a development of the eighteenth century, while Jean Delumeau observes that the ecclesial revolution was far from becoming a reality before that time: "in France and most Catholic countries," he writes, the influence of the seminaries "was almost unnoticeable until the late seventeenth century."[17]

Since our study ends at 1700, before the polarization of two distinct religious cultures, it does not seem necessary to belabor the point that we must be careful not to equate the perceptions of clerical hagiographers with the general laity's ideas about saints. Neither should we undermine the value of hagiographic evidence by overemphasizing the disjuncture between clergy and laity. One important trend in recent studies is the reconsideration of the deeply embedded assumption that channels between elite and popular culture ran in a single direction—from the top down. On the contrary, the flow was multidirectional, and often the lines are so intertwined as to suggest that the structure of religiousness was not purely hierarchical. Bakhtin's brilliant study of Rabelais's masterpiece showed how it vibrated with popular motifs and perceptions.[18] Rothkrug's work on German shrines illuminates the ways popular piety furnished intellectual problems and subject matter for such lofty theologians as Aquinas and Ockham. The hagiographer was no less—and probably more—enmeshed in this complex circuitry. More often than not, even before he had begun to write the story of his saint, fact was already being transmuted into legend; the holy life was being recreated by the imagination and the needs of the faithful. The hagiographer's main contribution was to shape the received material according to the current, partly implicit, pressures of the saint-making process, including the tastes of his bishop, the interests of his house or order, political interests, and, not least, the expectations of local devotees, both clerical and lay. In short, as Delehaye pointed out, the hagiographer was not a biographer, at least in the modern sense. He was an agent of a mythmaking mechanism that served a variety of publics, and he took his cues where he found them, often from very modest, nonclerical sources.[19]

Thus, in interpreting the hagiographic materials that constitute our sources we have followed a pragmatic and flexible set of procedural guidelines. Our stance is cautious: we are aware, and hope our readers are aware, that in hagiography legend presides over fact, and that the end product is as often myth as history. We try to turn this to our advantage by setting our sights on the collective mentality rather than on the uncertain empirical record. Our "facts," then, are perceptions. Our perceptions are largely those of clerics, the compilers and shapers of the saint's story, and this too dictates caution, particularly as we proceed into the last century and a half of our study, the Counter Reformation period when piety was moving, albeit unevenly, into a dimorphic mode. The more closely the hagiographer confined himself to delineating the pattern of virtues the holy person shared with the entire community of saints, the more we are inclined to interpret this as an "official," or at least clerical, view. However, when his account departs from the routine pattern, when he furnished evidence of the saint's special qualities, and when his portrait conveys information about the secular aspects of the saint's life, such as details about family, we feel justified in interpreting the material more freely.

The distinction is roughly analogous to the difference between a thirteenth-century and a late-fifteenth-century altarpiece. The earlier painting—most likely commissioned, if not painted, by a cleric—is strictly iconic. It serves its devotional purpose by presenting a virtually abstract, symbolic image—Madonna, or crucifixion, or saint—with a very limited range of historical references. The fifteenth-century painting, very possibly commissioned by a lay patron or a confraternity of laymen, is richly allusive. It retains a religious purpose, but its images resonate with political, social, ideological, even private references. The first painting is of great interest to historians of art and religion. The second is additionally valuable to historians of lay culture and society. While some saints' vitae resemble the first type, a great many more are like the second, containing a wealth of allusions to the social context of the hagiographer as well as of his subject. We must still ask ourselves whether the hagiographer's allusion to marriage or the family or whatever social reference he is making represents a strictly clerical perspective or whether we may generalize from it to the broader society. As always, caution is in order, but for all the reasons we have already adduced we go on the assumption that the hagiographer's clerical status did not altogether isolate him from his lay roots or from the experiences of the society around him.[20]

A Note on Terminology

Our use of the term "saint" includes those whose official title is "Blessed" as well as those more properly titled "Saint." The distinction between the two terms came into wide use only in the seventeenth century and has to do with technical questions that do not concern this study: "Blessed" refers to those whose cult has a more limited observance than "Saint" and whose full canonization awaits further investigation and official approval. We also use the term "saint" in describing the holy men and women of our study during their lifetimes, though obviously they were not canonized until after they died. Some saints were referred to as such even during their lifetimes, but our usage is only a matter of stylistic convenience. In using the term "saint" or the expression "would-be saint" or "future saint" or "holy person" we do not mean to imply that the individual in question was consciously or actively promoting a reputation for sanctity.

We have allowed ourselves considerable license in using the terms "medieval" and "Middle Ages." The Middle Ages is a period designation with vaguely defined—indeed, hotly disputed—beginning and ending dates. Our study begins in the eleventh century, well in the midst of the medieval period, and ends in the seventeenth, well out of it. Nonetheless, we sometimes use the term "medieval" to cover this entire period to avoid resorting to a series of awkward and equally ill-defined terms such as "premodern," "early modern," and "postmedieval." When we are making time comparisons we use such terms as "late Middle Ages," "Renaissance," and "Reformation" to indicate the conventional divisions of our long and difficult-to-define period.

In referring to the written texts of saints' lives we use the Latin words "vita" and "vitae" to distinguish them from the "life" or "lives" of saints in the more general sense. In the literature the terms hagiographer, hagiography, and hagiographical are ambiguous. They may refer to: (1) the practice of writing saints' lives, and its practitioners; (2) the product, that is, the actual texts; (3) the scholarly study of these writings; and (4) the study of the entire history of sainthood and the cult of saints. In this book we will reserve the term and its variants for the first two meanings, though when we refer to "hagiographical scholarship" we have in mind meanings three and four. In short, in this book hagiography is the writing of saints' lives, and hagiographical scholarship is the study of the writing of saints' lives.

1

The Call to Holiness

Saints' vitae nearly always include some reference to the familial and societal contexts in which people found themselves at the point of their conversion to unusual holiness. Often the conversion was less a dramatic turning point than a lengthy process of spiritual questioning and growth. The written record of the call to holiness, whether sudden or protracted, even when related by a clerical hagiographer well aware of the didactic conventions of his profession, is a rich source for exploring the social history of the medieval and early modern family. Our method is the traditional one of examining the texts and letting the stories speak for themselves wherever possible. What matters in this endeavor is not so much whether the stories are true as that they were told and retold. Stories of Aquinas's bitter conflict with his family and of Dominic's loving, supportive mother circulated throughout Western Christendom. We explore the meaning of these accounts for the history of family relations. Because we are concerned primarily with the perception of behavior rather than the behavior itself (and also because of our reservations about the state of psychohistory), we generally eschew an intrapersonal psychobiographical approach. In assessing perceptions, however, we do offer interpretations of communal values that build upon but necessarily go beyond the immediate evidence.

Except in the brief statistical profiles at the end of each chapter we are not primarily concerned with typicality, that great nemesis of the quantitative historian. Rather, we try to convey the texture of changing human relations in the medieval family. For example, in our first chapter we note that hagiographers present several strikingly different types of children—

the old child, the innocent child, the guilt-ridden child, to name three. We try to analyze the conceptions of childhood that may underlie the different types, then to relate them to the concrete realities of medieval society. It bears repeating that we are less concerned with the authenticity of any particular vita than with the underlying perceptions about children that the account conveys. At the same time, the strategy of the account dictates that our attention be drawn first to the call to holiness—the conversion experience or the process that leads to a life of perfection-seeking.

We begin with children, advance to adolescents, and conclude part 1 with a chapter on adults. At all times we are concerned with the insights about life stages and family relations that saints' vitae provide. Some saints felt the religious impulse very early in childhood; indeed, stories of supernatural signs before birth or in early infancy are not uncommon. With adolescence appears the phenomenon of conversion to the pursuit of holiness, a change of life direction from an earlier state described variously as wicked, aimless, spiritually empty, or merely conventional. Sometimes conversion did not occur until adulthood, and in such cases it tended to be sudden and caused the future saint enormous difficulties in extricating himself or herself from worldly attachments. In the call to holiness, as in the resultant quest for spiritual perfection, chastity was central, both literally and symbolically, and to chastity we devote a separate chapter.

Whenever it came, the call to holiness found the individual in a social setting. Mothers, fathers, sisters, brothers, husbands, wives, and children were invariably affected by the saint's desire for a radical alteration of life—sometimes as protagonists, sometimes as antagonists, almost never as indifferent bystanders. In short, the family was the first context in which the religious impulse was manifested. The theater of the saint's pursuit of holiness soon widened—to the streets of the village or town, to the pilgrim road, the monastery, or even to the courts of princes or bishops. Saintliness interested everyone, and however much the pursuit was a highly individualistic experience, it had inescapable social ramifications and consequences.

It is this interaction between the holy aspirant and society that is the subject of part 1. We are interested in what saints' lives tell us about childhood, adolescence, and adulthood, about parental affection and authority, about the impact of religious inspiration upon family bonds, and, conversely, about family influences on religious behavior. Our interest extends to saints in the broader social context, and we take up such matters as the treatment of women, the effects of town development and commercial expansion, the impact of the mendicant movement, the rise of lay piety, and the changing roles of the clergy.

1 ⊙ *Children*

Medieval society knew the age of childhood. The widely held view that a concept of childhood did not emerge until the early modern period is emphatically contradicted by our reading of the evidence on saints, where we find a clear sense of what it was to be a child.[1] Saints, of course, were exceptional; more often than not their childhoods reflected what the society viewed as unusual, sometimes strange, occasionally bizarre, so that the saint's early years may appear as the reverse of the experiences of lesser mortals. Both positively, as evidence of society's expectations, and negatively, as evidence of the abnormal, stories about holy children confirm that a concept of childhood existed. In the Middle Ages childhood was understood to be a process of development, not a fixed state. Child psychology did not begin with Rousseau; medieval people were not ignorant of the dynamics of growth. Whether the somewhat elliptical evidence on early childhood that we have extracted from the thickets of hagiographical convention justifies the use of Freudian or Eriksonian analysis is another matter; but, however conjectural our theories of explanation, we are confident that a process of development was observed and that its observation is worth examining.

Variety, not uniformity, characterized the childhood of saints. It has long been a commonplace of scholarship that hagiographic accounts of the saints' early lives follow a set pattern dominated by a few nearly universal conventions that are almost interchangeable between one saint and another because, at bottom, the saint's life is a supernatural construct.[2] This view we reject. Grace may have determined the heavenly destination, but not how the saint arrived there. Divine election did not make a regiment of

19

holy automatons, not even in the formulaic constructions of hagiography. As early as the eleventh century (and more commonly in later centuries), saints' lives displayed childhood struggles of conscience worthy of a Martin Luther. The extremes of sainthood ranged from perfect children, too innocent and angelic to live on earth, to conscience-ridden penitents who scourged their bodies, starved themselves, tortured their flesh with belts and hair shirts, and shed rivers of guilty tears.

Biblical precedent and the need to establish the divine election of the saint combine to explain why many accounts of saints' lives begin with the story of how God answered the prayers of a childless couple by sending them a son or daughter. For the most part such tales reveal more about the universal concerns of parents than about medieval children, but they are worth a pause before we enter the world of saintly childhood proper. While there are not enough of these stories to permit us to trace their historical development or to relate them specifically to their social context, yet there are enough to suggest that the tales of barren women, mothers who could not suckle their babies, and wondrous infants throw light upon the vicissitudes and joys of medieval life. We may begin with two stories from southern Italy.

Like the biblical Sarah and Abraham, the parents of the fourteenth-century St. Nicholas of Tolentino had reached an advanced age without a longed-for son. The would-be mother's prayers were answered by an angel who appeared to the sleeping couple and directed them to the shrine of St. Nicholas of Bari. To the shrine they went as poor pilgrims, and while they were asleep on the church steps they saw an apparition of Nicholas dressed in papal robes. The saint instructed them to name their son Nicholas and promised that miracles would attend his life. (See fig. 1.)

A similar story is told of the noble Matilda of Calafato, who was granted a daughter in response to her prayers. Shortly before her child was born, Matilda encountered a stranger who told her that she must deliver the babe in a stable, in honor of Mary. This she did, giving birth in 1432 to an extraordinarily beautiful daughter, the Blessed Eustochio of Messina. The barrenness of the woman, her failure to fulfill the fundamental responsibility of her sex, and, correspondingly, her denial of her husband's potency were spectacularly overcome in these cases by supernatural intervention. To the theologian the mother was merely a vessel of grace, but to her husband, to his family, to their friends and neighbors, she now must have been something more. Her faith and the fervor of her devotion were such that she could summon heavenly power to her side. For the Sicilian faithful who venerate Eustochio, the age-old drama of miraculous fertility replayed in her story has direct, concrete relevance.

According to historical demographers, at least 10 percent, perhaps 20

Fig. 1. The parents of Nicholas of Tolentino have a vision of St. Nicholas of Bari dressed as pope. He tells them they will have a son whom they are to call Nicholas. Tolentino, Basilica of St. Nicholas, fourteenth-century fresco. Photograph from Alinari/Editorial Photocolor Archives.

Fig. 2. Juana de Aza dreams she has given birth to a dog with a burning torch in its mouth. In the foreground her infant son, Dominic de Guzmán, is being bathed. Pisa, Church of St. Catherine, detail of the Francesco Traini polyptych. Photograph from Alinari/ Editorial Photocolor Archives.

percent, of married couples in premodern societies remained childless, a condition the culture invariably blamed on the wife.[3] To the childless woman and her family, miraculous fertility offered a sustaining hope; but to their more fortunate neighbors the mother's barrenness appeared to be due to some hidden sin, or at least to a lack of religious fervor. With endless variations, the saints' lives present this powerful dialectic: upon the outcome of prayer hangs a moral and spiritual judgment; the successful suppliant is one who has found favor with God, while the others are denied because of some defect, a defect that carries the further peril of being made public.

The stories of Nicholas and Eustochio are typical in showing the saints' parents united in supplication. After this the mother usually plays the more important part, beginning with her bearing and nurturing of the saintly infant. The father may well disappear from the story almost entirely, as did the father of Dominic de Guzmán, whose correct name is a matter of concern only to a few hagiographical specialists. His mother, the Blessed Juana de Aza, however, became a cult figure in her own right. To Juana alone, as to Mary, God foretold the coming of a son and his future greatness. Already the mother of several grown children, Juana must have been in her forties and near the end of her fertile years when she prayed for another son. After a nighttime vision in which St. Domingo de Silos told her that she would bear a son who would be a shining light to the church, she became pregnant. One night Juana dreamed of a dog in her womb with a burning torch in its mouth, which broke away from her and set the world afire. (See fig. 2.) Still a third vision, either to Juana or to Dominic's godmother, revealed the babe with a shining star on his forehead.

The dog and the shining star became important symbols in pictorial representations of the Dominican order—in a famous pun, Dominic's preachers are the *domini canes*, the hounds of the Lord. But our interest in the story centers on Juana and her significance to the faithful. As in the biographies of such major saints as Clare of Assisi, Rose of Viterbo, Bernard of Clairvaux (interestingly, his story also includes a vision with dog symbolism), Thomas Aquinas, Hugh of Cluny, and Gilbert of Sempringham, the mother stands alone. It is she who prays, she who receives the supernatural message, she who reveals it to the world, and she who takes charge of its fulfillment. These are paler reflections of Mary's story; the father's physical contribution is not—as it was in the case of Joseph—denied, but for all other purposes he is absent, and the maternal role is powerfully emphasized. In some of these accounts the father, invisible in the prenatal events, even appears during the saint's childhood as an opposing force. In the contest between saint and father the mother marshals her prenatal visions and vows to reinforce *her* child's religious vocation.

Like other women, the saint's mother is shown as fearing the pain and danger of childbirth, and like many she turns to prayer. The mother of Blessed Queen Cunegund of Poland had given birth at least eight previous times, always with great suffering. Pregnant again, she went to church to pray to the Virgin and the saints. A divine voice promised her an easy delivery of a wonderful daughter who would be honored by all nations. In due course the babe was born and immediately sang out a greeting to the Queen of Heaven in a remarkably mature voice. All the attendants were awestruck, but her mother took this as proof of her vision. The linking of devotion to the Virgin with safe delivery is here affirmed in a dramatic way.

Modern psychologists observe that women who have an easy, natural delivery tend not to suffer postpartum depression and that they adapt well to motherhood.[4] Mothers who have a happy delivery are even inclined to endow their babies with special goodness. Did Cunegund's first outcry reflect her mother's joy at a safe and easy delivery? In the medieval view Cunegund's cry confirmed her mother's sense of self-worth and demonstrated it to the world. Supported by such signs of divine favor, the saint's mother was all the more able·to persuade others to share her conviction that this was a special child. Cunegund's mother continued to receive heavenly signs of her child's divine election. At the breast Cunegund already began to practice abstinence in a manner, we are told, reminiscent of "the Blessed Nicola [Tolentino]." On Wednesdays and Fridays she abused her tender little body by contenting herself with only one breast at each feeding. The text preserved for us in the *Acta Sanctorum* suggests that the mother nursed her child herself (*maternis mamillis*), an unusual practice for a queen and a further indication that she knew this was a very special relationship.

Stories of infants rejecting the breast also appear in the lives of saints from Italy, France, and Iberia. Most, like that of Nicholas of Tolentino, simply tell of abstinence on Fridays, but others are more elaborate. Gonçalo de Amarante refused to nurse until he had been carried to church and allowed to gaze at the images of other saints. Guillaume de St. Bénigne, an eleventh-century saint whose mother's first sign was a ray of sunlight shining on her right breast, restored milk to an old woman who had been brought to take charge of him. Robert de la Chaise-Dieu refused to suckle from an immoral wet nurse, as did Ursulina di Parma, who had been put out to nurse with an adulterous woman.

Catherine of Sweden, daughter of the great prophetess St. Bridget and, though never formally canonized, also popularly regarded as a saint, was the fourth of eight children. Put out to a wet nurse, she refused to suckle because of the woman's sinful life. Bridget then took the babe to her own breast, only to find that her infant daughter was now a judge of her mother's conduct: Catherine nursed happily when Bridget had been sexually continent but refused the breast "as though it were absinthe" when the saint had had sexual relations.

Like the stories of conception and childbirth, these nursing stories deal with a human function fraught with uncertainty and apprehension and therefore charged with symbolic meaning.[5] Necessarily the stories involve two protagonists, the woman who provides and the child who receives. The woman without milk suffers some of the same opprobrium as the woman who cannot conceive or bear. The child is merely a victim of the mother's fault. But with the saint everything is turned around. The child who rejects the breast on certain days is inspired to begin an ascetic and penitential life and is joined by the mother in religious sacrifice. What others might well interpret as personal failure, she explains as a great portent. Less fortunate is the wet nurse. The saintly child who refuses her nurture is revealing and condemning her secret sin. Already the infant is a champion of morality.

In part these stories serve merely to create a supernatural aura about a religious hero. The tale of Robert's restoration of milk to an old woman seems to have no further function. Others fulfill a moral purpose. The consequence of sin was to have bad milk, to be rendered helpless in carrying out the maternal function. And bad milk was a sign of sinfulness. Moreover, God knew all, and sin could not be hidden from him and from his agents, the saints. Some stories also serve as inspiration. Holy children who began to abuse their tender little bodies by self-denial set an example for early and rigorous asceticism. Emphasis on Friday abstinence provided a practical guideline for lay people who could not pursue more extreme forms of penitence. And, whatever the moral tale, a mother was its author. Even in these seemingly fanciful and manifestly unverifiable nursing stories, the social historian sees a confluence of old wives' tales, folk wisdom, and hagiographic duty that reveals something of the quality of infant care in the Middle Ages. The accounts suggest that parents, especially mothers, were responsible for nurturing their innocent children, and that this duty was not taken lightly.

Although a few nursing stories contain hints that the infant saint exercised conscious judgment, the primary theme is a commentary on adult morality. The holy infant, even when endowed with special gifts and surrounded by supernatural signs, is essentially passive. Early in childhood, however, by age seven and in some cases even earlier, the saintly child begins to make conscious choices concerning the journey toward sanctity and to act on its own behalf. Here our study of childhood properly speaking may be said to begin.

After the rather hackneyed stories of devout yet barren women, what strikes us very quickly about childhood stories is their great variety, a variety that defies conventional hagiographic typing. The patron saint of youth, Louis of Gonzaga, is an outstanding example of the range of youthful spirituality. According to his four confessors, Louis never committed a mortal sin or lost his baptismal grace, and even demons testified to his boyhood sanctity. Yet his biographer tells us that in Louis's own mind he was imperfect; once the young boy uttered a string of bad words he had learned from his father's troops, and he repented the sin for the rest of his short life. Louis's penances could take extreme form—as a boy he scourged himself until the blood ran, three times a week at first, then every day. Beginning by whipping himself with cane branches, he progressed to lengths of rope and then to an iron chain. In place of a hair shirt he wrapped his naked body with bands studded with sharp riding spurs that dug into his flesh. Even in an age when the service of spirituality frequently led to extremism, such behavior was not taken for granted. When servants showed the bloodied garments to the boy's father, the distraught man lamented to his wife that their son wanted to kill himself. Paternal distress turned to anger when Louis preferred to wear rags rather than the clothes appropriate to his noble station. At fifteen he decided to enter the Jesuit order instead of pursuing the worldly career his father intended for him. Louis's mother was relieved that he had not chosen one of the more rigorous clerical orders, but his father was unforgiving until at last his anger gave way to admiration for the boy's constancy of purpose.

Rich in imagery, this sixteenth-century spiritual biography is an amalgam of themes that appear in many earlier stories of saints, though it is unusual to find so many themes combined in the life of a single young man. Louis is the child without sin, too perfect for this world. He died at twenty-three. But Louis is also a penitential child, driven by guilt to practice increasingly drastic self-mortifications that weakened him and helped bring on his early death. Finally, Louis is the rebellious child who destroys his parents, rejects their plans for him, and ultimately bends them to his will. (When we were working in central-western Mexico we were struck by the ubiquity of representations of Louis of Gonzaga, especially in small rural churches, conveying both extreme boyish innocence and severe, bloody penance. While this is not the place to digress to consider the sort of anthropological work we hope ultimately will complement our present study, we may at least express our confidence that the hagiographic record generally is not an esoteric clerical form of devotion divorced from popular piety. What was written of Louis in the sixteenth century is visible to faithful Tarascan villagers in the twentieth.)

To be sure, most stories of saintly boys and girls report much less eventful childhoods. Parents, usually mothers, encouraged by a sign or by some clue in the child's behavior to believe that this was a child intended for a religious life, took the decisive first step: boys were sent to school to learn to read and write Latin, and girls were enrolled in a convent. The future saint obeyed, demonstrating steady and untroubled growth in his spiritual life. For the most part saintly schoolboys were reported as adept at learning, serious to the point of gravity, and attractive to their peers as well as their elders. Girls adapted easily to the regimen of the convent, practiced austerity and obedience, displayed great humility, and distinguished themselves by a special gift for prayer. Many are the stories of girlish rapture and ecstasy. Growth toward perfection was steady and uncomplicated, marvelous and serene.

Some boys and girls were not merely good, they were spectacularly good. Their worldly innocence shone through their faces and graced their movements. Hagiographers portrayed them strewing blossoms on their favorite shrines, or as preternaturally beautiful babies whose parents gave them names reflective of their divine gift of beauty. Eustochio of Messina was such a child. Her parents had named her Smaragda (Emerald) in recognition of her loveliness, but in religion she discarded this reminder of worldly vanity. The parents of Rose of Lima, on the other hand, refused to acknowledge her special beauty until she was three months old, then they changed her name from Elizabeth to Rose, symbol of the Blessed Virgin.

In hagiography as in popular piety, beauty had, so to speak, two faces. A sign of supernatural endowment, it was also a worldly temptation, to her who possessed it as well as to those who beheld it. To Rose of Lima her very name, symbolic of this ambiguous blessing, became a burden for which she is reported to have received consolation from the Blessed Virgin herself. Rose also came to hate her beautiful hair because her brother teased her when she combed it, and, though she revered her parents, she resisted when her mother tried to persuade her to enhance her natural beauty with adornments. Instead, imitating her spiritual heroine Catherine of Siena, she disfigured herself.[6]

Angelic beauty and goodness marked boys as well as girls. St. Bernardino da Siena, whose toothless and hollow-cheeked old man's face gazes at us sternly from many a fifteenth-century altarpiece and wall painting, was reported to have been a child of remarkable beauty, with a delicate complexion that blushed at the very hint of blasphemy. As virtuous as he was handsome, little Bernardino punched the face of a local citizen who invited him to perform some unnamed act of vice. Apparently this did not discourage the seducer, for later we find Bernardino and his friends pelting the evil man with mud and stones. Other children were less militant in their innocence. As a child Costanzo da Fabriano was so good that his parents wondered whether he was actually an angel, and Berengar de St. Papoul, the eleventh-century French saint, was so gentle as to be thought feminine.

The beauty of Margaret the Barefooted combined rustic and unsophisticated simplicity with the ethereal delicacy of an icon. The connection between natural beauty and supernatural power exemplified in holy images in Margaret's biography is made unusually explicit. Just as the icon was not merely a symbolic aid to prayer but also a holy object with its own power, so the saint's body was not just a vessel of spiritual perfection but also a holy, wonder-working agent. The faithful elbowed forward to touch the saint's living body; they schemed and paid cash to obtain pieces of the corpse for their altars. And just as the beauty of the icon was a manifestation of its power, so the beauty of the saintly child revealed the mystery of divine election.[7]

Some saints did not outlive their childhood purity. Among these were the child martyrs, invariably portrayed as victims of Jewish ritual murder.[8] In their obvious anti-Jewish purpose these stories tell us something of medieval feelings about children. Jews were never accused of ritually killing adults, only innocent children. As targets of Christian hatred, Jews were believed to be especially addicted to the most odious crime medieval people could imagine—child murder.

We ought to be skeptical about the widespread notion that medieval people could not afford to invest much affection in children and the related notion that they had no conception of childhood as a distinct life stage.[9] Both propositions seem to founder on the evidence that shows people of medieval Europe treating children with loving concern. Often love of children was mixed with a certain awe; for all its imperfections, childhood could be a state of holy innocence. Innocence had its unique power, envied by Jews, who schemed to possess it, cherished by Christians, who both nurtured it and were protected by it. Even the innocence of children who did not display the special gifts of divine charisma might be a spiritual treasure. In moments of crisis, when ordinary prayer failed and it came time to try special measures, communities organized processions of their children in the hope that their angelic innocence would move the heavenly host to pity.[10]

In medieval language innocence meant above all sexual purity. Casimir, the late-fifteenth-century prince of Poland whose saintliness shone through features his biographer described as both beautiful and venerable, was reared by his parents to be a model of virtue and learning. When they directed him to take a bride he refused, declaring that he had already decided to dedicate himself to a life of chastity and hard penance. During his nightly vigils Casimir was so moved by the thought of Christ's suffering that he bathed his bed in tears. "In the middle of the flower of his youth" he became chronically ill. All his physicians prescribed sexual intercourse as a remedy. When his parents attempted to follow the doctors' orders by placing a beautiful virgin in his bed, Casimir refused to embrace her, saying that he preferred death to surrendering his innocence.[11] Shortly thereafter he died. Like Casimir, most saints were described as protecting their chaste innocence throughout their lives, although seldom do we encounter such graphic symbolism as in the story of William, Bishop of St. Brieuc. After a lifetime of defending himself against the assaults of women made avid by his great beauty, he died, and when he was being prepared for burial he was discovered to have the underdeveloped penis of a child.

Though stories of childhood innocence are very common in the hagiographic literature, and, though the condition was often associated with children in general, innocence was not invariably attributed to children, nor did it by any means always reign supreme. Hagiographers used the commonly accepted notion that ordinary childhood was a time of mischief and irresponsibility to set their young heroes and heroines apart, by depicting them as at odds with the frivolity, even sensuousness, of ordinary children. Some saints' lives tell of early years marked by an extraordinary seriousness of speech and manner, by gravity of countenance, and by precocious devoutness. The theme of the "old child" is prominent as early as the eleventh century in accounts from Germany, France, and Italy.[12] Nicholas the Pilgrim is described as *venerabilis puer*; Gautier de l'Estep, Adelaide of Bellich, Benno of Osnabrück, and William of Montevergine, all of the eleventh century, are noted as having had the grave manner of old age, and the "old child" continues to appear frequently in the accounts of later centuries. As a child the thirteenth-century William of St. Brieuc (he of the boyish penis) already had the heart of an old man. If the "old child" is a hagiographic convention it is nonetheless revealing, for it suggests by contrast—indeed, it often explicitly states—the attributes of most children, frivolity and sensuality. The old child avoids the company of other children, preferring solitude. He does not play games, engage in horseplay, or tell or listen to dirty stories. He does not indulge in what hagiographers refer to as the common sensuality of ordinary children (masturbation?). The old child studies hard, prays regularly, and attends church gladly.

It is hard to escape the conclusion that medieval people knew childhood as a stage distinct from adulthood, distinct even from adolescence, as a time of self-indulgence and relatively harmless frivolity. Even so, none of its characteristic vices were regarded as incompatible with angelic innocence, probably because, despite the stirrings of the flesh, which stories of saintly children frequently refer to as common, children did not engage in sexual intercourse.

Against these commonsense ideas about childhood stood the Augustinian teaching that childish misbehavior evinced the original sinfulness of humankind. The contradiction turned upon the conflicting views of human nature that Christian culture sucked in through its tangled roots. It was fairly generally held that children existed in a state of nature and entered society only as adults, but there agreement ended. In one view, prevalent in the western Mediterranean and rooted in pre-Christian autocthonous beliefs, nature was good, incapable of evil intention, and even endowed with divinity. In another view, derived from Neoplatonism, gnosticism, and perhaps ultimately Eastern dualism, nature as the opposite pole of divinity was incapable of good. Although this dualism was rejected in its more extreme form (to reappear later in the Manichaean heresy), its influence is evident in the official Catholic doctrine that without the gift of divine grace there is only sin.[13]

Saints' lives reflect the continuing tension between these fundamentally opposed conceptions. The saint as innocent child alternated with the "old child" who shunned immature sinfulness. For some, a child's physical beauty could not be accepted as a gift of nature; it could only be a sign of divine grace, of the supernatural. Medieval society did not resolve this conflict. The tension of two natures continued in a kind of fitful equilibrium until the Reformation, when Luther, Zwingli, and Calvin revived the Augustinian concept of human nature and the Anabaptists carried it to its logical conclusion: born in sin, children were corrupt. Only as adults might they join the community of saints. Protestant Augustinianism made the child saint a philosophical impossibility and cast childhood itself into a kind of theological limbo.[14]

The innocent child is important in understanding the social context of medieval piety, but so too is the hagiographers' fondness for dwelling on the struggles of the penitent child, preoccupied by temptations, sinful conscience, and the need for expiation. Often at the age of seven, occasionally even earlier, these saintly children would begin intense penitential activity, spending their nights kneeling in prayer and whipping themselves until they were bloody. They welcomed illness as a punishment and a test of faith. They suffered the pains of Christ's scourging and crucifixion. They had visions of Christ, the Virgin, and angels. Longing for the life of a hermit, they vowed they would be always chaste and continually penitent. "From the age of reason," Giovanni da Matera wanted to be a hermit. According to a twelfth-century account, he fled from his family to a barren and uninhabited island off the coast of southern Italy, where he almost died. A celestial voice restored his strength and directed him to a boat that he sailed to Calabria. In that more favorable environment he was able to take up again his life of solitude and repentance.

The story of the youthful penitent Giovanni da Matera was unusual for the saints of his time, most of whose lives followed a less tumultuous and guilt-ridden path into the routine ascetic life of the monastery; but with the thirteenth century, perhaps a bit earlier, guilt-ridden piety began to appear in much more dramatic and personal forms. Pioneering this new religious sensibility—for it clearly was more than just a shift of hagiographic style or conventions—were Italian girls, particularly girls from the regions of Tuscany and Umbria. One of the earliest was Bona of Pisa. Born in 1156 to a Pisan father and a Corsican mother, Bona's future sanctity was revealed by an angel to a priest named John who was at that time a student in Paris. Nothing further is related of Bona or her family until she was about three, when her father went on a sea voyage from which he never returned. Four years later Jesus appeared to Bona while she was sleeping with her mother and told her that she should no longer share her bed with anyone, not even her mother.

Having first been abandoned by her father and now ordered from above to give up maternal comfort, the seven-year-old girl embarked on a life of austerities and penance. She gave up meat and fasted on bread and water three days a week. In imitation of the baby Jesus, she slept in a manger on straw, denying herself sheets and blankets. When she was ten Bona had a second vision in which Christ gave her money to buy a hair shirt. By this time she already had fulfilled the prophecy of the Paris priest and had joined the Canons of St. Martin in Pisa.

Three years later Bona's mother had a vision in which Jesus came to her as one of a group of pilgrims to tell her that her husband was alive and well across the sea, and that she could send Bona to him in their company. With her mother's consent Bona embarked for the Holy Land, unaware that she was sailing into a sea of divinely ordered trials. Many years before his union with Bona's mother, her father had married a noblewoman in the Levant who had borne him three sons. Now, reunited with his first wife and his sons (one of whom was patriarch of Jerusalem, another master of the Templars!), he was ashamed of his irregular behavior and his connection with a lowly Corsican woman, and with his sons he plotted to kidnap Bona before she could land. With divine help Bona escaped her would-be kidnappers and made her way to shore, where she took refuge with a hermit. Some time later she set out to see the holy places, but she was wounded and captured by Saracens. After many adventures Bona managed to return to Pisa, where she lived a life rich in mystical experiences that included visions of spiritual marriage with Christ and of the bearing of spiritual children. Her reputation as a visionary brought her great respect in the city of Pisa, and she became the religious counselor to a group of devout men.

Bona's story is less a moral tale than a spiritual odyssey of heroic proportions, and its rich detail, interwoven with hagiographic legend and visionary fantasy, strikingly evokes a historical time and real places. Twelfth century Pisa and the Holy Land come alive with ethnic prejudice, class snobbery, Levantine merchants, and marauding Saracens. We discern an emerging bourgeois religious life, in which spirituality was leaving the cloister and seeking new forms, both associative and personal.[15] The confraternity movement was beginning to appear, and the intensely personal mystical phenomenon of spiritual marriage, which one hundred and fifty years later would have its greatest exemplar in another Tuscan saint, Catherine of Siena, is here already in practice. Like Catherine, Bona was a spiritual counselor to the laity. Fortified by her communication with St. James the Apostle and with Christ, as well as by her rigorous austerities and heroic sufferings as a pilgrim, Bona transcended the usual limitations of her sex and created a place as a leader in the public religious life of her city. Before we reflect more fully upon the connection between childhood guilt and adult achievement, let us look at a few more biographies of saintly girls.

Four years after Bona's death another Pisan girl described as destined for sainthood was born. The story of Gerardesca of Pisa also gives us much personal detail. Before her seventh year, we are told, she too gave up "family delights"; but the parallel with Bona goes no further. Gerardesca fled to a convent, where her devotions seem not to have been spectacular. When her mother entreated her to come home she obeyed, and she obeyed again when her mother chose a husband for her. Filial obedience was the central virtue of Gerardesca's early years; but her biographer lets us know that God helped her strike out on her own course to achieve spiritual satisfaction. When her mother continued to meddle in her daughter's life by praying that Gerardesca would bear a child, God replied that her daughter would indeed have a child and that he would be St. John the Evangelist. When the mother ignored this portent she was punished by painful fistulas for two years before she received a miraculous cure. By this time Gerardesca had persuaded her husband to become a monk so that she was free to pursue an intense mystical life. Now a great change came over her. She became joyful and her eyes shone. Like Bona, she entered into a close personal union with Christ and also became a spiritual counselor.

Another contemporary who achieved renown as a visionary and public figure was Sperandea, born in the nearby Umbrian town of Gubbio. At the age of nine Sperandea began to practice such extreme austerities that her parents intervened, whereupon she ran away from home. Directed by a vision of Jesus Christ, she wandered from place to place, preaching against vice and displaying an image of the red cross that had appeared to her in a vision.

But Sperandea's story is overshadowed by that of another Tuscan girl. In the Church of the Collegiata, in many-towered San Gimignano, a series of frescoes narrates the thirteenth-century life of a famous local saint, Serafina, or Fina as she was familiarly known. A hundred years later her biographer described her in the now-hackneyed terms of the beautiful but grave girl who avoided children's games and abhorred vanity. Fina wore a hair shirt, devoted herself to chastity, and practiced the usual penitential routines. But she also struck out in the newer directions of thirteenth-century female piety, laboring with her hands, nursing the sick, and cultivating celestial marriage. In her efforts to emulate Christ's passion she punished her body so harshly that she became paralyzed, welcoming her suffering as a means of perfecting her virtues. Her paralysis did not restrain her biographer from asserting that it was the profundity of her meditation that kept her from rising to help her mother when she was gravely injured in a fall down a flight of stairs. Fina's attention, it seems, was riveted by a huge serpent that she finally understood to be the devil, "the deceiver of our first parents." When Fina made the sign of the cross the serpent disappeared, but by then her poor mother had expired. It is difficult to escape the inference that Fina's mother had not approved, perhaps had tried to block, Fina's ascetic practices, and that in the mind of the girl (or at least of the hagiographer) the mother's painful death was divine retribution. Five years later Fina followed her mother to the grave to become an object of intense local veneration, especially powerful in guarding the Sangimignanesi against the plague. (See fig. 3.)

Intense private devotions and austerities also filled the girlhood of Chiara di Montefalco. From the age of four (according to an account written within a decade of her death by the bishop of Spoleto) Chiara was gripped by divine love. When she was nine her older sister reproved her for leaving her bare foot partly uncovered while she slept, an instance of immodesty for which Chiara suffered great shame. Shortly after this Chiara followed her sister into a local hermitage, and in 1291 she became its head. (See fig. 4.) Austerity, silence, and even flagellation continued to be the main preoccupation of Chiara's religious life well into adulthood, but, as with other thirteenth-century Umbrian and Tuscan holy women, private penance was less an alternative than an avenue to fame and public influence. Against the heretics of her time Chiara waged unrelenting warfare. She took part in public disputations and displayed great knowledge of theology, despite

Fig. 3. Scenes from the life of Serafina (or Fina) of San Gimignano. *Upper right:* Fina lies ill while rats gnaw at her; her mother feeds her. *Lower right:* Fina's mother falls down a flight of stairs while Fina contemplates the devil in the form of a serpent hovering over the stricken woman. *Upper and lower left:* scenes of the veneration of Fina

her lack of formal education. Her compatriots called upon her to be a peacemaker, and she ranged from Spoleto to Arezzo, from Trebbia to Perugia, preaching peace, settling civic discords, and freeing war captives.

The lives of Bona, Gerardesca, Sperandea, Serafina, and Chiara have much in common. Most obviously, the stories all have female heroines, and the theme of guilt-ridden childhood is more frequently associated with girls than boys, whereas adolescent and adult guilt are not specific to one sex. The historical setting of these girls' lives breaks through the hagiographer's tale at every point. All of them came from just that central Italian region where civic life had been quickening since the eleventh century, and their religious lives were intertwined with the lives of the city-republics.[16]

by the townsfolk. *Right center:* Fina as protectress of the city of San Gimignano. San Gimignano, Civic Museum. Altarpiece by Lorenzo di Nicolò di Pietro Gerini. Photograph from Alinari/Editorial Photocolor Archives.

Preaching, fighting heretics, giving spiritual counsel, peacemaking, and helping the poor and sick, these young women took a vigorous part in the public, communal world. They were much esteemed and sought after by their compatriots, and their vigorous activities also led to envy and opposition from other religious activists. Chiara's confutation of heretics led one member of the radical Franciscan, or Fraticelli, sect—a certain Petrus di Salomone—to attack her as a fraud by casting doubt on her claim that she had the instruments of Christ's passion engraved on her heart. Early in life most of these saintly girls began to suffer attacks from demons which they countered with fasting, vigils, and other more extreme austerities. But neither private demons nor public slanderers could defeat these young women. Rigorous prayer and penance, begun early in childhood, may have weakened their bodies, but they toughened their spirits and steeled their wills.

While we may reserve judgment about certain fantastic details, the great spiritual intensity of these girls' lives has the ring of authenticity. Hagiographers were challenged to convey more vivid, highly personal religious experience, and they refined their literary skills accordingly. Authors took pains to furnish the details of everyday life and to color their drama with the emotional tones of authentic feeling. Visionary miracle and epic fantasy were set in real landscapes and cityscapes, while hagiographic stereotypes

Fig. 4. Chiara di Montefalco begs her sister to receive her into her religious community. Montefalco, Church of St. Clare, Chapel of the Holy Cross. Fresco of the Umbrian school, fourteenth century. Photograph courtesy of Ministero Beni Culturali e Ambientali: Istituto Centrale per il Catalogo e la Documentazione. Number F614.

paled under the vivid imprint of powerful individual personality. As a result of this growing hagiographic realism, we have an increasingly rich documentation of the mentality of the period. And the realism itself is an expression of what we have called a new sensibility.[17]

These accounts furnish ample hints and often direct evidence that what the holy boys and girls took to be signs of divine election their families received with considerable doubt and much anguish. Even in the so-called age of faith and miracle, parents who discovered their seven-year-old children whipping themselves until the blood ran or praying all night on their knees took alarm. Often, believing the children were sick, they sought medical advice. For their part, ascetic children knew they would encounter parental distress and opposition, and invariably they practiced their austerities in secret. Nor was there to be a single definitive instant when the world would become totally persuaded, a single act that would demonstrate to everyone's satisfaction that this was indeed a saint and not an imposter, a witch, or a lunatic. The struggle with protective parents, commonsense doubters, and officious clerics went on until saintly children could strike out on their own. Holy children ultimately moved beyond the world of the family to a wider environment, but here too they met with uncertainty and skepticism, especially if they were female. The monastery, the convent, or the busy Italian town viewed the holy youth with a mixture of awe and doubt that might not be resolved until after death by miracles at the tomb. Even then the church might remain skeptical, as attested by the hundreds of canonization cases that remain incomplete.[18]

Doubtful though they might be, medieval people were drawn by the aura of power that emanated from holy penitents. Most penitents sought privacy and silence; few holy ascetics began their careers by preaching publicly or by claiming they were divinely elected. But no cloister or forest cell was remote enough to hide them from a society that thirsted after wonder-workers. And if they were effective, anything they did, however bizarre, was seen by their contemporaries as an added sign of sanctity.

This connection between wonder-working and a reputation for sanctity is especially striking in the lives of female penitents. Girls and women were considered particularly susceptible to demonic possession and hysteria;[19] moreover, they did not normally engage in public activity, especially not as religious advisers to men or as political counselors. Thus the holy female penitent had to overcome skepticism based on the prejudice against her sex as well as the usual reservations about extreme ascetic behavior. She built upon the strength she had begun to muster in early childhood as she forged her will in contests against inner temptation and family resistance. Contrary to the modern propensity to regard inner voices, self-castigation, and a feeling of unworthiness as pathological and dysfunctional, we suggest that for Bona of Pisa, Chiara di Montefalco, and the others such manifestations were crucial to their personality development and ultimately proof to their communities of their saintliness. Any useful application of modern social or psychological theory should regard the saint's development as a series of outcomes that were positive and effective for medieval society.[20]

Such a late-medieval Italian archetype of female saintliness, which combines extreme private penitence with vigorous public activity, is nowhere better represented than in the biography of the great mystic Catherine of Siena. Written by Raymond of Capua, her confessor and spiritual adviser, and supplemented by her own letters as well as by other contemporary documentation, it also has the virtue of being full of individual and reliable detail. Born in 1347, just as Italy was about to suffer the first great wave of bubonic plague, Catherine was the twenty-third child of the dyer Giacomo Benincasa and his wife Lapa. Many of her brothers and sisters had died, including a twin sister, and for this reason Mona Lapa nursed Catherine at her own breast, although she had not done so with any of the other children. Catherine's confessor tells us that at about the age of five she was sometimes found praying in lonely corners of the house or heard walking slowly up the stairs saying a Hail Mary with each step. At six, returning to the city after a visit to her older sister Bonaventura, she had a vision of Christ. He was wearing papal robes and the pope's triple crown, and he was seated on an imperial throne attended by Saint Peter and Saint Paul. Christ blessed the girl, and from that moment Catherine grew silent, began to abstain from food and cruelly to whip her flesh, and wandered to woods and caves to imitate St. Dominic and the ancient fathers of the desert. In that same seventh year she consecrated her virginity to Christ. So far Catherine followed the typical path of the penitential girl who turned to asceticism at about the age of seven. But Catherine was unusual; already she was a leader, gathering other girls of her age around her to join her in prayer and "to discipline [i.e., flagellate] themselves together with her."

Catherine's early religious dedication did not form itself into a specific program for another decade. In fact, between her twelfth and fifteenth years she wavered ever so slightly, under pressure from her mother and Bonaventura, and there seems to have been a possibility that she might reconsider her vow of chastity and accede to her family's urgings that she take a husband. But her vacillation ended abruptly when Bonaventura died. Catherine took her sister's death to be God's punishment not of the worldly Bonaventura, but of herself, for her apostasy. Determined now to persist in her spiritual vocation, she faced the renewed efforts of her family to break her will. Not yet sixteen, she flung down the gauntlet by cutting off her hair. The entire family responded by treating her as a servant, dealing severely with her so she would see the foolishness of her ways and agree to marry. But Catherine's spiritual genius and determination were equal to the test: she took her punishment to be an opportunity for spiritual growth, and she imagined that the place of her servitude was the holy house of Nazareth, her father Jesus Christ, her mother the Blessed Virgin, and the rest of the household the apostles and disciples of the Lord.

Thus Catherine became the joyful servant of Christ and transmuted her punishment into a great instrument of interior prayer. Giacomo admitted defeat and gave orders that no one was to torment the girl any longer so that she would be able to serve her bridegroom in peace and pray for the Benincasa family. For her part also Catherine adjusted to the realities, for the time being accepting the decision of a local Dominican congregation of widows, the Mantellata, that it would not be proper for a young virgin to join them. Instead, her father gave her a room below the kitchen as a cell where she could practice her solitary penances and devotions. But the next year she came down with chicken pox and persuaded her mother that she could get well only if she were allowed to join the Mantellata; otherwise, she warned, St. Dominic would take her from this life. Terrified by this suicidal threat, Mona Lapa went to the prioress of the Mantellata and persuaded her to accept Catherine.

Still more obstacles blocked the mystic's path to spiritual peace. Having overcome her family's opposition and impatient for the day when she was to join the Mantellata, Catherine was now tormented by demons who paraded before her the earthly and womanly pleasures she was giving up. It was carnival, when, before the austerities of Lent, the world was turned topsy-turvy and for a few hours fantasy swept away life's harsh realities and loosened its restraints. The Sienese were in the streets eating, drinking, playing at love, and mocking their betters.[21] In her dark cell Catherine heard the carnival riot while her demons continued to torture her. Suddenly Christ appeared with his mother and a host of saints. Placing a gold ring on her finger, he took Catherine as his bride. The ultimate mystic joy was hers. While Catherine alone could see the ring of her spiritual marriage, all Christendom was soon to feel the force of this young woman's will, tempered in a succession of crises she had transformed into spiritual triumphs. Catherine had built within herself an oratory to which she could always repair for renewed strength and from which she would sally forth again and again to do battle against sin, to help the sick, and even to remonstrate with popes in the church's trial of the Great Schism.

Of the many other Italian female penitents, we select one more from the following century, Francesca de' Ponziani, the patroness of Rome. For her too our source is a life composed by her confessor. Francesca's revulsion against the world began in early childhood. She could not bear to be near any man, even her father, and she shunned normal embraces not only from him but also from her playmates, girls as well as boys. Francesca made herself practically a hermit in her own home, absorbed in prayer, fasting, and good works. When she was eleven (the age of puberty, her biographer tells us), she declared that she wished to serve God in chastity, apparently intending to enter a convent. When her father opposed her plan she became paralyzed, and after a lengthy illness she was cured by an apparition of St. Alessio Romano, a ninth-century saint whose cult was popular in Rome.

If Catherine of Siena was the greatest example of girlish religiousness triumphant, Francesca was a striking case of defeat and its traumatic consequences. The transaction between her and St. Alessio is obscure. All we are told is that after she recovered from her illness Francesca gave in to her father, took a husband, and bore several children—despite her abhorrence of the male touch. It was not until she had been married for sixteen years that Francesca was allowed to fulfill her girlhood aspiration, finally persuading her husband to live with her in chastity. Like Catherine, Francesca was attacked by demons, but the adolescent Catherine had defeated hers by the use of her mystical imagination; Francesca's demons persisted throughout her life. Her torments were obviously connected with the frustrated spiritual impulses of her childhood. Demons appeared to her in the form of lions, snakes, humans, and angels. They beat her, knocked her about, cut her, hung her by her hair, tempted her sexually, and dumped her into a privy. (See figs. 5–7.)

Like Catherine, Francesca experienced ecstasy in prayer; but whereas Catherine had managed to build for herself an interior oratory and people it with figures of joy, Francesca's visions more often were filled with portents of punishment. And where Catherine saw the divine household, Francesca saw purgatory, hellfire, and the apocalypse. Catherine too could speak of her wretchedness and unworthiness before God, but this did not keep her from believing she was Christ's bride or from assuming the role of God's agent in her letters to the pope. Francesca founded a congregation of oblates, cured the sick, miraculously provided food to the poor, gave spiritual counsel, in short, led a fairly active and even vigorous public life; but her self-doubts, her sense of guilt, and her obsession with punishment for herself and catastrophe for her city dominated her thoughts. A female saint was more likely than a male to undergo such intense spiritual suffering, but when she resolved these trials in childhood or adolescence the woman often went on to achieve a prominent and powerful position. Even when self-doubt continued, as in Francesca's case, a woman could find remedies for her private sufferings in public activity and translate her sense of personal sin into apocalyptic vision. Such a woman makes a powerful impression upon her age.

With Teresa of Avila, one of the best known of those saints whose spiritual conflicts began in girlhood, our attention shifts from Italy to Spain. Teresa's autobiography is one of the most important spiritual documents of the sixteenth century. Like Catherine, she was reared in a religious family and began to exhibit signs of unusual piety before she was seven. The willingness to die for religion, noted in so many other girl penitents, in Teresa took the extreme form of an explicit longing for martyrdom, an inspiration she shared with her older brother. She ran away from home to be a hermit, then came back and lived in a cell in the family garden. When Teresa was barely fourteen her beautiful young mother died. For a time she tried to cope with this loss by taking the Blessed Virgin as her mother; but the devil seduced her, as she put it: Teresa began reading books about the heroes of chivalry, became vain about her appearance, and decked herself with cosmetics and jewelry. Her hagiographer asserted that her natural aversion to sin and her fear of losing her honor held her back from greater evils he only hinted at; nonetheless, her father deplored her worldliness and was sufficiently worried to send her to a convent school, where she returned to better ways.

After six years Teresa returned home. She was now about twenty, and a pattern seems to have established itself: alternation between periods of intense religious dedication and backsliding into temptation, worldliness, and self-doubt; so, at any rate, Teresa described her life in retrospect. She joined the Carmelite order, became ill, returned home at her father's insistence, and suffered a paralytic stroke. During her three-year illness Satan led her to gossip excessively with secular people, and, until the image of the crucified Christ jolted her back to seriousness, she neglected her prayers.

As Teresa reported, her decisive conversion did not come until middle life when, at the rather advanced age of forty-two, she became Christ's bride. Her struggles to reform her order, her travels throughout Spain on behalf of religion, her conflict with the Inquisition, her tutelage of St. John of the Cross, highlight a life of extraordinary vigor and accomplishment. What Catherine of Siena was to fourteenth-century Christendom in the age of the great papal schism, Teresa was to the sixteenth century in the age of the Catholic Reformation. Ridden with guilt over her sinfulness, she energetically attacked the imperfections of others; constantly fearful of her own backsliding, she urged the church ahead; humble before God, she rejected the judgment of his vicars.

Teresa's life displays one of the many variations of that same pattern of feminine inner humility and external dynamism we observed in Catherine and her Italian predecessors. It was not a new pattern, nor was it exclusive to women, for we can trace it at least as far back as St. Augustine's *Confessions*; but from the thirteenth century women began to make this kind of spirituality their own. The seventh year was the favored one for the onset of religious impulses for many girl saints, a fact that may not be attributed merely to the medieval liking for mystical numbers. From dozens of cases, we have pieced together the following composite picture. Between the ages of four and seven, occasionally a bit later, a medieval girl began to be aware of what society had in store for her. From her peers, from the church, but most especially from her parents, she learned the norms of her class and sex. She might be allowed a few more years of frivolous play, but already she was being subtly cued for courtship, marriage, and motherhood. If, as was often the case, there was a new baby, she was put in charge unless her family was rich enough to employ a nurse. At the same time she was becoming aware of a drastic alternative: the life of the spirit in perpetual chastity, humility, and charity. This was also the time of her first communion, when she began to encounter the images of miracles and sacrifice. The lives of the saints, the image of the Blessed Virgin Mother seated in

Fig. 5. Francesca Romana (de' Ponziani) thrown on a cadaver by the devil. Vienna. Predella panel by Girolamo de Cremona(?). Photograph courtesy of Fototeca Berenson.

Fig. 6. (opposite, top) Francesca Romana (de' Ponziani) tormented by demons. Rome, Monastery of the Oblates de' Specchi. Fifteenth-century fresco. Photograph courtesy of Ministero Beni Culturali e Ambientali: Istituto Centrale per il Catalogo e la Documentazione. Number C2244.

Fig. 7. (opposite, bottom) Francesca Romana (de' Ponziani) whipped by demons. Rome, Monastery of the Oblates de' Specchi. Fifteenth-century fresco. Photograph courtesy of Ministero Beni Culturali e Ambientali: Istituto Centrale per il Catalogo e la Documentazione. Number C2245.

heaven next to her Son, the delicacy of white-robed nuns picking their way through the cluttered streets of her town—these beckoned the girl away from her mother's path and toward the way of the Virgin. At her tender age they offered a sweet refuge from the worldly obligations she felt closing in on her. Her budding awareness of physical intimacy was filled with disgust and dread. To her childish perception, motherhood with its disfigurement in pregnancy, screams of labor, filth of afterbirth, and early decay of beauty—offered no joy that could be compared with the ethereal serenity of the Madonna.[22]

For however many girls this experience was typical, for most it was a temporary stage on the way to puberty and adolescence. Physical squeamishness was banished by inner biological changes and outward social pressure. If the responsibilities of marriage and motherhood were heavy or painful, there were always the consolations of the spiritual world one had begun to imagine as a girl. The comforts of prayerful identification with the Madonna were always available. For the exceptional girls who were unwilling or unable to accept this compromise, however, adolescence would be still more painful than childhood. Bodily afflictions, demonic temptations, flagellation, longing for martyrdom, however formulaic and conventional they appear in the hagiographic stories, were the common responses provided by the culture to the culture's own dilemmas.

The call to sainthood emerged out of a psychic contest rooted in the deepest tensions of Christian culture. In its characteristic medieval form this was the tension between the world of the flesh and the world of the spirit. It began early in life. Neither a philosophical abstraction nor a child's fairy tale, the world of the spirit seemed substantial, immediate, and obtainable. The possibility of transcending material existence was a cornerstone of the basic religious fabric, dramatized over and over again by the saints, repeated daily in the mass, promised for the future in the Resurrection. However sweet the promise of spiritual perfection might seem to a young girl first becoming aware of the world of the flesh, it was yet no easy escape. She had to rid herself of childish impetuosity and overcome pride and desire, convincing herself of her utter worthlessness before God. She had to tame the most ordinary bodily desires, abstain from food and drink, deny herself all mundane comforts, and even inflict severe pain on herself. If she was successful in her course of self-abasement and denial, she was very likely to find herself in a struggle with her parents, even before her will could have been fully tempered for the unequal contest. She was driven to secretiveness, perhaps to outright lying, often to running away from home. Invariably the conflict escalated: against the parents' greater worldly strength the child needed greater spiritual resources, resources sought in ever greater extremes of self-mortification.

To the stark reality of everyday life medieval culture offered only stark alternatives—the hermitage, the crusade, the renunciation of home, of bodily warmth, of family love. Radical enough to a boy, to a girl just beginning to grope toward femininity the ideal of sainthood was a siren call beckoning her to a life so extreme that even contemporaries were prone to look upon it as madness, unless and until she could demonstrate that here was a divine madness confounding the wisdom of the world. She did this through the sheer force of her personality—sometimes, but not always supported by miracles and signs—which turned her antagonists into supporters and the rest of the world into believers. Temptation, self-doubt, disbelief, scorn, and persecution were the crucible in which her will was tempered and tested. The religious ideology of medieval Christendom was demanding, but its rewards were great—not merely fame but fame eternal, a place at God's table, and the power to dispense God's grace.

Statistical Profile of Child Saints

While other historians of sainthood have pointed out that the thirteenth century saw a proliferation of childhood crises in the lives of the saints,[23] a glance at table 1 (p. 123) shows that this phenomenon extended to the fourteenth century and continued to be substantial in the fifteenth. We might have thought this could be explained by the fact that detail about saintly children increased as the sources improved over time; but the decreasing frequency of stories of saintly children in the sixteenth and seventeenth centuries makes this explanation unlikely. Roughly between 1200 and 1500, independent of the changing quality of the sources, childhood received a special emphasis in hagiography. Again, some will argue that we are dealing with hagiographical conventions about saintliness in childhood, and no doubt this is true to a degree; but this does not explain why conventional stories about the saints' childhood became widespread just at this time, why they assumed the particular configurations they did, and why they declined sharply in the sixteenth century.

Certain facts are clear. The stories came from every country of Europe, perhaps with a slightly greater frequency from Mediterranean areas, but not overwhelmingly so. Nor are they limited to saints of a particular religious order, with the possible exception of a tendency toward the Dominicans. Figures for family status defy efforts to arrange child saints along a spectrum from rich to poor or highborn to humble. Relatively, peasants nearly equal kings, the urban poor outnumber patricians, and artisans appear more frequently than nobles. We began by suggesting that medieval society knew childhood; we can now add that this knowledge extended to every class.

Of what this knowledge consisted is suggested in the section of table 1 labeled family dynamics. What we have tried to demonstrate in individual cases is confirmed in the profile. A family that had a saintly child was likely to be put under great strain, even to the breaking point, particularly if the child was a girl. Frequently parents joined in vigorously opposing a child who aspired to the ascetic life; somewhat less often, the child's aspirations drove the parents apart, with the mother as the more important force. Mothers might exert a powerful influence toward sanctity in their children (230), but their opposition could also be awesome (280). Fathers appear to have been less intimately involved in the process of early childhood development. Sometimes the father simply did not appear in the story at all, as in the case of Dominic de Guzmán. More often the father appeared, but as a secondary figure. Following our early suggestion—that the path of sanctity, particularly for girls, meant a departure from the normal path of socialization—it is not surprising that mothers dominated, since they provided the feminine model.

Seven-year-old girls, of course, understood not role models but people; they rejected not an abstraction but their mothers. Where the mother supported rather than opposed her daughter's aspirations to sanctity against the opposition of her husband, a modern reader may suspect that she was vicariously rejecting her own femininity; the maternal path she had chosen—or had been forced into—was not good enough for her child. Whether or not she was rejecting her own femininity, however, she was surely helping her daughter to do so. According to the notion of spiritual hierarchy that the mother shared with most medieval people, a child who could throw off the burden of sex might aspire to a level of perfection that the mother could only dream of. And frequently the mother had supernatural signs to armor her in her struggle against her husband. If this was her only child, or her last child, as was frequently the case in the accounts analyzed earlier, the mother's emotional involvement in the struggle for saintliness is even more understandable, for this was her one hope of transcending her own destiny.

Whether these stories are fact or fiction is less important than what they reveal about social realities. (To come closer to home, Horatio Alger stories tell us as much about late-nineteenth-century American values as does a biography of Andrew Carnegie.)[24] Medieval adults expected children to behave in certain ways and to go through certain stages of development. Parents were intensely involved with their children's upbringing and concerned with their welfare. They reared them in accordance with their station and conscientiously tried to prepare them for life tasks. Even if they designated their children for a life in religion, they had socially conventional notions of what that kind of life entailed. They felt love for their children and expressed their affection and concern with praise and with punishment.

This picture of a close-knit, affective family, in which children were caringly treated in their own terms while being prepared for adulthood, conflicts with the usual description of the medieval family as set forth by social scientists including Philippe Ariès, Lawrence Stone, and François Lebrun. They maintain that the concept of childhood became defined only in the seventeenth century, that the affective family was a late-seventeenth- and eighteenth-century phenomenon that emerged among the gentry and was quickly taken over by the bourgeoisie, and that parents had so many children that the death of "this or that member" did not cause the living much grief.[25]

Our conclusion, based on a select and relatively small group of children in their family settings, does not permit us to claim that we have overthrown the work of these scholars, but it does suggest that their composite picture is less than universal. At the very least, those who knew these stories, and presumably understood and relished them (for hagiography was one of the principal genres of medieval literature), had before them a vivid portrayal of the affective family with all its tribulations, pressures, and joys. Were we to concede that hagiographers made up these stories from whole cloth, we would still have to explain where they found their material, and why this pattern became fashionable in the thirteenth century and went out of fashion in the sixteenth. Whatever the explanation for this rise and fall, which we find less in variations of social class, place, or nationality than in the dynamics of family structure, the transition to the modern nuclear family with its strong affective bonds was not a simple linear one.[26]

2 ⊕ *Adolescents*

For many saints adolescence was not a period of special crisis. Saints' vitae record many dutiful sons who more or less obediently followed the religious path set out for them by their parents. In many cases the parents' decision was influenced by heavenly signs foretelling great holiness for their unborn or newborn son. Often the parents recognized special gifts in the young boy and set him on the road to an ecclesiastical career by sending him to school.

If for many young men the road to religion, and even to saintliness, was smooth, young women generally did not find it so. This is not to say that medieval families seldom chose a religious career for daughters; obviously they did. Many were the convents populated by noble girls whose parents regarded a life in religion as a socially worthy alternative to marriage, while other houses accepted girls whose harassed parents could not find the price of a dowry.[1] But such girls seem not often to have achieved a state of noble holiness. The female saint had to come by a different route, through the torments of a childhood beset by fears of marriage or of an adolescence ridden with sexual guilt.

Among boys too there are distinctions to be observed. The pattern of the dutiful son who followed parental wishes as they took him into a religious education, then to ecclesiastical office, and ultimately to sainthood was more common early in the period of our study, and more frequent in the north of Europe than south of the Alps or Pyrenees. A typical case is that of the eleventh-century bishop Bernwald of Hildesheim, son of a Saxon count. Bernwald's life was written by Thangmar, his schoolmaster and later his confessor, who detailed the boy's early aptitude for learning, both in philosophy and in "the lighter or mechanical arts" of writing, drawing, and designing. Ordained a deacon while still *adolescens*, Bernwald made his way first by the patronage of his uncle, a future bishop, then by distinguishing himself in the household of the emperor. Except for a brief reference to the celestial aura that seemed to radiate from his face, Bernwald's vita contains no hint of the supernatural, nor does it record any spiritual struggle. A good boy became a good bishop, and a powerful one. Good birth, ability, and family support were in German society the normal requisites for success in an ecclesiastical career, and, in the eleventh and twelfth centuries especially, prelacy was one of the highroads to sainthood.[2]

The parents' decision to send a son to school did not necessarily mean that the boy had a religious vocation.[3] Only when the future saint Wolfhelm met Saint Heribert, bishop of Cologne, sometime about 1030, was he attracted to the contemplative life, ultimately to become an abbot. Arnoul, the future bishop of Gap, got his start on the path to sainthood as a favorite of his abbot, whom he accompanied to Rome. On the other hand, a boyhood impulse toward extreme asceticism sometimes had to be curbed and deflected into a more respectable channel. As a boy in late-eleventh-century Bergerac, Géraud de Salles burned to become a hermit, a career most unsuitable for a nobleman's son. But the Blessed Robert d'Abrissel influenced him to join the Augustinian Canons Regular, and from there Geraud became a famous preacher. The future saint need not have been distinguished by any great success at school. Power, rather than intellectual or religious ability, was the key to veneration, as, for example, in the case of the English bishop Wulfstan in the eleventh century. He "knew no more than was absolutely necessary for the discharge of his duties," but when he died he received a rare papal canonization as a fighter for the rights of the church.

The importance of ecclesiastical careerism as a path to sainthood was to decline in the thirteenth and succeeding centuries. Italians came to dominate the ranks of sainthood, while this shift toward the Mediterranean continued with the prominence of the Spaniards in the Catholic Reformation. At the same time—and, as we intend to show, not coincidentally—the number of women saints increased, more saints came from nonnoble and humbler origins, fewer saints were prelates, and the story of the saint who had been a dutiful adolescent gave way to the drama of conversion crisis, family conflict, and sexual temptation.

Nothing suggests the growing intensity of religious consciousness in the thirteenth century so much as the increasing reference to conversion, and nothing better demonstrates the connection between changing religious ideas and new social patterns. Everyone knows the story of Francesco Bernardone, the merchant's son born in 1181 who stripped off his elegant clothes in Assisi's public square and turned from dissolute ways to a life of humility and poverty. (See fig. 8.) The story of Francis of Assisi became the classic example of youthful conversion, although the paradigm could claim scriptural precedents and even in the Middle Ages was not unknown before Francis. Nearly two centuries earlier, in a Flemish town, a young man named Arnolf, who had begun to pursue a knightly career, suddenly gave it up to devote himself to a life of contemplation and severe penance. Refusing election to abbot, he fled into the forest to seek a life of solitude. There he communed with the animals, even taming wild beasts, but, like so many of the great holy figures of this earlier time, he finally was lured back into the world, serving as a political adviser and accepting a bishopric. From late-tenth-century England comes the story of St. Walstan of Baw-burgh, a young noble perhaps related to royalty, who renounced his entire inheritance, disguised himself, and lived for thirty years as a humble farm laborer. Having given up his chances of worldly power, Walstan gained the greater gift of miracle. In the eleventh and twelfth centuries he was the special protector of the working people of Norfolk and other English localities.

These tenth- and eleventh-century stories of world renunciation are heav-ily legendary; they make a simple equation between giving up temporal power and acquiring supernatural grace to be used for the benefit of the community. While they begin with a youthful crisis and conversion, they tell us very little about its circumstances, moving quickly to the details of the saint's subsequent miracle-working and healing. About the time of Francis, however, the adolescent crisis becomes a major part of the story. The details of spiritual growth and the circumstances of conversion are dealt with at greater length, and the texture of the narrative becomes richer with situations and emotions that connect to ordinary lives.[4]

Two stories of thirteenth-century saints illustrate the point. John the Spaniard left home at thirteen to study in Provence. There he spent all his father's money and had to be rescued by a local rich man. Two years later, as Lent approached, he began to feel remorse for his spendthrift ways. He sought out a pious hermit to hear his confession and decided upon a rigorous course of penance. At about the age of seventeen he took the Carthusian habit and eventually acquired a reputation for sanctity. Andrea Corsini, later bishop of Fiesole, was, according to his biographer, already contentious, disobedient, and licentious at the age of twelve. He grew to love arms and hunting instead of the church. After years of scolding him, his distraught mother at last burst out with a revelation: before Andrea was born, she said, she had dreamed of a wolf who invaded a church but then turned into a lamb. Now she knew that the wolf had been her unborn son. His mother's confession pierced Andrea's heart like an arrow, and he

Fig. 8. The bishop of Assisi covers the nakedness of
Francis, who has stripped off his clothes and flung
them at his father. Assisi, Basilica of St. Francis of
Assisi (upper church). Fresco by Giotto. Photograph
from Alinari/Editorial Photocolor Archives.

accepted the implication of her premonition. The next day he went to the Carmelites to dedicate himself to the Blessed Virgin. Bearing the scorn of former companions who mocked his newfound holiness, and resisting the temptations of the devil, who came disguised as a visitor, Andrea took humility as his special virtue.

The conversion to the spiritual life of the great fourteenth-century English mystic Richard Rolle was sudden and unexplained. Yet, as in thirteenth-century accounts, there is a richness of detail not usually found in the vitae of earlier centuries. Rolle began his religious career while a university student. Quitting school at about the age of eighteen (it is uncertain whether he was at Oxford or at the Sorbonne), Richard returned home and begged two gowns from his sister. These he cut up and sewed into a crude hermit's robe that he put on, to the horror of his sister, who thought he had gone mad. To avoid his friends, lest they try to stop him, and afraid of his father's wrath, Richard slipped out to sing and pray in the local churches dressed in his homemade religious robes. In one church he delivered a sermon that brought tears to the eyes of his listeners, including a local squire, John of Dalton, who provided him with the means to become a hermit.

The sixteenth-century Spaniard Pedro de Alcantara rejected the world even more totally than had Richard Rolle. At sixteen he left his noble family, gave up his education, and joined the discalced Capuchins. To guard himself from temptation he seldom opened his eyes for three years, and for the whole of his religious life he never looked at the face of a woman or even at women's clothes.

If the usual theater of crisis for adolescent boys was school, for girls it was marriage or the prospect of marriage. As a future saint, Umiliana Cerchi (b. 1219) of Florence was unusual in that she displayed no special piety or distaste for married life until after she had taken a husband at the age of sixteen (according to some accounts she was only twelve). Within a month of her marriage she began to spurn facial makeup and ornate clothes and to attend mass daily "for her sins." Umiliana spent her money on alms for the poor, visited the sick, and even cut off parts of her own garments to clothe the naked. Apparently this behavior offended the sensibilities of some of the townspeople, because she would return home with signs of having been beaten. She experienced pains in her stomach and womb that were like birth pangs, but accepted everything with great patience and humility. She paid "the marriage debt" (as theologians called the legitimate sexual demands of one's marriage partner) and bore several children, but she must have had misgivings.[5] When her children were ill Umiliana would tell them that it was better for them to die in purity and virginity than to recover and marry. She also suffered guilt for her husband's business dealings; when he lay dying she tried to persuade him to restore his usurious profits.

After her husband's death Umiliana returned to her father's house but resisted all pressures to remarry. Still, despite a vision of herself in white among columns of white-robed children, Umiliana found no peace. Yielding control of her husband's estate to her father, she had to beg alms in order to continue giving to the poor. Now that she had given up the last of her earthly connections, she was ready to enter a cloistered convent; but God had a harder duty in store, commanding her to stay in her father's house, where she would be an example to all, a chosen vessel in the church militant, a pillar of the celestial Jerusalem.

From then on the story of Umiliana's travails became an object lesson in how to live the contemplative life in the world. In her father's house she continually resisted diversions that she understood to be temptations of Lucifer. She took a vow of silence, whereupon the devil sent her daughter to entice her into speaking. She fasted for days and prayed that she might be made deaf and blind so that she could cut out the world. She flagellated herself and longed for martyrdom for Jesus' sake, but God would grant her only the death-to-the-world of long ecstasies. Umiliana levitated, gave off a divine fragrance, had a vision of a dove in her nocturnal chamber, and worked miracles. In 1246 God granted her a last consolation by taking her to him on a Sunday, as she had requested. Umiliana was immediately venerated as a saint in Florence, and her body was eagerly dismembered for relics. It is worth noting that in the contemporary accounts of her holy life and miracles all the witnesses were women; Umiliana's story was quintessentially a woman's.

One of the most prominent occasions of youthful crisis and conversion, for boys as for girls, was, not surprisingly, the death of a parent. The theme is common in saints' vitae from all centuries. What modern psychologists might variously interpret as a denial reaction or survivor guilt or a feeling of abandonment, the hagiographers describe as a sudden perception of the fleetingness of life and the vanity of worldly desires.[6] But grief worked differently in different cases. For the twelfth century's greatest saint, Bernard of Clairvaux, grief was the occasion of a long, debilitating spiritual malaise. When he was seventeen Bernard suffered the loss of his mother, Aleth. Mother and son had been extremely close, and Aleth had had premonitions of Bernard's saintliness. With her death, Bernard became brooding and passive. His sister rallied him from his despondency, but Bernard forsook the path of sainthood set forth in his mother's dream, steadily becoming lukewarm and even indifferent to religion and turning to a worldly, if not irremediably sinful, life. This period of mourning followed by spiritual indifference lasted about five years, until one day Bernard found himself again through prayer. Now he decided to become a monk and to follow the strict Cistercian rule, of which he became the unshakable champion for the rest of his extraordinary life in religion.

More often the connection between the loss of a parent and renunciation of the world was direct and immediate. For Peter Nolasco, the thirteenth-century founder of the Mercedarian order, conversion seems to have been the way for an adolescent boy to escape from adult responsibilities prematurely thrust upon him. Peter was fifteen when he inherited the family estate upon his father's death and, as the bearer of the family name and fortunes, was urged to marry. This led him to meditate upon the vanity of worldly desires in effect, to choose between life as a Barcelona patrician and life as a servant of God. Filled with such thoughts, he spent the night prostrate in prayer. By morning Peter had made his decision: he would dedicate both his patrimony and his virginity to God's service.

For others the death of a parent meant the final breaking of worldly ties. Angelo di Furcio, a thirteenth-century saint from the Abruzzi, was a bright youth who seemed destined for a career in religion by his considerable aptitude for learning. Encouraged by his family, Angelo had made a vow to enter the religious life, but he continued to postpone a decision until he was twenty. His father seems to have exercised remarkable understanding and tact in allowing Angelo time to make up his mind. As the father lay dying, he gently advised Angelo to fulfill his vow, but he made it clear that the choice belonged to the boy. This restrained deathbed counsel was effective. When his father died, Angelo rejoiced that he now knew his way, bemoaned his lost time, and prepared to leave the family home for an Augustinian monastery.

For Raimondo di Palmerio, born in Piacenza about 1140 of modest parentage, conversion was less a drawn-out process than a series of reversals. After a pious upbringing, he was set to learn a trade at the age of twelve. The vocation was not to Raimondo's liking, but he tolerated it out of obedience to his parents. When his father died the fourteen-year-old Raimondo left his apprenticeship to go on pilgrimage to the Holy Land, apparently as a way of escaping his unhappy condition rather than from any burning religious zeal. When he returned Raimondo married and had children. But the death of a son caused him to lose interest in worldly things. He urged his wife to accept a life of continence. When she hesitated, God intervened; the woman died. Raimondo went on pilgrimage again until Christ appeared to him and told him to give up his wandering, return to his native city, and occupy himself with works of charity.

Conversion could also be the restraining of wild religious impulses. In his youth the thirteenth-century Thomas of Ely was something of a religious vagrant who affected long hair and a beard and did not trouble to bathe.

After the death of his "simple parents" he was taken in hand by the bishop of Constance, who persuaded him to wash, behave more decorously, and settle down. Thomas went to Paris to study for the priesthood. Although he did not abandon all the extreme penitential practices he had begun in boyhood (for instance, he still whipped himself until, in the hagiographer's phrase, the blood ran down to his feet), Thomas was best known as a very effective preacher.

Sometimes after the death of a loved one a vision precipitated the turning to the religious life. Angela Merici, founder of the Ursulines, was the daughter of poor parents who lived on the shore of Lake Garda. She was only ten when they died, and she soon became strongly attached to her elder sister. Three years later the sister also died. Angela was despondent, especially since her sister had died without the sacrament. Grief mingled with fear, both for herself and for her sister, until she received a vision reassuring her that her sister was among the saved. Overflowing with gratitude, Angela consecrated herself more completely to God, joining the Franciscan Tertiaries and living a life of austerity, mystical experiences, and charity.

Death looms large in the literature of the medieval conversion experience. The simple formula displays a youth undergoing a period of despondency after the death of a parent, more often the father, then resolving the sense of loss in religion.[7] But it would be all too facile to accept a simple cause and effect relationship between mourning and turning to God. To conclude that Bernard found in the Blessed Virgin a replacement for the dead Aleth merely replaces a hagiographical convention with a psychological one. Death of a parent was indeed a turning point for many saints, but the circumstances of conversion varied widely. The period of despondency and uncertainty might be extended, as in Bernard's case, or fairly brief, as with Peter Nolasco. Resolution might be occasioned by supernatural intervention, as with Angela Merici, or by the wise counsel of a relative, as when the Blessed Humbeline spoke with Bernard. Conversion might be permanent, as with Thomas of Ely, or more temporary and fitful, as with Raimondo di Palmerio.

The death of a parent was a practical as well as an emotional problem. When a saint's biographer describes the youth as rejecting the toils of worldly affairs, this is no mere abstraction or philosophical reflection. The fifteen-year-old Peter Nolasco suddenly had to cope with the problems of managing a wealthy patrimony; Raimondo di Palmerio was faced with the burden of being a breadwinner at the age of fourteen. In these and many other instances death thrust youthful survivors into the world and they flinched. Peter gave away his patrimony and Raimondo decamped to the Holy Land.

This is not to say that all conversion should be explained as a rejection of adult social responsibilities, though such a motive is too often overlooked. The life of religion, whether in a monastery, in a hermitage, or on the pilgrim road, was a compelling alternative to that of a soldier, a housewife, or a peasant—even to the life of a prince—and countless young men and women responded to its attractions during their years of formation and decision. Like ourselves, medieval people referred to these years as adolescence, *adolescentia*, the time of growing up. While the formal age of maturity was usually twelve for girls and fourteen for boys—the age at which they might join a religious order, marry, or enter into a legal contract—it was not unusual to allow a much longer time after puberty for emotional, intellectual, and even physical maturity.[8] The death of a parent abruptly ended this time of growth and telescoped the normal period of adolescence into the confines of a "sudden" conversion. Our information is only about those who became saints, but the crisis of youth cut short was a very common one in this age of early and sudden death. No doubt many adolescents took the death of a parent as a call to religion, even if only a few became saints.

A fair number of young people came to religion as a result of an encounter with a holy person. While the accounts invariably describe the event in terms of the future saint's decision to reject the world, clearly another element was at work here: the personality of the holy man or woman was the force that turned the youth to religion. The spiritual state of the youth before conversion varied greatly; some had unfulfilled religious yearnings, others were more or less content with a normal life in society, and a few were dissolute and actively hostile to piety. Edwin Starbuck's statistical, empirical study explored numerous avenues to conversion and tabulated various age and gender correlates of the experience, but ultimately he was unable to explain fully the process of conversion, nor does a psychoanalytic explanation take us much further.[9] In some cases, to be sure, the youth placed himself under the tutelage of a father figure, or the young girl under a mother substitute, but more often youths responded to someone of their own age and circumstances, as did the followers of Bernard, Dominic, and Francis.

In Christian culture the prototypical charismatic religious leader was Jesus himself. At all times of Christian history the youth searching for a path in life might hear the Master's voice and heed his call. And in every period there were prophets who issued the call to repentence and worldly rejection in Jesus' name.[10] From time to time magnetic figures appeared to lead their followers away into the Egyptian desert, the forests of the Abruzzi, or the highways of Umbria. Then the column of youthful converts swelled, as it did during the thirteenth century in response to the rise of the mendicant orders.

Protective parents viewed the holy evangelist with awe and fear, many resisting a power that seemed to them magical or diabolical. Their unsuccessful efforts were part of the drama of the saint's story, as, indeed, of religious movements generally. The strength of the mendicant movement in the thirteenth century, as well as of movements like the Gesuati in the fourteenth and the Jesuit and other missionaries in the sixteenth, was built on a combination of charismatic appeal and youthful ardor.[11] Just as the death of a parent might produce the moment that suddenly ended an adolescent's search for identity, so also did the encounter with the holy evangelist, an encounter that might take many forms. The youth may have been one of a crowd who listened to Dominic de Guzmán in the public square and watched as flames seemed to shoot from his eyes, or, like Clare of Assisi, she may have stolen away from her family to receive the private benediction of Francis. Or he may have been one of the many British youths who came to watch the disembowelment of a Catholic and was so struck by the martyr's heroism that he vowed to brave the same fate. Whatever the particular circumstances, the youth found himself by associating with an important, even heroic, cause embodied in a great person. Religious conversion resolved the uncertainties of adolescence. Why one youth took this path and another did not is at present beyond the reach of scientific explanation, if not of hagiography. Still, the historian can identify times in which the religious solution to adolescent dilemmas was more common. The late Middle Ages was such a time, when adolescence increasingly became a battleground between worldly parents and ascetic children.

The thirteenth-century conjuncture of dramatic public issues—the agony of the Holy Land, the growth of commercial greed and its challenge to Christian community, warfare between pope and emperor, Guelf and Ghibelline, orthodox Christian and heretic—spurred new religious impulses.[12] It also inspired a radical set of religious choices. While there would always be many who thirsted for the contemplative life, others now burned to follow Francis and Dominic into the maelstrom of a militant religious life in the world. To those who had heard the romance of the gospel, preaching to unbelievers and confounding heretics seemed more exciting than singing in the convent choir or reading one's breviary in the gloom of a monk's cell. Begging bread in the streets seemed more spiritual than pouring over Peter Lombard's *Sentences* in the monastery library. The figure of the great bishop-saint was now rivaled by those of the lowly begging and preaching friar and the layman who resolutely tried to combine a secular life with spiritual discipline. Confraternities, Beguinages, and irregular groups of wanderers took up some of the space between a strictly ordered conventual life and the profane life of noble, merchant, or peasant.[13]

Catholic hagiography accounts for only a tiny part of the new popular piety of the late twelfth and thirteenth centuries. Besides the saints there were men and women who were driven by similar religious impulses to the fringes of orthodoxy and even further, into the outer darkness of heresy. Waldensians, Cathars, Beguines, Fraticelli, and Bretheren of the Free Spirit competed with Dominic, Francis, and Clare for the minds and spirits of Europe's youth.[14] The early life of Peter Martyr of Verona is a case in point. Peter was born in 1205 to Cathar parents who tried to force him to accept their faith. He resisted their beatings and the pressure of a heretical uncle and responded instead to the call of Dominic, from whose hands he took the habit of the Order of Preachers. Peter thus fulfilled his parents' early premonition that he would become an enemy of their religion.

In the sixteenth century the adolescent was once again presented with a rapidly expanding range of religious alternatives. As in the thirteenth century, traditional religious teaching failed to provide satisfactory directions for the spiritual hunger of youth, and a religious revolution followed. The central figure in the early stage of this new explosion was, of course, Martin Luther, a young monk who had tried to calm his troubled conscience with every resource offered by a monastic vocation. Luther too listened at length to the counsel of a spiritual teacher, his superior, Martin Staupitz.[15] But Staupitz could lead Luther only in the path of traditional doctrine; the rest of the way young Martin had to find for himself. Luther, not Staupitz, became the great evangelical teacher and opened the floodgates of new religious options, not only his own but also those of Calvinists, Anabaptists, Spirituals, Anglicans, Puritans, and many others. Catholicism too responded to the challenge of sixteenth-century Reformation with a variety of new or reinvigorated vocations. The common element was a new evangelism: apostolic faith, the word of the gospel, and the return to a community of saints were the themes of preachers in the streets and in the pulpit. For youth this was another time when the holy evangelist marked out a path from uncertainty to vocation.[16]

Whether turning away from the world out of grief for a dead parent, responding to the call of an evangelical preacher, or impelled by some inner spiritual urge, the future saint reached a decision within the intimacy of the family. In the previous chapter we used saints' lives as a basis for our conclusion that medieval society knew the age of childhood. We now offer what may seem to some an equally controversial suggestion, that medieval society recognized adolescence, not simply as an arbitrary number of years between puberty and young adulthood, but more positively as a period with a unique set of social and emotional characteristics. In the medieval view an adolescent was capable of rational choice and was responsible for the consequences. Parents recognized that youthful decision making might be painful, and even when they took the steps to countermand what they considered a rash decision they were likely to do so with some restraint and to exhibit a measure of respect for the child who was a child no longer. There are some instances of brutal parental opposition to the adolescent's decision to seek a holy life, even a few cases of murder; but more often what we see is a contest of wills, a power struggle between parent and adolescent. The contest was the essence. Parents did not as a rule engage in open struggles for power with younger children, nor did adults need to undertake contests of will with their parents. Adolescence was the appointed time for battles of that sort, certainly in the lives of saints and, we believe, among ordinary medieval people as well.

Even as early as the eleventh and twelfth centuries, when adolescents were usually more dutiful, there were a few stories of conflict between teenager and parent. Aelfheâh, archbishop of Canterbury (d. 1012), had been brought up piously by his mother, but he encountered her strong resistance when he proposed to enter a monastery after his father's death. The decision of thirteen-year-old Benno of Hildesheim to become a monk involved this eleventh-century saint in a family contest that pitted mother against father. Only the father's death brought an end to the struggle, and at twenty-two Benno became a Benedictine. A not uncommon variation of the family conflict theme appears in the story of Hanno of Cologne, the eleventh-century youth who had to run away from both his parents with the collusion of his uncle to pursue a religious vocation.

The life story of another eleventh-century saint, the French hermit Theobaldus, contains an interview between father and adolescent son that is as poignant as if it took place today. Young Theobaldus longed to become a hermit and to model himself after Elijah and John the Baptist. As with Hanno of Cologne, his uncle (also a future saint) urged him on; but his parents were adamant. Theobaldus fled from home with his father in hot pursuit. When they met the following conversation took place (according to family relatives whose testimony forms the basis of a life written within six years of Theobaldus's death):

> Father (tearfully): Son, why do you run away? This is your father you are fleeing, not the devil. I don't want to recall you from your vocation, but I am happy to have seen you, to have spoken with you directly even if only to see my son reject his grieving parents.
> Theobaldus (unmoved): Sir, don't upset me. Go in peace and let me remain in peace, in the peace of Christ.

Then Theobaldus turned his back on his father and walked away. The father, still sorrowing, returned home to his family, but Theobaldus's mother entered a convent to be near her son.

Not all parents were as forebearing as the father of Theobaldus or as open to persuasion as his mother. Nicholas the Pilgrim, born near the

Greek monastery of Štira, was an eleventh-century wanderer, a spiritual Pied Piper, regarded as crazy during his lifetime, at least by the parents of the young boys who flocked to him as he went about endlessly repeating *Kyrie eleison*. In contrast to the biography of Theobaldus, with its sympathetic portrayal of a troubled family, the story of Nicholas, also recounted by an eyewitness, portrays a vicious mother. The woman could not bear Nicholas's obsessive chanting, so she beat him repeatedly. When he was twelve, and still chanting, she threw him out. He went to live in a cave in the mountains, where he tamed a ferocious bear with the sign of the cross. When Nicholas returned home his mother decided he was possessed and had him exorcised, then beat him again. All of this, we are told, he bore patiently. Nicholas shut himself in a high tower, but he was dragged out, beaten, chained, and imprisoned. Still Nicholas chanted, even when he was thrown into the sea! Somehow he reached the shores of Apulia, near Trani, the town that later took him as its patron saint. Nicholas died at the age of nineteen, and miracles were soon recorded at his tomb. Four years after his death he received a papal canonization.

Whether Nicholas was the source of the stories of his mother's vile behavior or whether they were invented, we are left to wonder why eleventh-century southern Italians were pleased to repeat them, depicting the mother in such an unfavorable light.[17] More often it was fathers who bore the opprobrium of having misunderstood and mistreated their saintly progeny, from which we might infer that fathers were more likely to beat their children than were mothers. At the very least the story was cautionary, a warning to mothers as well as to fathers not to judge too quickly the extreme behavior of their children as they entered adolescence. Perhaps there is something more specific to the cult of Nicholas the Pilgrim. His cruel mother may have stood for all the mothers of Trani who had refused to believe that their children were running after a saint rather than a crazed seducer of young boys. By painting her in such brutal colors, they were punishing themselves vicariously for their lack of faith, for their own acts of violence against their willful children. (See figs. 9 and 10.)

In saints' vitae stepmothers come in for even less flattering treatment than did the mother of Nicholas the Pilgrim.[18] In late-fourteenth-century Lombardy the saintly Panacea, who had lost her mother at the age of three, suffered domestic persecution worthy of a Cinderella. Content to tend her flocks, gather wood, and share her crust of bread with the poor, she patiently bore her stepmother's beatings. So devout was Panacea at fifteen that one time when praying she forgot to stable the animals for the night. Although the animals returned home by themselves, the stepmother was so enraged that she set upon Panacea and killed her, then pretended she had died from other causes. But the girl's "martyrdom" could not be

Fig. 9. (left) Nicholas the Pilgrim, with scenes from his life. Trani, cathedral crypt. Altarpiece, Puglie school. Photographs courtesy of Ministero Beni Culturali e Ambientali: Istituto Centrale per il Catalogo e la Documentazione. Number E56537.

Fig. 10. (right) Details from figure 9. *Above:* Nicholas miraculously provides apples for his youthful followers. *Below:* Nicholas instructs the children while an amazed bishop looks on. Number E56691.

concealed. Her body became as heavy as lead, a sign that brought great crowds to her funeral. Miraculous cures took place at her tomb, and a cult grew up that continued for six centuries, culminating in Panacea's beatification in 1867.

Equally a subject of reproach was the mother of the Blessed Alpais, a late-twelfth-century French girl who cheerfully tended her father's two cows and carefully guarded her virtue. Sometime after the age of twelve Alpais suffered a double catastrophe; her father died and she fell ill. The illness caused her to give off such a vile odor that her mother and brothers refused to go near her. So disgusting was Alpais's condition that her mother withheld food from her in the hope that she would die. The girl's stomach shrank until she was unable to eat; her limbs became ulcerous and putrid, and everyone abhorred her. Finally the Blessed Virgin answered Alpais's prayers and cured her. From then on she had no need for food, although she ate and drank just enough to prevent the suspicion that she was possessed by demons. Having overcome the incomprehension and cruelty of her family with supernatural help, Alpais became a visionary and worked miracles.

The story of Alpais, written by a friend during her lifetime, is one of a relatively small but by no means insignificant number of saints' lives that tell of family cruelty. These are stories told by contemporaries, and often they are presented in such a way as to suggest that the saint was the source of the shocking details of parental abuse. Two features are worth considering. Almost all these stories describe rural families, and in none of them does the holy adolescent show any hint of Christian forgiveness for having been so cruelly treated. Departing from the tedious convention of saints whose parents were poor but spiritually noble, the biographies of Nicholas, Panacea and Alpais, along with the others of their kind, suggest the existence of a type counter to the usual pattern in which families treat the youthful religious vocation with respect, even when they oppose it. Countertypical parents who grossly violated this norm were beyond the limit of Christian charity, even the charity of a saint. No adolescent behavior, however bizarre, nor any disgusting physical deformity justified such brutality—this is the lesson of these stories.

That cruel parents were usually poor and rural suggests not so much that life among the rural poor was more brutal, but that they had far greater difficulty coping with the burden of children who suffered from a hideous illness or of adolescents who engaged in extreme behavior.[19] It may also be that medieval people could not bear to think about such degrees of cruelty within families of higher social quality. As all readers of saints' vitae know, the term "noble" in hagiography connotes a moral as well as a social condition, and many a family of humble peasants is described as noble in spirit. But a family that behaved as did the mother and brothers of Alpais forfeited any claim to such distinction. Mistreatment of adolescents of any class was condemned.

At the other extreme from the stories of parental cruelty are two twelfth-century accounts of parents who were overly zealous in their efforts to further their children's spiritual vocations, or at least their ecclesiastical careers. The father of Domenico Loricato used a bribe to have his son ordained as a priest. When Domenico learned of his simoniacal ordination he was so revolted that he could not or would not say mass for the rest of his life. Burning with a kind of "divine fire" in his breast, he became a hermit and searched for ever more intense forms of penance and self-castigation. Domenico would stand for hours with his arms extended in the form of a cross; he wore an iron tunic next to his flesh (hence the nickname "Loricato" or cuirass); he scourged himself, inventing new forms of flagellation that amazed even his biographer Peter Damian, the great battler again simony. In the case of Ulrich of Zell, the overzealous parent was the mother, who began to dress him in clerical costume when he was still a baby, apparently in response to a dream that prophesied he would be a bishop. Brought up in the court of his godfather, the Emperor Henry III, Ulrich preferred the chapel to the palace. Nevertheless his uncle, a bishop, realized that clerical robes did not protect a youth from the temptations of court life, so he removed Ulrich from the company of women until "he had had sufficient exercise in chastity." Both stories emphasize that parental management was not the way to the religious life. Vocations, even when they had been divinely prophesied, were not considered to be automatic or induced; they came out of conscious adolescent decision, and they flowered with the development of reason and will.

An extraordinarily rich account of maternal zeal, familial interplay, and the adolescent quest for religious identity is contained in the autobiography of Peter Celestine, the thirteenth century Abruzzi hermit who briefly served as pope. Peter's mother was determined that one of her twelve sons would become a cleric. After five died in childhood and her next choice showed no aptitude for a religious vocation, she picked six-year-old Peter to fulfill her ambition. In him she now saw wondrous signs of divine grace and arranged for his education. But the devil tempted Peter from his studies and incited his older brothers to oppose their mother's wishes. The brothers insisted that Peter leave school to work for a local magnate who had promised to make Peter his heir, no small matter in view of the family's poverty. The mother, fortified by supernatural signs that encouraged her to believe it was God's wish, resisted the brothers' pressure and paid for Peter's education with the family's meager funds. Peter now returned to his studies with zeal, he too being encouraged by visions of the Virgin Mary and the Apostle John.

Peter was now twelve. At this point the autobiography contains an intense dialogue in which Peter and his mother exchange accounts of their prophetic dreams and agree to keep them secret from others. By persuading him to keep silent about his supernatural dreams, Peter's mother guaranteed that she alone would be able to regulate his progress toward the religious life; but she may also have so undermined his independence as to render him unfit to pursue the very goal she had chosen for him. For the next eight years Peter was torn by anxiety and indecision, accepting his destiny as a servant of God but unable to make the break that would initiate the service. Not until he was twenty, and then only with the encouragement of an older friend, did Peter leave home to embark upon a religious career. Still unable to act independently, he decided to go to Rome to seek ecclesiastical direction; but after a day on the road his friend turned back and Peter was suddenly, for the first time in his life, alone and in sole charge of his spiritual vocation. Not in Rome but in the mountains of the Abruzzi, not as a priest (as his mother had wished) but as a hermit, he found his destiny.

Yet indecision remained with Peter all his life. His holy reputation as a hermit and his founding of the Celestines were to inspire a cult and induce the church to recognize him as a saint; but as Pope Celestine V he made "*il gran rifiuto*," abdicating the office and leaving the papacy to the simoniac Boniface VIII, a betrayal of responsibility for which Dante placed him in hell.[20]

It is not too much to say that the prevailing, although by no means unique, pattern in the hagiography of the eleventh and twelfth centuries showed teenagers dutifully following the path laid out from infancy by pious parents. This pattern was flanked by two extreme variants: violent mistreatment of bizarre adolescents on one hand and overzealous mothering on the other. As we have suggested, the extremes served to emphasize normal expectations and set limits to parental dominance. Still, such dominance was the major underlying theme of all these cases.

With the thirteenth century and even more prominently in the fifteenth, however, a new trend emerged. Adolescents were less likely to be docile and parents were less likely to be violent and smothering. Conflict between parents and teenagers over religious vocations was frequent and intense, but for the most part it was confined within more moderate, socially acceptable limits. In the stories of this later period we found no brutality to match that of Nicholas the Pilgrim's mother. Even while Catherine of

Siena's parents were trying to break her will by forcing her into a kind of family servitude, they were concerned for her well-being. At the same time, increasingly in the later period, the youthful convert seized the freedom to establish an identity and defended it vigorously. Parental authority remained a force to be reckoned with, but the balance of power shifted toward the adolescent.

This was true for young women as well as for young men, although perhaps to a lesser degree. When, for instance, Giuliana Falconeri announced her intention to join the Servites, her widowed mother was greatly distressed at the prospect of "losing" her only child. Like so many mothers before her, she opposed her daughter's decision; but two of the Servite founders, Giuliana's uncle Alessio and Philip Benizi, supported the girl, and during her novitiate Giuliana's mother gave her approval. Venturino di Bergamo's father opposed his entry into the Order of Preachers. Although Venturino had no saintly relatives to help him put his case, he was able to overcome his father's objections and win his blessing.

When parents refused their consent, children might run off, as did Pietro Petroni, who had begun to "preach" to his mother and brother at the age of two! Neither this nor his studious boyhood, his demonic attacks at the age of ten, and his nightly contemplation of Christ persuaded his parents to allow him to join the Carthusians. Nevertheless, at seventeen he applied to a nearby house of that order and, after some delay on account of his youth, he was accepted. Pietro's rejection of his parents was total; he refused to see them or even to hear anything about them again. Separation from one's family was, of course, part of the rejection of the world central to the monastic vocation. But it is not common to find such explicit repudiation with clear overtones of hostility until we come to these fourteenth-century accounts.

More typical even in the late fourteenth century is the situation of Giovanni Dominici, the future cardinal and opponent of Renaissance humanism. He was the son of poor working parents, so his labor was essential to the family economy. Nevertheless, while unhappy about his choice of the religious life, his parents did nothing to stop him from joining the Order of Preachers. The Dominican friars acknowledged the plight of Giovanni's parents and debated among themselves whether they should accept him. At last they decided the youth's vocation should take priority over the parents' material need and allowed him to enter.

When Pietro Geremia decided to follow the advice of a repeated nighttime apparition and turn from the legal career his lawyer father had chosen for him to embrace religion instead, his father was furious and stormed up to Bologna determined to bring Pietro back to Palermo. The lad stood his ground, refusing even to see his father. Returning alone to Palermo, the distraught man realized that if he was to have a son at all it would have to be on the boy's terms, so he gave Pietro his blessing.

Even when it was the parents who chose a religious career for a child this did not guarantee that adolescence would go smoothly. We saw the eleventh-century Domenico Loricato reject his father's simoniacal purchase of a priesthood and spend a whole life repenting his father's sin. Fifteenth-century Spain produced a saintly life with similar circumstances but a less extreme outcome. The story of Juan de Sahagún, as it comes to us from his brother, dwells upon the father's love for his son and his special care for the boy's career. At an early age, even before he was able to take orders, his father secured a benefice for him. Juan felt this was wrong and persuaded his father to let him resign. His uncle recommended him to the bishop of Burgos, and after a period in the episcopal household Juan left to make his own way as a preacher and theologian who won renown as a peacemaker and miracle-working healer.

The shift in power relations between parents and teenagers continued markedly during the sixteenth and seventeenth centuries, with fathers and mothers increasingly obliged to accommodate their children in the matter of conversion. Luis Bertran's father blocked his son's entry into the Dominican order with the formal objection that Luis had been ill from infancy. But when he turned eighteen Luis was able to enter without his parents' consent and to resist their efforts to get him back. Luis had the satisfaction of a vision in which his dying father accepted his decision before going to purgatory to do penance.

A new note of rational decision begins to appear in the adolescent conversions of the later period as well. That choosing a religious life was no mere childish escape fantasy is underlined by the hagiographer who set down the story of Serafino di Montegranaro, a saint from the province of Piceno in the second half of the sixteenth century. The story begins conventionally, with Serafino aspiring to a life of prayer and solitude but being forced by his poverty-ridden father to work as a herdsman. Upon his father's death the youth's situation became even more desperate. His brothers forced him to work as a stonecutter and cruelly mistreated him. Serafino longed to escape by becoming a hermit, but the daughter of a local builder who befriended him suggested that instead he join the relatively new order of Capuchins. Serafino investigated the order and entered it. Whereupon the author comments upon the wonderful wisdom of God, who used a young girl as his agent of spiritual direction rather than some mysterious form of supernatural intervention.

Rational choice is also a central theme of the early life of Francis de Sales, the great seventeenth-century French saint. Having grown up in a closely knit family, much attached to his parents, brothers, and sisters, Francis received clerical tonsure at the College of Annecy when still a schoolboy of nine or ten and planned to follow a religious career. His father, however, believed the boy was too young to understand the meaning of such a choice at this early age and, while allowing Francis to indulge himself in his priestly fantasies, continued to make plans for his son's secular career. But when boyhood fantasy turned into teenage determination, Francis was able to persuade his father of the validity of his vocation and to reject parental plans in favor of his own.

We have been saying that a study of saints' lives suggests the emergence of a new attitude toward adolescent behavior in the later Middle Ages that strengthened and flourished through the fifteenth century and beyond. Not merely a transitional phase between childhood and adulthood, nor a period of sexual limbo between puberty and marriage, the years between eleven and seventeen came to be understood as a time for self-discovery and commitment, regularly described in the sources as a period characterized by both internal conflict and family contest. The drama of internal conflict was played out over the teenager's acceptance or rejection of the world, symbolized most typically by the choice between chastity and unchastity. (This choice is so important that it deserves more extensive treatment, and to it we devote the next chapter.) The family contest was chiefly over the issue of career and turned on the question of who was to decide, the parents or the adolescent. In earlier times, if there had been any contest at all it generally had not been very severe, with the adolescent more likely to accept, even to internalize, the parents' choice of career. The teenager who refused to accept the parental decision had to be prepared to suffer the consequences, for power rested with the older generation.

With the fourteenth century—although already foreshadowed by some famous thirteenth-century cases, most notably that of Francis of Assisi—parental goals and teenage aspirations began to draw apart. Wealthy parents envisioned a successful worldly career for their progeny, while poor parents had little choice but to demand that their children remain at home to work. Even when parents planned a religious career for their son or daughter, they were likely to be guided by considerations of comfort and prestige. For their part, teenage children inclined to the religious life were more likely to aim at a more austere or strenuous form of religiousness—the life of a hermit, recluse, or missionary. At that point began a contest that might take myriad forms and find a variety of resolutions but, given the fact that these are saints' lives, could have only one outcome—the triumph of the future saint. Now the parent who refused to accept the youth's decision had to be prepared to suffer the consequences, for teenagers had discovered that in the end power rested with them.

It was less that adolescents of the early Renaissance had seized power than that parents had surrendered it. They had done so, in a word, for love. Stories of saints' lives, veiled though they are by religious metaphor, invocation of the supernatural, hagiographical convention, and the requirements of heroic biography, suggest close bonds of affection in the premodern family. In our previous chapter we suggested that the sharp contrast drawn by some historians between premodern open families of biosocial convenience and modern affective families is only partially correct. Our findings on adolescents tell the same story.[21] To be sure, the conflict between teenagers and parents was a struggle involving family wealth, prestige, honor, and security. But however crass or mundane the issues, however material the stakes in the contest, the struggle gained its intensity from the love that parents were depicted as bearing for their children. Without that love there might well have been no contest at all. When Theobaldus's father went tearfully to the young man's hermitage he went not to drag his son home but for the joy of seeing him again. When Giuliana Falconeri's mother bewailed her daughter's decision to join the Servites she was expressing her grief at losing not merely the caretaker of the household but also a beloved companion. Pietro Geremia's father was no doubt as domineering as any Sicilian patriarch, but he had a soft spot in his tender love for his son.

For their part the children were shown to be harsher, fully ready, in a way that their parents were not, to deny the family bond, to withhold love, and to condemn anyone who stood in their path. Their hostility suggests the strength of the bond of love they had to break. Future saints, their hagiographers ascribed their vehemence to their otherworldly ardor: Luis Bertran envisioned his father in purgatory, and Pietro Petroni refused even to hear word of his parents. Faced with determined adolescents who were ready to hate them if they blocked the path of righteousness, worldly Renaissance parents gave way.

Whether families of the period before the fourteenth century were less tightly knit than this, and whether they contained less love, we are in no position to say. The docility of those earlier saints who accepted parental direction in no way excludes the possibility that real affection existed between parents and children. Nor, conversely, does the shift from obedience to rebellion, from authoritarian parents to power-wielding children, imply a weakening of affective bonds. We do suggest that, within a tightly knit family structure filled with emotion, conflict developed over a changing set of cultural norms and social conditions.

One fact we have noted is an increasing recognition of adolescence as a distinct period with its own problems and needs, a recognition abetted by such diverse factors as the rise of universities and the formalization of guild apprenticeship, the rise of the mendicant movement with its conscious appeal to adolescent youth, and the reappearance of Greek educational ideas with their emphasis upon rationality and *paedaia*.[22] These fundamental trends of the twelfth and thirteenth centuries both reflected and encouraged the notion of adolescence as a period of personality formation. The Goliardic poets, with their celebration of youthful wandering and dissipation, are unthinkable without the rise of the universities, and, as the secular counterparts of would-be saints, they underscore the appearance of a youth culture.[23] Adolescence became an explicit concern of the Italian humanist educators of the fourteenth and fifteenth centuries, both among such theorists as Pier Paolo Vergerio and Leonardo Bruni and among schoolmasters of the importance of Vittorino da Feltre and Guarino da Verona.[24]

Another widely noted fact was the increasing emphasis in piety upon personal responsibility and active involvement. The mysticism of a St. Bernard, the strongly personal and emotional character of the cults of the Virgin and of the crucified Christ, the flowering of the confraternity movement as well as of mendicancy, all attest to the rise of new forms of spirituality that required thought, choice, examination of conscience, and individual commitment. Neither supernatural intervention nor vicarious atonement for sin disappeared from the spectrum of Christian religious experience; but the saint as a purely passive vessel of supernatural grace or as a target of divine intervention gave way to the evangelical activist and the mystic penitent. These were forms especially appealing to a youthful romantic imagination.

While adolescents of the later Middle Ages harkened to the spiritual sirens of the new piety, their parents were awakening to opportunities of a more material sort: economic and social changes provided new opportunities for enrichment and worldly success. A land-based and static manorial economy made room for a society of towns and commerce. Eleventh-century parents, whether noble or servile, could plan with some certainty the future of their children. For the most part children would follow in the footsteps of their fathers and mothers; the major alternative was to take religious vows. For poor sons and daughters the monastery was a sanctuary not only for the spirit but for the body as well; in an economy of scarcity monks were not the greatest sufferers, and in the great Benedictine estates life could be positively comfortable. To nobles the church offered benefices, professional careers, and honors. Clerical connections extended the range of family influence and power. In the thirteenth century parents had lost few of the older options and also had begun to enjoy newer ones. The range of professional careers extended to include law, medicine, and the academy. Commerce broadened horizons beyond the village to the city, the region, ultimately to the world overseas. Merchant, banker, master craftsman—a father could see virtually endless possibilities for his son. Nobles and patricians envisioned avenues of expansion, peasants and laborers paths of escape. The locus of both expansion and escape was the town, the great clearinghouse for information about new ways, the great theater of change.[25]

The new piety and the new economy converged to form a wedge between parents and children. Parents, calculating opportunities for enrichment and influence, may now have been more likely to set their hearts upon secular careers for their children. Teenagers, drawn by champions of the new piety and supported by a youth culture that gave them a sense of worth, set their hearts upon heroic spirituality. One is immediately tempted to describe this polarization as due to a new teenage rebellion, but the opposite may be true. What had changed for the teenager was not the introduction of a new religious impulse, but only its style and tone. In a heavily religious culture such as medieval Christendom, choosing the life of the spirit was a common form of adolescent world rejection. What had changed for the parent was something more fundamental, the dramatic expansion of secular options. No doubt parents always wanted "the best" for their children, but now "the best" was less likely to be a career in religion. No doubt a life of the spirit had always been a powerful attraction to the medieval adolescent, but now a son or daughter was likely to find parents blocking the way.

Statistical Profile of Adolescent Saints

Whereas the statistical findings on child saints presented in the preceding chapter conveyed a rather clear profile (prevalence of females, emergence in the thirteenth century and decline in the sixteenth, major family dynamics, adulthood marked by extreme penitential practice and mystical experiences), the patterns for adolescent saints are much more complex, ambiguous, and even contradictory. The most that can be said for some of the purely numerical findings is that they do not contradict what we have concluded about teenage saints. That much said, we suggest that the summary profile deepens our understanding of adolescence and the impulse to religion in several significant ways. Table 2 (p. 126) summarizes data on the 415 saints whose stories record their decision for the holy life as occurring during adolescence. Our analysis of individual cases noted the emergence of the teenage saint, especially the one who had to overcome parental opposition, as an important type as early as the thirteenth century, a fact we tried to relate to cultural, intellectual, social, and economic factors in Europe generally. But this type became statistically significant only in the fifteenth century, when it spread from Italy to southern France and especially to Spain. The Iberian peninsula, of course, was at this very time experiencing social and economic changes, simultaneously fueled by and fueling transoceanic expansion, on a scale that matched the growth of the Italian city two centuries earlier.[26] In each case economic conditions (which were radically different even though they produced similar levels of disruption) did not "cause" the emergence of a particular type of saint, but they did provide a milieu conducive to changes in the ways society understood the adolescent. But in all centuries adolescence was the life stage during which a decision for a religious vocation was most likely to be made (48 percent of all cases); it was the response, parental and societal, to that decision that varied greatly with time and place.

Compared with the stories told about saintly children, those concerning adolescents assign a lesser role to the family. Figures on the status of the parental family and on occupational category suggest one reason for this difference: in many cases very little information is provided about family background; instead, we meet the saint as a young man or woman (more often a young man) ready to take religious vows and begin a career in the church. Among those stories that do tell of parents, there is a further reversal of the pattern for children. It is the father, not the mother, who plays the major role, whether as a supporter or as an opponent of the adolescent's decision. Fathers, far from being absent on business, killed in war, or dead from a plague, as has been suggested for some thirteenth-century saints' lives, were present and active.[27] The eleventh century, when most boys and girls obediently followed careers planned by their parents, was nevertheless a time when the few who did not quickly encountered fierce, sometimes violent opposition. During the next three centuries, on balance, the families of future saints did not strongly resist their adolescents' impulses, though here the exceptions may be historically more important than the rule. In any event the fifteenth and sixteenth centuries, more commonly in Mediterranean areas than in northern Europe, witnessed the triumph of the rebellious teenager. While in the eleventh century teenage rebellion frequently was met with physical brutality, which in turn led to flight, by the fifteenth century holy adolescents more often stood their ground and ended by converting their parents. Other important influences on the adolescent saint's quest for perfection were advanced religious education, pilgrimage, direct contact with another saint, and his or her peer group. This cluster of factors (especially when compared with the figures for children, which suggest more spontaneous response to visionary experiences, personal crises, and the effect of religious rites) suggests a thoughtful decision by a maturing individual who was faced with a variety of options and who carefully selected among them. Parental wishes and advice counted, but so did informed experience of wider societal values. Consideration as well as inspiration, reason as well as emotion, were increasingly decisive elements in conversion, or so it was perceived by hagiographers.

In the remainders of their holy lives these adolescents continued to be known less for their supernatural powers, charity, and extreme asceticism than for their work on behalf of the church. In every category of supernatural activity during the saint's lifetime, this group ranks well below the norm for all saints; note especially the low index numbers for supernatural signs (58), visionary experiences (67), and prophecies (74). Nor are these saints known primarily for their involvement in the world, whether as healers (79), church leaders (74), or founders of new orders (58). Rather, these are the "lesser" saints, venerated mostly within an order or fairly locally, because they suffered martyrdom or because their causes were heavily promoted by influential groups within the church. Generally they did not achieve wide popularity in their lifetimes, and a majority were canonized only locally or not at all. A comparison of multivariate analysis results shown in table 2 for adolescents with parallel figures for children shown earlier in table 1, whether one examines "grand means" or percentage variation by subcategories, reveals a consistent pattern of sharply lower scores for the adolescent group, especially in the areas of supernatural activity, chastity, and asceticism. But we do not suggest that these saints are somehow unimportant in the history of popular piety. Less spectacular to be sure, their lives were more intelligible to the faithful as models of religious and social behavior. Of course most children were not born with shining stars on their foreheads or inspired by divine wisdom to begin preaching and confounding heretics at the age of nine. But any adolescent, at least one sufficiently devoted to prayer and study, might with God's grace achieve a high spiritual state and faithfully serve the needs of the church.

3 ⊕ *Chastity*

Between the world of the spirit and the world of the flesh chastity was the great divide. No other virtue—not humility or poverty or charity—was so essential to either the performance or the perception of a holy life. Children who aspired to the religious life took a vow of chastity long before the onset of puberty made it a practical issue, and for both boys and girls the decision to remain virgin marked a turning point. In stories of adolescents who aspired to holiness the battle over chastity was a central drama—an internal struggle against temptations of the flesh and a social conflict with parents who wanted them to marry.

The peculiar nature of the virtue of chastity accounts for the intensity of the struggle. Other virtues were goals to be approached by degrees: perfect humility and perfect poverty were rare even among saints; a transgression of charity was not irredeemable, and fortitude and patience came gradually with self-discipline and practice. Such virtues were inherently ambiguous, their recognition a matter of subjective judgment, and in cultivating them saints were forever examining their consciences. But chastity was different. The boy or girl who practiced it had to remain virginal, and virginity admitted of no degrees; its loss was irrevocable.

While virginity was a physical fact, a state of never having "known" the flesh, chastity was a state of mind, a facet of the Christian mentality pruned to its metaphysical roots. The ideal of chastity, like so much else in Christianity, tapped into Hellenistic culture, itself an amalgam of Eastern and Greek components. The ancient dualism of mind and body, of the need to overcome the flesh and live in the spirit, was a major concern of Hellenized Jews like St. Paul, and with Paul began the Christian preoccupation with chastity and with virginity, its highest spiritual expression. Christian culture internalized the belief that the body polluted the spirit, and that nothing polluted the body more than sex. Nowhere is this notion more strikingly displayed than in the biographies of saints.[1]

By far the greater number of saints preserved their virginity. Many saints' lives record no struggle, either internal or external, to maintain this holy state. Pious boys went to school in monasteries and pious girls entered convents; nothing was mentioned of sexual desire, much less of temptation or transgression. Pehaps some of these future saints never experienced any sexual problems, at least none that were serious enough to come to the attention of their biographers. Perhaps some hagiographers believed it more fitting to eliminate recollections of sexual details from a life intended to be exemplary. But in the stories of many saints, lust, virginity, and chastity were central issues.

If a vow of chastity expressed spiritual commitment, it was also a professional consideration, for it was a prerequisite for clerical careers. By the late eleventh century the Roman church attempted to enforce sacerdotal celibacy for secular priests as well as for monks.[2] If many circumvented the injunction, many did not. The Catholic Reformation brought a renewed emphasis on priestly celibacy and chastity, especially for those who aspired to high levels of ecclesiastical preferment. Thomas More's childhood contained themes common to the early lives of many future saints—prodigies before birth, a great talent for learning, extraordinary youthful piety—but More had to give up his early ambition to become a priest because he felt unable to be celibate. Good Christian that he was, More's life as a married layman would hardly have brought him veneration as a saint had he not died a martyr's death.

The choice of celibacy had social consequences as well. Niccolò Giustiniani, a twelfth-century Venetian noble, originally had chosen the monastic life, but when all his brothers were killed he obtained a papal release from his vows for the express purpose of continuing the Giustiniani family name. He married the daughter of a doge, Anna Michela, and fathered six sons and three daughters. Then, his family obligations fulfilled, Giustiniani returned to the monastery and spent his remaining twenty years as a humble penitent who achieved beatification. The claims of family were not always persuasive. Ubaldo, a twelfth-century bishop of Gubbio, was well along in a monastic career when a crisis threatened his family estate. Some friends secretly came to him and urged him to marry and recover his patrimony. But Ubaldo replied that he would not pollute himself with the pleasures of women. Presumably the family inheritance was sacrificed in the pursuit of the higher goals of spiritual perfection.

Stories of parental pressure to marry, and they are many, frequently show the aspiring saint's family acting on its sense of its practical needs.

The noble father of the future Pope Victor III acknowledged his son's flaming contempt for the world but felt compelled to restrain him from entering religion, for this was an only son and a father had to consider the family's future. When his father died Victor fled to become a hermit, but his mother, now solely responsible for guarding the family's estate, had him returned by force and kept him in custody for a year. At the age of twenty-two the future pope fled again, this time to a monastery beyond his mother's reach.

Contests between children and parents did not display an opposition so much between religion and irreligion as between two different cultural values, the individual's need for spiritual expression and the family's need to perpetuate itself.

Family duty might mean siring children, or it might mean protecting the family's wealth, promoting its interests, or maintaining its prestige. When these interests could be furthered by an ecclesiastical career, the parents did not oppose a child's vow of chastity. The mother of Thomas Aquinas, for example, supported a religious vocation for her son, but she was violently against his choice of the Dominicans because she regarded them as socially inferior to the Benedictines.

Tension between the ideal of sexual purity and societal pressures was not always played out within the privacy of family. Simon de Crépy began life as a noble knight, much patronized by Duke William of Normandy, the future Conqueror. When he was already a well-established magnate of twenty-seven his father died, and the sight of his decaying corpse so terrified Simon that he resolved to become a spiritual soldier of Christ, to wear a hair shirt and cultivate humility. Although he had taken betrothal vows with a beautiful noblewoman, he persuaded her to join him in giving up the world. Despite King William's efforts to dissuade him, both Simon and his betrothed entered religious orders.

The constraint of feudal obligations hinted at in Simon's story is set forth even more clearly in the life of the eleventh-century Poppo of Flanders. Having chosen a military career and ambitious for martial glory, Poppo gradually underwent a change of heart. Nevertheless, he concealed his new religious interests and continued to serve as a knight until forced to make a decisive choice about celibacy. One of Poppo's comrades-in-arms, Frumoldus, urged him to marry his daughter. Poppo was disgusted with the prospect of marriage, but he hesitated to offend Frumoldus, so he pretended he was assenting to the match. Riding during the night, he was engulfed by a celestial light and his lance seemed to be enflamed. This persuaded Poppo that he must put an end to vacillation, confess to his comrades that he had already chosen a path different from theirs, and from then on do only God's will.

While hagiographical stories that tell of social pressure more frequently deal with the propertied classes, who seemingly had so much more at stake, there is an occasional parallel in stories of humbler people. The future saint Teobaldo Roggeri was apprenticed to a shoemaker who offered him his daughter in marriage. But Teobaldo was determined to live a life of simple piety and chastity even though he remained a layman. His refusal ended any chance to take over his master's business and forced Teobaldo to accept a lowly job as a porter. Richard of Chichester, the future thirteenth-century bishop, began his religious life by giving to his envious brother not only his meager family land but his betrothed as well, assuring his brother that he had not so much as kissed the girl. In all of these stories the main theme is social position and the claims of worldly obligation that the saint must sacrifice as he turns to a life of the spirit. In many vitae, however, while the subject matter remains chastity, the theme shifts to the quest for purity. Rife with clerical misogyny as the stories often are, they nevertheless shed light on medieval attitudes about sexuality, procreation, and the obligations and trials both of married and of celibate people.

Many saintly young men, unable to resist parental pressures, feudal obligations, well-meaning friends, would-be fathers-in-law, or alluring careers, gave in and married. Marriage was the central social and economic bond of medieval society, and even future saints were not always immune to its attractions and advantages.[3] A few who let themselves be led to the altar still stopped short of the marriage bed, thereby turning marriage into a private theater for spiritual heroism. Medieval people believed that a chaste marriage was possible and that it was a sign not of sickness but of sanctity, a self-administered spiritual test of the most severe and relentless sort. In most vitae the men who insisted on a chaste marriage (as distinct from those who were trapped in one by a virginal wife) were highborn. Perhaps this was because nobles had greater social visibility; if there was no heir everyone would soon know it and speculate on the reason. Normally the woman was blamed for a lack of progeny, in which case a noble husband could find several recourses.[4] Besides, the nobleman's sexual activity outside marriage touched the wives and daughters of the community, becoming a delicious subject of common gossip.

Chastity ran counter to every expectation of noble behavior, and, because the behavior of highborn people was a matter of lively interest and scrutiny, a nobleman who lived in continence with his lawful wife was a subject of wonder. The hagiographer, working against a background of social experience, knew that nobles were expected to produce heirs who would continue their lines, also that sexual indulgence was as much a part of the culture of magnates as were gluttony and violence. He knew, then, what a pearl he had discovered in the story of a noble husband who was chaste. Just in the measure that it was a total inversion of the magnate's world,

Fig. 11. Prince Henry of Hungary and his wife make
a vow of continence while the king looks on. Florence,
St. Martin of Mensola. Predella panel in the manner
of Orcagna, 1391. Photograph courtesy of Gabinetto
Fotografico Soprintendenza ai Beni Artistici e Storici
di Firenze.

a chaste marriage was unworldly—but not so unworldly as to be beyond
the reach of good Christians. Continence was a virtue to which all could
aspire. Unlike holy miracle-working, which was a power granted by God,
chastity was a state of spiritual health requiring only human effort. (In
urging modern Catholics to practice prolonged sexual abstinence rather
than artificial contraception or even the "rhythm method," Pope Pius XII
was to say that heroism in marriage is not too much to expect, even in our
times.) (See fig. 11.)

It was rumored throughout England that Edward the Confessor refused
to have sexual intercourse with his wife. He had postponed marriage until
he was about forty-two, when he had wed Edith Godwin, the daughter
of the king-maker, for reasons of state. During the next two decades, until
his death in 1066, he produced no heirs, inspiring a national orgy of gossip.
Chroniclers offered a variety of speculations for the king's extreme behavior, of which his well-known piety was only one. The king was famous for

his humility and charity, and he was said to have been a great prophet and visionary, even to have performed a few miracles. Loved and revered throughout the land, Edward was considered a saint during his lifetime, a belief quickly verified after death by miracles at his tomb. Nonetheless, William of Malmesbury speculated that something besides sanctity governed Edward's sexual coldness toward his wife, notably a dislike of the Godwin family. Another chronicler, Roger of Wendover, asserted that Edward's marital continence was due to his unwillingness to beget successors of traitorous stock.[5]

Whether Edward's continence was clinical, spiritual, or political is, from our perspective, less important than the contrast implied in this and other stories between the aggressiveness of typical aristocrats and the renunciation of sexuality by their more saintly peers. The violence in the life and death of Magnus, count of Orkney, in legends recorded long after his death in 1106 forms a stark backdrop to the tale of his religious conversion and sexual renunciation. Magnus had been instructed in divine grace as a child, and he indulged in none of the usual boyish sins. As a teenager, however, he fell into worldliness before returning to the way of the gospel. Marrying when he was about twenty-two, he preserved his wife's virginity and lived with her for ten years in total continence. Magnus's reputation for having martyred the flesh in his lifetime may help explain why he was reputed to have suffered a martyr's death when in fact the evidence indicates that he was murdered by a cousin in a family feud. Although no miracles were recorded at his tomb, his cult received official approval only thirty-five years after he died, another indication that sexually inactive nobles were regarded as extraordinary.

One way for a noble to avoid the sexual aggressiveness commonly linked to the general violence of his class was total abstinence. But this could have disastrous social and political consequences: Edward's childlessness paved the way for the crisis that led to the Norman Conquest, and Cardinal Humbert saw Emperor Henry II's sterile union with Cunegund as divine punishment for Henry's exploitation of the church. Most married saints, though they may have longed to be chaste, could not refuse to pay the marriage debt. Their way, according to their hagiographers, was to follow the church's teaching of restraint; they engaged in sexual intercourse without yielding to passion and solely for the purpose of procreation.

Since the life of Margrave Leopold, the patron saint of Austria, was not written down until several centuries after his death, the sections that describe his intimate relations with his wife must be taken as moral commentary rather than historical fact. But the attitudes expressed were as prevalent in the literature of the early twelfth century, when Leopold lived, as in 1591, the date of Balthasar Poltzmann's *Compendium Vitae Miraculorum*

S. Leopoldi. As prince of Austria and a relative of the imperial line, Leopold understood fully the need to continue his father's name. He married Agnes, the emperor's daughter, not out of lust, Poltzmann assures us, but to have children who would succeed him on the throne and carry on his defense of the church. That Leopold had twenty-two children (another account says eighteen) did not confound his hagiographer. Only half the children survived, and of these some were girls; Leopold dedicated several of his sons to church careers, leaving ample but not excessive provision for dynastic needs. Although Leopold thus fulfilled family obligations, he nonetheless observed strict sexual discipline; he copulated soberly, never libidinously, and only after long intervals.

Prince Maurice of Hungary was one of those who attempted to follow the middle way Leopold traversed with such great success, but he fell by the wayside, overcome by longings for a more extreme life of purity. Born about 1280, he decided to marry after both his parents died. But after three years of a childless union (whether the marriage was consummated the hagiographer does not say), Maurice persuaded his wife to enter a cloister so he could join the Order of Preachers in Bologna. He became a humble penitent, wearing a hair shirt, taking "the discipline," and exercising the gift of clairvoyance. Although never officially canonized, he is venerated throughout Hungary.

Another story that should be read as social and moral commentary is Pietromaria Campi's *Vita di S. Corrado Eremita* (1613). Corrado too had the impulse to live in continence, but only with great difficulty did he separate from his wife. Born in Piacenza about 1290 to a Guelf family, Corrado led the conventional life of a Lombard noble until he accidentally started a raging forest fire while out hunting. This led to a string of difficulties, including a charge that he had started the fire out of opposition to the Ghibelline *podestà*, a member of the powerful Visconti family of Milan. Filled with remorse, Corrado repented the vanity of the world, political factionalism, and his own aristocratic carelessness. His first efforts at self-reform were moderate; he donated generously to the victims of the fire and humbled himself before the Visconti *podestà* but this did not satisfy Corrado's need for penance. He began to beg his wife to let him give his life to God's service, proposing that she return to her parents, and citing examples of other wives who had done this. Since they had no children and because Corrado was determined, his wife agreed to separate and entered a Franciscan convent.

But Corrado found that putting away his wife did not end his struggle for self-mastery. As soon as she was out of the way he began to suffer attacks from demons urging him to bring her back. He worried about his honor and feared the ridicule of friends who pursued him—inspired by the devil, according to Campi. First he fled to some hermits, then to Rome, but he found no escape; thoughts of his wife continued to torment him. Finally Corrado reached Sicily (perhaps the birthplace of his mother), and here his story takes on a different flavor. Demonic temptations to return to his noble life in Piacenza and to his abandoned wife give way to Sicilian tales of trial and heroism. The devil aroused the peasants against him, but in a time of famine he miraculously saved them from starvation. A local magnate helped him to settle as a holy man outside the city of Noto, where he especially revered a sacred crucifix believed to have been painted by St. Luke; but the devil incited his patron's son and servant to make some unspecified charge against him, and he fled to the remote grotto of Pizzoni. Beaten by hunters, Corrado refused, in what seems an early expression of Sicilian *omertà*, to accuse them. (Justice was nonetheless served when God visited them with horrible deaths.) Attacks by pirates, miraculous cures, mysterious provision of food, the attentions of birds—such events round out the life of this Lombard noble become Sicilian rural wonder-worker.[6]

Even such an obviousiy fanciful account may provide insights into the underlying connection between medieval sexuality and religiousness, and also into the relation between saintliness and its social context. The tale of the husband who wanted to live in chaste marriage is characteristically a story about a noble or a prince. In the few cases where it concerns common folk it lacks the note of heroic sacrifice that inspired the self-denial of a noble. Bourgeois or peasant husbands who gave up the pleasures of the marriage bed, or went so far as to put aside their wives, generally did so after they had reached middle age. Pietro Pettinaio, the thirteenth-century Sienese comb vendor who sold goods of such high quality at so fair a price that he had to limit his appearances at the market so as not to ruin his competitors, joined with his wife in a vow of chastity only after they had established that she was sterile. The fourteenth-century Florentine burgher Chiarito was something of an exception, turning to the cult of chastity after a vision at the relatively early age of twenty-eight. While living continently with his wife, who had already borne him several children, Chiarito organized a group of maidens dedicated to virginity.

More typically, the Sienese Giovanni Colombini, whose conversion we will examine in the next chapter, did not hear the call to chastity until he was fifty-one. Throughout the life of Sebastian of the Apparition women tried to seduce him, so that he finally fled his native Spain for Mexico, where he is patron of carters and florists. Only at the age of sixty did Sebastian agree to marry a poor girl who needed his support, with the proviso that he need not consummate the union. When she died he granted the same favor to another impoverished girl, who also died "intact." His biographer suggests that continence may have been an aid to longevity, for Sebastian lived to the age of ninety-eight, having long since given his remaining wealth to the Franciscan convent where he had gone at the age of seventy-two to work as a servant.

While the stories of saints who struggled with their sexual desires in the context of marriage show the interplay among religious ideal, hagiographic convention, and social reality, a similar interplay occurs in the life of the celibate male who is assaulted by lewd women, a story so common as to suggest that this was another standard topos of medieval hagiography. It was a form of spiritual heroism particularly relished by hagiographers, virtually all celibate clerics, who loved to dwell on the length and persistence of the attacks, the voluptuousness of the women, the difficulty of resisting. Prurient and shallow though the stories often are, they probably served to enhance the stature of the saint powerfully, especially among his clerical devotees. Like accounts of miracles, stories of heroic resistance to blatant sexual seduction could never be repeated often enough. Chastity stories, however, convey a strong flavor of natural passion. The holy man beleaguered in his cell by a temptress might call upon divine help, but his encounter with the woman was loaded with human tension, and the victory was a most personal and human one.

Even trite priests' tales may provide insight into broader social perceptions. The stories are premised upon a set of attitudes toward women that clerics shared with the laity they instructed.[7] Women were sexually charged and morally lax, ready agents for the devil's work. Celibate males were fair and delectable game, not only for prostitutes and outwardly lewd women, but even for normally respectable matrons. Any woman might suddenly become inflamed by a man's looks, or even by his aura of innocence, and scheme to encounter him alone so she could seduce him. The drama of the story lay in the hero's anguished trial and his victory over temptation. If the woman is presented as a stock figure whose behavior is entirely conventional for her sex, the man is treated with more depth and individuality. We are made to feel his torments and understand the heroism of his resistance.

Male responses to the lewd allurements of women could take many forms. Juan Cirita stemmed from a noble Galician family and was active with Count Henry of Portugal in the twelfth-century wars against the Moors. Severely wounded, he turned from his former life, first becoming a hermit and then helping to establish the Cistercian order in Portugal. But the transition to an ascetic life did not come easily to Juan. The memory of the pleasures of his former ways tormented him, while a succession of women came to his hermitage and inflamed him with lust. There is some suggestion that Juan's attacks were apparitions, but his reaction was real enough. He thrust his left arm into a fire until the flesh was burned away from his bones. Lust troubled him no longer.

One of Juan's Italian contemporaries also fought fire with fire. Born near the end of the eleventh century and religious since the age of fourteen, William of Montevergine (Vercelli) appeared at the court of Roger II of Naples, who took him into his intimate counsels. Jealous courtiers persuaded Roger to let them test the holy man by sending a prostitute to his chamber. The woman tried to tempt him into fornication, whereupon William walked calmly to the flaming hearth, parted the coals with his bare hands, lay down in their midst, and invited the woman to join him. The prostitute took this as a miracle and gave up her evil life to become a nun. King Roger, now convinced of William's holiness, gave him money to found the Benedictine Congregation of Montevergine.

One of the most outrageous of such stories was told of Thomas Aquinas, whose own family engineered the attempted seduction. When his mother learned that Thomas intended to join the Order of Preachers, recently founded by St. Dominic and as yet undistinguished, she tried to persuade him to change his mind. On her instruction his brothers kidnapped him on his way to Rome. Imprisoned in a family castle, Thomas spent his time reading the Bible, studying Aristotle, and preaching to his sister, who soon took the veil at S. Maria di Capua. The family battle over his own vocation continued, with the future Angelic Doctor holding firm to his intention and his brothers growing ever more exasperated by his determination to become a Dominican.

So incensed were they over their brother's stubbornness that they resolved to break his chastity by sending a beautiful girl to his chamber. The woman, made up lasciviously, entered the youth's room and tried by looks, caresses, and other unspecified "tricks" to lead him to sin. For a moment at least, Thomas felt the surge of the flesh (*in se carnis insurgere stimulum*), which until then he had always been able to master through reason. Now reason was not enough, and after violently thrusting the woman out of his room he fell prostrate, tearfully beseeching God to grant him the girdle of perpetual virginity. Weeping and praying, he fell asleep and saw two angels, who said that God had heard his prayer and that he had won his struggle. Pressing Thomas around the waist, they bestowed upon him the spiritual girdle for which he had prayed and promised that he would preserve his hard-won chastity until death. From then on Thomas abhorred the sight of women and avoided their conversation. (See fig. 12.)

William of St. Brieuc, whose corpse, it may be remembered, bore unmistakable anatomical proof of his chastity, was troubled for many years by importunate women who were attracted by his sanctity, his good looks, and his gracious bearing (at least so he told his deathbed confessor). Once, when he was still a youth and in minor orders, he was a guest in the house of a rich man when a woman, who seems to have been his host's wife, "vibrated fiery rays" of wanton desire and attempted to lie with him. She came to William during the night and climbed into his bed. Excited in a way that was new to him, William sprang up as from a fire and hid from "the face of the serpent." Even after he became a bishop women continued to pursue him. Once a noblewoman involved in litigation in the episcopal court tried to lie with him, hoping to persuade him to judge her case in her favor. When the woman made her intentions known, William seized the edge of his episcopal robe and made as if to shut out the fire from his bosom, while reproving her for trying to seduce her pastor.

The great Spanish mystic John of the Cross was much troubled by women who had designs on him. But instead of rebuffing them with strong words or violent gestures, as even the cerebral Thomas Aquinas had done, John was so controlled as to be able to reason gently with his temptresses and even to convert them.

Since these are stories about saints, chastity invariably wins over lust. And yet the tales conveyed a fearful respect for the power of sex, if not for the female who was its embodiment. The devil, ever on the lookout for ways to undermine a holy vocation, used sexual temptation as the chief weapon of his arsenal.[8] The holy man felt the stirrings of lust, understood

Fig. 12. Imprisoned in a dungeon by his brothers, Thomas Aquinas receives the girdle of chastity from two angels while the courtesan his brothers have employed to seduce him exits. Location unknown. Fifteenth-century panel. Photograph courtesy of Gabinetto Fotografico Soprintendenza ai Beni Artistici e Storici di Firenze.

the baleful power of women, and responded with tears, rage, even self-immolation. Divine help was regularly invoked. To a cleric looking for inspiration, perhaps for practical guidance, the stories carried an ambiguous message. Certainly there was room for taking great pride in tales of heroic chastity, even seeing them as chronicles of supernatural grace. But for those whose flesh was weak the stories at least provided the comfort of knowing that it took a saint to resist the wiles of a female in league with the devil, and that even saints wavered.

For many holy men the problem of chastity was less dramatic than for an Aquinas; their struggles, more frequent and longer-lasting, came not from whores paid to seduce them but from their own sexual desires. The price of virginity was an ever-chaste vigilance, a constant monitoring of thought as well as deed, and this was difficult for most ordinary men as well as for some saintly ones. As long as they lived on earth they were prisoners of their bodies. Against this domestic enemy the saint's weapons were prayer and willpower. In a real sense the whole problem of holy austerity was played out in the effort to cleanse the mind of impurities leaching into it from the body. Taming the flesh was not so much a technical problem of refraining from sexual intercourse and masturbation—for saints that was relatively easy—as of emptying the mind of desire, the false idol whose presence made it impossible to dedicate oneself entirely to God, to desire only him. In theological terms concupiscence was, as Luther so poignantly recognized, much more than lust; it was the desire for any part of the world, any need of the self that stood in the way of loving God.[9] The heroic saint had to conquer concupiscence in this full sense of the term, yet most often the conquest was presented as a sexual one. Lust was metaphor for all impurity, for all worldliness, and it could be so only because lust was a universal experience.

The struggle with concupiscence is to be found in saints' lives from all centuries and in all parts of Europe, and everywhere the sexual struggle was central. Heimerad, a typical contemplative ascetic, spent an entire life subduing lust.

When he felt the stings of the flesh he would sing a psalm or some part of the divine office while he soaked in a pool until his carnal urge became quiet. It is reported that he once dragged his nude body through thorns so that, burning with pain outwardly, he put out the fire that raged in his mind.

Heimerad, as it happens, was a Swabian monk who died in 1019, but his struggle could as well have taken place in fourteenth-century England or seventeenth-century Portugal. Ignatius Loyola, the great sixteenth-century mystic and reformer, once jumped into a lake to cool his sexual ardor.

Saints of the eleventh century displayed a wide range of sexual temptations. The dangers of the classical revival were manifest in the trials of the Abbot Gervin of Rheims, who was lured by poetry and its sensuous charms.[10] The sexual problems attended by wealth and position are half-revealed in Peter Damian's life of Romuald, the founder of the Camaldolese order, who, when he arrived at adolescence, "began to live in proclivity to fleshly sin, the vice that vehemently attacks men at that age, especially rich men." Whether Damian meant that rich men had a greater proclivity for masturbation, frequenting brothels, homosexuality, or all three, he does not tell us.

Although as a teenager Placido di Rosi (d. 1248) donned an iron belt to chastise his flesh, sexual temptation literally pursued him throughout his life. Fleeing from women, including a nun, Placido tried to find peace in the rural Casentino region of Tuscany. But after five months, still feeling temptation, he fled to higher ground to live an even more austere life, subsisting on roots and herbs and practicing "the discipline." For thirty-seven years he never slept in a bed or lying down but always rested sitting or standing, as if to avoid even the hint of carnality. Placido took no wine and little water, for he feared these liquids might provoke his libido. So great was the fear of sexuality suffered by Thomas of Cantilupe, the thirteenth-century bishop of Hereford, that he would not allow his own sisters to kiss him or to remain under his roof. John Berchmans, who died in 1621 at the age of twenty-three, to preserve his chastity took a vow when he was ten that he would allow no woman to touch him, not even his mother.

A more usual device to deal with temptation was scourging, such as was practiced by Guglielmo di Polizzi, the early-fourteenth-century Sicilian who repulsed recurrent attacks of carnality by flagellating himself. A more imaginative remedy was devised by Giovanni Bono of Mantua, who, though he had left the world, still harbored fond thoughts of a woman he had much loved. When temptation became too much for him to bear he seized some gravel and ground it into sharp particles that he wedged beneath his fingernails; then, striking his fingertips against a rock, he forced the gravel down to the quick, suffering such agony that he fainted and lay "half-alive" on the ground for three days. Only then did God appear to Giovanni in a dream and grant him freedom from temptation for the remainder of his life.

Hugues de Grenoble regarded lust as a disease that might be transmitted through the eyes; therefore he refused to look at the faces even of male clerics, not because he feared his desire for them but because their lust might somehow spread to him. Torello, a native of the same Casentino region of the upper Arno that for a time harbored Placido di Rosi, dealt with his recurring bouts of carnality by practicing severe austerities, tormenting his body with devices that tore into his flesh. Though he slept only three hours a night on a bed of thorns and with his head on a rock, he could not ward off his sexual demons. One came as a beautiful woman whom he was able to repel only by beating himself with a rod until his blood flowed to the ground. Then he threw himself into icy water and fasted for days.

Just as the Catholic Reformation drew upon the devotional traditions formed over many years, so its saints inherited the sexual attitudes of generations of holy predecessors.[11] The story of Philip Neri's triumphant struggle to achieve total chastity, to obliterate the last trace of carnal desire, continues the themes we have been examining. Philip did not wrestle with his sexual demons in the stillness of the cloister or by escaping to the mountains. Like other leading saints of the Catholic Reformation, and carrying on a trend that had begun as early as the thirteenth century, he fought and won his spiritual battle in the streets. From his native Florence he went to Rome to study and to pray in her churches. Philip encountered temptations everywhere, and he fought them with tears and prayers. A particularly difficult test, related at some length, arose when Philip, on his way to pray at the Basilica of the Lateran, caught sight of a half-naked beggar near the Coliseum. The man's nude body aroused Philip to impure thoughts that by the grace of God he succeeded in dispelling with prayer. If his sexual excitement caused him any guilt, Philip banished it by asserting that his temptations came not from the naked flesh but from the devil, who had disguised himself as a beggar. Yet the incident remained in his mind, and he dwelt upon it in detail many years later.

The devil's next instrument of seduction was a woman or, to be precise, two women, who locked themselves into his room, blocking his escape. Philip had no choice but to face his tormentors, but the very force of his righteousness and purity made them cower before him. Fearing not only his touch but his very glance, the women gave up the game and retreated to a corner. Another sinful woman, a Roman courtesan named Caesaria, paid, we are told, by some agent of the devil, plotted to entrap Philip. Pretending she wanted to confess, Caesaria asked him to come to a private interview in her lodging. When Philip ascended the stairs and opened the door he found Caesaria all but naked, covered only by a transparent robe. Sensing that if the robe fell away he would be completely compromised, he turned and fled. The enraged and disappointed Caesaria picked up the first weapon that came to hand, a footstool, and hurled it after the retreating saint, but God protected him from harm. After this incident divine grace so infused Philip that his passion became inert. From about the age of fifty he no longer even suffered nocturnal pollution. Every libidinous ardor cooled in his body, and even his sense of touch deadened. As he told his close friends, for him a woman and a stone were the same. Philip was restored to the innocence of a newborn child, living his last thirty years more as a celestial than a mortal creature.

If, in the lives of male saints, women appear as sexual predators and allies of the devil, the lives of women saints tell a different story, whether that story was told by a man, as most were, or by the saint herself. To be sure, even a male biographer was not likely to describe a saintly woman as a sexual hunter; but neither did he go to the opposite extreme to describe her as a celestial creature who felt no bodily urges or who coolly resisted sexual temptation. More than their male counterparts, holy women were likely to be presented as flesh-and-blood creatures struggling to cope with conflicting demands of family and society, spiritual impulses, physical and emotional needs. Unlike male saints, of whom Philip Neri is a good example, women who described their own sexual problems did not often allow themselves the luxury of blaming them on the devil, perhaps being too deeply instilled with the prevalent notion that women were the lustful sex to think of shifting their responsibility to outside forces. For this reason the autobiographical accounts of the spiritual travails of female ascetics present the most convincing treatment of human sexuality to be found in hagiographic literature.

Hagiographic convention also reflects the special connection between women and sexuality—or, more accurately, men's obsession with it. For female saints but not for males, the official classification turned on sexual condition: women saints were recorded as either virgin or widow, while men were confessors, bishops, or whatever. For women virginity was everything—once having given up her maidenhood a woman was irrevocably excluded from the select company of those who lived in Mary's image. A woman who had married might become a saint, especially if she were a widow (or a good queen), but her path to holiness was arduous, and in her saintly title she would reveal the blemish of having known the flesh.[12]

The vitae of those the church calls virgin usually begin by placing the young girl in her family setting. Typically vowing chastity before the age of seven and reaffirming the decision after puberty, they lived lives we have already charted in our chapters on children and adolescents. Their decisions to reject the world by refusing to marry carried them into an ever escalating contest with their parents. Kennocha, an eleventh-century Scottish girl, had to endure punishment and even death threats from parents, who insisted that she accept one of her many noble suitors. Even the pope tried, unsuccessfully, to get the thirteenth-century princess Isabelle of France to marry. Edigna, the daughter of Henry I of France, spurned a family-ordered marriage and had to disguise herself as a pilgrim to escape in an oxcart to Bavaria, where she lived in a cave marked out for her by God. Margaret, a thirteenth-century Hungarian princess who had become a nun, was pursued even into the cloister by Ottokar, king of Bohemia. Only when she threatened to cut off her nose and lips if forced to marry did he leave her alone. A fall on the ice that left her permanently crippled saved Lidwige of Schiedam from a marriage ardently desired by her impoverished noble family. To Lidwige the disability was a gift from God. Although there are many other examples, some of them from the humbler social strata, family pressure to marry seems to have intensified in direct proportion to the wealth and power involved. Marriageable women were counters in a social game played for very high stakes. But these stories, while illustrating tensions between social needs and personal spiritual impulses, tell us much less about sexual feeling than do the stories of women who married.

Whereas men could be sanctimonious about their ability to resist sexual assaults, women, considered the lustful and morally weak sex, had great difficulty in establishing their credibility in the face of gossip and male ridicule. Even the holy Queen Cunegund, daughter of one saint and wife of another, having chosen the difficult way of virginity within marriage, was vilified by a story that a young man had been seen entering and leaving her bedchamber repeatedly for three days. Her biographer identified the youth as the devil, one of many demonic apparitions that troubled her throughout her days. But no such stories are told of her husband, the Emperor Henry II, whose supposed chastity, while remarkable, provoked no vulgar insinuations. When insinuation gave way to outright accusation, a woman had little hope of defending herself. The noble Agatha Hildegard was alone in her husband's castle when a kinsman tried to rape her. When she resisted, the kinsman accused her before her husband, who, refusing to believe in his wife's innocence, drove her from the castle. Agatha became a pilgrim and a recluse who flagellated herself and worked miracles, thereby rehabilitating her reputation. Few woman had such divine testimony to their purity.

While male hagiographers were not particularly concerned to convey the woman's feelings about her vulnerability, the hard realities of her situation make it possible to infer what she must have suffered. The case of Jutta de Huy is particularly valuable because her friend and biographer lets us share her experience. Jutta was born near Liège about 1160. Her parents began looking for a husband for her before she was thirteen. But Jutta shrank from the prospect, feeling that she lacked the experience and strength for marriage. The married state seemed to her a heavy yoke: she feared "the burden of the womb" and the dangers of childbirth; she was not ready to take on the responsibility of rearing children or the chores of running a household; above all, she had deep misgivings about the vagaries of husbands. Jutta rejected one suitor after another—apparently there were many, for she was a very pretty girl—until at last she was unable to resist the pressures of her father, her friends, indeed the whole town.

Married, Jutta found that she hated the sexual act (later, when freed from it, she said that nothing would compel her to do it again). Memories of her carefree childhood made her melancholy; she grew weary of life and, she confessed, even hoped her husband would die so that she would be free from the conjugal debt. For this grievous sin she repented, and God changed her heart of stone to one of flesh. She dedicated herself to charity, and there is a suggestion that she even overcame her abhorrence of sex, at least enough to make her life tolerable.

After five years her husband died, and Jutta, still in her teens, was left with two children. Her father wanted her to remarry and invoked his bishop to persuade her to this course. But Jutta managed to enlist the bishop's support for her resolve to take no husband but Jesus Christ. For a time she was tormented by demons who came to her in the shapes of lions, bears, and snakes even when she took refuge at night in church. These were followed by a human tormentor. A young relative of her dead husband surprised her alone in the passageway of her home and tried to rape her. Jutta was paralyzed by fear:

> What should she do? To whom should she turn? If she wished to escape there was no place to go. If she tried to resist, the man was stronger. If she cried out, she was afraid the aggression would become public and that the ensuing scandal would compromise both of them forever.

At the very moment of being overpowered Jutta was saved by the appearance of a woman whom she took to be the Blessed Virgin. Her attacker could not see the woman, but he heard the approaching footsteps and fled.[13]

Such insights into the complex feelings of a woman about to be violated, and more generally about the difficulties of accepting the burdens of womanhood, are not usually encountered in the male-dominated literature of the Middle Ages. More often we must make do with laconic narratives. The story of Paola Gambara-Costa has elements of a satirical Italian film script but should be read as an all-too-brief and unsympathetic account of another kind of trial for the married woman. Forced to give up her life of prayer, solitude, and penance to marry Count Lodovico Costa, Paola first surrendered to mundane attractions, then, recalled to piety by a spiritual adviser, found herself in difficulties with her dissolute husband, who showed his contempt for his pious wife by installing his mistress in the household. When the interloper became ill Paola was forced to nurse her, and when she died Paola was accused of poisoning her. Only with great difficulty was she able to persuade her husband of the falsity of the charge and at last to convert him from his wicked life. Paola ultimately became a Franciscan tertiary, so ascetic that she ruined her health and brought on an early death.

Jeanne de Valois, wife of King Louis XII of France, came to the religious life out of a similar state of domestic helplessness, but involving a very different set of circumstances. Politics, not amour, was Jeanne's enemy. When Louis decided upon divorce Jeanne had no recourse but to accept the decision cheerfully and to remove herself to a convent, where she took up a life of extreme penance. She wore a hair shirt, flagellated herself nightly, and drove sharp silver nails into her breasts. Having surrendered an earthly king, she rejoiced in the cult of the Eternal King.

Marriages between spiritually inspired women and worldly men were prone to conflicts recorded in detail, sometimes poignant, sometimes inadvertently humorous, in these vitae. Granted these were unusual women, still their stories give us some glimmerings of the plight of medieval wives, and their husbands as well, trapped in incompatible and loveless unions. Hedwige of Bavaria, a thirteenth-century noble married to a Silesian duke when she was twelve (another source says sixteen), seems to have found little satisfaction in the conjugal act, so she devised a series of ingenious ways to pay the marriage debt in tiny and infrequent installments. As soon as she felt she had conceived, she refrained from sexual intercourse until well after she had delivered the child. She also celebrated Lent, saints' days, Advent, and other religious holidays in continence. At other times she managed to avoid sex for six or eight weeks even without the excuse of pregnancy or a holiday. After more than a quarter-century of rationing sex to her husband, she was able to persuade him to solemnize a vow of complete continence before the bishop. From then on Hedwige spoke to her husband only when absolutely necessary, such as when they were in church.

Cunegund, daughter of the king of Hungary, postponed the consummation of her marriage to Boleslau, prince of Krakow, again and again while she worked to persuade her royal husband to live in continence. After three years of prayer and miracles (during which time Boleslau found his satisfaction with other women), Cunegund succeeded in winning him over, even though he was anxious to have children.

A daughter was her father's possession, to be disposed of according to the family's financial and social interests.[14] The father of the famous prophetess Bridget of Sweden, "seeing that she was as comely as Esther, wed her to a man noble, rich and prudent." In describing Bridget as an object to be married, the phrasing is typical, as is the complete lack of any recognition on the part of her father that Bridget had long since begun to aspire to a holy life. One of her contemporary biographers tells us that Bridget had preferred to die rather than wed, but that she had to obey her parents. Bridget was happy to discover that her husband shared her spiritual yearnings. For two years the young couple postponed consummation, earnestly seeking divine guidance in the face of their frankly acknowledged sexual desire. At last the thought of having a child whom they could dedicate to God's service outweighed their misgivings about the impurity of carnal union, but the decision told heavily on their consciences. Each time they had intercourse they preceded it with a prayer that the union would produce a child pleasing to God, in this way tempering the sinfulness of the act. During Lent Bridget slept on the floor so they both might avoid impurity. Apparently, despite all these efforts, Bridget continued to feel some guilt. She reported that after she had been incontinent her baby daughter Catherine refused to take the breast, and at other times she expiated her guilt for "marital pleasure" by secretly whipping herself.

Bridget's experience as an unwilling bride did not make her sympathetic toward her daughter Catherine's aspiration to a life of religious virginity. After a girlhood filled with spiritual events, Catherine followed parental wishes and married at the age of thirteen or fourteen. She managed to persuade her husband to live in chastity by convincing him that sexual abstinence was a sure way to prolong life. The prescription proved ineffective, for the man died less than a decade later, some time after Catherine had abandoned him and gone off to Rome to follow Bridget.

Even pious maidens who had no trouble accepting marriage and its attendant sensual pleasures might still feel some residue of guilt. Umiltà was a thirteenth-century matron of Faenza who lived piously and happily with her husband and their "many" sons and daughters until she became ill. After a miraculous recovery, she was suddenly "able to live in chastity." While the account is sparse in detail, it does not suggest that physical disability rendered Umiltà unable to continue her normal married life but rather indicates that she saw the illness as punishment for having given up her youthful inclinations against the married state and her recovery as a sign of the future direction she should take. As a girl Umiltà had secretly cultivated asceticism and humility, fearing her parents' opposition. After spurning marriage to Emperor Frederick II's cousin, she had given in and accepted the hand of a local nobleman, Ugo Caccianemici. Now, after nine years of marriage, Umiltà retreated to a cell near Vallombrosa to live a life of fasting and prayer, while her husband also embraced the monastic life. (See fig. 13.)

The feeling of guilt over having enjoyed marital sex is presented even

more graphically in the case of Elena di Udine. Married about 1410 at the age of fifteen to a member of the prominent Cavalcanti family of Florence, Elena enjoyed twenty-seven years of a happy and fruitful union. When her husband died, however, she underwent a spiritual crisis. Now every former pleasure became a burden upon her conscience. Deciding to become the bride of Christ, she joined the Augustinian order to practice extreme poverty and to become a "mirror of penitence." Elena's inventive expiations are recorded in her own words by her confessor:

> The glorious Elena used to contemplate the passion and torments of her sweet and most beloved Jesus which He bore for wretched sinners. Considering that He had been crucified in every member of His body while she, given to worldly pomp and vanity in her youth and marriage, had offended God in every one of her members, she wished to perform hard and severe penance in each one of them. She wore a wreath or crown of iron barbs on her head so that she might constantly remember the Lord's Passion. I have heard, indeed, a most marvelous and amazing thing, that she frequently would tie a thick rope around her neck and pull her arm behind her back for six days at a time; she would order her sister to lead her about tied this way because, she said, my love, Jesus, was led tied like this to His death on Mount Calvary.

Suddenly the account shifts to the first person:

> Let this be done to me, for the bracelets with which I decorated my arms and for the ropes which bound the hands of my sweet Jesus and for the nails which pierced Him on the Cross. On my legs let there be iron bands to expiate my vanity in the dances I used to do so often; and because my Jesus had His feet pierced with nails. I also bind my loins with bands because I used to decorate them with gold and silver belts in my worldly life and because out of love my beloved was bound to a post and whipped. I wear a hair shirt because of the silken undergarments and precious stuffs with which I used to clothe myself, and because my Love was despised by Herod because He wore a white gown. Thirty-three stones I put in the soles of my shoes because I have so often offended God with my leaping and dancing, the same number of years which Jesus walked the earth for love of me. I flagellate my body for the impious and carnal pleasures with which I indulged it during my marriage and out of regard for my Lord who was whipped

Fig. 13. Umiltà converting her husband in an anteroom of the nuptial chamber that they will both shortly abandon in favor of monastic lives. Florence. Fourteenth-century altarpiece, influenced by Bernardo Daddi and the St. Cecilia master. Photograph courtesy of Gabinetto Fotografico Soprintendenza ai Beni Artistici e Storici di Firenze.

at the post for me. I sleep on stones and rocks because before I slept on soft beds, and my Bridegroom used to seek sleep stretched on the ground, and for three days lay within a tomb of stone.

A variant pattern of spirituality deferred is evident in the fourteenth-century life of Jeanne Marie de Maillé, daughter of the lord of Maillac. At the age of six Jeanne began to have spiritual stirrings, but her parents tried to divert her from her ascetic impulses and even to prevent her from reading. After a vision of the Virgin and Child at the age of eleven, she consecrated herself to Christ's passion. When she was sixteen, however, her parents forced her to marry a childhood friend. Except that she persuaded him to live in chastity, Jeanne seems to have been totally dedicated to the marriage. When her husband was wounded and captured by the English, she spent their entire fortune to ransom him. He died in 1361, whereupon his family cast her out, perhaps because she had failed to provide them with heirs, perhaps also because she had begun to behave in disconcerting ways. She "miraculously fed the poor" and had a vision of Christ on the cross that led her to express contempt for the world. Returning to Maillac, Jeanne rejected new suitors and led a life of great charity and piety, including the experiences of numerous visions and levitation.

Stripped of its hagiographical and supernatural details, the story demonstrates the lack of autonomy and the economic vulnerability of at least one fourteenth-century woman. Married with no consideration for her wishes, impoverished by the fortunes of the Hundred Years War and her devotion in ransoming her husband, she was left by his death to the mercy of relatives who rewarded her marital loyalty by disowning her. Jeanne of course was noble and in no danger of starving, although it is worth noting that when she returned to Maillac her own family ignored her wishes and tried to remove her as a financial burden by urging her to marry again.

Most women had even fewer means to cope with this rather common situation. Both Keith Thomas and Alan Macfarlane suggest that the social vulnerability of lower-class women in late medieval society encouraged accusations of witchcraft against them.[15] Perhaps in a culture that believed deeply in the constant presence of supernatural forces of good and evil there were grounds for such suspicion: the witch entered into a pact with the devil so she could revenge herself against her tormentors and protect herself against enemies; the saint called upon heaven for help and consolation. The saint, like the witch, invoked supernatural power as a remedy against misfortune, and between the two there was a tenuous difference. As the compatriot and namesake of Jeanne Marie de Maillé, Joan of Arc, was to discover, society and sometimes the church had trouble making the distinction.

None of the husbands described above except Paola's seems to have been particularly vicious; it would be unfair to assign a major part of the blame to them for failed marriages. The husband of Catherine of Genoa was another matter. Catherine's marital troubles were not due simply to her distaste for marriage, although if her parents had allowed it she would have become a nun as her sister had done. At sixteen she entered into marriage, accepting it as a cross to be borne; but she was scarcely prepared for the burden she was to suffer. Her husband Giuliano Adorno was, to reverse the usual hagiographic phrase, noble in birth but not in character. Crude and insolent and totally antagonistic to his wife's pious leanings, he began to mistreat her from the very first days of their marriage. Fierce and restless, "he was anxious to cut a good figure in the world"; he loved the company of men and was a gambler and a voluptuary. Giuliano and Catherine were, in short, completely incompatible.

Catherine suffered her husband's persecution for five years, living virtually as a recluse in her own household, driven into herself by Giuliano's harsh words and manner, reduced to a physical and emotional shadow of her former self. At last her parents noted her unusual behavior and her physical deterioration and intervened. Their prescription for her malady, which they diagnosed as a suicidal depression, was to give up her asocial life and come back into the world. At no point does the account suggest that they condemned the husband's depravity or that they even understood that he might be the cause of Catherine's condition. Their concern was for appearances, and Catherine, like all women of her time, was expected to accept her lot and make the best of it. So incessantly did they nag her that Catherine, now afflicted with a double load of oppression, finally decided to lighten her burden by going through the motions of rejoining Genoese society. The pretense deceived her friends, who believed she was well on the road to becoming as worldly as they. But Catherine's inner torment only increased; she feared that this superficial reconciliation to society would trap her into mortal sin, and she was disgusted by the life itself.

Another five years passed in this manner, Catherine's misery steadily increasing, until one day in the Church of St. Benedict, on the vigil of that saint, she prayed for a long illness, hoping that bodily suffering might alleviate the travail of her spirit. Her wish was granted, and she seems to have undergone a new conversion, helped by the advice of her sister's confessor. She began again the struggle against bodily appetites by practicing extreme self-mortification, tormenting her flesh with hair shirts, sleeping on thorns, and praying on her bare knees for six hours a day. She abstained from meat and from any food she had formerly enjoyed. After four years of self-affliction she achieved perfect victory over all her natural appetites. No longer was there any question of healing her broken marriage. Her husband troubled her no more, reappearing in Catherine's life story only for a conventional deathbed conversion.

While Catherine managed to survive a vicious husband, a few holy women did not. Margaret of Roskilde, a twelfth-century Danish noble, was murdered by her adulterous husband, who tried to make her death appear a suicide and buried her in unconsecrated ground. But the murderer was found out when a bishop, prompted by reports of miracles, began to investigate. A local cult developed immediately. Godelieve, an eleventh-century Frenchwoman, suffered a similar fate that is reported in much greater detail. Bertulfus, a rich and noble Fleming, fell in love with Godelieve and won her hand, but as soon as they were married he conceived a hatred for her and began to torment her verbally and physically. Godelieve's biographer explains the man's dreadful change of heart as the result both of diabolic influence and of a meddling mother who resented her son's choice of a foreign wife. Godelieve daily suffered "contumely, injuries, opprobrium and derision," but the pious young woman rejoiced in being singled out for suffering and offered her body as a sacrifice to God. Enraged by his failure to break her spirit, Bertulfus tried to starve her until at last Godelieve fled barefoot to her parents' home. Her father was moved by her plight and consulted his lord, the count of Flanders, who in turn sought the advice of a bishop. The bishop's decision was that Godelieve should return to her husband and that he should be admonished to treat her lovingly.

Now Bertulfus hated her more than ever and became determined to do away with her. When her friends and relatives expressed their sympathy for her loneliness and lack of physical consolations, Godelieve replied that she had no need of bodily delights or of worldly pleasures, all of which were so fleeting. She asserted that she was the luckiest woman in Flanders for having been chosen to share Christ's passion. Frustrated in his efforts to starve her either emotionally or physically, Bertulfus decided upon outright murder. He came to his wife at night, caressed and kissed her, and pretended to repent his past cruelties. Then he told Godelieve that he had found a sorceress who claimed she could bind them together in love surpassing any love known to two people, and he promised to send the woman to her the following night. Carried away by this chance of reconciliation and forgetting that she had just rejected worldly pleasure, Godelieve agreed to let the woman in.

The next night Bertulfus commanded two of his trusted servants to rouse his wife from her bed. Dressed in her nightgown and with her hair undone, the unsuspecting woman obeyed the summons and came to her door to await the wonder-worker. But as soon as Godelieve came out the two servants seized her and strangled her. They held her underwater until they were sure she was dead, then placed her corpse back in bed to be discovered by her attendants in the morning. There were no signs of violence on the body except for a small red mark on the neck, and the crime went undetected until the occurrence of signs and miracles at Godelieve's grave pointed to martyrdom.

The vitae of female saints convey a picture of women's place in society that can only be described as dismal. They show women to have had little control over their lives and bodies and few defenses against neglect and oppression. However unwilling or unready, they were married when and to whom their fathers chose. Subject to their husbands, they could scarcely expect sympathy and support from their parental families, and they were lucky if they were not blamed for their own suffering. Marriage was no guarantee of security, for they had little recourse against being divorced, abandoned, or disowned. They were obliged to submit to their husbands' sexual demands, and they had little recourse against rape. Occasionally their physical subjection went beyond sexual oppression to assault and even to murder.

There is no way to tell from reading these lives whether this picture was typical, nor are there readily available sources that would give us an accurate statistical estimate of the frequency of such oppressive conditions.[16] But the lives reveal much about attitudes and values. Parents' control over daughters was unquestioned, as was husbands' control over wives. Nothing in the social circumstances reported in these stories seems to have been a matter for indignation, much less for protest—not even from the oppressed women themselves. Extreme suffering was pitied, as extreme cruelty was condemned, but the institutional arrangements that fostered cruelty and suffering were accepted as entirely normal. What was unusual—and it was the drama of the saint's story—was the inspired response of the holy woman to a set of circumstances to which almost no one else offered any objection.

Statistical Profile: Chastity

Altogether, 64 of 151, or 42 percent, of the female saints in our sample had conflicts of one sort or another arising from their sexual lives. For men the corresponding figures are 137 of 713, or just over 19 percent. The facts themselves, stated in this bare way, are eloquent. The differences bespeak both cultural prejudice and social reality. Some hagiographers portrayed women as sexually powerful, the preferred tool of the devil, morally weak where the flesh was concerned, predatory toward men. Other recorders of holy lives, particularly those who took down the saint's very words, told a story of revulsion against the carnal act, great moral strength, victimization by men, and divine inspiration. Hagiographers were perpetuators of cultural myth, but the mythography of female sexuality turned on this contradiction.

In the vitae of male saints, women (other than mothers and most sisters) invariably were portrayed as limbs of Satan; they had no other function than to enhance the stature of the saint by making futile efforts to induce him into sin. Even if these were only tales for the titillation and consolation of celibate clerics, they transmitted widely a stereotype of women deeply rooted in Christian culture, going back to Eve, the Serpent, and the Fall.[17] To what degrees women as well as men were influenced by these myths about their sex is problematical, but contemporary social psychology tells us that powerful stereotypes are internalized by their victims as well as by their perpetrators.[18]

To read the lives of female saints, however, is to discover a wholly different cultural idea, although one that had to coexist with its opposite. Here women are in the mold of Mary, virgin in spirit if not in body, longing for freedom from the importunities of the world—a more sympathetic image to be sure, but even more devastating. The woman who internalized the ideal of Mary and sought to achieve it was virtually assured of failure, not only because the flesh was weak but because the world demanded marriage and motherhood.

Hagiography makes a formal distinction between those saints who preserved their chastity against the assaults of family pressure or external temptation and those saints who, whatever their misgivings, lived unchastely for a time before converting to continence. Tables 3 and 4 (pp. 129, 132) indicate how this official distinction between virgins and others is reflected in the lives of each group of saints. In some respects saints who withstood challenges to their virginity (table 3) are not significantly different from nonvirgins (table 4). In both categories women appear in large numbers, and in both the class configurations are similar; both groups are about equally dedicated to austerity and equally suffer demonic attacks, and their distributions over time are similar (except for the eleventh and early twelfth centuries, when the roll of saints was still dominated by celibate prelates). These similarities of time, place, and social circumstance suggest that the virtue of chastity was essentially a constant in the history of sanctity. Some trends and concentrations exist, but these were never so strong as to suggest a time or place where the ideal of chastity was not central to the perception of sanctity.

Yet there are important differences between the two groups. One is in the ways they arrived at the holy life. In the stories of saints who preserve their chastity, parents played a dominant part. Fathers and mothers were deeply involved in the saint's decision to follow the celibate life, as we might expect, since these were mainly children and adolescents. In the stories of those who came to practice continence after a period of sexual activity, the dominant influences toward conversion were some kind of personal crisis (299), reaction to worldly involvement (294), and visions (238). For them the conversion to chastity was an adult decision, and this we will examine more fully in the next chapter.

The other major difference is suggested most clearly in the multivariate analysis segments of tables 3 and 4. Saints who preserved their virginity have much higher index scores on all five components of holy reputation, but especially on supernatural activity (50.77 versus 39.53), than those who converted to continence after having known the flesh. The major saints, those who received papal canonizations, those with great popular appeal, those whose shrines and tombs attracted multitudes of the faithful, those whose relics were eagerly sought, the great wielders of spiritual and temporal powers—these saints were virgins. Virginity, an ideal that derived ultimately from pre-Christian sources in Hellenistic dualism, pervaded every segment of medieval society.

4 ⊕ *Adults*

In *The Waning of the Middle Ages* the Dutch historian Johan Huizinga portrayed a society that "bore the mixed smell of blood and roses." Strong in contrasts of light and shade, his study showed people veering "between cruelty and tenderness, between harsh asceticism and insane attachment to the delights of this world, between hatred and goodness, always running to extremes." Vows of chastity gave way to sexual license, refined manners dissolved in coarse laughter, as acts and feelings agitated in "that perpetual oscillation between despair and protracted joy, between cruelty and pious tenderness which characterized life in the Middle Ages."[1] The Russian Marxist Mikhail Bakhtin, exploring uncharted depths of popular culture, found an even more pervasive and profoundly embedded dialectic in the medieval *mentalité*. As Bakhtin saw it, the extravagant metaphors of Rabelais's comedy *Gargantua and Pantagruel* captured its essence: all opposites were linked; the world could be turned upside down and inside out; the order of daily routine was prone to sudden reversal and disorder.[2]

Saints' lives confirm and amplify these insights. Yesterday's sinner became today's penitent; the greedy merchant suddenly gave away all his worldly goods; the prostitute abruptly entered a nunnery; the overproud knight decided to dedicate his sword to Mary, and the scholar pledged his pen to the Trinity. Such reversals made sense in a world where every crime seemed to have its appropriate expiation and every sin its corresponding virtue, where the flux of becoming did not totally conceal an underlying harmony of being. Belief in a divine symmetry composed of paired opposites meant that sudden conversion required no other explanation than that it followed the same profound rhythm to which all things moved.[3]

100

Conversion might be a sudden and total reversal, but for adults its consequences were much more difficult and painful than for young people.
Adolescents were only on the threshold of life, whereas adults were enmeshed in a web of established comforts and demands. Moving from the
sense of emptiness and drift so well described by young Bernard of Clairvaux, adolescents found an identity through passionate commitment. The
aimless adult who finds a new life through conversion is not totally unknown in hagiography; but more usually we see the grown man or woman
well established in the secular world as a merchant, queen, professor,
knight, or comfortable cleric. As a result, the typical pattern of adult conversion, a drastic shift from a former state or condition to its opposite,
while conforming to the dialectical rhythm of medieval conceptions of
action in time, was an occasion of intense personal conflict. To leave a mate
of some years was much more wrenching than to refuse a marriage offer
from a suitor who was a virtual stranger; to abandon one's business or
profession was a greater sacrifice than to give up an apprenticeship. Teenagers could blithely reject their parents, but parents nearly always shrank
from abandoning their children. The anguish of leaving the world was a
major theme in stories of adult conversion.

In their initial call to the holy life adults were not very different from
adolescent converts: the death of a loved one, a serious illness, the preaching of a holy evangelist, an acute sense of worldliness, a sudden experience
of the supernatural were the most usual precipitants. As we suggested
earlier, the conversion to a life in religion was a form of world rejection
especially appealing to adolescents in a deeply religious culture. But to the
adult no less than to the teenager the life of the spirit was a refuge as well
as a challenge, a rejection of family in favor of the community of saints,
a flight from social obligation as well as a shouldering of the yoke of Christ.

Adults were less likely to be precipitated into conversion by the call of
an evangelical preacher than were their sons and daughters, although they
were not deaf to such appeals. The mendicant movement of the thirteenth
century captured fathers and mothers as well as their teenage children, if
not in as great numbers.[4] More typical of adult conversion, however, was
the story of the eleventh-century Orléans teacher Odon, which subtly contrasts the calm of mature reason with the youthful passion of religious
commitment. We may suppose that, like most intellectuals, Odon was a
professional skeptic, more likely to see all sides of a question than to commit
himself to a single one. (Among his early writings was a work on sophism
that, while the term did not have the pejorative connotations we attach to
it today, nonetheless implied the subjectivity of intellectual reasoning.)
Students came from all over Europe to hear Master Odon lecture on canon
law. He was famous as a dialectician and wrote on metaphysics as well as

on sophism. Odon was no impulsive teenager, and the way to his heart was through his mind. His biographer explains his conversion as the result of his reading Augustine's *On True Religion* and *On the Freedom of the Will.* "At once he was changed into another man," and he began to hate what he had loved and to love what he had hated. Odon had always been truthful, patient, and chaste, we are told, but to these virtues he now added religious zeal. "What a change in a man!" exclaims his biographer. Odon was now a convert to works of charity and to chastisement of the flesh. Once too busy with his secular works to study theology, he now devoted his considerable talents to writing about the canon of the Mass, original sin, the sins against the Holy Spirit and to composing a dialogue with a Jew on the coming of Christ.

Since he was already celibate, Odon had relatively little difficulty in following his new religious quest for a life of holiness. But for others, especially women, it was not so easy to accept the call to break ties with the past. Filippa Mareri was no more than conventionally pious until she was twenty-five, when she met Francis of Assisi. Then she resolved to leave the world, taking a first step by shutting herself up in a room of the family house. Although she was a grown woman, her family, especially her brother Tommaso, seems to have tried to prevent Filippa from pursuing her vocation, so she ran away from home and lived in a cave. Finally Tommaso had a change of heart and built his sister a chapel and an adjoining dwelling where she could live in reclusion. Strengthened by her earlier trials, Filippa ultimately came into her own as a contemplative, healer, peacemaker, benefactor of the poor, and miracle-worker.

Another woman whose life was changed by Francis was Giacomina di Settesoli, a Roman noble married to a member of the ancient Frangipani family. After hearing Francis preach she invited him to her house, which then became a meeting place for *il poverello* and his early followers. The Romans regarded her with affection for her generosity and piety and called her Friar Jacopa. The story that she took Francis's lamb to church with her suggests that her devotion was regarded as a shade eccentric. But, though dedicated to the Franciscan cause, Friar Jacopa did not abandon the world all at once. In 1209 when she first met the holy man from Assisi she was a matron of thirty with at least two sons, and apparently the obligations of motherhood and household kept her from fully embracing his example. Not until fifteen years later, when she had a presentiment of Francis's death and hurried to Assisi to minister to him, did she fully begin to live the consequences of her conversion. After bathing the stigmata of the dead saint with her kisses and tears, she returned to Rome to dispose of her property and make provision for her sons; then she returned to Assisi to follow in humility and poverty the life of a Franciscan tertiary. Her portrait was painted opposite Francis's own in the lower church in Assisi that is dedicated to him.

The story of Guala of Bergamo is linked with another great mendicant whose charisma worked on adults as well as on teenagers. Guala was a Bergamese patrician who was received into the Order of Preachers by Dominic himself in 1219 and became bishop of Brescia. He was a formidable preacher and a solicitous shepherd of his flock but was by no means extraordinarily holy until he received a vision of Dominic's death. As with Friar Jacopa, the loss of his spiritual mentor led Guala to break his ties with the world. He abdicated his bishopric and retired to a monastery, and there is some evidence that he subsequently joined the order of the Vallombrosan hermits.

An encounter with Dominic is also the nub of the conversion story of Iazech, or Hyacinth, Odrovaz. A Silesian noble, Iazech owed his appointment as a canon of Krakow cathedral to his kinsman the bishop of Krakow, who continued to further his nephew's ecclesiastical career. Sent to Rome on church business in 1216, the thirty-one-year-old Iazech was dramatically converted when he saw Dominic raise a man from the dead. Along with his brother the Blessed Ceslaus and another relative, Iazech entered the Order of Preachers and returned to Poland to spread the gospel. Like Dominic he found he had a gift for moving the hearts of his listeners, and he brought many Poles into the order. The faithful attributed an extraordinary range of miracles to him, including revival of dead people and animals, miraculous healing of paralysis and blindness, restoration of crops, making women fecund, and walking on water.

The roster of saintly converts who turned from established careers to follow a holy leader was lengthiest in the thirteenth century, that great era of new religious movements. Dominic de Guzmán and Francis of Assisi were the brightest luminaries of this particular firmament, but many other evangelists also drew men and women into religion by their spiritual ardor.[5] Philip Benizi, one of the seven founders of the Servites, was remarkably effective in inducing solid citizens of Florence to cut their worldly ties. One of his disciples, Ubaldo Adimari, had been a leader of the antipapal party of the Ghibellines and prominent in the intensely competitive political life of Florence before he was converted in 1280. After his conversion Ubaldo retired to the woods to lead a life of severe penance, becoming known for his gentle ways with animals and his miracle-working.

After the mendicant tide subsided, evangelism began to sound a different note. Not that sacred oratory ran dry. Great preachers were legion in the fourteenth and fifteenth centuries—one thinks of Jan Hus, Jerome of Prague, the Lollards, Bernardino da Siena, John of Capistrano, Vincent Ferrer, Bernardino da Feltre, John Herolt, Girolamo Savonarola, Johannes

Nider, and many others—but their major impact was moral rather than ascetic. For the most part the later evangelists exhorted reform *in* the world rather than flight *from* the world. Even the preachers who founded movements, such as Hus and Savonarola, were not out to make hermits, penitential contemplatives, or even friars of their converts.[6]

The fourteenth century was tormented by economic depression, interminable warfare, and the Black Death.[7] Not coincidentally, it was galvanized to new religious life by zealots and magnetic personalities. In the Dominican convents of the Rhine Valley mystics felt and tasted God. In the Beguinages of the Scheldt they practiced spiritual exercises. Flagellants whipped themselves bloody as they dragged their heavy crosses over the highways of Europe. In Bohemia some of the followers of Hus joined together in holy *agape* to await the coming millennium. In Italy Catherine of Siena inspired young girls to take Christ as their bridegroom. In Toledo religious mobs called for Christian purification by expelling the Jews. Religious exaltation led some men and women who had already found their niche in the world to exchange it for a cloister or cell; but many men and women who needed more intense spiritual experience found other alternatives as the theater of action shifted from the monastery to the home, from the pilgrim road to the streets of the town, from the band of hermits to the confraternity.[8]

More broadly speaking, the fourteenth century saw the emergence of a lay culture. As champions of the vernacular, Dante and Chaucer were among its major proponents, while the humanists of the Renaissance gave it a neoclassical literary and educational program and forged many of its tools. In the universities and schools Scholasticism grudgingly made room for liberal and biblical studies. Priests and monks no longer monopolized the life of the spirit. Dante, a layman, had the audacity to journey to hell and spot there more than a few prelates, along with a saint or two, and William Langland presented a moral indictment of society from a plowman's perspective. Eucharistic devotion continued, even increased in fervor, but lay men and women were no longer satisfied merely to gaze in awe at the Host. They wished to participate more actively, but they needed to do so on their own terms, without breaking the ties of family or abandoning their shops and countinghouses. Lay people needed practical and immediate moral guidance, ways of dealing with illness and death, spiritual consolation, reassurance about the punishments of purgatory and the damnation of hell, and modes of penance and expiation that did not require them to leave the world or altogether subdue the claims of the flesh. The evangelists of lay piety set forth programs of accommodation between life in the world and the law of the gospel that were not merely copies of clerical guidelines for becoming a saint.[9]

World renunciation as a form of religious expression did not disappear in the fourteenth and fifteenth centuries. It continued to attract many, and it emerged again with considerable vigor during the Reformation, when new charismatic leaders rallied young men and women to the aid of the embattled church. The shift toward new lay-oriented forms of piety was gradual and never complete. It took place in stages that we may describe— with apologies for overschematizing—as follows. In the eleventh and twelfth centuries conversion meant completely renouncing life in the world by going off to a monastery, convent, or hermitage. By the thirteenth century conversion still meant giving up a worldly life but did not require leaving the world. Men and women might take a special vow of poverty and renounce their goods; but they served God by ministering to others, not by shutting themselves behind monastic walls to pray for their own souls. From the late thirteenth century, and continuing until the Reformation, worldly ties were proving more resistant, and lay piety became a new arena of religious innovation and expression. Structures developed that allowed men and women to engage in intense forms of devotion and expiation while carrying on their obligations to family, business, and country. With the Reformation, Catholic lay piety came under stricter clerical control. There was still room for the ardent and sudden adult convert, but only if spiritual zeal conformed to the more carefully defined prescriptions of the church militant.

The more dissolute the converted sinner, the more dramatically intense the conflict between the world and the spirit. The dialectical ontology of Catholic Europe gave ample room for a sudden shift from sinner to saint. Biblical prototypes existed: Mary Magdalene was honored throughout Christendom as the fallen woman who became one of the inner circle of Jesus.[10] The good thief on the cross who acknowledged the Savior also became a cult figure. Through them Christ guaranteed that repentance was never too late, that no sinner was beyond the pale of God's compassion.

Among sinner-saints the wickedness of Vladimir of Kiev was emblematic, he having begun life among a heathen people regarded as barbarous by Christians. Vladimir was depicted as brutal and bloodthirsty, with a special weakness for sexual sin, as attested by his five wives and the numerous female slaves he kept as concubines. The Chronicle of Nestor sententiously observed that "his desire for woman was too much for him." While the circumstances of Vladimir's conversion to Christianity are obscure, they apparently are connected with his marriage to Anne, the daughter of Emperor Basil II at Constantinople in 989. But not even Christianity could altogether tame Vladimir. He was ruthless and brutal in forcing the Russians to adopt his new faith, although no doubt this achievement made him a cult figure.

Christians too could be great sinners, although hagiographers seem to have been reluctant to record the sordid details. The twelfth-century

1

2

3

4

5

6

7

8

9

Sienese Galgano Guidotti was described as dissolute and ferocious for thirty-two of his thirty-three years, although this received less attention from his biographer than Galgano's stubborn refusal to heed the supernatural signs urging him to change his ways. Not only did he resist his mother's attempts to get him to marry and settle down, even two visits from the Archangel Michael failed to move him. Only after his horse twice had veered from its course and the second time carried him to a nearby mountain did he acknowledge the divine call and settle down on the mountain as a hermit. Galgano's contemporary, the Provençal knight Bernard the Penitent, referred darkly to a horrible sin that he tried to expiate by going barefoot for seven years. When this failed to allay his conscience he decided to become a pilgrim, wandering to Jerusalem and then to India to seek out the shrine of St. Thomas. He was profoundly charitable to the poor and chastised every part of his body with metal bands. Four years of strenuous austerities and great physical suffering killed him. Pedro Armengol, a fourteenth-century Catalan who became famous for redeeming Christian prisoners from the Moors as well as for his ecstasies and levitations, had been the head of a band of brigands as a teenager, but no further details of his sinful ways are recorded.

The biography of Margaret of Cortona by her confessor gives us only sparse details about her life before conversion. Only from other sources do we discover why she was known as the Second or New Magdalen. Born about 1247 to a peasant family near the Tuscan hill town of Cortona, Margaret suffered at the hands of an unkind stepmother. As a youth she went to live with a local noble, sharing his bed for nine years and bearing a son. When her lover was killed she returned home, but her father cast her out, and she had to seek shelter with the Franciscans. Two years later she joined the Franciscan Third Order, and in due course her son also entered the order. Margaret was a protector of the poor and sick and took special care of pregnant women, founding hospitals and houses of refuge. A great visionary and mystic, she also exercised her influence in the civic world as "the preacher of peace." (See fig. 14.)

Fig. 14. Margaret of Cortona with scenes from her life. (1) Margaret does penance after the death of her lover. (2) Margaret is vested as a tertiary. (3) Margaret gives all her possessions to the poor. (4) Margaret saves a man who has invoked her aid while hanging himself. (5) Margaret washes the feet of lepers. (6) Christ promises Margaret that he will protect the Franciscan order. (7) Margaret, ill, receives communion in her cell. (8) Christ, accompanied by the Virgin Mother, shows Margaret the throne she will have in heaven. (9) Margaret in her shrine; the faithful come to be cured. Note that none of the scenes depicts Margaret's sinful life before her conversion. Cortona, Diocesan Museum. Altarpiece in the Sienese style, second quarter of the fourteenth century. Photograph courtesy of Gabinetto Fotografico Soprintendenza ai Beni Artistici e Storici di Firenze.

We could present some other examples of great sinner-saints, but not many. Margaret of Cortona is almost unique as a second Magdalen, and there are relatively few Bernard the Penitents or Vladimirs. However many abject sinners may have repented and converted to a moral and pious life, few of them seem to have become objects of veneration. That popular cults seldom honored a sinner-saint suggests that the rigorous requirements of church authorities for proof that the candidate for sainthood had achieved heroic virtues were grounded in medieval notions of justice as well as in abstruse theology. For an evil man or woman suddenly to become a vehicle of divine grace, a dispenser of favor who could make crops grow or the sick well was hard to accept. God might be mysterious, but he could not be regarded as capricious. The faithful were in awe of all wonder-workers, but in the main hagiographers reserved veneration for those who had been uncommonly virtuous and ascetic from an early age, and they practically ruled out any one who turned to a holy life after many years of blatant sinning.[11]

While every degree of theological crudity and subtlety may be found in the lives of the saints, the most pervasive theme is a lofty one—the conjunction of divine grace and human merit. The great majority of saints were shown to have been designated for holiness before they had reached the age of discretion, yet saints earned their election by living lives of superhuman effort. For the most part saints' stories express this theme in stark and simple terms: the holy person achieved sanctification through extreme self-denial and extraordinary good works, and by doing so built a credit balance of merits against which very few debits for prior sinfulness had to be subtracted. Here again the perceptions of holiness expressed in saints' lives reveal some of the more general values of Catholic piety.

The system of credits that assigned so many years off for a meritorious act was the product of the fusion of the early Germanic notion of retributive justice with the Christian doctrine of free will. Carried to its extreme in the medieval penitential system and simplified by preachers of moral reform, the notion that man is both the beneficiary of Christ's redemption and the responsible agent of his own salvation, transformed God into a fact-finding judge with the church as his ledger-keeper.[12] When greedy prelates and unscrupulous indulgence sellers encouraged the popular belief that remission of penalties was equivalent to assured salvation, the cult of saints and the treasury of merits became sources of abuse.[13] Since the Reformation, indulgences and cult have been easy targets for satire by both Catholic and Protestant reformers, but it is worth remembering that these practices arose from and sustained a profound sense of Christian community. Patron saints personified the communal identity of their city, town, village, and nation; they cast their protective mantle across generations; they brought the faithful together in processions to commemorate past favors and im-plore future ones.[14] In the seventeenth century, terrified by a great plague epidemic, the Tuscan town of San Gimignano called upon Serafina, its native saint, just as it had been doing for the past four hundred years. When their country was paralyzed by the Nazi blitzkrieg, French patriots rallied to Charles de Gaulle's invocation of the Maid of Orléans, who had rescued the nation from an earlier disaster in the Hundred Years War.[15] Today as for centuries rural Maltese rally around their favorite saints to compete for the honor of setting off festival fireworks; their idea of com-munity is based less upon class, residence, or even kinship networks than upon a tradition of identification with a particular saint.[16]

If the story of the sinner-saint violated popular notions of retributive justice, the same may not be said for accounts of ordinary men and women who underwent sudden spiritual transformations. In all times and places hagiographers loved to tell about the crisis that interrupted a mundane existence and led to dramatic conversion. These vitae also vividly record the problems their heroes had had living in the world and their difficulties in leaving it. Sometimes the impetus came from outside, as it did to Anafrid of Utrecht, a high feudal noble of tenth-century Brabant. Anafrid was a trusted counselor of his lord, a man of known integrity (he never took a bribe, says his biographer) and of moderation, for which qualities he was called upon to assume the bishopric of Utrecht. Anafrid declined, explain-ing that he had been a soldier all his life and it would be absurd for him to become a cleric now. Besides, he was too old. But his lord persisted, and Anafrid felt compelled to obey. Placing his sword upon the altar, Anafrid dedicated the rest of his life to the Blessed Virgin. The good soldier became a priest and a holy bishop, but the transition was not entirely smooth. Although God helped Anafrid by shielding his eyes from desire and barring him from all further occasions of sin, the flesh was unruly and had to be chastised. It was Anafrid's special practice to retreat from the duties of his office to a Benedictine monastery he had built. There he took lepers into his cell and nursed them, and gradually knightly pride became saintly humility.

Another high cleric of the same time, Lanfranc, the great defender of the Eucharist and archbishop of Canterbury, also had become famous in a worldly career before turning to the path of holiness. Born in Pavia, Lanfranc studied in Bologna for many years. When he began to receive offers to teach at other famous schools, he humbly settled upon a minor post at Avranches in Normandy. Kidnapped by robbers during a journey, he was unable to pray and suffered acute depression until he vowed to rededicate his life. After he escaped, he joined the Benedictine abbey of Bec. Now free to act on the impulse to humility he had suppressed in his worldy life, Lanfranc spent three happy years in virtual solitude, until his fame as a scholar threatened to draw him back into public controversies. He thought of running away to an even more remote place, but his abbot persuaded him to stay, and soon he had to give up all hope of anonymity. Lanfranc was made abbot, and after he agreed to serve as a counselor to Duke William of Normandy he became embroiled in political controversy without end. All this was but a prelude to his famous dispute with the theologian Berengar, in which Lanfranc defended the doctrine of the Real Presence of the Mass.[17] He declined an offer of the archbishopric of Rouen but accepted the see of Canterbury after much pressure from King William. There he defended the autonomy of the church, undertook sweeping reforms, and fought magicians and soothsayers; but the solitude and anonymity Lanfranc had sought after his conversion always eluded him. It is this theme of humility thwarted and solitude denied that distinguishes Lanfranc's story from the more common one of the powerful eleventh- and twelfth-century prelate who achieved veneration through public service.

Tension between the world and the spirit also marks the story of Bruno of Cologne, though Bruno was able to make a cleaner break. Born in 1030, Bruno was a teacher at Paris as well as a canon of Rheims cathedral when a strange event changed his life. At the funeral of a famous Paris doctor that Bruno was attending a voice was heard crying "I am accused by the just judgment of God!" The voice seemed to come from the coffin, and it was heard for several days in succession. Bruno, then a man in his forties, was terrified, believing that the voice from the dead was a warning of God's judgment upon sinners. He begged his friends to escape God's wrath while there was still time to seek a better way. The condemned in hell had no use for knowledge; all their riches, he preached, counted for less than a drop of cool water on their parched tongues. Bruno threw up his own career and with two companions began a life of spiritual quest that ended many years later in the harsh mountains of Calabria. At Chartreuse he founded the heavily cloistered Order of Carthusian Hermits.

Saints' lives show medieval people dealing with their crises by turning to religion and, in the twelfth century, frequently abandoning the world altogether. It goes without saying that most twelfth-century people responded to their troubles in a far less dramatic way. Saints were by definition exceptional; for ordinary people there were the consolations of prayer and penance, and such lesser austerities as fasts and pilgrimages. Nevertheless, the stories we are examining reveal a great deal about medieval religious values and ideas about life. For the people of that earlier time it did not require a crisis as catastrophic as the death of a wife or the loss of family fortune to provide a motive for giving up the world. The seriousness of the catastrophe was measured less in concrete terms than by its symbolic and emotional value—by its power to evoke the ephemerality of this life and its credibility as a sign from God. If only a comparative few responded by becoming hermits or monks, the very conventionality of the action suggests that many regarded it as a believable, reasonable, and desirable thing to do. In the twelfth century it was presented as an especially feasible resolution of the spiritual crises of youth, but world renunciation could be the recourse of adults too, as we see in the following stories.

When the Welsh minstrel Caradoc was threatened with severe punishment for having lost two of his royal lord's best hunting dogs, he took clerical tonsure and ran off to a cell on the island of Ary. The great reformer Norbert of Xanten had been a pleasure-loving courtier of Emperor Henry V. As a canon he had had to take holy orders but shunned elevation to the priesthood until one day, riding through the Westphalian village of Wreden, he was thrown from his horse. Like Saul, he cried, "Lord, what will you have me do?" A voice that seemed to come from inside him replied, "Turn from evil and do good; seek after peace and pursue it." From that moment Norbert turned to a life of fasting and prayer, became a priest, and eventually founded the Order of Canons Regular of Prémontré. Berthold, the future abbot of Garsten, came from a family of counts who lived near the shores of Lake Constance. After his wife died he became a holy man and won fame as an exorcist and miracle-worker.

Gerlac of Valkenburg, in Holland, also was converted after the death of his wife. A celebrated soldier and horseman, he lived an immoral life until he was about forty. While he was in the midst of a tournament he received news of his wife's death. Immediately Gerlac announced to the crowd that he was leaving the world, dismounted from his horse, exchanged the noble steed for a donkey, and rode off. Gerlac's life in religion was virtually a step-by-step penitential inversion of his life in the world. When a thorn in his foot gave him great pain, he recalled that this was the foot with which in childish anger he had kicked his mother. In place of his knight's armor he now wore a hair shirt and a tight iron cuirass. Since the friars who had given him refuge considered him too highborn to do menial work, he left them to take up the humbling task of tending pigs and sheep. From the enjoyment of the pleasures of the flesh he now turned to abstemiousness, became "an inexorable castigator of his own body," and, his biographer reports, traded his feudal castle for a hollow oak tree.

Volkuin of Sittenbach was an ordinary priest of no particular distinction until a fire burned down his house and shocked him into renouncing the world. He decided to become a Cistercian monk and, after giving away a third of his remaining worldly goods, achieved fame by washing the feet of pilgrims and caring for the poor and sick, in imitation of Christ. Giovanni Bono led a thoroughly dissolute life for forty years until his miraculous recovery from an illness that had brought him to the point of death (according to one account he had been judged dead and then revived by the intercession of Giovanni da Matera) caused him to devote his last forty years totally to God's service. Obizio da Niardo renounced his way of life because of a dream about the pains of hell that came to him after he was almost killed in a battle between his native city of Brescia and neighboring Cremona. Leaving his worldly goods to his family, he devoted himself to a career of public good works. Whether leaving his wife and four children caused him any compunction or difficulty the account does not say.

Hroznata, a Bohemian noble who had a strong commitment to God as well as to his king, kept both these loyalties in careful balance and, according to his biographer, married only to produce an heir. But the son died in infancy, followed soon after by his grieving mother. This double loss convinced Hroznata that he should henceforth think only of how to please God. He started out on a pilgrimage to Jerusalem, but the sea terrified him and he went instead to Rome. There he consulted the pope, who advised him to join the Přemonstratensian order. Ultimately he found martyrdom at Alt-Kinsberg, near Eger, where he had been thrown into a dungeon, presumably because he was a great defender of ecclesiastical immunity against interference from temporal government.

Victory rather than tragedy turned the knight Gautier de Bierbeck to the religious life. On his way to a tournament he stopped to attend mass and prayed to the Virgin Mary. She favored him in the jousting and, says his biographer, sent him a golden cross. From that time on Gautier dedicated himself to Mary's service and became a monk at Hinnerode. The Queen of Heaven continued to look after Gautier all his life, helping him to escape from pirates, to find a valuable horse belonging to the monastery, and to work miracles.

Bernardo Calvò, a Catalan jurist and knight, decided to leave the world after recovering from a serious illness. For a year he had to resist efforts by his friends and family to dissuade him from his course. Since he was already in his thirties and had become prominent in legal and government affairs, they believed he would be more useful in the world; besides, they pointed out, he was deeply involved in litigation over a family estate. But Bernardo could not be dissuaded and became a monk. So complete was his rejection of worldliness that when some women praised the beauty of his teeth he bashed them in with a rock.

Accounts of men and women who turned to the religious life after some personal crisis or supernatural sign continued through the succeeding centuries, but the contours of the story changed; the conversion crisis was no longer so precipitous. Hagiographers took more pains to tell their readers about the events that led up to conversion and those that followed it. Perhaps tension between the two worlds had been as deep in the twelfth century as in the fourteenth and fifteenth, but it is in the later period that the accounts become rich with the drama of renunciation. From the very outset of the Renaissance there are some examples of a new emphasis upon inner discourse and reflection.[18] Biographers begin to use the device of dialogue to dramatize conflicts of conscience as well as of family resistance. In the late fourteenth century, classical literature provided models for the delineation of personality and the revelation of character, making humanist-influenced saints' lives easily distinguishable from more traditional examples.

New aesthetic sensibilities and the new requirements of literary style were the surface tremors of deeper shifts in the social and psychological fabric. The claims of the sacred order remained powerful, and conversion would continue to be a common option, but the temporal world of the new era had its own compelling reasons; its duties as well as its pleasures demanded growing recognition. The full range and consequences of these transformations, at least as related to religious ideas, we will take up in the second half of this book. For the moment we wish to concentrate on two cases of adult conversion that we have selected as much for their typicality as for the vivid way they illustrate the interplay between the worlds of the flesh and the spirit.

The earlier case is the life of Nevelone da Faenza, patron of shoemakers. Nevelone's conversion began with an illness in 1248 when he was twenty-four years old. Recovering, he "put on the new man" and began to practice charity and to mortify his flesh, but he did not abandon his family or his cobbler's bench. Nevertheless, wife and world soon impinged on Nevelone's new piety. His wife complained that he was too generous with his goods. No doubt she had cause, since the account says that Nevelone gave so much to the poor that he was left almost naked. Nevelone bore his wife's complaints patiently but did not change his ways; on the contrary, he persuaded her to accompany him on his next pilgrimage. An illness prevented her from going, however, and although she recovered "miraculously" she died soon afterward. Nevelone was now free to give his few remaining possessions to poor widows and to dedicate himself entirely to pious practices. He was especially devoted to pilgrimage; he made the long trip to the shrine of St. James of Compostela in Spain at least seven times. But if Nevelone was no longer of the world, he was still very much in it. He had to deal with sexual temptation (by jumping into an icy river) and with lascivious women (whom he converted by prayer). In Faenza he founded a society of Battuti, or self-flagellators, and only in his later years, perhaps when he was no longer strong enough to go on pilgrimage, did he find the spiritual strength to become a recluse under the aegis of the Franciscan tertiaries.

For our second case, which richly illustrates both the volatility of medieval personality and the counterpull of earthly affections, we move to the bourgeois world of Siena in the mid-fourteenth century. Giovanni Colombini, founder of the mendicant order of Gesuati, was a colorful figure in the life of his town. When we first see him Colombini was a successful merchant, a husband and father. He had been elected to the Sienese senate and had served as one of the twelve gonfaloniers or standard-bearers of the city. He was also "greedy for making money," hot-tempered, and impatient. One day he returned home hungry for his dinner. When he found that the meal was not ready, Giovanni cursed and stormed. To calm him, his wife Biagia thrust a book of saints' lives at him and told him to pass the time with it until she finished cooking. Giovanni threw the book to the floor, then picked it up and thumbed the pages until he came to a life of St. Mary of Egypt. Reading how she had become a hermit after leading a wicked life of the flesh, he grew fascinated and felt his own heart change. His anger subsided as he began to reflect on piety, and he felt swelling within him an impulse to change his life in imitation of the saint. When Biagia called him to dinner he was so absorbed that he told her to wait until he had finished reading. The good woman rejoiced and prayed to God to complete the work of conversion, open her irascible husband's eyes, turn him from greed, give him a docile heart, and prompt him to divine worship.

Giovanni began to attend mass and to take frequent communion. This spiritual food nourished him even in the marketplace, where he exchanged his greed for generosity. He began to debate with himself whether it was more harmful to the spirit to be a lender or a debtor, and he no longer tried to knock down the price of goods he bought or to force up the price of what he sold. On the contrary, he now sold below the just price and paid more than the seller asked. As the news of his unusual way of doing business spread around town Giovanni was besieged by buyers and sellers. The volume of his business multiplied, to the wonder of some and the envy of others. "Isn't this the man who yesterday and the day before haggled over piddling sums, who refused to pay his debts or keep his hands off others' property?" What had happened, it was asked, "so that his hands, once so tight-fisted to the needy, now open even to those who do not beg?" Some thought he had been persuaded to change his ways by a friend who had convinced him of the unseemliness of avarice and invoked the honor of his family. Others, contrasting his sudden liberality with his past greed, believed he was delirious. But a few wise persons, says his biographer, saw that they had a budding saint in their midst.

Totally wrapped up in love of the Savior, Giovanni was equally indifferent to the criticisms of his business rivals and the praise of his friends.

Untangling himself from his family proved more complicated than reforming his business methods. Giovanni began to think about living in chastity, but he was much troubled by the obligations of a husband, for which all manner of scriptural exhortations rang in his ears. One day he gently broached the subject to Biagia as follows:

> Beloved wife, give back to me the power over my body which I gave you freely, I beg you. Take back yours in freedom. Be my wife no longer, but my sister and I will no longer be your husband but your brother. We will be two, no longer of one flesh, and of no flesh except the Savior's. . . .
>
> We do not have many children, although we are not childless, and if none survive us our heir will be Christ who makes us coheirs in the Father's Kingdom. In the meantime our lives will be uncorrupt and angelic and our abstinence the joy of the angels.

As he spoke Biagia was wrung with emotion and broke into tears, but, the hagiographer assures us, God moved her heart to understanding and she gave her consent. "From the silver state of matrimony they passed into the golden one of celibacy." Throwing himself on his knees, Giovanni offered himself and his wife as a sacrifice while Biagia looked on and gave her silent assent.

The transition to his new state was not altogether easy, though God helped Giovanni dominate his carnal spirit and the temptations of the flesh. His libido waned, but he knew that he was not yet a fortress impenetrable to temptation and weakness, and he moved only gradually toward extreme asceticism. His was a day-by-day spiritual progress rather than a sudden and total metamorphosis. Continence prepared him for the new and higher level of spirituality to which God now lighted his way: Giovanni reflected upon Christ's call to poverty, and to his vow of chastity he now added the promise that he would divest himself of all his remaining possessions and "naked follow his naked Savior."

Soon thereafter Giovanni fell ill, welcoming his affliction as a special mark of divine favor sent to further his religious growth. But the loving ministrations of Biagia and his friend Francesco Vincenzio threatened to nullify any spiritual gain he hoped to realize from the illness. So one day he crept secretly from his sickbed and went to a poor little hospital in a remote corner of Siena, where only after much anxious searching Biagia and Francesco finally discovered him. To their expressions of concern he replied: "Why do you disturb me? Why do you trouble yourselves over me? I came here for one reason, because of your indulgence and your excessive care for this miserable body of mine. Softness is the enemy of the spirit, and I insist on the bridle of penitence even in sickness. This bed is fine for me. Please make way for this poor woman here. She is bringing me a plate of food more satisfying to my hunger than anything you have in your fine broth. Give up any hope of my returning."

Biagia and Francesco bombarded the sick penitent with objections: this was a wretched little hospital for beggars and it was neither right nor proper that a rich nobleman like himself should be there; God would be displeased, and his fellow citizens would laugh at him for so foolishly trying to assume the title of pauper. Giovanni gave in to their entreaties and came home.

Weakened by his persistent fever, he faced an even greater trial in Biagia's sudden change of heart. She had consented quickly, albeit passively, to give up her claim to the conjugal debt, but now, after eight years of living as Giovanni's sister, Biagia rebelled at being dragged down with him into ever deeper levels of poverty and humility. "How long am I to bear this disgusting and filthy life? Have I come to the point where I bear the name of wife but really live out my days in squalor and suffering as the unhappy maidservant of an unfortunate master?" Again taxing Giovanni for sanctimoniously pretending to be a rustic hermit, she alternated harsh recriminations with gentle appeals to his conscience, never ceasing to remind him of the scriptural obligations upon a married man. Exasperated and frustrated at her continued inability to move the athlete of Christ, and more than faintly aware that she herself had started him on the path to holiness, Biagia cried:

> Far be it from me who have always hoped for goodness to argue for evil, but just as those who want a fruitful rain in a time of drought do not want a flood, so I wanted a shower to water your dry spirit, not a deluge which would destroy your health, drown your civility and bury your humanity.

But the more she argued, the more Giovanni became aware of the unbridgeable gap between her views of worldly moderation and his path of penance.

Eight years earlier he had hoped to follow Christ as his new master without radically disturbing his civil and domestic arrangements. Now he saw that there could be no compromise with a world steeped in sin and darkened by the shadows of spiritual ignorance. He proposed to Biagia that they take the final step: she would retire to a convent for a life of prayer and good works; he would take to the streets and public squares to preach the name of Christ. Biagia was aghast:

> I wish I had never been so foolish as to consent to your first request! I'm not unaware that the Apostle says you should not try to dissolve

the bond with your wife. This final step of breaking up our household sounds to me like the howling of a wolf.

It took a miraculous apparition to solve the impasse between Giovanni and Biagia. More than once Biagia discovered Giovanni lying on a pallet bathed in a celestial light. But, says the hagiographer, who already had taxed Biagia for reverting to "woman's stupidity" Biagia's understanding remained clouded. Finally Christ himself persuaded her to drop all objections to Giovanni's request for dissolution of the marriage. Giovanni and his friend Francesco had come upon a group of beggars at the door of the cathedral where they had gone to attend mass. Giovanni felt a special compassion for the wretched leper lying half-naked and crippled in the dust. He and Francesco hauled the leper to his feet and helped him walk to Giovanni's own home. At the door they encountered Biagia, horrified and disgusted at this latest adventure in piety. Her clamorous objections unavailing, Biagia was forced not only to take the leper in, but also to put him in her bed (for Giovanni had long since given away his bed and slept on the floor) while her husband went out to buy some medicines and to find another bed. When Giovanni returned he went to the sickroom, only to find that the leper had disappeared, leaving behind a sweet odor.

No one doubted that the leper was Christ. Even Biagia was struck by this miracle of divine visitation and at last realized that in resisting her husband she had been denying the spirit of the Lord. Now she gave in to his request and set him free from his matrimonial obligation. For his part, Giovanni now felt sure that the will of God had been involved all these years, and he was ready to begin his new life. Placing their thirteen-year-old daughter Angelina in a convent where she changed her name to Magdalena, he divided his property in three parts, one for his daughter's convent, another for his favorite hospital, and the third for the sodality of the Blessed Virgin. In addition he designated a sum to maintain his wife and, together with his first disciple Francesco Vincenzio, who also left behind a wife and child, took to the road.[19]

Giovanni Colombini's conversion had been abrupt and clear-cut. He had displayed the most unattractive features of the commercial ethos, treating business associates, family, and friends as objects of his own gratification. The story is unequivocal: no repressed longings for the religious life troubled Colombini's conscience, and there is no hint that he had not been entirely content with a life of making money, climbing the ladder of Sienese politics, and lording it over his household. Yet he read a book and was instantly converted. Although it took him eight years to complete the break with his former existence, he was a new man from the day he happened upon the life of St. Mary of Egypt. To Giovanni, as to his biographer and his admirers, his transformation was edifying, inspiring, and reasonable.

But the next eight years of Giovanni's life revealed the limitations of this diadic world view. Switching from sharp dealing to liberality in his business, he increased his profit, while the skeptical Sienese believed he had come up with a clever scheme to drive out his competitors. His wife, who had prayed for a gentle rain to soften Giovanni's heart, lived to lament the flood of radical piety that engulfed their home. For his part, Giovanni too found the consequences of conversion troublesome. Conscience and the Bible told him that marriage was not to be broken, and he worried about the future of his wife and child. Religious zeal carried him into a succession of false starts; persuaded by his wife and even by his disciple that his retreat to a paupers' hospital was unseemly and probably hypocritical, he slunk home. The lengthy dialogue between Giovanni and Biagia expresses vividly a dialectic between impulses of the spirit and ties of the world, a struggle with no easy outcome because each had strong and legitimate claims.

Colombini's biographer, unfeeling as he often was about Biagia's plight, nevertheless betrayed the insight that being married to a would-be saint was a dubious privilege. What is more, his description of Giovanni and Biagia's domestic and civic world is so rich that the account almost defeats its purpose; conveying the full extent of Giovanni's entanglements, it manages to portray the jilted wife as more heroic than the saint and to generate sympathy for the world he sought to escape.

Colombini's midlife conversion brought him to an agonizing dilemma: intoxicated with the love of God and bent on imitating his saints, he could not go on with his old life as Giovanni, the husband of Biagia, and Messer Colombini, merchant and Sienese dignitary. But to decide what he no longer could be was one thing; to know what he should become was another. Eight years of experimenting with different modes of religiousness convinced Giovanni Colombini that the compromises acceptable to many of his contemporaries were not for him. One by one he rejected casual and part-time religious solutions. He was no more able to live as Biagia's brother than as her husband, nor could he maintain his integrity as a humble penitent while continuing to live under a comfortable roof. Frequent communion was not sufficient armor against the importunities of the marketplace. Ultimately he made the radical break. But he also rejected the standard alternative of taking vows and closing himself behind monastery walls. Instead, he chose to follow the way of Francis of Assisi, gather around him a band of like-minded devotees, and go out to beg for his bread. Like Francis, Colombini had no intention of founding an order and at first rejected clerical regulation. His Gesuati, or men of Jesus, were to be an informal and untonsured band of humble penitents. But like the Franciscans the Gesuati ultimately were co-opted, and before Giovanni's death he accepted a formal rule from the pope.

Colombini's search and its final outcome were part of the late medieval saga of lay piety. The aspirations of men and women to follow the dictates of conscience and to assuage their spiritual hunger were at odds wih a clerical hierarchy that encouraged reliance upon authority and upon a sacramental system that offered vicarious and formal avenues to communion with divinity. The Reformation shattered this precarious balance between lay inspiration and clerical authority. Luther's doctrine of the priesthood of all believers was the Emancipation Proclamation of lay piety, the climax of a long quest for spiritual equality and individual responsibility before God. Reformation Catholicism chose the opposite solution, reaffirming clerical authority and leadership. Lay piety was to flourish only within bounds set by the hierarchy; no amount of individual inspiration or mystical communion with the Godhead could replace the priest at the altar. Whereas Protestantism promoted what Max Weber termed "asceticism in the world," Catholicism reaffirmed the unbridgeable gulf between the world and the spirit. The Roman church continued to teach that the life of penance and humility could be achieved fully only by withdrawal from the world, and thus it perpetuated a spiritual hierarchy that ascended from sinner to saint.[20]

Statistical Profile: Adults

Table 5 (p. 135) displays a profile for saints who converted to the holy life as mature adults. We leave out those whose canonization or beatification rests solely upon their martyrdom, because the quality of information about them is not adequate for a full description. Since martyrs interested the church as well as the faithful mainly for the circumstances leading to and surrounding their deaths, much of the detail about their lives upon which our study depends was not recorded and is irrecoverable. To include martyrs in the profile, therefore, would skew the findings by overemphasizing lack of biographical detail. For example, no statistical statement on family dynamics among martyrs can be made. To include martyrs would lead the reader to infer that martyrs' families were indifferent to them when in fact it was their venerators and biographers who were indifferent to information of this sort.

Table 5 deals, then, with 225 nonmartyr saints who came to the holy life after they had passed the age of twenty. Unlike holy children and adolescent converts, the phenomenon of conversion in adulthood shows no great diversity over time and space. There is a significant cluster of adult converts in the seventeenth century, reflecting the impact of the Catholic Reformation with its emphasis upon struggles of conscience rather than upon supernatural intervention. But the total of seventeenth-century saints, excluding martyrs, is small, and the preceding six hundred years show little variation in this category. Nor did geographical origin make much difference. Italy, with its high degree of commercial development and town life, saw roughly the same incidence of adult conversion as Spain, these being only slightly above the rates of such conversions in France and Germany. England, for reasons we will examine in part 2, was an exception.

A stronger element of differentiation is social class. Among adult converts, urban patricians outweigh both kings and peasants. Although the trend is not so strong as to be reflected in the overall figures for citified Italy, it is nonetheless historically significant. The distinction in classes, taken together with the predominance of males, the uneven distribution among orders (an overrepresentation of Benedictines and Jesuits, an underrepresentation of Dominicans), the anticipated absence of a strong family influence, since these are mature adults, and, above all, the strongly positive scores of crisis, influence of a spouse, and reaction to worldly involvement, all confirm what we have seen in the individuals we have examined, quintessentially in the case of Giovanni Colombini. Adult converts were men who traded wealth and influence for a humble place in God's order. They were much less often favored with supernatural grace and power (31.10 grand mean versus 50.91 from table 1) than holy children. In many instances they came to be venerated because of their association with a famous saint rather than for their own spiritual achievements. A prominent way they expressed their religious inspirations was in the founding of new orders. They were saints who came to the holy life as mature men or women and found none of the available options of piety, such as confraternities and penitential processions, sufficiently fulfilling. Relying upon the talents and confidence they had acquired in their former lives, they were able to take initiatives that widened the range of spiritual expression available to others by founding new orders and new forms of devotional practice.

Appendix to Part 1
Statistical Profiles of Saints

The reader should note that in these profiles the vitae are *not* weighted: each saint "counts" equally, even though some obviously counted far more than others in capturing the attention of the faithful. The matter of a "weighted" sample is discussed fully in the Appendix on Method. In lieu of a weighted analysis, table 1 and the other statistical profiles that follow include a section on Multivariate Analysis showing the direction and magnitude of variance between "lesser" saints and those of "greater" reputation and importance.

Specific points in the tables are explained below (see table 1 for note indexes):

[a]"Index of representativeness," followed in parentheses by the total number of cases and the number of female cases; that is, (25, 3) means 25 saints, of whom 3 were female. Calculation of the index is described in the Appendix on Method. The *historical* significance of the index numbers (since a random sample is not involved here, it would be misleading to report *statistical* significance levels) depends not upon their absolute magnitude but upon the historical context. For example, the 208 figure for Gender = female is important, and we believe it justifies the lengthy attention we give to holy girls in chapter 1, not because it is a big number—208 percent of randomly expected distribution—but because such a large gender disparity points to qualitatively different paths to sanctity for girls and for boys. The figure for royalty is also high in an absolute sense, 161 percent, but we consider it low in a historical context, since for obvious reasons information about the childhood of the son or daughter of a king was so much more likely to find its way into the hagiographic record than details

of the childhood of someone who grew up in humble surroundings. In short, the index is meant to be interpreted only within a historical setting, and the description of that setting is not always amenable to precise quantitative portrayal.

Since the gender distinction is especially significant, we include separate figures on the absolute number of cases in each category for females. The overall proportion of females among holy children is 55 out of 151, or 36.4 percent, and it is against this yardstick that proportions in any category should be evaluated; so also in tables 2–5.

[b]The categorizations of "type of canonization" and "extent of cult" are the same as shown earlier in the table. For "quality of reputation and popularity," however, the number of cases in each category differs somewhat from the earlier entries because the categories are not discrete and also because here we use a more inclusive definition of "wide popularity." For example, a saint's reputation might have been heavily dependent upon promotion by influential groups, based primarily upon martyrdom, and yet the saint might have been widely popular during his or her lifetime. Whereas in the early segment of the table the saint is included in each appropriate category, for purposes of this ANOVA procedure and multiple classification analysis each case necessarily is assigned to only one category, with "association" taking precedence over "not exceptional" and so on through the category of highest precedence, "wide popularity."

[c]For the construction of these categories of activity and their respective indexes see the Appendix on Method.

[d]The figures give the percentages by which mean scores for the groups shown at the left vary from the overall mean and, in parentheses, variance of the mean when controlling for the other two variables in the analysis. For example, the tendency of saints who received papal canonizations to have higher than average scores in all categories of activity ($+9$, $+6$, $+3$, $+40$, $+11$) looks very different when the effects of reputation and cult are taken into account ($+1$, -7, -4, $+24$, $+5$). The preference by popes for power holders and those active in furthering the work of the church is "real" (statistically independent to a substantial degree), whereas high scores in the other three categories clearly reflect the impact of cult and reputation rather than the independent effect of papal canonization. Canonizations through the Congregation of Rites, on the other hand, show a strong, independent, and consistent trend toward saints who were not power holders but excelled in the more "spiritual" virtues.

Table 1

Children

(N = 151)

Century of death			Occupational category		
Eleventh	112	(25, 3)[a]*	High prelate	146	(15, 0)
Twelfth	64	(17, 1)	Bishop	102	(15, 0)
Thirteenth	126	(35, 13)	Abbot, abbess	104	(29, 10)
Fourteenth	128	(24, 10)	Canon, friar, monk, nun	101	(23, 7)
Fifteenth	118	(17, 11)	Priest	22	(4, 0)
Sixteenth	74	(15, 9)	Tertiary	174	(15, 11)
Seventeenth	87	(18, 8)	Royalty/nobility	135	(14, 10)
			Professional	36	(4, 0)
Geographic area of birth			Military	54	(2, 0)
Low Countries	87	(5, 1)	Urban worker	91	(3, 0)
Scandinavia	163	(4, 2)	Peasant	68	(2, 1)
British Isles	23	(6, 0)	Housewife	153	(7, 7)
France	137	(30, 7)	Youth	220	(15, 9)
Germany	120	(20, 9)	Marginal person	44	(3, 0)
Italy	110	(62, 29)			
Iberia	99	(15, 4)	Type of canonization		
Eastern Europe	106	(5, 1)	Papal	245	(47, 9)
Other	186	(4, 2)	Local	66	(15, 3)
			Congregation of Rites	136	(23, 14)
Gender			Beatified only	71	(42, 22)
Female	208	(55)	Popular or other	72	(24, 7)
Male	77	(96)			
			Time between death and canonization		
Membership in an order			Never canonized	67	(67, 30)
Benedictine	94	(22, 6)	Within 25 years	221	(19, 4)
Heavily cloistered	98	(9, 5)	Within 75 years	226	(16, 3)
Cistercian	66	(6, 1)	Within 175 years	139	(13, 3)
Augustinian canons	87	(7, 1)	More than 175 years	140	(36, 15)
Dominican	180	(22, 12)			
Franciscan	116	(21, 11)	Quality of reputation and popularity		
Jesuit	27	(2, 0)	Reputation largely		
Others	112	(30, 8)	by association with a major		
Not in an order	89	(32, 11)	saint	91	(29, 11)
			Reputation dependent upon		
Status of parental family			promotion by influential		
Royalty	161	(12, 7)	groups	65	(18, 7)
Titled nobles	131	(26, 13)	Martyrdom the primary		
Untitled nobles	128	(35, 6)	reason for reputation	34	(11, 0)
"Good family"	90	(14, 4)	Wide popularity during		
Urban patrician	95	(20, 7)	lifetime	283	(41, 12)
Other burghers	138	(5, 3)	Perceived by some		
Urban poor	159	(7, 2)	contemporaries as bizarre		
Peasantry	159	(13, 5)	or deviant	279	(16, 11)
Probably well-off	21	(4, 2)			
Probably urban	105	(9, 4)	Extent of cult		
Probably poor	42	(5, 2)	National and		
Unknown	21	(1, 0)	international	179	(46, 15)
			Patrons of cities,		
			protectors for specific		

conditions and classes	139	(36, 16)
Mostly in an order	88	(44, 16)
Local	51	(25, 8)

Nature of sources

Contemporary biography	157	(73, 28)
Contemporary notices	84	(27,10)
Other contemporary documents	52	(18, 9)
Later Information	108	(29, 8)
Weak, forged, or legendary	35	(4, 0)

Family dynamics and saint's quest for perfection

Only child	227	(23, 4)
Siblings noted	163	(74, 36)
No mention of siblings	57	(54, 15)
Never married	98	(127, 37)
Married	110	(24, 18)
Split family	331	(16, 10)
Bitter opposition	187	(22, 14)
Moderate opposition	124	(17, 9)
Neutral family	27	(20, 3)
Moderately supportive	149	(42, 12)
Heavily supportive	180	(34, 7)
Saint's influence on family		
extensive	191	(25, 13)
moderate	226	(28, 9)
none	78	(98, 26)

Split families

Father's influence		
major	331	(6, 2)
minor	471	(10, 8)
none	0	(0)
Mother's influence		
major	343	(12, 6)
minor	371	(4, 4)
none	0	(0)

Opposed families

Father's influence		
major	213	(17, 10)
minor	155	(14, 10)
none	102	(8, 3)
Mother's influence		
major	280	(19, 9)
minor	160	(14, 10)
none	61	(6, 4)

Supportive families

Father's influence		
major	207	(38, 8)
minor	97	(27, 9)
none	42	(31, 5)
Mother's influence		
major	230	(51, 11)
minor	73	(19, 7)
none	36	(26, 4)

Other family influences

Sibling's influence in		
split family	433	(4, 4)
opposed family	160	(6, 3)
supportive family	70	(5, 2)
Spouse's influence		
very supportive	162	(8, 7)
very opposed	146	(4, 4)
slight or none	70	(10, 6)
Other relatives very influential	157	(10, 2)

Other influences upon saint's quest for perfection

Friends very supportive	86	(6, 2)
Friends supportive	129	(4, 1)
Friends negative	98	(3, 1)
Direct influence of another saint	93	(28, 9)
Indirect influence of another saint	173	(37, 14)
Influenced by visions	181	(32, 20)
Suffered a major crisis	46	(5, 2)
Crisis a factor	195	(31, 16)
Pilgrimage a factor	75	(7, 0)
Wide travel	95	(34, 9)
Response to preaching, reading, etc.	145	(18, 13)
Early religious education	171	(57, 16)
Advanced religious education	54	(14, 1)
Escaping a worldly problem	92	(10, 4)

Major components of saint's reputation

Supernatural power

Mystic contemplation	200	(66, 39)
Visionary experiences	256	(54, 32)
Struggles with demons	215	(26, 14)
Famous prophecies	244	(35, 19)
Miracle-working	195	(35, 13)
Supernatural signs	269	(37, 26)
Intercessions	138	(111, 42)
Wonder-working relics	119	(19, 8)

Charitable activity

Comforting the sick	170	(32, 13)
Aiding the poor	174	(22, 7)
Aiding widows, children, prisoners, prostitutes, etc.	117	(36, 12)

Asceticism

Struggle to preserve chastity	225	(38, 15)
Extended periods of reclusion	103	(15, 6)
Flagellation	225	(37, 18)
Extreme austerities	183	(59, 26)
Fortitude in illness	220	(18, 17)
Extreme humility	167	(23, 9)
Extreme poverty	111	(15, 7)
Killed performing duties or by austerities	170	(29, 16)

Temporal power

Model ruler	119	(16, 5)
Peacemaker	169	(23, 3)
Temporal reformer	145	(18, 4)
Active in affairs of state	158	(26, 9)
Active in church affairs	152	(33, 4)

Evangelical activity

Moral teacher	132	(18, 9)
Spiritual confessor	135	(17, 10)
Extended pilgrimages	121	(15, 5)
Great preacher	112	(19, 1)
Dedicated to apostolate	61	(24, 5)
Church reformer	120	(35, 6)
Founder of an order	161	(16, 5)
Important religious writings	142	(20, 8)
Supported monasticism	84	(14, 1)
Supported scholarship	118	(21, 5)
Supported worship of Jesus	193	(84, 47)
Supported veneration of Mary	153	(46, 22)
Supported veneration of saints	110	(24, 10)
Supported other practices of worship and prayer	153	(37, 9)

Multivariate Analysis: Type of Canonization, Quality of Reputation and Popularity, Extent of Cult[b]

		Supernatural Power	Charitable Activity	Asceticism	Temporal Power	Evangelical Activity
Grand mean[c]		50.91 ($r = .44$)	45.39 ($r = .42$)	40.78 ($r = .44$)	28.01 ($r = .43$)	33.18 ($r = .40$)
Type of canonization						
N = 47	Papal	+ 9% (+ 1%)[d]	+ 6 (− 7)	+ 3 (− 4)	+40 (+24)	+11 (+ 5)
N = 15	Local	−14 (− 7)	+12 (+21)	−16 (−11)	+ 9 (+18)	− 8 (− 1)
N = 23	Congregation of Rites	+20 (+22)	+16 (+18)	+31 (+29)	−37 (−35)	+27 (+23)
N = 42	Beatified	− 8 (− 6)	− 5 (+ 2)	− 3 (+ 1)	−25 (−16)	−12 (− 9)
N = 24	Popular	−14 (− 9)	−26 (−20)	−20 (−15)	− 5 (+ 3)	−21 (−16)
Reputation						
N = 54	Not exceptional	0 (+ 6)	−10 (− 5)	− 4 (0)	−21 (−16)	−15 (−11)
N = 15	By association	− 7 (− 7)	0 (0)	+ 4 (+ 1)	−12 (− 1)	+24 (+21)
N = 9	Through promotion	−22 (−31)	-21 (−27)	+12 (+ 3)	−48 (−40)	+15 (+ 2)
N = 6	Martyrdom	−56 (−42)	−50 (−37)	−66 (−55)	−100 (−92)	−39 (−29)
N = 67	Wide popularity	+ 9 (+ 5)	+15 (+11)	+ 6 (+ 4)	+35 (+26)	+ 9 (+ 6)
Cult						
N = 46	National and international	+16 (+10)	+21 (+17)	+13 (+ 9)	+29 (+ 8)	+15 (+ 6)
N = 36	Patrons	+ 2 (+ 2)	+ 5 (+ 4)	+ 3 (+ 2)	− 3 (− 2)	−14 (−13)
N = 44	In an order	0 (+ 3)	−12 (− 9)	− 6 (− 5)	−18 (− 4)	+ 6 (+ 9)
N = 25	Local	−31 (−27)	−25 (−21)	−17 (−10)	−19 (− 4)	−18 (− 8)

*For notes, see opening of this appendix.

Table 2

Adolescents

(N = 415)

Century of death			Occupational category		
Eleventh	94	(58, 4)	High prelate	81	(23, 0)
Twelfth	108	(80, 12)	Bishop	111	(45, 0)
Thirteenth	93	(71, 16)	Abbot, abbess	111	(85, 10)
Fourteenth	93	(48, 10)	Canon, friar, monk, nun	117	(73, 15)
Fifteenth	113	(45, 7)	Priest	147	(71, 0)
Sixteenth	109	(61, 6)	Tertiary	60	(14, 4)
Seventeenth	91	(52, 3)	Royalty/nobility	62	(18, 11)
			Professional	67	(20, 0)
Geographic area of birth			Military	71	(7, 0)
Low Countries	108	(17, 6)	Urban worker	45	(4, 0)
Scandinavia	56	(4, 0)	Peasant	142	(11, 2)
British Isles	122	(87, 4)	Housewife	40	(5, 5)
France	94	(57, 10)	Youth	113	(21, 9)
Germany	90	(41, 9)	Marginal person	96	(18, 2)
Italy	99	(153, 20)			
Iberia	96	(40, 8)	Type of canonization		
Eastern Europe	94	(12, 1)	Papal	87	(46, 1)
Other	64	(4, 0)	Local	106	(66, 8)
			Congregation of Rites	79	(37, 4)
Gender			Beatified only	116	(188, 26)
Female	80	(58)	Popular or other	85	(78, 19)
Male	104	(357)			
			Time between death and canonization		
Membership in an order			Never canonized	105	(290, 51)
Benedictine	87	(56, 4)	Within 25 years	89	(21, 0)
Heavily cloistered	103	(26, 4)	Within 75 years	91	(18, 0)
Cistercian	107	(27, 7)	Within 175 years	89	(23, 2)
Augustinian canons	116	(27, 2)	More than 175 years	89	(63, 5)
Dominican	107	(36, 3)			
Franciscan	97	(48, 6)	Quality of reputation and popularity		
Jesuit	122	(25, 0)	Reputation largely		
Others	90	(66, 12)	by association with a major		
Not in an order	105	(104, 20)	saint	83	(73, 13)
			Reputation dependent upon		
Status of parental family			promotion by influential		
Royalty	84	(17, 8)	groups	124	(95, 6)
Titled nobles	90	(49, 8)	Martyrdom the primary		
Untitled nobles	101	(76, 10)	reason for reputation	113	(100, 5)
"Good family"	101	(43, 4)	Wide popularity during		
Urban patrician	91	(53, 5)	lifetime	68	(27, 3)
Other burghers	92	(9, 4)	Perceived by some		
Urban poor	76	(9, 1)	contemporaries as bizarre		
Peasantry	98	(22, 7)	or deviant	57	(9, 4)
Probably well-off	120	(61, 3)			
Probably urban	105	(25, 2)	Extent of cult		
Probably poor	105	(34, 6)	National and		
Unknown	121	(17, 0)	international	78	(55, 8)
			Patrons of cities, protectors		

for specific conditions and classes	103	(73, 11)
Mostly in an order	102	(141, 19)
Local	108	(146, 20)

Nature of sources

Contemporary biography	93	(118, 19)
Contemporary notices	100	(88, 10)
Other contemporary documents	103	(97, 6)
Later information	100	(74, 16)
Weak, forged, or legendary	124	(38, 7)

Family dynamics and saint's quest for perfection

Only child	94	(26, 4)
Siblings noted	88	(110, 25)
No mention of siblings	106	(279, 29)
Never married	109	(388, 46)
Married	45	(27, 12)
Split family	84	(11, 4)
Bitter opposition	90	(29, 11)
Moderate opposition	103	(39, 13)
Neutral family	102	(207, 18)
Moderately supportive	108	(86, 8)
Heavily supportive	83	(43, 4)
Saint's influence on family		
extensive	69	(25, 10)
moderate	73	(25, 8)
none	106	(365, 40)

Split families

Father's influence		
major	200	(4, 1)
minor	40	(2, 0)
none	80	(5, 3)
Mother's influence		
major	100	(8, 3)
minor	71	(2, 0)
none	83	(1, 1)

Opposed families

Father's influence		
major	104	(23, 7)
minor	86	(23, 7)
none	102	(22, 10)
Mother's influence		
major	76	(14, 7)
minor	83	(20, 6)
none	124	(34, 11)

Supportive families

Father's influence		
major	95	(48, 2)
minor	103	(79, 6)
none	102	(209, 22)
Mother's influence		
major	82	(50, 3)
minor	103	(74, 5)
none	107	(212, 22)

Other family influences

Sibling's influence in		
split family	33	(1, 1)
opposed family	104	(11, 3)
supportive family	102	(20, 6)
Spouse's influence		
very supportive	32	(4, 1)
very opposed	12	(1, 1)
slight or none	64	(24, 8)
Other relatives very influential	98	(17, 6)

Other influences upon saint's quest for perfection

Friends very supportive	114	(25, 2)
Friends supportive	130	(12, 3)
Friends negative	41	(4, 0)
Direct influence of another saint	100	(82, 9)
Indirect influence of another saint	90	(53, 5)
Influenced by visions	76	(37, 9)
Suffered a major crisis	44	(13, 2)
Crisis a factor	69	(30, 11)
Pilgrimage a factor	123	(31, 4)
Wide travel	87	(86, 3)
Response to preaching, reading, etc.	82	(28, 1)
Early religious education	114	(105, 4)
Advanced religious education	108	(77, 1)
Escaping a worldly problem	43	(13, 3)

Major components of saint's reputation
Supernatural power

Mystic contemplation	81	(73, 20)
Visionary experiences	67	(39, 11)
Struggles with demons	84	(28, 9)
Famous prophecies	74	(29, 8)
Miracle-working	91	(45, 7)
Supernatural signs	58	(22, 11)
Intercessions	101	(224, 28)
Wonder-working relics	102	(45, 10)

Charitable activity

Comforting the sick	79	(41, 7)
Aiding the poor	89	(31, 3)
Aiding widows, children, prisoners, prostitutes, etc.	93	(79, 14)

Asceticism

Struggle to preserve chastity	99	(46, 13)
Extended periods of reclusion	110	(44, 11)
Flagellation	88	(40, 5)
Extreme austerities	88	(78, 21)
Fortitude in illness	80	(18, 7)
Extreme humility	93	(35, 5)
Extreme poverty	100	(37, 6)
Killed performing duties or by austerities	92	(43, 6)

Temporal power

Model ruler	87	(32, 1)
Peacemaker	96	(36, 0)
Temporal reformer	91	(31, 2)
Active in affairs of state	77	(35, 3)
Active in church affairs	74	(44, 1)

Evangelical activity

Moral teacher	110	(41, 9)
Spiritual confessor	89	(31, 3)
Extended pilgrimages	109	(37, 3)
Great preacher	100	(47, 0)
Dedicated to apostolate	107	(115, 1)
Church reformer	94	(75, 10)
Founder of an order	58	(16, 3)
Important religious writings	111	(43, 4)
Supported monastacism	108	(50, 3)
Supported scholarship	92	(45, 5)
Supported worship of Jesus	72	(86, 23)
Supported veneration of Mary	83	(69, 15)
Supported veneration of saints	95	(57, 7)
Supported other practices of worship and prayer	86	(57, 7)

Multivariate Analysis: Type of Canonization, Quality of Reputation and Popularity, Extent of Cult

	Supernatural Power	Charitable Activity	Asceticism	Temporal Power	Evangelical Activity
Grand mean	29.28	32.67	26.24	19.47	27.52
	(r = .55)	(r = .44)	(r = .50)	(r = .52)	(r = .48)
Type of canonization					
N = 46 Papal	+59 (+43)	+11 (+ 1)	+30 (+21)	+114 (+86)	+34 (+28)
N = 66 Local	+ 6 (− 5)	+14 (+ 4)	− 3 (−11)	+12 (+10)	− 7 (− 4)
N = 37 Congregation of Rites	+46 (+43)	+60 (+61)	+41 (+38)	+17 (−16)	+51 (+34)
N = 188 Beatified	−21 (− 8)	−10 (− 1)	−16 (− 5)	−35 (−18)	− 7 (− 3)
N = 78 Popular	−12 (−22)	−22 (−30)	+ 3 (−10)	− 3 (− 9)	−20 (−23)
Reputation					
N = 143 Not exceptional	+14 (+19)	+11 (+17)	+13 (+17)	− 4 (− 5)	−12 (− 7)
N = 53 By association	− 8 (−14)	0 (− 9)	+12 (+ 4)	+20 (+24)	+30 (+22)
N = 33 Through promotion	+ 6 (+ 3)	− 3 (− 7)	+20 (+16)	+ 3 (0)	− 3 (− 8)
N = 88 Martyrdom	−67 (−57)	−43 (−42)	−61 (−57)	−81 (−60)	−25 (−19)
N = 98 Wide popularity	+40 (+29)	+23 (+20)	+22 (+19)	+66 (+47)	+25 (+19)
Cult					
N = 55 National and international	+15 (− 5)	+ 8 (− 5)	0 (−14)	+68 (+45)	+18 (+ 5)
N = 73 Patrons	+35 (+18)	+30 (+15)	+13 (+ 1)	+10 (− 5)	− 3 (−10)
N = 141 In an order	+ 6 (+ 5)	+ 1 (− 1)	+13 (+ 9)	+13 (+13)	+20 (+20)
N = 146 Local	−29 (−12)	−19 (− 4)	−20 (− 4)	−43 (−27)	−25 (−16)

Table 3

Chastity Assaulted

(N = 97)

Century of death			Occupational category		
Eleventh	126	(18, 3)	High prelate	46	(3, 0)
Twelfth	64	(11, 1)	Bishop	106	(10, 0)
Thirteenth	129	(23, 8)	Abbot, abbess	72	(13, 1)
Fourteenth	108	(13, 4)	Canon, friar, monk, nun	96	(14, 7)
Fifteenth	97	(9, 5)	Priest	62	(7, 0)
Sixteenth	84	(11, 4)	Tertiary	144	(8, 6)
Seventeenth	91	(12, 5)	Royalty/nobility	194	(13, 8)
			Professional	86	(6, 0)
Geographic area of birth			Military	129	(3, 0)
Low Countries	137	(5, 2)	Urban worker	94	(2, 0)
Scandinavia	131	(2, 1)	Peasant	109	(2, 0)
British Isles	54	(9, 1)	Housewife	103	(3, 3)
France	149	(21, 7)	Youth	182	(8, 5)
Germany	65	(7, 4)	Marginal person	116	(5, 0)
Italy	102	(37, 13)			
Iberia	113	(11, 1)	*Type of canonization*		
Eastern Europe	132	(4, 0)	Papal	243	(30, 4)
Other	71	(1, 1)	Local	62	(9, 1)
			Congregation of Rites	147	(16, 5)
Gender			Beatified only	69	(26, 15)
Female	177	(30)	Popular or other	74	(16, 5)
Male	84	(67)			
			Time between death and canonization		
Membership in an order			Never canonized	62	(40, 20)
Benedictine	72	(11, 2)	Within 25 years	235	(13, 1)
Heavily cloistered	85	(5, 1)	Within 75 years	285	(13, 2)
Cistercian	34	(2, 1)	Within 175 years	182	(11, 1)
Augustinian canons	146	(8, 0)	More than 175 years	121	(20, 6)
Dominican	115	(9, 5)			
Franciscan	120	(14, 5)	*Quality of reputation and popularity*		
Jesuit	20	(1, 0)	Reputation largely		
Others	105	(18, 7)	by association with a major		
Not in an order	126	(29, 9)	saint	88	(18, 7)
			Reputation dependent upon		
Status of parental family			promotion by influential		
Royalty	190	(9, 5)	groups	90	(16, 6)
Titled nobles	157	(20, 7)	Martyrdom the primary		
Untitled nobles	91	(16, 3)	reason for reputation	24	(5, 0)
"Good family"	70	(7, 2)	Wide popularity during		
Urban patrician	148	(20, 7)	lifetime	204	(19, 4)
Other burghers	258	(6, 3)	Perceived by some		
Urban poor	107	(3, 1)	contemporaries as bizarre		
Peasantry	133	(7, 0)	or deviant	297	(11, 6)
Probably well-off	33	(4, 0)			
Probably urban	18	(1, 1)	*Extent of cult*		
Probably poor	40	(3, 1)	National and		
Unknown	29	(1, 0)	international	152	(25, 8)
			Patrons of cities,		
			protectors for specific		

conditions and classes	157	(26, 8)
Mostly in an order	65	(21, 7)
Local	79	(25, 7)

Nature of sources

Contemporary biography	168	(50, 18)
Contemporary notices	68	(14, 6)
Other contemporary documents	36	(8, 1)
Later information	139	(24, 5)
Weak, forged, or legendary	14	(1, 0)

Family dynamics and saint's quest for perfection

Only child	246	(16, 4)
Siblings notes	175	(51, 20)
No mention of siblings	49	(30, 6)
Never married	98	(81, 21)
Married	120	(16, 9)
Split family	256	(8, 5)
Bitter opposition	304	(23, 13)
Moderate opposition	192	(17, 7)
Neutral family	34	(16, 1)
Moderately supportive	77	(14, 1)
Heavily supportive	157	(19, 3)
Saint's influence on family		
extensive	248	(21, 10)
moderate	214	(17, 9)
none	73	(59, 11)

Split families

Father's influence		
major	159	(2, 0)
minor	221	(3, 3)
none	517	(3, 2)
Mother's influence		
major	269	(6, 4)
minor	300	(2, 1)
none	0	(0)

Opposed families

Father's influence		
major	319	(17, 7)
minor	209	(13, 6)
none	198	(10, 7)
Mother's influence		
major	367	(16, 9)
minor	231	(13, 6)
none	171	(11, 5)

Supportive families

Father's influence		
major	194	(23, 4)
minor	61	(11, 0)
none	32	(15, 1)
Mother's influence		
major	182	(26, 4)
minor	66	(11, 0)
none	26	(12, 1)

Other family influences

Sibling's influence in		
split family	344	(2, 2)
opposed family	289	(7, 5)
supportive family	66	(3, 0)
Spouse's influence		
very supportive	127	(4, 1)
very opposed	57	(1, 1)
slight or none	99	(9, 6)
Other relatives very influential	124	(5, 2)

Other influences upon saint's quest for perfection

Friends very supportive	79	(4, 1)
Friends supportive	186	(4, 2)
Friends negative	178	(4, 1)
Direct influence of another saint	115	(22, 6)
Indirect influence of another saint	101	(14, 3)
Influenced by visions	174	(15, 5)
Suffered a major crisis	115	(8, 1)
Crisis a factor	226	(23, 9)
Pilgrimage a factor	169	(10, 0)
Wide travel	130	(30, 4)
Response to preaching, reading, etc.	151	(12, 2)
Early religious education	159	(34, 7)
Advanced religious education	78	(13, 1)
Escaping a worldly problem	172	(12, 1)

Major components of saint's reputation

Supernatural power

Mystic contemplation	170	(36, 20)
Visionary experiences	176	(24, 11)
Struggles with demons	141	(11, 6)
Famous prophecies	131	(12, 7)
Miracle-working	173	(20, 5)
Supernatural signs	260	(23, 13)
Intercessions	138	(71, 22)
Wonder-working relics	175	(18, 7)

Charitable activity

Comforting the sick	149	(18, 9)
Aiding the poor	123	(10, 3)
Aiding widows, children, prisoners, prostitutes, etc.	106	(21, 7)

Asceticism

Struggle to preserve chastity	—	—
Extended periods of reclusion	118	(11, 4)
Flagellation	170	(18, 8)
Extreme austerities	154	(32, 10)
Fortitude in illness	267	(14, 9)
Extreme humility	192	(17, 6)
Extreme poverty	151	(13, 7)
Killed performing duties or by austerities	165	(18, 7)

Temporal power

Model ruler	104	(9, 2)
Peacemaker	149	(13, 2)
Temporal reformer	138	(11, 2)
Active in affairs of state	151	(16, 4)
Active in church affairs	115	(16, 1)

Evangelical activity

Moral teacher	114	(10, 5)
Spiritual confessor	148	(12, 3)
Extended pilgrimages	100	(8, 3)
Great preacher	146	(16, 0)
Dedicated to apostolate	60	(15, 1)
Church reformer	144	(27, 3)
Founder of an order	141	(9, 3)
Important religious writings	188	(17, 3)
Supported monasticism	121	(13, 0)
Supported scholarship	122	(14, 3)
Supported worship of Jesus	179	(50, 25)
Supported veneration of Mary	134	(26, 9)
Supported veneration of saints	93	(13, 2)
Supported other practices of worship and prayer	129	(20, 5)

Multivariate Analysis: Type of Canonization, Quality of Reputation and Popularity, Extent of Cult

		Supernatural Power	Charitable Activity	Asceticism	Temporal Power	Evangelical Activity
Grand mean		50.77 ($r = .38$)	45.03 ($r = .47$)	40.09 ($r = .42$)	26.60 ($r = .50$)	34.68 ($r = .61$)
Type of canonization						
N = 30	Papal	+11 (+ 9)	− 3 (− 6)	− 7 (− 8)	+59 (+51)	+ 5 (− 1)
N = 9	Local	−24 (−22)	−21 (−14)	−25 (−24)	−35 (−28)	−12 (− 8)
N = 16	Congregation of Rites	+13 (+ 9)	+34 (+25)	+24 (+30)	−10 (−14)	+59 (+60)
N = 26	Beatified	− 5 (− 2)	+ 6 (+11)	0 (+ 1)	−29 (−23)	−34 (−31)
N = 16	Popular	−12 (− 9)	−27 (−24)	+ 3 (− 3)	−32 (−29)	− 7 (− 4)
Reputation						
N = 34	Not exceptional	− 3 (+ 5)	− 7 (+ 3)	0 (+ 2)	−23 (−18)	−23 (−14)
N = 11	By association	− 2 (−10)	+26 (+ 8)	− 5 (−21)	0 (+17)	+27 (+ 9)
N = 9	Through promotion	− 3 (+ 1)	+ 5 (− 2)	+ 3 (+ 2)	−11 (− 4)	+ 5 (−19)
N = 4	Martyrdom	−22 (−14)	−58 (−50)	−61 (−46)	−50 (−71)	−10 (− 7)
N = 39	Wide popularity	+ 6 (0)	+ 4 (0)	+ 7 (+ 9)	+28 (+18)	+13 (+15)
Cult						
N = 25	National and international	+16 (+12)	+15 (+18)	+ 1 (− 1)	+40 (+17)	+15 (+ 2)
N = 26	Patrons	+12 (+12)	+15 (+ 5)	+10 (+ 3)	−22 (−24)	0 (−13)
N = 21	In an order	−12 (−12)	−13 (−10)	−17 (−13)	− 4 (+ 5)	+ 4 (+13)
N = 25	Local	−18 (−15)	−20 (−14)	+ 3 (+ 9)	−14 (+ 5)	−19 (0)

Table 4
Converted to Chastity
(*N* = 104)

Century of death

Eleventh	65	(10, 2)
Twelfth	92	(17, 3)
Thirteenth	120	(23, 8)
Fourteenth	116	(15, 6)
Fifteenth	100	(10, 4)
Sixteenth	93	(13, 5)
Seventeenth	112	(16, 6)

Geographic area of birth

Low Countries	100	(4, 0)
Scandinavia	63	(1, 0)
British Isles	73	(13, 3)
France	86	(13, 7)
Germany	96	(11, 4)
Italy	126	(49, 17)
Iberia	106	(11, 3)
Eastern Europe	61	(2, 0)
Other	0	(0)

Gender

Female	187	(34)
Male	82	(70)

Membership in an order

Benedictine	104	(17, 4)
Heavily cloistered	157	(10, 5)
Cistercian	143	(9, 3)
Augustinian canons	18	(1, 0)
Dominican	23	(2, 1)
Franciscan	120	(15, 6)
Jesuit	98	(5, 0)
Others	120	(22, 8)
Not in an order	93	(23, 7)

Status of parental family

Royalty	178	(9, 5)
Titled nobles	169	(23, 11)
Untitled nobles	80	(15, 5)
"Good family"	65	(7, 2)
Urban patrician	97	(14, 5)
Other burghers	242	(6, 0)
Urban poor	166	(5, 0)
Peasantry	124	(7, 3)
Probably well-off	47	(6, 1)
Probably urban	102	(6, 1)
Probably poor	62	(5, 1)
Unknown	29	(1, 0)

Occupational category

High prelate	71	(5, 0)
Bishop	20	(2, 0)
Abbot, abbess	36	(7, 2)
Canon, friar, monk, nun	45	(7, 2)
Priest	33	(4, 0)
Tertiary	67	(4, 3)
Royalty/nobility	223	(16, 8)
Professional	133	(10, 0)
Military	363	(9, 0)
Urban worker	262	(6, 0)
Peasant	53	(1, 0)
Housewife	577	(18, 18)
Youth	42	(2, 1)
Marginal person	278	(13, 0)

Type of canonization

Papal	76	(10, 2)
Local	123	(19, 5)
Congregation of Rites	171	(20, 8)
Beatified only	81	(33, 11)
Popular or other	95	(22, 8)

Time between death and canonization

Never canonized	94	(65, 20)
Within 25 years	84	(5, 2)
Within 75 years	123	(6, 0)
Within 175 years	77	(5, 2)
More than 175 years	130	(23, 10)

Quality of reputation and popularity

Reputation largely by association with a major saint	118	(26, 8)
Reputation dependent upon promotion by influential groups	89	(17, 7)
Martyrdom the primary reason for reputation	63	(14, 1)
Wide popularity during lifetime	110	(11, 3)
Perceived by some contemporaries as bizarre or deviant	203	(8, 3)

Extent of cult

National and international	113	(20, 7)
Patrons of cities, protectors		

for specific conditions and		
classes	90	(16, 2)
Mostly in an order	113	(39, 16)
Local	86	(29, 9)

Nature of sources

Contemporary biography	119	(38, 13)
Contemporary notices	77	(17, 8)
Other contemporary		
documents	84	(20, 4)
Later information	124	(23, 8)
Weak, forged, or		
legendary	78	(6, 1)

Family dynamics and
saint's quest for perfection

Only child	87	(6, 2)
Siblings noted	125	(39, 17)
No mention of siblings	90	(59, 15)
Never married	52	(46, 1)
Married	387	(58, 33)
Split family	181	(6, 5)
Bitter opposition	99	(8, 6)
Moderate opposition	148	(14, 3)
Neutral family	103	(52, 11)
Moderately supportive	67	(13, 4)
Heavily supportive	85	(11, 5)
Saint's influence on family		
extensive	232	(21, 15)
moderate	106	(9, 5)
none	86	(74, 14)

Split families

Father's influence		
major	222	(3, 2)
minor	207	(3, 3)
none	0	(0)
Mother's influence		
major	125	(3, 2)
minor	271	(2, 2)
none	500	(1, 1)

Opposed families

Father's influence		
major	109	(6, 4)
minor	120	(8, 3)
none	148	(8, 2)
Mother's influence		
major	129	(6, 3)
minor	100	(6, 3)
none	145	(10, 3)

Supportive families

Father's influence		
major	63	(8, 2)

minor	115	(22, 6)
none	90	(45, 12)
Mother's influence		
major	52	(8, 1)
minor	134	(24, 9)
none	88	(44, 10)

Other family influences

Sibling's influence in		
split family	160	(1, 1)
opposed family	77	(2, 1)
supportive family	102	(5, 3)
Spouse's influence		
very supportive	137	(16, 12)
very opposed	154	(10, 8)
slight or none	77	(26, 12)
Other relatives very		
influential	90	(4, 3)

Other influences upon
saint's quest for perfection

Friends very supportive	56	(3, 0)
Friends supportive	132	(3, 0)
Friends negative	209	(5, 1)
Direct influence of another		
saint	107	(22, 6)
Indirect influence of another		
saint	129	(19, 9)
Influenced by visions	238	(22, 8)
Suffered a major crisis	299	(22, 4)
Crisis a factor	248	(27, 13)
Pilgrimage a factor	110	(7, 0)
Wide travel	125	(31, 7)
Response to preaching,		
reading, etc.	211	(18, 4)
Early religious education	35	(8, 3)
Advanced religious education	51	(9, 0)
Escaping a worldly problem	294	(22, 5)

Major components of saint's reputation

Supernatural power

Mystic contemplation	137	(31, 18)
Visionary experiences	124	(18, 10)
Struggles with demons	156	(13, 3)
Famous prophecies	121	(12, 4)
Miracle-working	129	(16, 8)
Supernatural signs	126	(12, 4)
Intercessions	103	(57, 21)
Wonder-working relics	100	(11, 3)

Charitable activity

Comforting the sick	170	(22, 9)
Aiding the poor	171	(15, 8)
Aiding widows, children,		
prisoners, prostitutes, etc.	118	(25, 7)

Asceticism

Struggle to preserve chastity	—	—
Extended periods of reclusion	170	(17, 2)
Flagellation	141	(16, 8)
Extreme austerities	153	(34, 12)
Fortitude in illness	89	(5, 1)
Extreme humility	169	(16, 8)
Extreme poverty	152	(14, 5)
Killed performing duties or by austerities	111	(13, 2)

Temporal power

Model ruler	55	(5, 2)
Peacemaker	97	(9, 2)
Temporal reformer	71	(6, 1)
Active in affairs of state	106	(12, 3)
Active in church affairs	47	(7, 0)

Evangelical activity

Moral teacher	86	(8, 1)
Spiritual confessor	149	(13, 6)
Extended pilgrimages	106	(9, 0)
Great preacher	51	(6, 0)
Dedicated to apostolate	63	(17, 0)
Church reformer	95	(19, 4)
Founder of an order	205	(14, 5)
Important religious writings	94	(9, 3)
Supported monasticism	95	(11, 3)
Supported scholarship	65	(8, 1)
Supported worship of Jesus	130	(39, 17)
Supported veneration of Mary	135	(28, 9)
Supported veneration of saints	113	(17, 8)
Supported other practices of worship and prayer	114	(19, 5)

Multivariate Analysis: Type of Canonization, Quality of Reputation and Popularity, Extent of Cult

		Supernatural Power	Charitable Activity	Asceticism	Temporal Power	Evangelical Activity
Grand mean		39.53 ($r = .58$)	39.91 ($r = .60$)	35.58 ($r = .55$)	16.63 ($r = .56$)	26.56 ($r = .61$)
Type of canonization						
$N = 10$	Papal	+41 (+28)	+31 (+37)	+44 (+47)	+147 (+97)	+37 (+20)
$N = 19$	Local	−30 (−22)	−39 (−30)	−33 (−25)	+24 (+35)	−25 (−14)
$N = 20$	Congregation of Rites	+33 (+16)	+47 (+41)	+24 (+16)	+13 (+ 1)	+57 (+48)
$N = 33$	Beatified	0 (+12)	+10 (+18)	− 2 (+ 2)	−32 (−21)	−16 (−13)
$N = 22$	Popular	−23 (−26)	−39 (−55)	−10 (−17)	−51 (−44)	−23 (−21)
Reputation						
$N = 43$	Not exceptional	− 5 (+ 5)	0 (+13)	− 1 (+ 6)	− 3 (+ 8)	−13 (− 5)
$N = 13$	By association	+ 2 (+11)	+25 (+39)	+13 (+16)	−30 (− 5)	+ 8 (+ 6)
$N = 10$	Through promotion	+ 9 (+ 6)	− 7 (−19)	−17 (−26)	−43 (−42)	− 6 (−25)
$N = 11$	Martyrdom	−65 (−66)	−77 (−81)	−50 (−43)	−37 (−31)	−34 (0)
$N = 27$	Wide popularity	+30 (+12)	+23 (+ 1)	+23 (+10)	+50 (+18)	+33 (+15)
Cult						
$N = 20$	National and international	+36 (+21)	+21 (+ 2)	+14 (− 4)	+126 (+92)	+52 (+32)
$N = 16$	Patrons	+16 (+21)	+ 4 (+ 7)	+11 (+14)	−34 (−36)	−13 (−25)
$N = 39$	In an order	− 6 (−11)	+ 4 (− 3)	+ 5 (+ 5)	−30 (−15)	+ 9 (+17)
$N = 29$	Local	−26 (−12)	−22 (− 1)	−22 (−11)	−28 (−23)	−41 (−31)

Table 5
Adults (Martyrs Excluded)
(N = 225)

Century of death			Occupational category		
Eleventh	101	(37, 3)	High prelate	101	(18, 0)
Twelfth	107	(49, 3)	Bishop	85	(22, 0)
Thirteenth	96	(45, 7)	Abbot, Abbess	83	(40, 4)
Fourteenth	96	(30, 5)	Canon, friar, monk, nun	72	(25, 4)
Fifteenth	75	(19, 5)	Priest	73	(6, 0)
Sixteenth	105	(20, 4)	Tertiary	121	(17, 6)
Seventeenth	126	(25, 5)	Royalty/nobility	112	(18, 6)
			Professional	182	(27, 0)
Geographic area of birth			Military	175	(11, 0)
Low Countries	110	(10, 0)	Urban worker	183	(10, 0)
Scandinavia	90	(2, 0)	Peasant	41	(2, 0)
British Isles	113	(18, 3)	Housewife	138	(10, 10)
France	90	(34, 7)	Youth	0	(0)
Germany	95	(26, 4)	Marginal person	88	(19, 2)
Italy	102	(102, 15)			
Iberia	107	(27, 2)	*Type of canonization*		
Eastern Europe	85	(5, 0)	Papal	34	(11, 1)
Other	44	(1, 1)	Local	110	(39, 4)
			Congregation of Rites	115	(32, 6)
Gender			Beatified only	88	(63, 11)
Female	69	(32)	Popular or other	139	(80, 10)
Male	108	(193)			
			Time between death and canonization		
Membership in an Order			Never canonized	113	(161, 22)
Benedictine	130	(51, 5)	Within 25 years	30	(4, 0)
Heavily cloistered	91	(15, 3)	Within 75 years	35	(4, 0)
Cistercian	119	(20, 4)	Within 175 years	91	(15, 2)
Augustinian canons	85	(12, 1)	More than 175 years	99	(41, 8)
Dominican	55	(12, 2)			
Franciscan	97	(28, 7)	*Quality of reputation and popularity*		
Jesuit	129	(6, 0)	Reputation largely by		
Others	112	(52, 7)	association with a major		
Not in an order	78	(29, 3)	saint	128	(69, 8)
			Reputation dependent upon		
Status of parental family			promotion by influential		
Royalty	74	(9, 3)	groups	79	(22, 4)
Titled nobles	94	(31, 9)	Martyrdom the primary		
Untitled nobles	80	(36, 6)	reason for reputation	—	—
"Good family"	92	(13, 3)	Wide popularity during		
Urban patrician	112	(38, 4)	lifetime	58	(15, 1)
Other burghers	104	(6, 0)	Perceived by some		
Urban poor	118	(9, 0)	contemporaries as bizarre		
Peasantry	82	(12, 1)	or deviant	66	(7, 2)
Probably well-off	133	(31, 2)			
Probably urban	89	(13, 2)	*Extent of cult*		
Probably poor	131	(22, 2)	National and		
Unknown	147	(5, 0)	international	90	(36, 6)
			Patrons of cities, protectors		

for specific conditions and		
classes	72	(31, 1)
Mostly in an order	107	(88, 16)
Local	117	(70, 9)

Nature of sources

Contemporary biography	76	(58, 9)
Contemporary notices	111	(56, 8)
Other contemporary		
documents	136	(47, 6)
Later information	100	(46, 6)
Weak, forged, or		
legendary	103	(18, 3)

Family dynamics and
saint's quest for perfection

Only child	41	(7, 1)
Siblings noted	80	(58, 14)
No mention of siblings	118	(160, 17)
Never married	90	(175, 11)
Married	161	(50, 21)
Split family	10	(1, 1)
Bitter opposition	36	(6, 4)
Moderate opposition	72	(15, 0)
Neutral family	142	(151, 17)
Moderately supportive	59	(26, 4)
Heavily supportive	91	(26, 6)
Saint's influence on family		
extensive	96	(23, 10)
moderate	72	(15, 5)
none	104	(187, 17)

Split families

Father's influence		
major	0	(0)
minor	40	(1, 1)
none	0	(0)
Mother's influence		
major	0	(0)
minor	0	(0)
none	400	(1, 1)

Opposed families

Father's influence		
major	30	(4, 1)
minor	63	(8, 2)
none	82	(9, 1)
Mother's influence		
major	51	(6, 1)
minor	57	(7, 2)
none	61	(8, 1)

Supportive families

Father's influence		
major	59	(17, 1)

minor	101	(43, 7)
none	134	(143, 19)
Mother's influence		
major	62	(22, 1)
minor	110	(44, 10)
none	133	(137, 16)

Other family influences

Sibling's influence in		
split family	0	(0)
opposed family	41	(2, 2)
supportive family	111	(12, 4)
Spouse's influence		
very supportive	101	(13, 6)
very opposed	120	(9, 6)
slight or none	95	(29, 8)
Other relatives very		
influential	77	(8, 3)

Other influences upon
saint's quest for perfection

Friends very supportive	69	(5, 0)
Friends supportive	54	(3, 0)
Friends negative	190	(9, 2)
Direct influence of another		
saint	103	(50, 7)
Indirect influence of another		
saint	80	(29, 5)
Influenced by visions	100	(24, 6)
Suffered a major crisis	206	(38, 6)
Crisis a factor	90	(24, 9)
Pilgrimage a factor	80	(12, 0)
Wide travel	120	(63, 4)
Response to preaching,		
reading, etc.	94	(18, 2)
Early religious education	41	(19, 2)
Advanced religious education	110	(43, 0)
Escaping a worldly problem	184	(34, 8)

Major components of saint's reputation

Supernatural power

Mystic contemplation	78	(48, 17)
Visionary experiences	72	(28, 9)
Struggles with demons	68	(15, 2)
Famous prophecies	68	(18, 2)
Miracle-working	68	(23, 3)
Supernatural signs	71	(18, 4)
Intercessions	77	(104, 11)
Wonder-working relics	86	(23, 3)

Charitable activity

Comforting the sick	98	(34, 7)
Aiding the poor	83	(19, 6)
Aiding widows, children,		
prisoners, prostitutes, etc.	103	(50, 5)

Asceticism

Struggle to preserve chastity	43	(13, 2)
Extended periods of reclusion	84	(23, 5)
Flagellation	57	(17, 4)
Extreme austerities	78	(47, 6)
Fortitude in illness	61	(9, 1)
Extreme humility	74	(19, 5)
Extreme poverty	101	(23, 5)
Killed performing duties or		
by austerities	81	(26, 1)

Temporal power

Model ruler	112	(27, 0)
Peacemaker	69	(17, 3)
Temporal reformer	92	(20, 2)
Active in affairs of state	100	(28, 0)
Active in church affairs	112	(43, 1)

Evangelical activity

Moral teacher	66	(16, 2)
Spiritual confessor	95	(20, 3)
Extended pilgrimages	78	(16, 1)
Great preacher	100	(26, 0)
Dedicated to apostolate	110	(38, 1)
Church reformer	100	(51, 2)
Founder of an order	132	(25, 5)
Important religious writings	90	(22, 3)
Supported monasticism	100	(31, 3)
Supported scholarship	108	(34, 2)
Supported worship of Jesus	93	(70, 13)
Supported veneration of Mary	83	(42, 8)
Supported veneration of saints	98	(37, 5)
Supported other practices of worship and prayer	86	(35, 3)

Multivariate Analysis: Type of Canonization, Quality of Reputation and Popularity, Extent of Cult

		Supernatural Power	Charitable Activity	Asceticism	Temporal Power	Evangelical Activity
Grand mean		31.10	35.20	28.72	24.88	28.38
		$(r = .38)$	$(r = .48)$	$(r = .48)$	$(r = .41)$	$(r = .55)$
Type of canonization						
N = 11	Papal	+31 (+18)	+13 (+10)	+40 (+47)	+51 (+17)	+56 (+40)
N = 39	Local	−16 (−17)	−25 (−21)	−31 (−28)	+47 (+51)	−15 (−11)
N = 32	Congregation of Rites	+47 (+40)	+75 (+67)	+52 (+52)	−14 (−47)	+72 (+55)
N = 63	Beatified	+14 (+16)	+18 (+15)	+15 (+13)	−18 (−16)	− 8 (− 9)
N = 80	Popular	−27 (−23)	−34 (−30)	−24 (−24)	−11 (+ 5)	−23 (−15)
Reputation						
N = 104	Not exceptional	− 9 (+ 2)	−16 (− 2)	−12 (− 2)	−19 (−22)	−24 (−12)
N = 48	By association	−10 (− 8)	0 (− 2)	+ 2 (+ 2)	− 3 (+ 2)	+ 7 (+ 7)
N = 17	Through promotion	+19 (+16)	− 8 (−13)	−15 (−25)	+ 7 (+ 9)	+12 (+ 6)
N = 56	Wide popularity	+19 (− 3)	+32 (+10)	+24 (+ 9)	+36 (+36)	+34 (+14)
Cult						
N = 36	National and international	+39 (+28)	+28 (+ 4)	+10 (−12)	+51 (+46)	+47 (+22)
N = 31	Patrons	+ 7 (0)	+16 (+ 5)	+ 2 (− 6)	+13 (+ 5)	+ 6 (− 2)
N = 88	In an order	− 3 (− 5)	+ 9 (+ 7)	+10 (+ 8)	−20 (−13)	+ 1 (+ 2)
N = 70	Local	−19 (− 8)	−32 (−13)	−19 (− 1)	− 7 (−10)	−28 (−13)

2

Perceptions of Sanctity

In part 2 we attempt to use saints' vitae as an index of the changing configurations of piety in Latin Christendom between the eleventh and seventeenth centuries. We try to understand the popular perception of holiness, and we find it was different from the evolving criteria of the official canonization process. Here, even more than in part 1, biographical detail and verification of supernatural phenomena are beside the point. Having presented the textual material of saints' lives in the first part, we now give more attention to questions of typicality and relationships among social factors and modes of religious expression. Here we rely more heavily on statistical methods.

We are examining very broad social and religious trends over wide expanses of time and place and deep divisions of sex and class. Although the individual lives are important and we can hardly think of a group of people more individualistic than saints, there is a collective perception of sainthood that transcends this or that particular case. Here we find Max Weber's concept of the ideal type very convenient. In the chapter "Who Was a Saint?" we present sainthood as an ideal type emerging out of the collective mentality of Latin Christendom. In subsequent chapters we look at how this abstract or ideal type was actually manifested in various areas of Europe, over several centuries, in men and women, and in different social classes. Both parts 1 and 2, different though they are in perspective and to some degree in method, approach religion as a part of social history.

5 ⊕ *Who Was a Saint?*

In the official procedures for canonization established by Pope Urban VIII in the early seventeenth century, all candidates except martyrs must satisfy three general requirements: doctrinal purity, heroic virtue, and miraculous intercession after death. Urban's decrees standardized practices that had developed in numerous locales over many centuries. The first concern, doctrinal purity, reflected the long-standing problem of how to make sure that no heretic or heterodox thinker was admitted into the community of saints, a possibility repugnant in itself as well as in its potential embarrassment to a church claiming the infallible guidance of the Holy Spirit.[1]

The second requirement, heroic virtue, was designed to separate bona fide miracle-workers from practitioners of magic and the black arts. As elaborated by Thomas Aquinas and other thirteenth-century theologians, the virtues were seven: the three theological virtues of faith, hope, and charity and the four cardinal virtues of prudence, temperance, justice, and fortitude.[2] Together they embraced all the requirements of a good Christian life. An agent of Satan might confound the laws of nature and by wizardry lure others into the diabolic path, but someone who practiced the Christian virtues to a heroic degree could not possibly be in the devil's employ—at least so the theologians reasoned.[3]

The third requirement, miraculous intercession, demonstrated that "the servant of God" (the dead saint) now sat in heaven among the community of saints and was able to intercede with Christ to answer the prayers of the faithful on earth. The distinction between miracle-working on earth, which was not an indispensable requirement, and miraculous intercession after death, which was a sine qua non, is important. Saints are not the only

141

mortals who can work miracles, but they are the only ones who are able to intercede on behalf of the faithful after they have departed this life.

While all three requirements had historical roots both in official thought and in popular practice, the extent to which they were applied varied widely. During almost the entire period of our study—that is, from the eleventh century into the seventeenth century—investigations varied greatly in their degree of thoroughness and in the manner in which they were conducted. A truly detailed and precedent-setting examination of heroic virtue first occurred in 1671 in the canonization process for Teresa of Avila.[4] Before that time, although popes and bishops were alert to testimony charging violations of chastity or of faith, they did not systematically insist upon positive evidence of heroic virtue. The investigation of doctrinal purity seems to have begun in the twelfth century with the proliferation of heretical movements; but official doctrine itself lacked the rigorous and authoritative uniformity it later came to have. In numerous cases of local cults ultimately "allowed" by the papacy, it is doubtful whether bishops and other clerics making on-the-spot investigations were sufficiently knowledgeable to recognize doctrinal error.[5]

As for miracles, the zeal and credulity of the faithful usually prevailed.[6] Before the advent of modern medicine any recovery from a serious illness might well have been seen as miraculous. Criteria with a claim to scientific objectivity in evaluating evidence of miraculous cures had to await the modern era, when medical experts proclaimed their scientific explanations of health and disease. On those infrequent occasions when the physicians admit to being baffled by a recovery that defies the known laws of nature, the church may conclude that a miraculous intercession has occurred.

Before the coming of the age of science, however, which coincided—not altogether fortuitously—with the decrees of Urban VIII, the major force in the establishment of saints' cults was veneration by a community of believers, whether that community was the populace of a particular town or nation or the membership of a monastery or order. Even today the initiative for canonization lies with the community, though the cult must be prepared to undergo rigorous screening in Rome. In short, the official criteria do not tell us very much about ideas of sanctity over the centuries or about the origins of a cult.

The lives of saints, with all their limitations and obscurities, suggest that people had their own ways of deciding whom they would venerate. Believers were little concerned with the theological ideas of their heroes, much less with questions of doctrinal purity. What interested the faithful was the holy life and, above everything else in that life, evidence of supernatural power. For example, while in examining a mystic the Congregation of Rites required a detailed analysis of the doctrinal implications of the candidate's mystical experience, most devotees were far more interested in the mystical event itself. Popes and princes were attentive to Catherine of Siena's visions of the church in crisis not because of the purity and accuracy of her doctrine but because they accepted her claim that God himself spoke through her. The same may be said for Francesca de' Ponziani, Bridget of Sweden, the Seven Founders of the Servites, and most of the noted visionaries we have encountered. Even Thomas Aquinas, doctor of the church and arguably its greatest theologian, attracted a cult during his lifetime not only because of his intellectual powers but because so many also bore witness to what they believed to be his supernatural graces. (See figs. 15 and 16.)

If not doctrinal purity, what persuaded believers that the claims of a holy person to supernatural communion were authentic? Here the second official criterion, heroic virtue, is crucial. While the church uses heroic virtue to distinguish saints from wizards and witches, in popular belief saintly virtue was less a legalistic than a charismatic matter. A combination of the force of personality, rigorous self-denial, humility, and good works led people to believe that a saint was in their midst. We are of course unable to account for all the factors that led to cultic veneration in every case, and we would not be so foolish as to try to assign mathematical scores to explain individual cases; subjectivity is at the core of cult formation, and the vagaries of fortune—as the circumstances of the moment—played no small part.[7] As we saw in our analysis of saintly children, no single act established sanctity; behavior initially perceived as bizarre by parents and friends only gradually came to be seen as divinely inspired. Many holy people were plagued throughout life by skeptics and doubters, acclaim coming to them only after death.

Yet a pattern of popular criteria does emerge, criteria that antedated the official definition of heroic virtue and always took precedence in the rise of popular cultic veneration. First among these was evidence of supernatural power. The most obvious and compelling form of such power was the ability to work miracles, to bring about an effect that confounded nature's laws or bent nature to the wonder-worker's command. To us some miracle stories seem comical, such as the tale of the saint who sat down to a chicken dinner and was about to carve a leg when he realized it was Friday. Making the sign of the cross, he restored the bird's feathers, and off it flew. Many other miracles resist a social or utilitarian interpretation. Why, except to persuade onlookers of their powers, did saints command flowers to bloom out of season, walk on water, change water to wine and back again, or, like Cristina of Stommeln, fly up to the church rafters? The majority of miracles and miracle-workers, however, addressed obvious human needs—many were the saints whose prayers sent rain or whose hands healed the

Fig. 15. The Madonna offers her breast to the praying
Bernard of Clairvaux. Faenza, Civic Gallery.
Emilian school, late fifteenth century. Photograph
courtesy of Ministero Beni Culturali e Ambientali: Is-
tituto Centrale per il Catalogo e la Documentazione.
Number F20060.

Fig. 16. (opposite) Spiritual graces in the life of Thomas Aquinas.
Above left: Thomas encounters a demon. *Above right:* As he lies ill,
a star shines through his window, restoring him. *Below:* En route to
the Council of Lyons, Thomas falls ill and craves sardines. Miraculously, a man appears with a load of sardines and offers them to
the saint, who refuses them. Loreto Aprotino, Church of St. Maria
del Piano. Fresco of the Abruzzi school, fourteenth century. Photograph courtesy of Frick Art Reference Library.

sick or lame, even revived the dead. Legion are the saints who protected
crops, rescued condemned men from the gallows, or provided food for the
hungry by multiplying loaves of bread. Such "useful" miracles outnumber
all other sorts of white magic and no doubt are the most important.[8] But
they share certain fundamental qualities with even the most trivial of miracles. Wonder-working in whatever form was power. While the future saint
might humbly deny possessing supernatural power, and the biographer

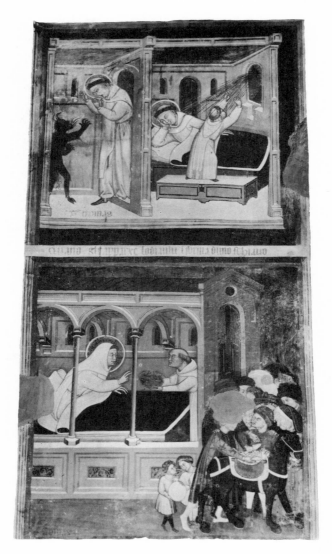

whose zeal did not propel him into doctrinal error would emphasize that God was working through the holy person, the believer saw only the result. A man or a woman not bound by the laws of nature commanded respect. (See figs. 17, 18, and 19.)

Awe of the wonder-worker stemmed from an ambivalent attitude toward nature, one not altogether in harmony with Christian teaching. Nature was the beneficent provider for human needs, but at the same time a capricious

Fig. 17. Dominic de Guzmán restores to life a young nobleman, Napoleone Orsini. Pisa, Church of St. Catherine. Altarpiece by Francesco Traini, 1344–45. Photograph courtesy of Gabinetto Fotografico Soprintendenza ai Beni Artistici e Storici di Firenze.

giant that brought starvation, illness, and death without reason or warning. The Christian view of a harmonious world order in which nature was guided by divine providence blended into a timeless folk belief that nature was not entirely benevolent. The person who could command the heavens to send rain, defy natural death, or make flowers bloom in wintertime took the place of God, as an accessible and tangible source of power. The church's distinction between worship, which belonged to God alone, and veneration, which might be accorded to his saints, meant little to the peasant whose fields gave abundant yield or the journeyman whose blind daughter was made to see by a local holy man.[9]

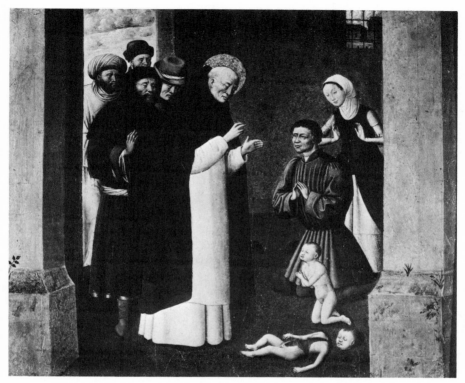

Fig. 18. Vincent Ferrer restores a baby to life. Naples, Church of St. Peter Martyr. Altarpiece by Colantonio. Photograph courtesy of Ministero Beni Culturali e Ambientali: Istituto Centrale per il Catalogo e la Documentazione. Number E56970.

Miracle-working was the most important but not the only form of supernatural power that attracted cultic veneration. Prophecy and clairvoyance, the ability to foretell the future and the ability to know people's thoughts, were also compelling proofs of supernatural power. As with miracle-working, awe of these phenomena sometimes passed the limits of Catholic doctrine. Fortune-tellers, "cunning" men and women, witches, geomancers, and necromancers competed with holy people in serving the universal human eagerness to transcend the bounds of time.[10] Clerical hagiographers were always concerned to link prophecy with religious purposes. The most common hagiographic prophecy attributed to holy people was the prediction of their own death, a foreknowledge that stressed the saint's acceptance of mortality and joyful anticipation of impending reunion with God.

The major prophets were those who played upon lofty apocalyptic and

Fig. 19. Nicholas of Tolentino rescues a ship in distress. Giovanni di Paolo. Photograph courtesy of the John G. Johnson Collection, Philadelphia.

eschatological themes: the Coming of Antichrist, the Flagellation and Reform of the Church, the Second Coming of Christ. But to ordinary folk
these were less interesting subjects than predictions of when a plague
would end, where an army would attack, or whether a woman would
conceive.[11] One of the reasons saints so often were called on as peacemakers
in the civil conflicts of thirteenth- and fourteenth-century Italy was the
belief that they were able to foresee the end of strife and its just solution.[12]
Just as miracle-workers had to establish that they were not witches or
wizards, so prophets and clairvoyants had to maintain their distinction
from soothsayers and fortune-tellers. This was not always easy, either for
them or for their public. When we later examine the interaction of supernatural power with other saintly attributes, we will suggest how people
distinguished divine from diabolic inspiration. For the moment, however,
we wish to look at some other aspects of the perception of supernatural
power.

The ears, the eyes, the nose, the mouth, the hands all gave witness to
supernatural power. Blood was the life force. A few saints received Christ's
stigmata in their foreheads, hands, and feet. Some, as if to convince new
doubting Thomases, bled from their sides, and blood flowed, dried up,
and poured out again from other wounds and orifices.[13] The blood of a
saint has always been among the most precious of relics, but any form of
bodily eruption might qualify as a sign of divine election. The suppurating
sore on Rita di Cascia's forehead disgusted her sister nuns, and Rita worried
that it would also offend the pope when she went to Rome. But the sore
disappeared during her pilgrimage, then came back when she returned to
her convent. This persuaded the sisters that Rita's lesion was a special sign
of divine favor. Giovanni Colombini's chamber pot emitted a fragrant odor
after he died. Attracted by its fragrance and believing it would work wonders, a young woman took some of the pot's contents to apply to her facial
disfigurement, whereupon the fragrance disappeared and was replaced by
the normal odor. Colombini's biographer explains that such a holy relic
was not to be perverted to the uses of vanity. Just as every vice had its
corresponding virtue and every sin its expiation, so every disgusting odor
might have its fragrance and every hideous scar its beauty. The most physical perceptions could be instantly transformed by supernatural energy,
while the withdrawal of divine approval immediately restored them to their
primal ugliness.

Not all signs involved a reversal of sense perception. God often showed
his divine choice by an outpouring of light: the countenances of holy children radiated light; a ball of fire shone from Philip Neri's breast, and fire
darted from Dominic de Guzmán's eyes. The rooms in which saints prayed,
suffered, and died often were filled with celestial light. Important moments

in the lives and at the death of many saints were signaled by mysterious sounds—bells rang, cocks crowed, music played, and voices came from the heavens. Eyes were witness to the hovering of white doves, overflights of birds, and the appearance of crosses where a saint had stopped to pray. Just as saintly souls were borne aloft by divine grace, so their bodies were often seen to defy gravity, especially while they were deep in contemplation or in the act of consecrating the Host. One of the most famous levitators was Thomas Aquinas: his companions bore witness as the chunky Dominican floated "two cubits" above the church floor while he prayed. The intangible and inexpressible experience of ecstatic communion could also have an external manifestation. Many saints were observed to go for hours, days, even weeks, without the normal signs of life. While they were communing with God they drank no water, ate no food, neither spoke nor moved. Dead to the world, they lived in God. And when they finally departed the earthly life, their bodies, remaining uncorrupted, gave still another testimony to their sanctity. (See fig. 20.)

Wonder-working, prophecy, stigmata, and illumination were tangible evidence of saintly election and power. Popular veneration thrived upon such manifestations because they provided divine aid and reassurance.[14] But saints' lives are also filled with accounts of intensely private forms of supernatural intervention. Whereas the saint's devotees demanded public performance, the initial inspiration to the holy life was usually a longing for private penance and contemplative prayer. The crown of the contemplative life was mystical communion. Union with the Godhead was reported by relatively few contemplatives and so was a powerful indication of saintliness. Supremely individualistic, mystical union was ineffable, so that very few who experienced it were able to describe it to others. (See fig. 21.)

Exclusive as well as esoteric, of intense interest only to a few, mysticism was not the stuff of everyday faith. To the great majority of believers Christianity's appeal was twofold: Christ's resurrection gave promise of immortality; God's providence provided help in this world. In itself mysticism neither guaranteed salvation nor provided for daily needs. Its consolations were far more subtle, and it met a need felt deeply only by a relative few. Even at the times of its greatest popularity, in the later Middle Ages and during the Catholic Reformation, the appreciation as well as the practice of mystical devotion was for the most part limited to the book-reading public.

Yet if mystical experience had been merely a form of private contemplation, it would be hard to account for its prominence in hagiography. In fact, however, mystics could also reach out to the world. The most impressive contemplatives were those who had achieved a powerful mastery

Fig. 20. Giuseppe di Cupertino levitating. Rome. En-
graving by Caspar Froij, 1781. Photograph courtesy
of the Franciscan Museum, Capuchin Historical In-
stitute.

over self, who had learned how to focus all energies and drives toward
one object. Great mystics made great reformers, peacemakers, preachers,
healers, miracle-workers. Moreover, while the content of their visionary
and ecstatic experience might be comprehensible only to the few, their
direct communion with divinity was another mark of their authenticity and
power. Besides, not all mystical visions were private. The prophetic power
of Bridget of Sweden or Francesca de' Ponziani was partly due to the
visionary form of their predictions.[15]

In confronting the supernatural power of a cult figure, the church's
problem was to determine whether this power came from God or the devil.
In their awe of the supernatural, believers may have been less rigorously
attentive to the origins of power, but they too were concerned to distinguish

between what came from the devil and what came from God. Aquinas's levitation was a sign of his saintliness, but witches too defied gravity when they flew to meet their satanic master in the Sabbath. Rita's suppurating sore was a talisman of God, but one of the prime evidences of witchcraft was the appearance of bodily marks where the witch had fed her demonic familiar. Ecstasy might be diabolic possession, and exorcism might be due to the black art rather than to divine healing. We may recall the case of Alpais, who, though she needed no physical nourishment, took an occasional crust to allay suspicion that she possessed demonic power.

Obviously one distinction lay in the effects of supernatural power; saints did not use their powers for evil purposes. But an employee of Satan could conceal evil behind the semblance of good. The devil's servants used wizardry to enhance their reputations and to establish their authority. Between the saintly miracle-worker and the demonic agent, however, there stretched another enormous gulf. The saint was invariably a deeply penitential ascetic who regarded miracle-working as incidental, even an embarrassing obstacle in the drive to self-abasement. Many a lone hermit or recluse who shunned society to practice austerities and to contemplate God had to be dragged into the limelight, for the faithful were convinced that the most world-denying ascetics possessed the greatest supernatural power, not only for healing the flesh but also for divining the perplexities of the human condition.

Even when they did not work miracles or wield some other instrument of supernatural power during their lifetimes, extreme ascetics were likely to be regarded as holy. When such a one died, the faithful flocked to the grave hoping to see the heavenly sign that would tell them this was a saint whose soul now rested with God. In a society where the overwhelming majority of people ate meat two or three times a year if at all, seldom tasted wine, suffered chronic illnesses, saw hideous deformities on every side, slept on hard mats or on the floor, and engaged in backbreaking labor, those men and women who willingly, even eagerly, pursued still greater physical deprivation and suffering in the name of their God seemed indeed to be "athletes of Christ."[16]

To the awe and respect their strenuous austerities earned them, Christian doctrine added the assurance that penitential ascetics suffered not only to bring themselves closer to heaven but also to expiate the sins of all. More

Fig. 21. Bridget of Sweden sees a flame from Christ and Mary in heaven. In the hands of a priest the figure of Christ emerges from the Host to explain the mystery. New York, Pierpont Morgan Library, miniature MS. 498, f. 4v, 343v. Neapolitan school, early fifteenth century. Photograph courtesy of the trustees of the Pierpont Morgan Library.

than models of the perfection that most lay people could not hope to achieve, ascetics were advocates, protectors, and intercessors who, like Christ himself, took on the burden of sin for their flocks. Every community, whether of town, occupation, or condition, had its special protector, its holy ascetic who had once walked its streets, sweated at the same toil, or experienced the same catastrophe. "Their" saint had shared their condition yet had transcended it by making human suffering into a holy profession. For the spiritual elite, mastery over bodily demands was the avenue of communion with the Godhead; for the humble believer it was the outer sign of supernatural election.

To be sure, not every devout penitent was a saint, and the faithful often were uncertain whether their would-be hero was holy or mad. Some of the crowd at the tomb were there out of curiosity, others to scoff, but the great majority came with hope. If no miracle of healing took place the crowd would disperse, only to reassemble the next day or in a week, a month, or a decade. Sometimes the miracle came only after many years; sometimes not at all. For every miracle-working tomb that attested to the presence of a saint, there must have been many dry wells, lost to the sight and memory of the faithful and of the hagiographer as well.[17]

Extreme asceticism by itself did not guarantee the authenticity of a cult figure, but it was a powerful magnet to draw believers to the tomb. The sine qua non of an ascetic life was renunciation of sexual activity; chastity was the universally understood symbol of rejection of the flesh and the world and hence the indispensable first step toward spiritual perfection. To lay folk chastity was a seal of authenticity. Renunciation of sex did not make a person a saint, but yielding to sexual temptation was a sure way to be disqualified, the first and most important of a series of negative tests designed to separate the sheep from the goats. In all the stories of temptations of saintly young men, the agency is not a plate of delicious food, a soft bed, or a bribe of money; always the devil's tool is a beautiful and lascivious woman. The common wisdom as well as the religious ideology of society identified sexual intercourse as the fundamental division between innocence and worldliness; it admitted of no degrees or compromises. Even the most abstemious saint had to eat and drink occasionally, but there was no such thing as an almost virginal saint.

Eating and drinking too could reveal a failure or an imposter. A putative saint who even once failed to observe the taboos on Friday meat or Lenten indulgence quickly lost public respect; the hagiographer almost always carefully notes the saint's rigid observance of ritual abstention. In addition to being chaste and abstemious the saint had to be humble, most particularly about his or her spiritual perfection. A saint who vaunted holiness was not only an imposter but a contradiction in terms.

Saintly ascetics, of course, went far beyond these negative sanctions to

ever-greater heights of self-denial and penance. Saints not only gave up
sexual intercourse, they cultivated solitude. Some chose to live as recluses;
a few gave themselves entirely to the hermit life; many more retired only
in their later years or retreated from the world from time to time for periods
of spiritual renewal. In all degrees the aim was penitential and contemplative; penance required deep prayer and meditation, away from conversation and interaction with other people. Women sought holiness by
shutting themselves up in a barren cell next to a church or even in a corner
of someone's house. Men more often took to the woods or caves by themselves or joined eremitical communities designed to support solitude.

The impulse to penitential solitude was at odds with society's need to
have holy contemplatives in its midst. Wherever the recluse or hermit
went, people followed, seeking prayers, advice, or miraculous cures, or
merely wishing to bask in the saint's aura. Every monastic house had its
celebrated brother or sister who had managed to achieve the life of solitary
contemplation. Yet holy men and women seeking salvation through prayer
and penance became objects of veneration not so much for what they had
accomplished for their own souls as for what they might do for the faithful.
The paradox went further still. The greater the reluctance of venerable
recluses to open their doors to the world, the more the world wanted to
enter. Reluctance was evidence of saintly humility; the humble walked with
God.[18]

Unlike chastity, humility admitted of degrees. In the lives of many prelate
saints of the eleventh and twelfth centuries traces of humility are hard to
find; nonetheless, humility was one of the central virtues of the apostolic
life, institutionalized by Benedictine monks and reinvigorated by Cluniac
and Cistercian reforms. Just as pride was virtually synonymous with
aristocracy, so humility was its paired opposite. The Benedictines cultivated
humility through obedience and discipline: the monk's will must be subordinated in all things to the will of his superior; perfect humility was to
be achieved through systematic discipline of the unruly body.[19]

Whereas Benedict's rule provided a controlled, measured approach to
the *vita apostolica*, prudently adapted to the rigors of the European climate
and wisely cognizant of human frailty, many seekers of holiness were
impatient with its moderation. Whether inside the monastery or in villages
and towns from the North Sea to the Mediterranean, inspired men and
women sought ever more extreme forms of self-abasement. Colombini
stealing off to the paupers' hospital, Juan de Dios tearing at his hair and
beard so that people would think him mad and heap abuse upon him,
Francis of Assisi eagerly kissing the wounds of lepers, Catherine of Siena
drinking a cupful of cancerous pus from a sick woman who abused her—
these were efforts to eradicate the last vestiges of worldly honor, to expunge
all regard for self, whether of the spirit's pride or the body's health.[20]

One aspect of the striving for humility was expressed in interaction with others: obedience tamed the will. Another was turned toward the self: discipline tamed the body. The physical manifestations of humility crossed over into the realm of penitence. Both might begin with ritualized prayer— a night before the altar on one's knees, hours spent praying with arms outstretched in the form of a cross either standing rigidly or lying prone. Was it humility or penitence that led ascetics to sleep on the cold ground with a rock for a pillow, to walk barefoot in the snow, to sit in a tree for days or years, to insist on cleaning the pigsty, to disfigure their faces and smash in their teeth? Obviously both impulses were involved, just as they were in using such ascetic devices as the ubiquitous hair shirt, or the more elaborate tight metal corselet fitted with iron studs, or again by placing sharp stones in their shoes to make every step a painful reminder of Christ's suffering for human sin. The humble penitents who whipped themselves to reenact one of the episodes of Christ's passion constantly tried new refinements. Louis of Gonzaga progressed from cane branches to ropes to iron chains as his instruments of flagellation. We may also recall Domenico Loricato, who amazed Peter Damian with his resourcefulness in finding new instruments of self-punishment. So popular was flagellation that it became one of the chief activities in the confraternities of lay people that burgeoned in the thirteenth century, and flagellating processions were a common sight in the dark days of the Black Death. Nor was the "discipline" strictly a male practice. Countless are the stories of young girls who whipped themselves until the blood ran.[21]

In the lives of holy penitents illness played a prominent role. Medieval society was all too well acquainted with sickness; it carried away perhaps half of all children, stalked the most robust adult, and turned old age into lingering agony. Illness was both chronic and episodic; present everywhere in every time, it also mounted massive assaults upon entire populations. Sickness was a most unwelcome visitor to everyone but a saint, who turned it into an occasion of spiritual triumph and rejoiced at receiving such a special sign. The faithful watched the chronic sufferer carefully and marveled at those who were able to bear the burden not merely with resignation but with joy. Illness became the occasion for sharing Christ's suffering and for glorifying the will of the Father, for taming the body and bringing nearer the prospect of death and reunion with God. To transform the universal experience of physical affliction into spiritual triumph and joy was to be numbered among the bearers of supernatural power.

Nothing more sharply set saints apart from the rest of the community of the faithful than the way they dealt with their bodies. Saints eradicated bodily desire, whether for sexual satisfaction or for health, thereby gaining extraordinary power. Most believers wanted precisely those things the saint gave up—fecundity, a full belly, good health. And the saints understood and responded, interceding in response to prayer by bestowing upon others what they had spurned for themselves. However much the saints' vocation propelled them from the world and toward God, the needs of the faithful drew them back. The body of Christ embraced not only saints but sinners of every degree. God's elect understood this and knew they had a responsibility to serve the needs of their weaker brethren. Sometimes their drive toward holiness caused them to neglect the sufferings of the faithful while they were alive; but once they had ascended to sit with the Father, saints heard the prayers of their suppliants for worldly needs.

Some saints were already a part of the community during their lifetimes. The saint who labored in charity for the needy and the sick acquired a reputation for holiness that did not rest solely on the exercise of supernatural power. Miraculous healing, to be sure, riveted the attention of the faithful, but believers might also revere men and women who, even without the gift of miracle, practiced charity to extraordinary degrees. What they did any human being might do, but they were the ones who projected superhuman dedication, thoroughness, and effect. Great nurturing saints came to the fore in every era and for every kind of human need: Bononio and Margaret of Scotland were among those eleventh-century saints dedicated to ransoming Christian prisoners. Domingo de la Calzada and Peregrinus were two of many twelfth-century saints who gave aid to pilgrims. Helping widows and orphans, a characteristic saintly activity in the twelfth and thirteenth centuries, enhanced the reputations of Nevelone da Faenza, Alberto di Bergamo, Yves Helory, and William of Rochester, among others. With the fourteenth century, helping children become an especially popular virtue; Marina Villarina, Pietro Petroni, and Simone di Rimini were famous for it. In the sixteenth and seventeenth centuries charity became specifically associated with moral uplift; such saints as Juan de Dios and Juan Grande (Pecador) were celebrated for ministering to prostitutes, while Giacinta Marescotti, Bernardino Realino, and Jean François Régis visited prisoners. A very few saints stood up against Spain's enslavement of New World natives and imported Africans.

Saintly charity could also take more conventional forms. In the lives of wealthy princes or merchants who became saints, founding a monastery or endowing a chapel did not automatically earn veneration, but it was duly noted and cited as evidence of holy charity. More inspiring to the faithful, for whom the story of the widow's mite came closer to home, were the converts to penitence who took a vow of poverty and gave all their goods to the needy. Most of all, believers loved to hear about the holy beggar who shared his crust or gave his cloak to someone more in need of earthly comforts. Clearly saints were voices of social concern, models who aroused the conscience of their times. Again the paradox: saints might remove themselves from the world to seek a timeless union with God, but they remained infused with the values and mores of their social fabric, and often they responded to the needs of their Christian brethren.

In addition to supernatural power, penitential asceticism, and charitable works (the intercorrelation of these will be discussed later), saints often engaged their energies in wielding power on earth and spreading the Christian message. Neither in the official criteria of canonization nor in the popular canons of saintliness, however, do these two activities have much status. In the gospel as well as in the popular mind worldly power was sometimes seen as an obstacle to holiness. Like wealth, it was the antithesis of the Christlike virtues. Nonetheless, a great many saints spent a substantial portion of their lives on earth as princes, bishops, abbots, and abbesses, or as influential ministers to the powerful, a significant aspect of their holy lives.

The consistent association of temporal power with saintliness, while it contradicted one aspect of the legacy of the gospel, was congruent with another theme of Catholic theology. In Christian thought power is an attribute of God, and medieval thinkers tended to acknowledge that kings as well as priests exercised a sacramental function. Royal anointing was a seal of divine grace, a delegation of Christ's kingly authority to do justice and to promote the welfare of the people. The divine gift of miraculous healing, the "king's touch," was associated with royalty down to the eighteenth century.[22] Power was ambiguous: profane, yet sacred; an occasion for corruption, yet also for holiness. Popes and bishops also wielded great power on earth. Their primary mission was the care of souls, and the prelate who kept this aim foremost in spite of worldly temptations and distractions was held up as a model for his successors and as an image of the church militant. For both princes and prelates the possession of power was an opportunity to cultivate the virtue of humility; to command obedience and yet to remain as humble as the lowliest of one's subjects was a saintly manifestation of that Christlike virtue.

Power created opportunities for displaying saintly virtue in still another way, for it provided an occasion for heroism to those who had it as well as to those who opposed it. The bishop who defended the church's rights against the encroachment of royal authority, the missionary who ignored the infidel prince's injunction against preaching the word of God, the English martyr who defied the Tudor and Stuart kings, the holy counselor who was banished for daring to censure the immoral behavior of an emperor were all caught up in the web of temporal power. And more than a few saints during their lifetimes suffered the opposition or condemnation of misguided, narrow-minded, and ungodly high clerics. Short of martyrdom, suffering at the hands of kings or prelates did not make a saint, but stories of persecution fueled the ardor of the faithful and enhanced the aura of holiness.

Those who spread the word of God—reformers of morals, preachers of the apocalypse, apostles to heretics and unbelievers—often became objects of cult in their own lifetimes. The word was charismatic, and its great voices carried the authority of divine inspiration. Preachers like Dominic de Guzmán, Bernardino da Siena, and Vincent Ferrer, who could keep audiences of hundreds, even thousands, spellbound for days, were celebrities whose presence and touch captivated the faithful. Their preaching seemed imbued with divine intelligence, clairvoyance, and prophecy. They were much sought after to deliver judgments, settle controversies, lend their special prayers to heal the sick, or ward off fearful catastrophes. Believers clutched at their garments, scooped up the earth they trod, and, when they died, eagerly collected their relics and awaited miracles.

Sharing in the evangelical work of disseminating and revitalizing the faith were the great writers on doctrine and morals as well as those who propagated new forms of devotion, sometimes by establishing whole new orders. Such men and women were less likely to be known to the laity. Their contributions were not as quickly or fully understood and appreciated by the masses of the faithful, so they were less likely to become objects of popular cult. But inside monastic walls the memory of the great founders, reformers, and writers of the order was assiduously preserved, intensely venerated, and zealously promoted.

In the perception of sanctity over the centuries, these five aspects of the holy life—supernatural grace, asceticism, good works, worldly power, and evangelical activity—were universals. They were virtually the definition of sanctity, not in the church's regulations, but nonetheless in the perception of most believers. Appearing over and over in the veneration of the faithful wherever Latin Christendom took root, this aggregate of perceptions forms a saintly icon, shapes an ideal type that transcends time, place, class, and sex. As with any ideal type, however, its actual manifestations were varied. While distinctions of gender have no place in the ideal of sanctity, it is a fact that there were significantly more female saints in thirteenth-century Italy than in eleventh-century Germany. Although nationality or ethnic identity is unrelated to God's election, English saints were very different from Spanish saints. And, despite Jesus' promise that the last would be first in the kingdom of heaven, the Christian faithful preferred kings to peasants for their saints and expected very different things from each.

In part 1 we explored conversion to the holy life. In the chapters that follow we consider the holy reputation and how it varied over time and place, sex and class, employing a set of procedures designed to measure statistical variation (see the Appendix on Method). These allow us to deal concretely with the historical sociology of sanctity.

Thus far we have said nothing about a path to sainthood that stands dramatically apart from the others—martyrdom. In the early church saintliness was synonymous with martyrdom; saints were those who gave their lives in witness to the true faith of Christ. The church perpetuated that recognition in the liturgy of the mass, while Pope Urban VIII's decrees formalized martyrdom as a distinct type requiring no additional proofs of sanctity.[23] The church officially places all martyrs in a single category, but certain distinctions among them are worth noting. The child martyrs of the Middle Ages were little more than names, their lives in hagiography beginning only with the stories of their murder by wicked Jews who wanted their blood. Next to nothing is known of them, therefore, nor is knowledge of their lives relevant here. In contrast, adult martyrs in the Middle Ages, like their earlier models, were purposeful heroes of dramatic and mortal struggles for the faith. Even in those few cases, stemming particularly from the eleventh and twelfth centuries, where a violent death was the only evidence of martyrdom, legend held that the victim had died in defense of the rights or interests of the church. One example is the cult that grew up around Knut, a Danish king's bastard son whose brothers probably murdered him for political reasons. Another is the veneration of Helen of Skövde in Sweden. A twelfth-century noblewoman, Helen was murdered by her husband's family, who suspected her of complicity in his death. Even when we cannot say that martyrs deliberately decided to die for the faith, clearly they chose their course knowing its dangers as did Thomas Becket, the mendicant and Jesuit missionaries to Asia, Africa, and the New World, Thomas More, and the English recusants. (See figs. 22 and 23.)

This motif of human agency, in which the Christian decides upon a spiritual course and follows it to an ultimate conclusion despite all worldly considerations, is the essence of the martyr's story. In marked contrast to popular notions of the saint as a miracle-working vessel of supernatural power, the martyr is a hero honored as a supreme example of how men and women by the exercise of their own will can further God's work.

In the period of our study martyrs were not so universally and fervently venerated as were miracle-working healers and intercessors (excluding the early church martyrs who were incorporated in the canon of the mass and a few political martyrs such as Becket and Joan of Arc). At the end of the Middle Ages, however, the martyrs once again came to the fore in popular veneration. Wherever Christianity encountered a frontier, it had need of martyrs. Whether in carrying the faith to infidel and heathen lands, combating the encroachments of kings and princes, or fighting heresy in Europe itself, martyrs there would be. In the eleventh and twelfth centuries the frontier of Christendom was beyond the Danube and in the lands washed by the North and Baltic seas. The thirteenth century saw Christianity on the defensive, hemmed in by Islam on its southern frontier and weakened from within from the Alps to the Pyrenees by the cancer of heresy. In the lands of the Moors, Franciscan missionaries met bloody deaths so often that a friar's very decision to go there was tantamount to a choice of dying for the faith. Against the Albigensian heretics in southern France and northern Italy it was mainly the Dominicans who carried the fight and sometimes made the supreme sacrifice.

Only in the sixteenth and seventeenth centuries, however, did martyrdom again dominate the ranks of the saints to a degree approaching their importance in the early church. The frontiers were now England and the new lands of Europe's expansion overseas. In Asia, in Africa, and in North and South America, Franciscans and Jesuits, together with Dominicans, Servites, and others, courted death at the hands of the heathen, and literally hundreds of them won the martyr's crown. In England, where the Tudors and Stuarts were forging a national church, Catholic exiles, mostly Jesuits and secular priests, stole back into the country in a doomed effort to restore the old faith. Ordinary lay men and women who came to the attention of the authorities as devotees of Catholicism might also be martyred if they refused to take an oath of allegiance. Never since the days of the early church was the choice of martyrdom so clear as it was for the English recusants, who merely had to utter a few words to save their lives.

At the same time that the ranks of saints came to be filled by martyrs, appeals for saintly intercession declined as a form of popular piety. The trend has continued to this day. The decline of cultic veneration has been neither absolute nor uniform, being less pronounced in Mexico City and Palermo than in Paris and New York. Devotion to saints is still capable of great bursts of excitement, as in the canonization of a Mother Seaton, and it persists in such practices as stringing St. Christopher medals on rearview mirrors of automobiles. But it is undeniable that there has been an overall great decline in the role of cult and of saints as intermediaries between the faithful and their God.[24] The increase in the frequency of martyrdom and the decline of hagiology are related to a great shift in Christian piety. The extreme form of this shift came with Protestantism, which—often forcibly— eliminated saints from its devotional practice. Catholics, to be sure, did not go as far; indeed, the Counter Reformation employed cultic veneration as an instrument for rallying the faithful to the Roman church, and the cult of saints still plays a very important role in the church's official life. But the long-range tendency of the Counter Reformation church was toward tighter control of popular cult. Whereas Protestants came to place emphasis upon the individual's relation to God, the Catholic church assumed for

Fig. 22. Stanislas of Krakow is murdered at the altar and his limbs are torn off because he has tried to reform his king's morals. Assisi, Basilica of St. Francis of Assisi (lower church). Fresco by followers of Giotto. Photograph from Alinari/Editorial Photocolor Archives.

itself the role of intermediary, allowing much less leeway for indiscriminate dependence upon supernatural folk heroes.

In the history of hagiology the early seventeenth century marks the culmination of this tendency, with prohibitions against any form of cult activity not sanctioned by the papacy itself. The papacy has been far more skeptical about the validity of miracles and about wonder-working people than the rank and file ever had been. On the other hand, it has been

Fig. 23. Martyrdom of Thomas Becket (upper scene). Ramsey Abbey, East Anglia, Psalter illustration, ca. 1300. Pierpont Morgan Library, miniature 302, f. 4v. Photograph courtesy of the trustees of the Pierpont Morgan Library.

generous in granting the crown of martyrdom to its defenders and propagators. Whatever their attractive qualities, martyrs are not easy models to emulate, nor do most of them dispense favors. Their path toward sainthood is neither available nor relevant to the lives of most of the faithful. Their lesson is rather the lesson of self-reliance and indomitable will, which is less likely to inspire the peasant or the tradesman than it is the cleric honoring the heroes of his order. (See fig. 24.)

Fig. 24. Life, miracles, and the canonization of Peter Martyr. The scenes illustrate varied aspects of the reputation of a popular saint. *Left to right from top:* (1) The child Peter, returning from school, is questioned by his heretic uncle. Peter recites the Creed. (2) Peter is vested with clerical robes. (3, to right of central image) Kneeling before a statue of the Virgin Mary, Peter prays for help and hears her say, "I have interceded for you, Peter, and your faith will not fail you." (4) From lengthy penance, the muscles of Peter's jaw are contracted so that his mouth must be opened by force before he can eat. (5) Peter leaves his companions to go into the world to preach. (6) A youth kicks his mother in a fit of temper. He confesses his sin to Peter and cuts off his leg in remorse. Importuned by the youth's parents, Peter replaces the severed leg, which heals instantly. (7) Persecuted by heretics, Peter is fortified and consoled by the crucifix. (8) While Peter is disputing with a heretical bishop in Milan on a very hot day, the bishop promises to abjure heresy if Peter will make a cloud appear to shelter them from the scorching sun. The saint prays, and a large cloud appears in the blue sky. (9) Peter exorcizes a possessed woman. (10) Preaching in the Piazza Mercato Nuovo in Florence, Peter makes the devil, who has appeared in the form of a wild horse to stop his sermon, jump over the piazza without harming anyone. (11) Peter cures a paralytic nun, Carasia. (12) Heretics invite Peter to see the apparition of the Madonna and child in their church, hoping this will convert him to their faith. Peter displays the consecrated host before the apparition, thus unmasking the devil, who had taken the appearance of the Madonna. (13) The devil causes a child to fall into a boiling cauldron, but Peter heals the scalded child. (14, tentative identification) A mother brings Peter her child, born shapeless. Peter blesses the lump of meat, which takes the shape of a normal child. (15) In Piacenza the saint goes with the bishop to the house of Count Gaufredo di Lumello and cures the tumor of the count's son by covering him with his cloak. (16) Struck in the head and shoulder by the dagger of the heretic Carinus, Peter dies, writing the Credo on the ground with his blood. His companion, the blessed Dominic, is being struck by another dagger. Angels carry the saint's soul to heaven. (17) Peter's remains are taken to Milan. (18) Miraculous cures occur at Peter's tomb. (19) Peter's canonization. Altarpiece by Simone Lamberti. Photograph courtesy of Gabinetto Fotografico Soprintendenza per i Beni Artistici e Storici di Parma.

6 ☩ *Place*

Neither in the heyday of the Gregorian Reform nor yet when the Crusades were in full swing, not even in the reign of Innocent III, when the papacy was at the peak of its power, or in the Conciliar era, was Latin Christendom truly united. Not one but many Christendoms flourished in Europe and its overseas outposts between the eleventh and the seventeenth centuries. The unity of the Christian commonwealth was hard to come by in a world where loyalties were pulled this way and that by cultural, political, and geographical diversity. The parish—the very nucleus of Christendom—was a closed, exclusive community, unfriendly to outsiders, jealously guarding both the privileges and the obligations of its inhabitants. Christian belief and practice also varied, and piety meant different things to different people. If all believers were theoretically united in the "body of Christ," they were actually separated by the divergent spiritual needs that stemmed from being men or women, nobles or peasants, clerics or penitents, Latins or Germans.[1]

Yet Christian belief unified as well as divided, and hagiography illustrates this complicated balancing. Saintly lives reflected the divisive factors of sex, class, culture, and place. But saints' cults could cut across these barriers to strengthen communities as broad as Christendom itself, or to foster loyalties as specialized as those of a new town or craft. The life of the saint was closely intertwined with the community, and above all community had a territorial dimension. Tuscan hill towns tended to provide the setting for guilt-ridden conversions of adolescent girls, while Rhinelanders seem to have been inclined to venerate great bishops who had been pious and obedient boys. Place not only influenced the configuration of saintly careers

166

but also set spatial limits around cultic veneration. Such limits, of course, had no warrant in theology; whatever the territorial confines of saints' earthly lives, their supernatural afterlives were universal and their graces available to all. But Christian practice has always been inclined to accommodate the human need to create structures of identity—to separate "us" from "them." Many are the saints who have won church recognition on the basis of a strictly local veneration, whose cults serve the needs of a particular town, order, or people for a unifying symbol.

In the eleventh and twelfth centuries every part of Europe contributed its saints in numbers roughly comparable to geographical extent (see table 6). Powerful bishops, ascetic monks, and prophetic nuns from every region constituted an elite spiritual community that reflected Christendom's vision of a unified body of Christ.[2] But most saints who lived and died between the early thirteenth and the mid-sixteenth centuries were Italian. During that period the proportion of saints who were Italian rose from about one-fifth in the eleventh and twelfth centuries to nearly three-fourths in the fourteenth before dropping back to one-fifth in the sixteenth century.

With respect to virtually every aspect of sainthood we shall examine—from conversion to the differentiation of sex and class—the years from about 1200 to about 1540, that is, from the advent of mendicancy to the Reformation, emerge as a coherent period in the history of Catholic piety. This was the period when conversion was a conscious choice fraught with anxiety and conflict, when the female contemplative came into her own, when the saint's favored place was the town, when austerity and good works were powerful signs of holiness. These were the years when lay people actively joined the pursuit of spiritual perfection and developed

Table 6
Saint's Birthplaces over Time
(number in each category)

	Century of Saint's Death						
Place	11th	12th	13th	14th	15th	16th	17th
British Isles	19	20	10	2	2	54	42
Scandinavia	1	9	1	3	0	0	0
Low Countries	8	11	6	1	2	3	2
Holy Roman Empire and Switzerland	32	27	22	7	4	1	2
France	23	37	24	11	7	4	19
Iberia	11	13	12	3	9	16	22
Italy	26	35	79	74	53	33	23
Eastern Europe	7	0	4	5	4	4	3
Non-European	1	1	1	1	2	1	5
Total	128	153	159	107	83	116	118

new forms of religious expression. This was the era of the Italian saint, more specifically the northern Italian urban saint.

All these trends are aspects of a set of related developments. In the second quarter of the thirteenth century popes relied heavily on the Franciscans in their fight against heresy and favored the order's efforts to raise its heroes to the honors of the altar. With the growing split between Spiritual and Conventual Franciscans over the question of poverty, popes tended to shift their support to the Dominicans, who were especially active in preaching against the Cathar heresy in southern France and northern and central Italy. Papal support of the mendicants inevitably meant a heavier concentration of urban Italian saints, since this was the mendicant stronghold.[3] To a less pronounced degree mendicancy's appeal to women also helps explain the rise in numbers of female saints, just as the Franciscan and Dominican concentration on adolescent recruiting helps explain the importance of conversion in hagiographic literature of the period.

Increased participation by the papacy in thirteenth-century canonization proceedings by no means explains everything, however. In many respects the popular piety represented by mendicancy was a challenge to the very hierarchical and sacerdotal structures that thirteenth-century popes were in the process of fostering. Above all, Franciscan calls to apostolic poverty opened a Pandora's box not only for the order but for the church as a whole, and Pope John XXII's condemnation of this doctrine in 1322 by no means laid radical poverty to rest.[4] While the papacy ultimately saw mendicancy as a weapon in its fight against heresy as well as in the effort to shore up the crumbling walls of ecclesiastical popularity, the rise of mendicancy was not a response to papal needs so much as it was an expression of popular piety.[5] Moreover, when all is said and done, papal canonizations account for only about one in ten of the widely recognized saints of the thirteenth century, most of whose cults flourished by popular enthusiasm under the approving or merely tolerant eyes of local authority. In this great majority of saints' cults, papal involvement at most amounted to approval of an existing cult; more often it meant tolerating a veneration that did not flagrantly violate papal canons.

The idea of papal primacy in the recognition of sanctity becomes even more questionable when we consider ecclesiastical history in the next century and a half. The era of urban, mendicant, female, lay, and Italian saints that began in the thirteenth century reached its zenith in the fourteenth and remained very substantial in the fifteenth century. Meanwhile, the papacy suffered Boniface VIII's humiliation at Anagni in 1302 and saw the election of a French pope in 1305 who took up residence in Avignon. Whatever else it was for the authority and prestige of the papacy, the Babylonian Captivity was a time when Rome and Italy lost their primacy in church affairs.[6] Moreover, barely a year after the papacy returned to

Rome in 1377, French cardinals seceded and returned to Avignon, where they elected a competing pope and inaugurated the dismal period of the Great Schism.[7] The papacy's nadir is also seen in its shrinking part in authorizing new cults. In the whole of the fourteenth century there were only eight canonizations by popes, and there were only sixteen in the following century. All the rest were local. The role of the papacy, which even in the thirteenth century was limited, explains virtually nothing about changing cultic activity in the two centuries that followed.

Even the mendicant movement was not so much a cause of changing ideas of holiness as it was a channel for their expression. Francis of Assisi, Dominic de Guzmán, Philip Benizi, and the other founders of mendicant orders were innovators of genius whose work shaped the forms that piety was to take. Like most great founders, they crystallized needs and promoted aspirations that without them would have been channeled differently or perhaps not at all. But needs and aspirations had more diffuse origins.

The theater for innovative piety in the thirteenth century was the town. Occupational guilds frequently served to focus religious activities, while in the latter part of the century towns fostered confraternities dedicated primarily to religious observances and practices for lay people. Low Country towns gave rise to Beguinages where women could retire for periods of meditation and prayer without taking lifelong vows. These were followed by a parallel movement, the Beghards, for lay men. In southern France and northern Italy, Waldensians, Brethren of the Free Spirit, and other lay groups dedicated to the imitation of Christ through poverty, charity, and free preaching earned the church's condemnation by seeming to attack the fundamentals of clerical power. These heretical movements grew up with the rising towns of the eleventh and twelfth centuries, went underground as they began to be suppressed, and continued a fitful existence throughout the period we are studying.[8] The origins of the more radical Cathars, or Albigensians, who denied the visible church altogether, are obscure, perhaps stemming from dualist movements in southeastern Europe, but their heyday in Western Europe was the twelfth and early thirteenth centuries, and there are some traces of a continued existence in more remote areas of France and Spain in the fourteenth century.[9]

Thirteenth-century town populations were also galvanized by apocalyptic prophecies that combined social protest with radical religious schemes. Millenarians predicted an end to the existing order; the Antichrist would appear and begin a new era of the Spirit, either preceded or followed by the Second Coming of Christ. The intense excitement attending the rise of the Franciscan order was fueled in part by its association with the millenarian prophecies of the Joachimites, who applied the ideas of the Calabrian abbot Joachim of Fiore to contemporary events. Antichrist was variously identified with Emperor Frederick II or with the papacy, and Enoch and Elijah, the prophets of the New Order, with Francis and Dominic.[10] Spinning off from the Spiritual Franciscan movement were radicals identified by the loose term Fraticelli, preaching strict discipline and doctrines of total poverty.[11] Some Fraticelli mingled with the town poor and seem to have had a certain influence in the worker movements of the late fourteenth century.[12]

Everywhere towns offered religious association, spiritual community, popular preaching, and mutual consolation in a variety of forms, from the staid public ceremonies in which members of the Venetian elite ritually flagellated themselves, to the more spontaneous processions of Bianchi, Disciplinati, and other lay penitent groups, to the underground cells of Fraticelli, Umiliati, Free Spiriters, and Cathars.[13] The burgeoning of saints' cults in the thirteenth century was only one feature of this wider explosion of popular piety, a medium for expressing religious ideas as well as for seeking spiritual solace and divine help. Towns marshaled relics, built shrines and chapels, and promoted confraternities dedicated to the celebration of their favorite saints.[14]

To the extent that towns fostered new economic activities, new social relations, and new cultural forms, urban growth was responsible for the rise of new expressions of piety and new religious movements. For lay people the pursuit of holiness could no longer be confined or channeled into monastic life, hitherto the chief symbol and avenue of religious conversion. Town dwellers sought ways to express their religious needs while they continued to pursue the more satisfying and absorbing pleasures of civic living for which they or their parents had left their rural villages. Town life weakened or dissolved personal bonds of lordship and certainties of caste. New forms of allegiance and association—civic pride, guilds, confraternities, neighborhood churches—provided important substitutes. All these agencies used religious symbols and practices to seal the bonds of fraternity and solidarity: patron saints, special cults, obligations of alms, participation in feasts and processions. These were for the most part voluntary organizations that required considerable personal spiritual initiative and involvement.[15]

In a rural village personal decision was confined within narrow limits. For lord as for peasant, for rich as for poor, providence determined whether it was to be feast or famine, and in the outcome human choice played little part. A matter of praying for the best and expecting the worst, piety was essentially supplication, vicarious, turning upon the ritual function of priest and the intervention of saints.[16] Not that this was uniquely rural; to a considerable extent medieval religion everywhere shared these qualities. The elaboration of a clerical order with indispensable sacramental functions was both cause and effect of an essentially collective relation to divinity and salvation. But the more fluid life of towns and individualistic activities promoted by a commercial economy could not fail to affect religious attitudes and practices, to emphasize human responsibility, individual conscience and initiative, and a personal relation to the divine source.

Urban activities such as moneymaking and moneylending brought tension between traditional and established values, and the resulting anxieties and guilt help explain the special intensity that marks much of the religious behavior of lay townfolk in the late Middle Ages. Insecurity was the basis of collective strivings by medieval townsfolk for spiritual as well as secular legitimation through saints' cults and religious endowments and their hospitality to living holy men and women. The flowering of late medieval and Renaissance religious architecture, painting, and sculpture was predominantly a phenomenon of the towns. Merchants and bankers gave enormous sums for chapels, churches, and altarpieces, for the liturgical objects, religious sculpture, and church windows by which they made restitution for the profits of their spiritually questionable enterprises.[17] Material symbols of religious culture were vehicles for the expression of civic pride, personal conscience, and emotional identification with the saints and the Godhead. The individualism so often seen as the essence of Renaissance modernism had a religious dimension that grew out of the interaction of medieval town society with traditional Christian imperatives.

If individualism was one pole of the innovations of town society, public association was the other. Between these two poles stood the medieval family with its network of loyalties and obligations. Civic government grew at the expense of extended family bonds that encumbered the growth of public authority.[18] At the same time, the commercial and industrial activities of the middle class threatened the solidarity of the family as a unit of producers. The loosening of the bonds of caste and estate, the shift away from family as the principal form of economic and social organization, freed—perhaps forced—people to seek alternative ways of establishing identity. Besides, even a heightened sense of individual religious awareness needed supportive structures.[19] The largest of these was the town itself, with its panoply of civic cult and public ritual. Civic patriotism was permeated by religious symbols and myths promoting public consciousness. A sense of moral solidarity with the town's welfare granted authenticity to its undertakings and legitimated the demands it made upon its citizens. Saints' days and other festivals made up the order of civic time and gave occasion for the further elaboration of patriotic symbols.[20] Below the level of civic organization, occupational guilds and confraternities brought men, and in some cases women, together for the expression of common spiritual and social needs. Even these were integrated into the structure of civic community; thus the Guild of Woolen Craftsmen (Arte della Lana) had the primary responsibility for maintaining the fabric of the Florentine cathedral.[21] The Venetian flagellant societies, or *scuole,* were integrated into the public ceremonies of the civic liturgy.[22] However we look at it, then, we see that as a force for association the town was a medium for the communication of religious as well as intellectual ideas and a vehicle for religious as well as political and social innovation and dissent.

The broad forces of economic and social change that fostered the rise of towns and the establishment of new class relations were at work in all parts of European Christendom in the twelfth and thirteenth centuries. Flanders and Brabant, the Rhine Valley, Provence, Aragon, Tuscany, Umbria, and the Po Valley were but the most important areas where towns, commerce, and manufacturing sprang up together. The piety of individual conscience and personal participation found expression in these same areas.[23]

The steady growth and optimism of the thirteenth century came to a sudden halt. Crop failure, famine, war, mercenary raids, declining markets, and the Black Death were the lot of Europe's people in the fourteenth century.[24] Religious leadership failed to provide adequate consolation or direction. While catastrophe spread from one end of Europe to another, the popes at Avignon were earning their infamous reputation as the most effective tax collectors of Christendom, and after the Great Schism of 1378 the prestige and influence of Christ's vicar sank even lower. In response to the Ottoman Turks' threat to Constantinople, the papacy could merely wave the cross of crusade. Princes and knights responded with hollow pledges, having more pressing concerns at home.[25]

Bodies weakened by famine and spirits demoralized by economic scarcity could hardly withstand the onslaught of the Black Death that first struck in 1348 and returned with terrifying frequency over the next 350 years. Reports by fourteenth-century chroniclers of death rates ranging from one-third to one-half of local populations, once dismissed by historians as typical examples of the Middle Ages' loose way with figures, now tend to be confirmed by demographic studies.[26] Some villages disappeared entirely.[27] Survivors lived with the horror of corpse-lined streets, the loss of their loved ones, and the constant fear that plague would return. According to Boccaccio (who borrowed from a traditional literature of catastrophe), the proximity and uncertainty of death impelled people to extremes of gaiety and despair, moral heroism and frivolity.[28] Melancholy was the dominant mood of the fourteenth century expressed in such themes as *de contemptu mundi,* the Dance of Death, and the Fifteen Last Signs of Christ, in dancing and flagellation manias, grotesque cemetery art, and the literatures of consolation. Millard Meiss has demonstrated the impact of the Black Death on popular piety through late-fourteenth-century Florentine and Sienese painting. Benjamin Kedar has shown how Genoese and Venetian merchants lost confidence in their business initiative, retrenched, and sought ways to protect themselves against fortune. In naming their children and their ships after saints, they expressed their helpless dependence on providence.[29]

Fourteenth-century events bred a sense of the cruelty of fate and the weakness of human endeavor. This mentality persisted in Europe for a long time to come.[30] Material effects of depression lasted throughout the fifteenth century, emotional ones perhaps longer as recurrences of plague continued to terrify and decimate populations. Towns recovered, but some shifts of economic activity and power were permanent. Antwerp, then Amsterdam, replaced Bruges and the Brabantine towns as centers of banking, trade, and industry. Venice outstripped Genoa as a power in the eastern Mediterranean. Great banking and commercial families disappeared and were replaced by others. In the Italian communes the late fourteenth century saw the rise of *gente nuova,* the new rich who thrust themselves forward into places of wealth and power made vacant by the catastrophes of plague and depression.[31]

Fitful economic recovery in towns was accompanied by renewed efforts to know God's will and to do his work. Urban centers once more welcomed wandering preachers who sought to interpret misfortune and give spiritual direction to workers and patricians alike. The homely moralism of San Bernardino da Siena made him one of the most beloved and welcome visitors to early-fifteenth-century towns.[32] (See fig. 25.) The Spaniard Vincent Ferrer had a sterner message of divine judgment.[33] Some preachers sought scapegoats in the Jews or in witches; some raised the issue of poor against rich. In the last decade of the fifteenth century Savonarola briefly succeeded in organizing the city of Florence as a New Jerusalem dedicated to the reform of both private and civic morality as a prelude to unifying the world in a single sheepfold under a single shepherd.[34] In Bohemia the Taborites awaited the coming of a millennial new order.[35] Papal schism ended through the combined pressures of lay rulers and reformers who launched a movement to relocate church sovereignty in ecumenical councils representing the whole body faithful. Conciliarism failed of its objectives to reform the church "in head and members" and to seize control from the papacy; but it focused lay aspirations and criticism, and it might be argued that its ultimate defeat paved the way for the coming of the Reformation.[36]

Developments in popular piety in the two centuries between Francis of Assisi and Francesco di Paola were closely connected with the achievements as well as the vicissitudes of town life. This is particularly to be seen in the towns of northern and central Italy, leaders in the formation of new saints' cults. The same towns were centers of the successful communal movements from the early twelfth century onward.[37] Most European towns emerged within the context of feudalism, and their history is one of a struggle for autonomy. Towns sought charters of liberties to restrain intervention in their affairs by local or regional magnates, bishops, abbots, and sometimes kings. External autonomy went hand in hand with control over their own populations. Nobles brawling in the streets, clergy shrugging off the jurisdiction of town courts, merchants buying cheaply and selling dearly, rustics swarming in for work and freedom—all had to be molded into citizens. The history of the medieval town in its drive to sovereignty condensed, in the brief span of decades, the history of state formation in early modern Europe. But in most of Europe towns enjoyed only brief moments of autonomy and only partially completed the process

Fig. 25. Bernardino da Siena preaching. Siena, Palace of the Commune. Panel by Neroccio di Landi. Photograph courtesy of Soprintendenza alle Gallerie e Opere d'Arte Siena.

of consolidation before they were absorbed into larger structures by dynastic states.

In Jacob Burckhardt's dictum, the city-state of the Italian Renaissance was "the first-born of the modern sons of Europe."[38] Burckhardt recognized that, whereas in the north feudalism gave way to territorial states, in Italy the rivalries of papacy and Holy Roman Empire made such political centralization impossible. Italian towns allied with pope or emperor according to the dictates of their political and economic needs—Guelf if papal, Ghibelline if imperial. In the vacuum left by two exhausted "world" powers after the mid-thirteenth century, towns made good their claims to territory, autonomy, and legitimacy, usually under the leadership of a "despot," a ruthless, amoral new man who in seizing power forged the Renaissance city-state with its brilliant amalgam of politics and high culture.

Burckhardt, however, passed too lightly over the continuity of Italian society with its urban past.[39] Many medieval Italian towns proudly traced their origins to Roman and even pre-Roman foundations, origins powerfully and visibly present in their very streets and buildings. Roman government survived in the diocesan structure of the medieval episcopacy centered in towns, and in canon and civil law. Roman culture survived in the Italian language and, however altered, in popular religious beliefs and public festivals. Out of this Roman heritage, taking strength from a history still living, appeared the commune of the medieval Italian town. By the late eleventh century Italian urban elites were forming sworn associations to deal with their common needs, giving rise to the term "commune." Within a century communal government spread to most population centers in northern and central Italy. Dozens of republican constitutions emerged, with town consuls and assemblies based on the model of ancient Rome. Fortified by well-articulated communal organizations built upon rich traditional foundations, and blessed with the advantages of great commercial wealth, Italian city-republics were in a much better position than their northern counterparts to overcome the forces of ecclesiastical and temporal lordship and establish their sovereignty.

The summer of the Italian city-republics was also the flowering time of Italian saints. Cults of holy men and women, predominantly urban, proliferated in the thirteenth century as never before and never since. To the growing panoply of devotions to Mary, Christ, and apostolic founders, thirteenth-century Italian townspeople added saintly heroes and heroines from their own midst. Every town had its holy penitent, its miraculous healer, its protector and intercessor. Thirteenth-century towns had similar spiritual needs; whether a town was in Flanders or in Tuscany, its people sought supernatural help in times of famine and disease, in expiating sins of avarice, in ministering to the poor and to orphans and widows made more vulnerable by the anonymity and uncertainty of the sex-differentiated market economy of urban centers. In short, a new society required a new piety, and cults were one effective way changing spiritual impulses found concrete expression and recognition.

Yet only Italy saw a rise in cult formation in the thirteenth century. Why? An explanation can only lie in the special set of conditions and circum-stances that differentiate Italian communal society from town society in the rest of Europe. Intense involvement by Italian cities in papal politics and, conversely, of the papacy in city politics provides one reason. Although the number of papal canonizations remained low in the thirteenth century, popes actively exerted influence over cult approval at the episcopal level, supporting candidates of Guelf proclivities and barring those tainted by Ghibelline associations. But there is much more to the politics of sainthood than papal intervention in Italian town cult.

In Italy popular piety and civic patriotism were fused to a degree rare in the north. The very success of the Italian communes provided resources that were exploited to promote the recognition of local heroes. Italian towns were more successful than northern urban centers in integrating their cler-ical components into a civic polity. Bishops and other clergy were expected to promote civic as well as spiritual interests. They were inclined to listen with sympathy and to take action when local citizens petitioned for rec-ognition of a favorite cult. For their part, communes, like religious orders, had the stamina and the means with which to press the cases of their holy men and women. In securing recognition of sanctity, organization and funds were essential along with enthusiasm, and communes had all three. Religious traditions were incorporated with civic patriotism, and religious symbols served political as well as spiritual functions—indeed, in a city like Florence, which regarded itself as the Christian daughter of Rome, destined to spread the twin blessings of liberty and salvation to the rest of Italy if not the world, political and spiritual aims were often intertwined. The civic myth that claimed for Venice equality with pope and emperor also traded on a combination of political and religious elements. The in-tegration of crusading motifs in the civic traditions of maritime cities such as Pisa and Genoa derived from the fusion of political and economic with religious aspirations.[40] Communes that hauled wagons displaying sacred banners into battle and regarded their capture as a catastrophic omen celebrated the discovery of a saint in their midst as a civic triumph.[41]

A native holy man or woman sanctified the very ground and space of the city, demonstrated to the world the superiority of the commune, and endowed its history with religious authority. The intense rivalry for saints' relics was not merely the competition of Italian business enterprise, but a recognition that possession of wonder-working remains provided a moral and spiritual as well as a material advantage. The late thirteenth century witnessed a surge of building in Italian communes; cathedrals, bell towers, and churches as well as government palaces, all were seen as public enterprises. The church that housed the saint's relics and images was as much a civic center as the palace where solons gathered to make law and spend the people's tax money.[42]

The Italian commune's religious heroes were not the saintly prelates and holy monks of the eleventh and twelfth centuries. In all times and places saints worked miracles in their lifetimes and served as intercessors after their deaths; but the later communal protectors, unlike those of the earlier period, in which manifestations of power were everything, were more often heroic models who had less to do with practical power than with the struggle toward individual spiritual perfection. These later town saints were ascetic penitents dedicated to expiating not only their own sins but also those of their community. They were contemplatives seeking consolation and joy in the ecstatic experience of mystical union. They were imitators of Christ who devoted their lives to poverty and ministered to the poor and sick of their towns. More than ever before, they were women and lay folk, and more than before they came from the humbler classes of society. Worldly power was incidental, even antithetical, to their quest for individual perfection. Yet, being townspeople, they were highly visible, and their spiritual journeys were witnessed by a community composed of both skeptics and admirers. Their parents, brothers, and sisters consulted priests about them; their confessors watched carefully over the orthodoxy of their spiritual travails; each advance toward perfection, every supernatural sign was noted, discussed, remembered, recorded. In a sense, even before they died they belonged to the community. Those who overcame internal doubts and hesitations and steeled their wills through spiritual discipline became counselors to sinners in need of moral direction and consolation, to civic leaders torn between private virtue and the demands of political action, to peacemakers seeking an end to constant warfare. (See fig. 26.)

The life of Giovanni dalle Celle vividly exemplifies the career of a four-teenth-century saint. A member of a Florentine patrician family, Giovanni had committed some dreadful but unnamed sin for which he was condemned to a tower to live on a diet of bread and water. During his imprisonment he corresponded with Simone da Cascia, a spiritual counselor of much fame in Florentine territory. A year later when Giovanni was released he went to the local abbey of Santa Trinità, and from there he retired to a hermitage in the nearby mountain forest of Vallombrosa. Acquiring renown for his holiness, he issued a steady stream of letters of spiritual consolation and advice to members of the Florentine oligarchy.

Like many other urban holy men, Giovanni was also the object of scandal, perhaps an echo of his sinful past. A story circulated in Florence that he had used the black arts to have a virgin brought into his cell for illicit purposes. But the rumor had no effect upon Giovanni's standing as a public counselor. When the Florentine commune went to war against the papacy in 1375 some city leaders were troubled by the prospect of taking up arms against the vicar of Christ, and they consulted Giovanni, who reassured them of the lawfulness of the contest. The ensuing War of the Eight Saints was a crucible for the amalgam of piety and politics that fostered the myth of Florence as the New Jerusalem.[43]

The steep rise in the proportion of Italian cults in the thirteenth century

Fig. 26. Nicholas of Tolentino making peace between two combatants. Perugia, Civic Gallery. Photograph courtesy of Gabinetto Fotografico Soprintendenza: Galleria Nazionale dell'Umbria. Number 715.

continued in the fourteenth and only slightly leveled off in the fifteenth century. By the early 1500s virtually every Italian commune had its special protector, a saint whose holy life had been lived inside its walls within the preceding three hundred years. During the age of the Italian commune, saints had come to legitimize all manner of civic enterprises. The saint made communal autonomy a holy cause and, as in the case of Florence, lent a religious aura to territorial aggrandizement. Saints continued to serve the timeless need of the weak for miracle and intercession, but they also spearheaded newer forms of religious individualism and moral activism that corresponded to the changing ambience of town life. Communal saints gave expression to the intense moral and spiritual anxieties of the urban middle classes and personified the aspirations of lay piety. They ministered to the victims of bourgeois economy and established standards of humanitarian concern that were in direct contrast to the medieval glorification of poverty. (See fig. 27.)

Like the communes themselves, the Italian saints of the late Middle Ages and Renaissance combined continuity and change. Both exemplified the indivisibility of tradition and innovation, both attempted to link the temporal with the sacred order. If the secularizing commune found religious legitimacy indispensable, the spiritualizing saint found the worldly town a receptive context in which to do God's work.

In the previous chapter we tried to answer the question "Who was a saint?" and we proposed an ideal type exhibiting five salient characteristics: supernatural grace, penitential asceticism, charitable work, worldly power, and evangelical activity. While these elements were universal in the perception of sanctity, no two saints displayed them in quite the same combination of degrees. Precise numerical scores and even the simplest arithmetic comparisons are not appropriate when applied to an individual saint, but if the reader is persuaded that a generalized perception of sanctity existed and that it is worthy of historical explanation, then the figures in table 7 should merit some analysis. (For statistical analysis of urban/rural perceptions of sanctity see chap. 7, on class.) The percentages isolate the saints of the British Isles as a composite group sharply different from the holy men and women of the Continent. A large majority of British saints were martyrs, and for this reason their cohort scores well below the average in all five components of sanctity. On the Continent, however, saints were anything but uniform. Supernatural activity, penitential asceticism, and charitable work—the three attributes most central to the popular as well as the clerical understanding of holiness—were especially prominent among Iberia's saints, least noted among those of Northern Europe. To a less pronounced degree, the Italian configuration is like that of Iberia,

Fig. 27. The sick and crippled at the tomb of Peter Martyr. Florence, Church of Santa Maria Novella, Spanish Chapel. Fresco by Andrea Bonaiuti da Firenze. Photograph from Alinari/Editorial Photocolor Archives.

Table 7
Components of Saintly Reputation by Place and Time
(percentage above or below grand mean for the component)

	Supernatural Power	Asceticism	Charitable Activity	Temporal Power	Evangelical Activity
Place					
Italy	18	17	12	9	3
Iberia	32	24	19	2	25
France	5	3	8	18	13
British Isles	− 54	− 46	− 31	− 43	− 20
Northern Europe	− 6	− 5	− 10	6	− 10
Century of death					
Eleventh	− 1	− 11	− 10	46	− 4
Twelfth	− 6	− 8	− 9	37	− 8
Thirteenth	20	10	2	11	− 1
Fourteenth	9	12	3	− 38	− 12
Fifteenth	20	13	8	19	10
Sixteenth	− 19	− 11	− 3	− 42	5
Seventeenth	− 22	− 1	14	− 50	14

whereas among French saints the most distinguishing characteristic is worldly power, a reflection of the close historical connection in that region between spiritual grace and expanding royal authority.

Taken as a whole, the figures suggest that hagiology distinguished Northern Europe from the Mediterranean at least as early as the thirteenth century, well before the age of expansion and of reformation. In Germany and the Low Countries the ranks of saints were dominated by great prelates and princes rather than by miracle-workers. Even when supernatural activity did become prominent in the north, beginning with the twelfth century and particularly along the lower Rhine, a holy reputation was more likely to rest upon private visionary experiences than upon miracle-working. In these regions, the twelfth century was indeed the time of the saintly mystic, often a person of lower-class origin. For the most part these were women; however they were unlike the zealous Tuscans such as Bona of Pisa and Catherine of Siena, who sallied forth from their cells to bring the gospel and spiritual nurture to the world. Rather, they were quiet contemplatives who spent their lives in meditation and prayer and who were known chiefly through their confessors and the admiring sisters of their orders. The biographies of these northern mystics are often thin, devoid of the rich detail that illuminates the personalities of their more active Mediterranean counterparts. Little is known of their childhood and adolescence apparently because their devotees and biographers were primarily interested in these women for their mystical experiences.

Supernatural activity among saints from the predominately French culture area between the Rhine and the Pyrenees reflects the character of this region as a geographical and cultural crossroads. With respect to supernatural activity and other characteristics as well, saintly French men and women ranged from powerful princes and prelates to visionaries and miracle-workers, some showing strong similarities to their Germanic neighbors to the north and east, others to their Mediterranean neighbors to the south.

The "typical" Germanic saint was male, a high prelate, born in the first half of the seven-hundred-year period of this study. His supernatural power, if he displayed it at all during his lifetime, was most likely to take the form of miracle-working. The typical Mediterranean saint, on the other hand, whether Iberian or Italian, was more likely to come from the lower classes, and far more likely to have been involved in intense family conflict, whether with parent or spouse. The Mediterranean saint was more likely to have had problems with chastity and sexual temptation and invariably (the exceptions are statistically insignificant) lived a lifetime full of wonder-working, surrounded by celestial signs.

French saints were of both these types, a fact reflected in table 7 by the roughly average indexes for this group. The French ideal of saintliness served the purposes of national state formation and the self-interests of an elite power structure; but France was also a land of intense popular religiousness in which saints' cults personified and marked out new directions in piety.[44] France shared with Mediterranean lands every new religious enthusiasm, be it the movements of thirteenth-century flagellants, the fourteenth-century Bianchi penitents, or the rise of mendicancy, the cult of the Sacred Heart and Catholic Reformation mysticism; these enthusiasms were amply reflected in the cults of French saints.[45]

Whereas in France the veneration of saints served both to further the interests of the elite classes and to channel and promote popular religious enthusiasm, in the Mediterranean the latter function was dominant. There were of course popes, Tuscan and Umbrian bishops, princes of Aragon and queens of Castile who came to be venerated as saints, but even among these public figures supernatural activity was paramount. In the Mediterranean it was not enough to be a prince or a prelate; the town of Gubbio venerated not Ubaldus the good bishop and defender of the church but Ubaldo the miracle-worker. Innocent III, perhaps the most formidable pope of the Middle Ages, was never honored by a cult, whereas Victor III and Celestine V, neither of whom achieved much for the church but both of whom were believed to be in close touch with the supernatural, received spontaneous veneration, while Gregory VII, the eleventh-century champion of ecclesiastical liberties, was not canonized until 1728, when clerical leaders once more came into their own. Spain and Portugal provide many additional examples to illustrate the Mediterranean preferences for the miracle-worker over the power holder, for celestial signs over doctrinal purity, for graces over charitable works.[46]

The predominance of supernatural activity of all kinds in the lives of Mediterranean saints compared with the saints north of the Alps and Pyrenees suggests that, from the standpoint of popular piety, Christian Europe was polarized centuries before the Reformation. According to Fernand Braudel, Europe divides along the line of the olive trees. Agricultural historians make the distinction between southern dry, extensive and northern wet, intensive farming, and the appropriate rotation patterns, whereas students of maritime commerce refer to the Baltic and Tyrrhenian zones and glottologists draw a horizontal line separating the Latin tongues from the Germanic and Slavic. Braudel's distinction between the Mediterranean and the northern European field holds good not only for geography and economy but also for the complex amalgam of symbols, values, and behavior for which we usually reserve the term culture.[47]

Material and spiritual culture interacted. Among Mediterranean people the relationship to nature was deeply ambiguous, and surely this ambiguity contributed to their supernaturalism. In the coastal plains below Barcelona and in the valleys of Apulia nature was good; rainfall was sufficient to provide an abundant harvest, and no frost threatened the vines and fruit trees. Nature's benevolence encouraged an outlook in which divine providence made human intervention superfluous. Olive trees planted by one's ancestors were as much a part of the providential landscape as rainfall and sunshine; the little labor they required bore no immediate or tangible relation to their yield. But Mediterranean nature had another, less benevolent face. Over vast stretches of central Spain and Sicily the sun was scorching, the prevailing southern winds erosive, and the rainfall inadequate; sandy soils could not be irrigated effectively or tolerate deep plowing; a good wheat crop was possible no more than one year in five. In much of the rest of the region harsh mountains, from which the trees had been progressively stripped away over the preceding two millennia, with consequent soil erosion and landslides, afforded meager pasturage at best. From these zones that so poorly repaid human labor, hungry men and women went down to the coasts and plains, where their numbers swelled the native populations and nullified nature's abundance, making poverty the norm everywhere. The splendor of commercial enclaves brought little solace to the multitude who had nothing to barter.[48]

Throughout the rural Mediterranean, society's injustice magnified nature's harshness. A small and inbred aristocracy not only consumed a disproportionate share of the region's produce, but did so under arrangements that dehumanized the peasantry. The ancient institution of the latifundium reinforced a sense of fatalism, already induced by natural conditions, and strengthened the peasants' perception that no human means would improve their condition.[49] A sense of helplessness encouraged resort to the supernatural in every class and region, and obviously this was true in Northern Europe as well. By definition all saints but martyrs displayed supernatural powers, if not in their lifetimes at least after death. But the intensity of the supernatural in those saints' cults that flourished in the Mediterranean was extraordinary. Throughout Europe most people lived close to nature, but in the north a combination of social institutions and physical conditions encouraged a stronger faith in the efficacy of human agency. Whereas in the north society was understood to be a cooperative agency to cope with and perhaps overcome nature's vicissitudes, in the rural south social arrangements tended to confirm the belief that uncontrollable natural and supernatural forces were at work, forces subject only to miracle and magic.[50]

In addition to a fundamental division between the Mediterranean and Northern Europe, the figures in table 7 suggest a closely related chronological divide, one that marks off the distinct time from the thirteenth century through the sixteenth century when popular piety and religious enthusiasm swelled the ranks of new saints, especially in Italy. The early sixteenth century, however, was a time of crisis for the cult of saints. Saints had embodied religious innovation and given direction to popular piety for the preceding three hundred years, but with the Reformation the traditional structures of belief and organization came under fire as never before. Protestantism was the climax of a long tide of lay religiousness that sought to give expression to new levels of personal conscience as well as to a deep sense of human sin and helplessness before almighty God. Luther's doctrine of justification by faith alone rendered superfluous the saint's efforts to earn divine grace by acts of charity and personal asceticism. The abject sinfulness of man, helpless since the Fall to justify himself before God, rendered the saints' quest for perfection not merely useless but even a sign of pride and an affront to divine power. With Everyman's salvation a matter between himself and God, there could be no miraculous intercession through cults, no treasury of merits, no indulgences, indeed, no purgatory. Denying the old Catholic distinction between veneration and worship, Protestants held that prayers to the saints violated the divine injunction of the first commandment. Saintly images were idols to be desecrated, torn out of churches, smashed. Luther's God was the *deus absconditus*, the hidden God, so awesome and awful in his majesty as to discourage any homely appeals for easing life's pain, which was a well-deserved result of man's innate depravity. Protestantism scorned a religion that seemed to concentrate on the sale of grace and the practice of magic rather than upon the state of one's immortal soul.

Even among reformers who remained loyal to Catholicism, most notably Erasmus, the "superstitious" extremes of saints' cults were held up to satire and ridicule. The response of the Counter Reformation church to humanist satire and Protestant contempt was to assume increasing control of cult formation and then to make it less accessible to popular and spontaneous religious enthusiasm.[51] Pope and bishops continued to foster cult where it seemed to serve hierarchical purposes, but they were much more careful in determining the spiritual zeal of candidates for canonization as well as that of their devotees. The decrees of Urban VIII in the early seventeenth century clarified papal requirements for canonization and gave the papacy absolute control in determining who was a saint. This was more than a process of bureaucratic centralization. It was also an important aspect of the church's drive against spontaneous and autonomous manifestations of lay piety, so often expressed in cultic veneration. The saints challenged the clerical hierarchy on several fronts. Their very heroism was a standing reproach to the human frailties of the clergy, whether of the priest sorely tempted by the flesh or of the bishop who lived in ostentatious splendor. The saints' display of supernatural power, so direct and efficacious, often overshadowed the more remote and mysterious priestly miracle of the Blessed Sacrament. Saints' cults could divide as well as unify the body of Christ. Relic mongering set monasteries and towns against each other, and religious orders competed in adding to the roster of their saintly champions. We have just seen how communes driving for autonomy used cults of local saints to enhance their standing as well as to focus civic patriotism. Some of the more powerful, like Venice, even had pretensions to religious authority independent of and equal to that of the papacy.[52]

The church thus had both theological and practical reasons for bringing the veneration of saints under strict papal control. Fewer were admitted to the roster of new saints, and those who were were likely to be champions of Rome—heroes martyred in the effort to bring England back to the Catholic fold, missionaries to the natives of the New World. The Counter Reformation church sought to renew and extend the universal mandate given to it by Christ and transmitted through the successors of Peter. Reestablishing the Church as a unified and universal structure required a reversal of the medieval trend toward fragmentation of loyalties, practices, and beliefs. Saints' cults were a key element; too often they had served as instruments of localism, but under careful papal guidance they could now serve as symbols of unification.

In the course of this papal takeover, however, there was a reduction in the number of new cults and a diminution of the role of sainthood as a feature of Catholic religiousness. One of the main voices of popular piety was henceforth to be muted if not silenced. Just as the perception of sanctity had never been uniform throughout Latin Christendom, so also did the decline of sainthood and cultic veneration, whether by Protestant attack or papal control, vary by region. Table 8 provides statistical data that point to this important set of relationships among sainthood, popular piety, and reformation.

In some Protestant areas people gave up their saints with alacrity, turning against shrines and images with violent resentment as though at last they could throw down a hateful barrier between themselves and God. In other places believers were much more reluctant to give up intercessors and resisted their elimination even while publicly accepting a theology and a church that denied the possibility of intercession.[53] No single factor can explain the later history of sainthood in each area of Latin Christendom. Past practice was important, but tradition was modified by new political configurations, economic factors, and religious impulses.

In northern Germany and in Scandinavia, where Lutheranism became a state-supported church, the elimination of cultic veneration was thorough and complete, partly because it was carried out by organized visitations backed by the power of the state. But even before officials stepped in, crowds incited by Lutheran and radical preachers had stormed into churches to vent their spleen upon saints' images and other symbols of the old faith. Here popular resentment was fueled by xenophobia—the old faith being represented as a foreign intrusion calculated to exploit the honest peasant or town worker. Even the saints were regarded as foreign agents of exploitation. In northern Germany and especially in Scandinavia, few local holy men and women had won recognition as saints from prelates who were too often seen as representatives of Rome rather than as local champions. The roster of German and Scandinavian saints had been largely completed by the end of the twelfth century (see table 6) and consisted of princely (39 percent in the Holy Roman Empire) and clerical power holders (54 percent) who had little in common with the later aspirations of lay piety. Even such an exceptional figure as Bridget of Sweden, the fourteenth-century prophet, became much more an object of veneration in her adopted Italy than in her native land. Scandinavians, unlike Magyars and Poles, never gave up their attachments to epic pre-Christian heroes in favor of saints canonized by medieval popes as part of the campaign of Christianization.

In the Low Countries, along the Rhine, in southern Germany, and in Switzerland, new saints' cults also declined after the twelfth century, although not so precipitously as in northern Germany and Scandinavia. But the cults of such saints—for the most part Dominican mystics, Beguines, and unworldly young princes—had a limited popular appeal, unlike the saints of Italy during this time, who were visible public figures closely involved with the life of the commune and the urban populace. (Note in table 8 the high scores of Low Country saints for activities such as demonic struggles and extended reclusion and the low scores for charity and miracle-working.) Searchers after individual perfection, Rhineland saints stood apart from the spiritual needs of ordinary lay people, as well as from ecclesiastical or secular politics. As cult objects they counted neither strongly against the old faith, as in Scandinavia, nor very strongly in its favor, as in Italy.[54] In the north cultic veneration was less central to popular piety than in Mediterranean lands, and the violent iconoclasm that the Reformation elicited may have expressed a long-standing cultural bias. North of the Alps the choice between Catholicism and Protestantism depended largely on the decisions of temporal power holders and the presence of charismatic Reformation preachers.

In England even more than in Germany the decision to break with Rome and establish a separate church was related to dynastic and national politics. Popular piety remained attached to the older faith, as did certain great noble houses and state officials. The Tudors had considerable difficulty in rooting out "popery," while Anglican theology hovered between Protestantism and Catholicism with a royal pope. It was easier to arouse the English people against nefarious Rome than to persuade them to give up their affection for the old liturgy, easier to incite action against monastic landholders than to do away with the saints. Ultimately, Mary and the apostles were placed in a doctrinal limbo, losing their roles as intercessors but not banished from reverence. Saints' cults were abolished, but such saints as Edward the Confessor and Thomas Becket continued to hold a place in the national memory of secular heroes. The new martyrs, from Thomas More and John Fisher to Edmund Campion and Robert Persons, were officially condemned for lese majesty and treason, but neither Anglicans nor Catholics have withheld their admiration from these heroes who embodied the English national ideals of moral courage and noble sense of duty.

The Europe that remained Catholic was as subject to variation as was the Europe that became Protestant. France is a case in point; regional differences, national politics, and Calvinist proselytizing all contributed to a century of conflict in which first one trend and than another came to the fore. As we have seen, saints' cults in France served two very different functions. On the one hand there were any number of cults closely connected with national pride and enhancement of the monarchy. There were also many cults of substantial local popularity but little national importance that expressed the changing needs of lay piety. Thus, on the eve of the Reformation in France, to a much greater degree than in Germany, cultic veneration contributed to the strength of the old faith. By itself hagiology was never enough to determine the outcome of the battle between French

Table 8
Statistical Profiles by Geographic Region
(percentages)

	Eastern Europe (N = 27)	Scandinavia (N = 14)	Holy Roman Empire (N = 95)	Low Countries (N = 33)	France (N = 125)	Italy (N = 323)	Iberia (N = 86)	British Isles (N = 149)
Order								
Benedictine	4	7	36	27	17	12	9	15
Cloistered	7	0	2	0	2	13	6	0
Cistercian	0	0	12	24	14	1	7	5
Augustinian	4	21	5	0	13	4	6	3
Dominican	19	0	5	3	2	14	10	0
Franciscan	11	0	4	3	6	22	16	1
Jesuit	11	0	1	9	4	1	8	11
Other orders	4	14	14	15	24	21	24	7
Type of canonization								
Papal	15	36	21	3	16	11	13	9
Local	15	14	26	18	14	13	12	13
Congregation of Rites	19	0	3	9	11	12	30	2
Beatified only	32	14	15	18	28	46	29	63
Popular	19	36	35	52	31	18	16	13
Extent of cult								
National and international	44	72	24	15	13	10	28	12
Patrons	15	7	17	9	18	21	24	7
In an order	30	0	31	36	42	44	33	9
Local	11	21	28	40	27	25	15	72
Gender								
Male	93	72	77	79	80	80	84	93
Female	7	28	23	21	20	20	16	7
Class								
Royalty	15	14	12	0	6	1	6	6
Titled nobles	11	14	27	9	16	12	12	7

Lesser nobles	22	7	15	31	25	19	27	5
"Good family"	11	23	5	3	8	6	7	29
Urban patrician	11	7	6	18	13	21	8	8
Other burghers	4	0	1	3	1	3	3	1
Urban poor	4	0	3	3	1	4	7	0
Peasantry	7	14	3	3	5	7	10	0
Probably well-off	7	14	13	9	14	6	7	28
Probably urban	4	0	5	3	3	10	3	1
Probably poor	4	7	8	12	6	8	7	10
Unknown	0	0	2	6	2	3	3	5
Supernatural power								
Mystic contemplation	22	14	20	18	19	29	35	3
Visionary experiences	11	14	14	9	10	20	19	3
Struggles with demons	33	21	17	36	24	26	23	5
Famous prophecies	4	7	6	9	6	13	17	3
Miracle-working	26	14	19	12	28	33	40	7
Supernatural signs	19	14	17	18	20	24	29	3
Intercessions	67	72	57	45	58	59	70	22
Wonder-working relics	22	14	29	36	31	32	31	27
Charitable activity								
Comforting the sick	19	7	24	18	29	31	30	7
Aiding the poor	15	29	25	9	24	29	30	9
Aiding widows, orphans, prisoners, etc.	41	29	17	21	20	20	30	15
Asceticism								
Struggle to preserve chastity	22	21	9	24	21	20	20	13
Extended reclusion	11	0	12	24	14	18	12	6
Flagellation	22	7	14	0	8	15	14	1
Extreme austerities	48	14	38	33	40	45	44	13
Fortitude in illness	7	0	6	6	5	7	6	2
Extreme humility	26	36	23	33	27	34	38	5
Extreme poverty	11	14	18	21	18	28	27	4
Killed performing duties or austerities	15	7	9	9	14	10	21	5

Temporal power

Model ruler	4	29	14	3	11	8	7	7
Peacemaker	7	14	7	12	7	13	6	4
Temporal reformer	7	21	21	18	30	19	24	11
Active in church affairs	30	36	54	48	59	47	47	15
Active in state affairs	22	14	38	24	31	26	33	14

Evangelical activity

Moral teacher	7	0	8	9	9	12	10	3
Spiritual confessor	0	0	6	9	10	9	20	5
Extended pilgrimages	11	21	11	9	14	7	8	4
Great preacher	44	0	13	9	26	28	30	11
Dedicated to apostolate	41	21	15	6	20	19	31	50
Church reformer	11	29	5	3	12	11	6	3
Founder of an order	0	0	2	0	13	8	9	1
Important religious writings	7	0	13	6	8	11	13	5
Supported monasticism	0	0	15	15	15	6	6	6
supported scholarship	7	7	8	6	7	7	8	7
Supported worship of Jesus	30	14	16	12	18	23	16	9
Supported veneration of Mary	15	7	12	12	13	14	21	3
Supported veneration of saints	11	14	7	21	6	7	10	4
Supported other practices of worship	15	14	12	6	14	9	10	5

Protestant and Catholic, but it was not an insignificant element. Whereas in Germany Catholicism meant the church and the hierarchy and little else, in France, as in England, Catholicism was no less hierarchical but offered more ways believers could combine their religious with their social lives. The percentages in table 8 show that, despite the relatively lesser prominence of mendicancy among French saints than among those of Italy and Iberia, French saints were active in charity and in the kinds of public religious expressions usually associated with the mendicant movement. Much in Catholic belief and practice was vulnerable to Huguenot criticism, but France's religious identity was Catholic, forged by saintly heroes, both royal and peasant, who over centuries had come to symbolize the fusion of religion and nation.

Iberia brings us to the land of the Mediterranean wonder-worker and the military champion of the truth faith. In Spain and Portugal the crown, firmly in control of the church, made certain that the old faith would remain unchallenged. Iberian kings were ready to use the Inquisition not only to root out heresy but to turn against Moriscos and Jews, thereby diverting a religious question into racial and ethnic channels. By insisting upon purity of blood, Portuguese and Spanish rulers not only satisfied the people's ethnic chauvinism but also held a deadly weapon over the heads of the nobility, so many of whom had Jewish ancestry.

Mystics, Illuminati, Erasmians, and Valdesians might have made some inroads into the religious culture of Hispanic elites, but they could never shake the devotion of the faithful to their miracle-working saints. Again, figures in table 8 for various aspects of supernatural power suggest the special quality of Iberian piety. Nor could they shake the loyalties of hidalgos, with their proud tradition of fighting for the nation of Santiago. In Iberia as perhaps nowhere else in Europe, after centuries of the domestic crusade known as Reconquest, the cause of Catholicism and of civilization had become one. Not only was Hispanic Christianity immune to Protestant alternatives, but it became a central resource for the renewal of Catholicism and its counterattack against the north. Teresa of Avila and John of the Cross combined mystical contemplation with militant reform and contributed mightily to making Catholicism a revitalized intellectual and political force in Europe and throughout the world.

Nonetheless, there may never have been much likelihood that the Iberian empire would opt for Teresa over Santiago. From the mid-sixteenth to the mid-seventeenth century Spanish troops, the famous tercios, spearheaded the Catholic effort to drive back Protestantism in Germany, the Low Countries, even in France, while the conquistadores, followed all too closely by the clergy, won Latin America for Spain and the cross. In forming the Company of Jesus, Loyola had drawn upon his aristocratic and military background, and the Jesuit combination of Spanish militarism and religious

zeal explains the extraordinary success of the order in establishing its in-
fluence in virtually every aspect of European and Latin American culture.
The soldiers and saints of Iberia put Catholicism on the offensive in the
Old World and the New. They also made Hispanic Catholicism the well-
spring of Counter Reformation piety.[55] New World saints reflected the pre-
dominant values of Hispanic religiousness. The vitae of Rose of Lima,
Martin of Porres, Pedro Claver, and Maria Anna de Jesus de Paredes y
Flores ("the Lily of Quito") recalled the supernatural elements of Mediterranean wonder-workers, visionaries, and penitents as these had been
elaborated in the hagiography and cultic activity of the thirteenth and
fourteenth centuries. In some cases New World saints patterned themselves
explicitly after their European models, but even where the kinship appears
to be more general it is unmistakable.

In eastern Europe the survival of Catholicism was heavily indebted to
religious nationalism. Hungarians and Poles venerated the saintly kings
who had led them to Catholicism and thereby contributed a major component in their national identities. Protestantism made some headway in
the sixteenth century, but it carried the stigma of foreign, and particularly
of German, interference.[56] As in the New World, new cults arose around
religious heroes whose lives formed a bridge between the Counter Reformation, especially in its Jesuit form, and traditional medieval piety. Stanislas Kostka, for example, became a national cult figure after his death at
the age of eighteen in 1568. The story of his life revolves around his
eagerness to receive the Blessed Sacrament, which apparently was denied
him on account of his illness. Through the miraculous intervention of Saint
Barbara he was able to take communion, and he was cured completely
when the Madonna brought him the Christ child to hold. After this she
ordered him to join the Society of Jesus. Because his father and brother
opposed this course, he ran away and was admitted to the order by Peter
Canisius; even then he had to flee to Rome to avoid his still-unreconciled
father. After nine months of life in religion the Blessed Virgin decided to
"pick this flower of paradise"; he became ill and died. Beatified within half
a century of his death, Stanislas shares with the chaste Casimir the honor
of being a patron saint of Poland. In eastern Europe Catholic piety showed
less interest in the Counter Reformation themes of individual conscience
and revitalized contemplative experience than in older preoccupations with
boyish innocence and celestial signs of divine intervention. In the face of
Protestant incursions, a reaffirmation by the church of the sacraments and
of the religion of miracle and otherworldly purity strengthened the Poles'
ties to a simpler national heritage.

In Italy the presence of the papacy ensured the continuing dominance
of Catholicism. But in the 1540s this by no means seemed a foregone

conclusion. Lutheranism and various forms of evangelical radicalism appeared to be making inroads. The theology of justification by faith alone won support in Catholic humanist circles, and the need to reform the church in head and members was seen as urgent. The mercantile and silk-producing city of Lucca was a hotbed of radical ideas, while heterodox literature rolled off Venetian presses.[57] High officials of monastic orders, like Bernardo Ochino, head of the Capuchins, and Peter Martyr Vermigli of the Augustinians, converted to the evangelical faith and went into exile. But the tide soon turned. The papacy shook off its lethargy, instituted reforms, convoked the Council of Trent, and recognized new orders. Bishops renewed their dedication to the dioceses, and newly established seminaries revitalized the training of priests.[58] As part of their self-appointed responsibility of policing Christendom, the Spaniards intervened directly in Italian politics to support such conservative Catholic princes as the Medici grand dukes.

The success of Catholicism in Italy was not merely a matter of papal politics and military incursions. In every commune of the north and every village of the south believers in the old faith clung to their saints, venerated holy relics with undiminished devotion, carried wonder-working images through the streets as before, and found satisfaction in a religion of miraculous intervention. The profusion of new cults in Italy in the preceding three centuries, unmatched in any other part of Christendom, ensured that developments in popular piety had found expression under the umbrella of the church of Rome. The communes and the mendicant orders had been the two major vehicles of innovation, and both these institutions had been extremely effective in gaining official recognition for their galleries of heroes.

However uncertain, even suspicious, the hierarchy may have been about the proliferation of popular cults, saints welded the loyalties of their devotees to the traditional church, helping Catholicism survive as a living religion. Made up of many peoples and traditions, embracing many lands and social conditions, Catholicism never was nor ever could be an unchanging or undifferentiated body of doctrine and practice. Believers would continue to find many ways to express their diverse impulses within the overarching unity of the single faith; if they could not, they would break away or be cast out. In fostering saints' cults the church tacitly recognized that Catholicism was no seamless web but a web with many seams.

7 ⊕ *Class*

The God of a religion that emphasized the free gift of divine grace, the equality of believers, and the dignity of each individual soul, the God of a religion founded among the poor and humble, might be expected to make no distinctions of class. Christian theology and popular piety agreed that on Judgment Day he would reward all according to their merits rather than to their worldly status or wealth. In paintings of Judgment Day rich and poor weigh equally in the scales of justice; their nakedness emphasizes Christ's indifference to their former worldly state.[1]

Equality and the irrelevance of worldly position in the matter of salvation is just one of the several conclusions that might be drawn from the gospel, however. Jesus' promise that in his father's kingdom the last would be first expresses a hope of social reversal that may be construed for this world or the next. In Christianity as in all religions with inversion myths, hope for the future may promote revolution or it may postpone social action by encouraging subordinate people to accept inequality in this world.[2] Augustine resolved the contradiction for orthodox Catholic thought by rejecting a revolutionary reading of the biblical apocalypse. For him the millennium was the Christian order founded by Christ and presided over by the church in the world. Jesus had never intended to subvert the social order but rather established his church to alleviate suffering and provide the means of salvation. There is no hope of social inversion in this world or even of significant progress before the end of time. City of God and earthly city were metaphors for the states of grace and sin, not alternatives of political order.[3]

194

It is hardly surprising that Augustine's position became the orthodox doctrine of the medieval church, for he emphasized the importance of spiritual over temporal reality and sustained the claims of a clerical hierarchy to unique and indispensable sacramental powers. At the same time, the medieval church enjoyed and supported the advantages of worldly wealth and distinction. As successors of Rome and as the self-styled heirs of Constantine's Donation, the popes were lords in this world as well as gatekeepers to the next, while at every level, from village priest to abbot and bishop, the clergy was enmeshed in the economic and social order. As landlords, rentiers, owners of serfs, wielders of temporal power, and ministers of kings, and as princes in their own right, the clergy could not, however, be fully content with Augustine's slighting of the temporal order as a mere interval between Christ's first and second comings.

Nor could they be comfortable with Augustine's deep pessimism and his association of all that was worldly with all that was sinful. Christian thinkers came to regard lordship more positively, as the surrogate of divine power, and worldly hierarchy as the mirror of God's order. In the medieval church's organic view of society, all believers were members of the mystical body of Christ; but the head of that corporate entity was more dignified than the belly, and it controlled the arms and feet. The simplest division of Christian society was tripartite—those who prayed, those who fought, those who labored. Because each part was indispensable to the others and contributed to the common work of salvation, labor was no less valuable than prayer and might. But if labor was noble, laborers were not; priests and knights were honorable; plowmen and herders were base. The holy state of poverty was similarly ambivalent. To be poor was to be like Christ, yet also to be despised.

Thus, while medieval clerical thinkers tended to use organic images in explaining social divisions, they could scarcely avoid hierarchical ordering. Master was better than serf, prayer better than labor, rich better than poor. Power was dangerous to the spirit but somehow it was close to God, and, if poverty was a holy estate, the poor were no more respectable for it. Moreover, changes in medieval economic and social arrangements weakened the force of the prevailing organic image. Juridical definitions of status and estate may have hardened in the later Middle Ages precisely to defend the privileges of birth against an increasingly complex economic order. A place in the social hierarchy had to be found for merchants, bankers, judges, professors, urban workers, and farm laborers who were no longer simply burghers, slaves, or serfs. Some theorists were content with a catch-all "middle" category, while others made elaborate listings of occupational differences. During most of the period we are studying three distinct modes of social ordering coexisted: a tripartite organic distinction of prayers, fight-ers, and workers; a juridical estate grouping of clergy, nobility, burgher, and peasant; a wealth ordering descending from rich to poor.[4]

The intricate history and interaction of these different modes of analysis, with all their variants over time and place, obviously complicates our effort to examine the importance of class in the historical sociology of sainthood. We have chosen to employ a schema based on family status and occupation, one that we find to be fairly workable given our span of seven centuries and our scope that includes all of Western Christendom. While no classi-fication scheme for medieval society can be entirely free of ambiguity, ours (which the reader may consider more fully in the section at the end of this chapter, p. 218) is adequate to demonstrate two significant points: one, that social origins helped determine who achieved reputation as a saint; two, that once such a determination was made social origins had—with a pair of exceptions—little to do with how the faithful perceived their saints. We begin with a tabulation, shown in table 9, of the distribution of saints by class origin according to century.

At all times many more saints originated in the upper than in the lower classes. Over 40 percent of the total number of saints in our sample came from noble or "good family" backgrounds. Whatever the imprecision of designating nobility, it is clear that these saints were from the landed elite, not peasants. If we add those classified as urban patrician, royalty, and probably well-off to the nobility and those of good family, the ratio mounts to roughly three to one in favor of upper-class groups. Naturally this ratio should be treated as an order of magnitude rather than as an absolute count.

Why so many saints from the upper classes? An obvious answer is that the church, especially in the Middle Ages, was an elite institution that protected its class interest and rewarded its own. Most high prelates came from the upper classes, and in the eleventh and twelfth centuries bishops, archbishops, and abbots figure prominently in the ranks of saints.[5] Clearly their cults were based upon clerical perceptions of holiness, so that the whole process was self-serving. Moreover, the saintly bishop who staunchly defended the church's rights in an era of great struggle against temporal control was defending the interest of a class as well as of a spiritual institution. At the same time, however, many such great prelates were also popular heroes—conscientious pastors, defenders of the poor closely iden-tified with the economic and social interests of their communities. The faithful were less interested in the class origin of such figures than in their effectiveness during their lifetimes and their intercession after death.

Just as most bishops came from the upper classes, so did most abbots and abbesses. This reflects both the predominance of the aristocracy in the

Table 9
Family Status over Time
(percentage in each category)

Family Status	11th	12th	13th	14th	15th	16th	17th
				Century of Saint's Death			
Royalty (N = 42)	10.2	3.9	8.8	3.7	2.4	2.6	0.0
Titled nobles (N = 113)	17.2	12.4	13.2	11.2	14.5	13.8	9.3
Untitled nobles (N = 156)	21.9	28.8	18.2	17.8	16.9	6.9	11.9
Good family (N = 89)	4.7	5.9	5.0	8.4	7.2	21.6	22.0
Urban patrician (N = 120)	3.9	14.4	17.0	20.6	13.3	13.8	14.4
Other burghers (N = 21)	0.0	.7	3.8	.9	2.4	4.3	5.1
Urban poor (N = 25)	3.9	1.3	1.3	2.8	4.8	4.3	3.4
Peasantry (N = 47)	2.3	3.9	3.8	4.7	13.3	6.9	6.8
Probably well-off (N = 106)	18.8	12.4	9.4	6.5	7.2	17.2	12.7
Probably poor (N = 67)	8.6	9.2	8.8	7.5	4.8	2.6	11.0
Probabably urban (N = 49)	5.5	3.9	8.8	12.1	8.4	0.0	1.7
Unknown (N = 29)	3.1	3.3	1.9	3.7	4.8	6.0	1.7
Number of cases by century	128	153	159	107	83	116	118

$p \leq .0001$
Contingency coefficient = .42

Benedictine order, the principal monastic order down to the thirteenth century, and the great power that feudal classes exercised in clerical elections during the same period. The Rule devised by Benedict of Norcia in the year 529 gave monks the right to elect their abbots.[6] Of the seventy-nine abbots and abbesses in our sample, fully fifty-eight were of aristocratic origin, whereas of thirty-three monks and nuns aristocrats numbered nineteen. In short, there was an abundance of aristocrats in the rank and file of the houses governed by the Benedictine rule, but an even greater imbalance among its abbots and abbesses.

The mendicant orders, which arose in the thirteenth century, made a strong recruiting appeal to people of humbler origins, particularly in the towns. But of seventy Dominican saints in our sample fifty-one were from the upper classes, a ratio that almost exactly mirrors the sample as a whole and is little different from the proportion of Benedictine monks and nuns who were well-to-do. Servite saints too were for the most part from elite families (15 of 18). Only among Franciscans (60 of 104) and Carmelites (11 of 20) did the preponderance of the highborn diminish in a significant way, but considering the egalitarian leanings of these two orders the decline is not very impressive. When we look at Dominican priors and prioresses we find that twelve of thirteen were upper class; the corresponding figures for Franciscans are ten of fourteen. Thus, even with the decline of lay investiture and the rise of religious orders that consciously appealed to all classes, high position remained associated with high social status, at least among those holy men and women of the orders who came to be venerated.

Neither the social fluidity of high medieval and Renaissance town life nor the coming of the friars fundamentally altered the disposition of clergy and laity alike to ignore apostolic egalitarianism in favor of social hierarchy. The prejudice in favor of rich over poor and aristocrat over peasant continued even during a time when commercialization was transforming the nature of economic activity and altering the composition of both elite and subaltern classes. Among the ranks of saints, counts and bishops were joined by merchants, and serfs by cobblers, but the well-to-do continued to dominate all others to a degree essentially unchanged.

In the fifteenth century as in the eleventh, among Dominicans as among Benedictines, and even among Franciscans, the saintly aristocracy was drawn predominantly from the aristocracy of society. Since the orders played the greatest single role of any group in promoting saints' cults, their social biases go a long way to explain why so many saints were of elite origins. The imbalance of upper-class religious leadership, among saints as among others, was due not only to social preference for aristocrats but also to such practical reasons as the need for educated clerics. The mission of Dominic's Order of Preachers was to promote correct doctrine against the errors of heretics and infidels, and from the outset the Dominicans' program gave an important place to higher education. The order founded its own schools of higher learning and made use of the existing universities. Francis's call to a holy life of apostolic simplicity and poverty had some of the egalitarian and anti-intellectual overtones so often associated with such appeals, but scarcely was Francis in his grave before his order took on assignments that sent its friars into the universities, where they soon began to distinguish themselves as theologians and canonists.[7] Franciscans as well as Dominicans and Benedictines became bishops, popes, professors, inquisitors, ecclesiastical statesmen, and counselors to princes and kings. In short, mendicancy as well as Benedictine monasticism and the secular priesthood provided opportunities for prestigious careers, and such opportunities were bound to attract affluent youths who had some schooling. The development of so-called third order, or auxiliary, components made it possible for Dominicans and Franciscans to recruit the poor and uneducated who did not aspire to priestly ordination or to higher education;

but leadership in the orders and professional careers generally went to those who had the advantage of good birth and good education.

Among lay saints as well as priests and monks a similar class advantage prevailed. Of 206 lay saints in our sample, 158 were of the upper classes. Of these, twenty-five were royal. The special characteristics and charismatic qualities that induced people to regard kings and queens as holy we have already discussed. High titled nobles shared some of these same qualities, though to a lesser degree. Power commanded respect, attention, and awe. But we think there are still more profound factors that explain why the faithful tended to venerate their social betters. The spectacle of reversal, of sacrifice, of inversion of worldly status was crucial to the perception of sanctity. Inherited poverty was commonplace; voluntary poverty was sanctifying. Chastity was a greater virtue for nobles, who were expected to behave licentiously, than for commoners, who were not. Humility and abstemiousness meant so much more when practiced by members of an aristocracy known for its haughtiness and gluttony. Giovanni Colombini's dedication to charity and poverty was all the more awe-inspiring because it was an inversion of the ways of his urban patrician class, just as it was for his model, Francis. For a farm laborer or a town worker to take a vow of poverty or of humility was little more than to affirm an existing condition. But the whole point of conversion to holiness was rejection of the world and its values, overturning one way of life in favor of its opposite, shedding the "old man" and putting on the new. The very material circumstances of the upper classes gave them the means to demonstrate to the world the fervor of their conversions.

The surrender of material goods and worldly status in the name of a newly assumed spirituality was the outer, visible symbol of an inner, invisible event. Hagiographers and other believers who observed the conversion to sanctity tended to see it as a dramatic and sudden reversal. Autobiographical accounts suggest that saints themselves saw their call to holiness in this way. Even when conversion was more drawn out, as in the case of Teresa of Avila, she and her observers regarded her spiritual quest as a series of sharp reversals of her initial intention. The treatment of religious renewal as a sudden event rather than a process of growth suggests that the medieval idea of adult personality was as a fixed quantity that might be modified only by some powerful outside force such as a demonic attack, a celestial vision, or the death of a loved one. In the medieval perception, states of being were much more "real" than stages of becoming, since the structure of reality was static, not dynamic. The world consisted of absolute qualities, not relative quantities.[8]

Time too was qualitative, not a linear transition from "then" through "now" to "someday," but a pendular or cyclical alternation between good times and bad, times of work and of play, or, in Le Roy Ladurie's phrase, times of feast and times of famine.[9]

Augustine's rejection of the idea of spiritual progress in history and his belief that sin confounded moral growth were in accord with the medieval sense that time was organized into distinct epochs, a perception that derived from the Genesis account of the world's creation. In a universe of established qualities and ordained states, a change of direction such as a spiritual conversion was perceived as sudden, dramatic, and divinely inspired. In the drama of sudden reversal and spectacular moral alteration, conversions of the poor and humble could not match those of the highborn. The poor did not have much to lose and, perhaps for this reason, seemed to have less to win.

It is at least possible that both the hagiographer's tendency to ennoble his heroes and the preponderance of stories of aristocratic saints reflected something more tangible than social and metaphysical bias—that members of the upper classes were in fact more likely to pursue holiness than were the poor. Some modern social historians have argued that class-related family differences led to different types of personality and different styles of behavior among their young.[10] The enormous chasm between the material circumstances of aristocrats and peasants is not at issue; the question is how and to what degree material circumstances and social position fostered different child-rearing practices, family relations, and personalities.

A case for a psychosocial explanation of aristocratic religiousness might go as follows. Highborn infants had wet nurses, poor children did not. Poor children grew up in more crowded proximity with their parents and siblings than did the children of the rich, while the practice of sending noble boys off to receive their educations in other noble households and then away to school was common in medieval times. The children of aristocrats learned to command, those of peasants to obey. Upper-class children were confronted with role models, both religious and secular, that emphasized high moral and social purpose, achievement, and dedication. The poor had few expectations beyond following in the weary footsteps of their fathers and mothers. It also has been argued that in the late Middle Ages both aristocratic and merchant fathers frequently were absent from home, the first because they were away fighting, the second because they traveled extensively on business.[11] These and other aspects of child-rearing suggest a coherent set of psychosocial circumstances that may have inspired religious enthusiasm among medieval aristocratic and upper-class children more than among children of the poor. Abandoned by their mothers, then by their wet nurses, then by their fathers, upperclass adolescents may have sought refuge in God. Brought up to command and to marshal all their resources to achieve high goals, they may have been better equipped emotionally to withstand their parents' opposition. Having been taught that no horizon was too far, no lofty task too arduous, they may not have thought it presumptuous to aspire to spiritual perfection. Denied nothing but love as children, they may have been more prepared to deny everything for the love of God.

However plausible this chain of psychosocial reasoning, the evidence does not suggest significant differences in the family relations of saints from the upper and lower classes. Adolescents battled their families to about the same degree in one group as in the other and won them over about as frequently. True, stories of family conflict among the poor were more likely to be violent and even brutal, but there is little evidence to show that the issues or the outcomes were very different from those of socially superior families. Given the paucity of evidence for supporting a psychosocial explanation of class differences among saints, we conclude that the three-to-one preponderance of aristocratic and upper-class saints over those from middling and poor origins is to be explained by a series of more concrete factors, including the institutional bias of the medieval church, the material advantages of the upper classes, the prominence of the religious orders in promoting cultic veneration, the denial of literacy to the poor, and the greater opportunities of the upper classes to make dramatic gestures of world renunciation. In addition to these reasons, we suggest that two modes of cultural perception were also instrumental: the medieval tendency to understand changes of behavior in terms of sudden inspiration and dramatic reversal rather than of internal process of growth, and the medieval disposition to equate social and moral nobility, an equation internalized by all classes.

These factors, of course, were not unvarying in either their application or their effect. To see just how they did apply, we refer again to the tabulation of the class origins of saints by century (table 9). The eleventh and thirteenth centuries stand out as times when a disproportionate number of saints came from royal houses. But these two peak times represent strikingly different conditions. Most eleventh-century royal saints were male rulers who came from the border areas of Latin Christendom, achieving renown for instituting or spreading the faith among their peoples or defending it against unbelievers. To this group belong Vladimir of Kiev, already noted for his inordinate sexual appetite and his brutality, Stephen of Hungary, the Russian Boris, and others. Faced with the problem of converting entire populations, the church found it expedient to work through heathen princes who thus became cult heroes shortly after they became Christians.

In the thirteenth century, by contrast, a disproportionate number of royal saints were female and came from areas where Catholicism had been established for centuries. These were queens and princesses whose reputation for saintliness consisted of their rejection of worldly power and vanity in favor of extreme austerity and contemplation. The males among them, such royal saints as Louis IX of France and Louis of Anjou, typify the infusion of the Christian ideals of faith and justice into the military and chivalric virtues. By the thirteenth century the church, which had long since declared its emancipation from temporal control, tended to bestow its highest honors not on power holders but on those who turned from the world or who sought to combine their worldly duties with the values of Christ and the apostles. Kings and queens were still in the limelight, but their sanctity now depended upon their spiritual rather than their political virtues. (See fig. 28.)

The trend away from sainthood as a confirmation of power exercised on behalf of the church and toward sainthood as an expression of unworldly virtues was true of saints of all classes. Nobility, both titled and untitled, declined from about 40 percent in the eleventh and twelfth centuries to about 30 percent in the thirteenth through fifteenth centuries. Urban artisans and shopkeepers were particularly prominent in the thirteenth century, peasants in the fifteenth. Social elites continued to dominate, but there was increasing room for the middle and lower classes. We have discussed at some length the growth of lay piety and the ways Christians began to assume more responsibility for their religious practices and beliefs. The shift away from saints of elite backgrounds toward those of humbler status is one reflection of this main trend. It was not that the faithful suddenly began to seek out peasants and urban workers as religious heroes. Rather, the perception of sanctity came to emphasize an integration of supernatural power, asceticism, and charity. Belief in the royal healing power and in the wonder-working bishop's staff did not disappear, but more and more the faithful were inclined to look to the holy penitent or the world-shunning contemplative for miracles. Moreover, beginning in the thirteenth century, not only were saints more often of middle- and lower-class origin, but even those from the elite strata now came to be venerated for activities that had little to do with their social origins.

One of the most direct ways to examine the perception of sanctity is to look at the numbers of saints who were high prelates and of those who were rank-and-file clergy or lay people. The figures in table 10 provide such a breakdown and help us compare saints from the ecclesiastical hierarchy with the social ordering shown in table 9. The decline in representation of the prelacy is obvious in all sectors of ecclesiastical leadership except that of popes and cardinals, who constituted a small and rather unvarying proportion. Between the twelfth and the thirteenth centuries the drop in the number of saintly archbishops, bishops, and heads of monastic houses is unmistakable, and the trend continued through the seventeenth century. Clearly mendicancy and lay piety reinforced each

Fig. 28. Scenes from the life of Elizabeth of Hungary. Note especially, *upper left:* Elizabeth presenting her crown to the crucifix; *upper right·* at table with her husband, Louis IV, landgrave of Thuringia, Elizabeth refuses food; *lower left:* Elizabeth kneels beside her bed and receives the discipline from her maidservant. Naples, Church of St. Maria Donna Regina. Fresco in the style of Cavallini. Photograph from Alinari/Editorial Photocolor Archives.

other in establishing the ascendancy of a new range of spiritual values as well as in breaking the monopoly of the prelacy in at least this aspect of religious leadership.

The sixteenth and seventeenth centuries—the period of the Reformation, Counter Reformation, and the spread of Christianity to Asia and the New World—was the time of the martyr saint. Percentages like those shown in table 9 and absolute figures like those given in table 10 for lesser clerics and lay people largely reflect the high incidence of martyrdom among the saints of this era. Lesser clerics, predominantly secular priests and Jesuits, were church heroes in the struggle against English Protestantism. Often the family origins of these martyred priests and lay recusants were passed over in silence or described in such vague terms as "of good family." Percentages for other classes did not change very drastically. There were fewer members of royalty, continuing the steady decline that had begun in the fourteenth century, but the paucity of those described as noble, with or without title, was counterbalanced by increases in the categories "good family" and "probably upper." While the number of saints from the titled nobility may have declined, a broader definition of social elites such as those used by Robert Anderson and Peter Laslett would lead us to conclude that in sainthood the aristocracy held its own through the end of the seventeenth century. The proportion of saints of peasant origin fell off to about 7 percent in the sixteenth and seventeenth centuries; but this appears as a decrease only when measured against the unusually high level of peasants for the fifteenth century.

All in all, there was only one great shift in the class configuration of saints, and it came in the thirteenth century. None of the great developments on the threshold of the modern age, neither the Catholic Reformation

Table 10
Prelates, Lesser Clerics, and Lay People over Time
(numbers in each category)

Category	Century of Saint's Death						
	11th	12th	13th	14th	15th	16th	17th
Popes and cardinals	4	3	4	2	3	4	2
Bishops and archbishops	31	42	28	8	7	1	4
Abbots, abbesses, priors, prioresses	34	49	26	14	20	12	5
Lesser clerics	19	18	35	32	18	53	55
Tertiaries	5	0	8	15	5	9	7
Lay people	35	41	58	36	30	37	45
Total	128	153	159	107	83	116	118

nor the overseas apostolate, for example, changed the social dimensions of sainthood to a significant degree. Whatever may have been the social trends of the early modern period, their impact upon Catholic piety was blunted by the church's rededication to its sacramental and pastoral functions, which inevitably underscored the *magisterium* of the clerical hierarchy. The Catholic Reformation and Counter Reformation were not movements that involved widespread popular participation. Indeed, lay and popular piety, suspected of having contributed to the agony of Protestant schism and heresy, were brought under strict clerical supervision and direction. Once more the initiative for religious innovation passed to the clergy. With the Counter Reformation's stress on doctrinal clarity and refutation of heresy, there was a new emphasis on literary and theological education. All these developments favored a resurgence of elites in the ranks of the saints, as in church leadership.

Thus far we have treated class origin as a factor that may have determined who became a saint. Shifting the perspective, let us now ask a somewhat different but closely related question: Was class origin significant in people's perception of the saintly life after conversion? Was there an aristocratic or a peasant *type* of saint? The answer depends upon the particular class from which the saint came. The fact of royalty powerfully shaped the believers' image of a saint. At the opposite end of the social scale, so did the fact (or the myth) of peasant birth. It is difficult to think of Joan of Arc without identifying her as "the peasant maid" (although she was not a peasant), just as the veneration of Louis IX was based on the image of the saintly king. On the other hand, while the story of Francis's rejection of his father's wealth is extremely important in understanding his conversion, his urban elite status is scarcely relevant to his holy reputation, and we doubt that most of the faithful cared one way or the other about the class origin of Teresa of Avila.

Except at the two extremes of the social scale, kings and peasants, whose class was usually germane to the perception of their holy lives, saints, especially if they had taken monastic or clerical vows, tended to be seen as classless—which is to say that the perception of their saintly activities did not give prominence to whether they bore a title or came from a good family. Hagiographers, unlike ordinary believers, paid more attention to class, apparently because they felt it necessary to connect the beginnings of sainthood with the social (and in the medieval view, therefore moral) influences of the saint's family.[12] Historians may display a somewhat similar bias when they try to link every activity of the saint to his or her class origins. But by doing so we risk misrepresenting the significance of class, treating it as a persistent part of the saint's identity when in fact it seldom counted for much in the popular image of the holy life.

The relation between class and culture is a central issue in social history and in anthropology, for European as for other societies. Some scholars believe that there is a distinct culture of the poor, while others suggest a rural culture or, more explicitly, a peasant culture. Still others deny the utility of the urban-rural distinction or the division of culture by classes preferring, for example, to speak of an "Italian culture" or a "Yiddish culture." The American reader knows the complexity of this question because of the extensive discussion of "black culture," a culture that was once rural, is now urban, always has been poor, and is both ethnic and racial. The question is central in our study because sainthood was central to medieval religion and religion was central to European culture. To the extent that class was a relevant factor in saintly activity and its perception in cult, it follows that Christianity was in some measure not one culture but several.[13]

One way to approach this problem is to look at the five aspects of saintly reputation we set forth in tables 1–5 and more fully in our analysis of "who was a saint?" and to use some fairly simple statistical measures designed to show whether, for example, royal saints were more ascetic than peasants, or nobles more inclined to charity than burghers. Supernatural power was for the faithful the primary attribute of sanctity, and it is in this area of holy work that we find the sharpest divisions of class. We have constructed an index (for details see the appendix on method) that measures how central were miracle-working, prophecy, visionary experience, mystical union, exorcism, and celestial signs in the perception of the saint's life. Employing the same class divisions we discussed earlier, but concentrating on saints whose family origins were stated clearly in the texts, we have obtained the following index scores for the prominence of supernatural activity:

Upper Class		Lower Class	
Royalty	61	Urban artisans and workers	91
Titled nobles	67	Peasants and rural workers	100
Untitled nobles	66		
Good family/gentry	42		
Urban patrician	66		

The index number of 100 for peasants and rural laborers indicates that among saints of this class supernatural power occurred more prominently than for any other class. Thus peasants became the standard against which we indexed the other classes. The score of forty-two for the good family category, for example, indicates that among saints of this group supernatural power was 42 percent as prominent as among peasant saints. Obviously these numbers by themselves explain nothing; but they suggest what it is that we have to explain.

Saints emerged from a social context that they seldom abandoned entirely. Moreover, they were protectors of diverse kinds of communities—geographical, political, and occupational. The occupational communities most frequently mentioned were those connected with a specific craft or activity; thus we have Omobono the patron of tailors, Raymond Nonnatus the protector of midwives, Albert the Great the patron of students, and so forth. But to be a peasant, whether serf or free, was more than to engage in an occupation. *Agricolus, contadino, villein, Bauer* specified a social condition, widely recognized and sometimes legally defined.[14] In a word, peasantry was a class. While this class had no specific patron, peasant saints were significantly different from saints of the upper classes.

Whether peasant culture was part of a more embracing "culture of the poor" is a question we will address shortly; for the moment we wish to examine perceptions of sanctity as they relate to the peasantry. The most important characteristic was supernatural activity, which was far more central to the stories of peasant saints than to others. One explanation might be that peasants had a distinct culture and formed a correspondingly distinct religious community; but there is no statistically significant correlation between the class origin of a saint and the class of the faithful who participated in the saint's cult. Here the example of the "peasant" maid Joan of Arc is not the exception but the rule. Even in less prominent cases, canonization documents make it clear that the formation of a cult brought together people of distinct classes. The local noble joined his peasants on his knees at the tomb of the saint and secured the help of the bishop in documenting the wonders performed by someone who in life may have been his bondsman.

Another assumption, that the transmission of culture is largely one-directional, downward from elites to have-nots and from town to countryside, is also contradicted by patterns of cult formation, where often the order was the reverse. Religious practices and beliefs begun among humble folk and embodied in lowly wonder-workers found their way to the manor house and the cathedral. This movement of religious impulses from peasantry to nobility was a significant channel of cultural transmission, because everywhere peasant saints were venerated and everywhere the cultic practices of humble people had to be reckoned with by kings and prelates alike.[15]

Furthermore, the question whether religious impulses moved on a vertical axis is based on a model of culture as an exact reflection of social organization. Such a model implies that culture has no historical autonomy; it becomes a mere adjunct of the social order, a limitation particularly inappropriate for the study of piety. Medieval society was, to be sure, hierarchical; the church, the court, and the marketplace all maintained class barriers. Hierarchy was buttressed by a religious ideology that stressed divine lordship as the pattern of the universe and by a metaphysic that subordinated the visible world to the higher degrees of intellectual and spiritual being. Obviously medieval religious culture was related to social organization and shared many of its hierarchical features. A tiny clerical elite had an inordinate influence upon doctrine, liturgy, morals, and art.

Still, the relics of the martyrs and saints beneath every altar were eloquent testimony to the power of popular religious needs. Whether or not it originated as a concession of a monotheistic church to polytheistic beliefs from outside Christianity, the cult of saints became virtually the fiber of which piety was woven by priests, monks, and the faithful of every class and condition.[16] The gathering of the faithful at the shrine of a favored saint attenuated class barriers. The lord may have taken a special place at the head of the ranks of the venerators, and perhaps he knelt on a silken cushion, but he was a humble suppliant like the rest. The peasant saint not only transcended class barriers but turned them upside down. The noble who joined the serfs in supplication before a saint who in life had toiled in the fields acknowledged that in the community of Christians riches and titles counted for nothing.[17]

If the veneration of saints subverted, or at least inverted, social distinctions, this does not mean that class had nothing to do with perceptions of sainthood. Supernatural power dominated the life stories of peasant saints just as magic, miracle, and sorcery pervaded the everyday lives of rural people. Particularly subject to the vicissitudes of nature, as to the arbitrary will of their overlords, peasants accurately guaged the impossibility of improving their lives in any significant degree. Only supernatural intervention explained why one child died and another survived, why crops flourished one year and withered the next two or three. Receptive to miracle and magic, peasants sought wonder-workers. For them a saint who could not answer their prayers was no saint at all, while, conversely, a beneficent wonder-worker was an immediate object of awe and veneration. For peasants the holy and the miraculous were interchangeable.

Not the peasants' rusticity but their powerlessness explains their resort to the supernatural. In all places and among persons of every class, magic and miracle are the special province of the helpless; even a noble resorted to the supernatural to cure a lame child or to protect himself in battle. But occasions of helplessness were far more frequent for the peasant than the lord and for the town laborer than the merchant. The humble carter or woolen worker, as unsure of his daily bread as the poor cottager, and perhaps even more terrified about the onslaught of illness, was a ready client of the supernatural and almost as likely as his rural cousin to identify saintliness with miracle-working. Among the cults of saints of the urban middle and lower classes, supernatural power was almost as central as in the cults of peasant saints and much more so than for saints from the wealthy classes.

Town workers shared with peasants not only poverty and powerlessness but also a common origin. Medieval towns were populated and constantly replenished by immigrants from the countryside as well as by migrant workers and vagabonds who divided their time between town and country.[18] The poor of medieval Europe, whether they lived in rural hamlets or walled towns, shared a culture in which supernatural forces controlled every aspect of life. Physical well-being, the struggle against hunger, pain, cold, and illness, was life's paramount concern, but other needs such as vengeance, love, and reassurance about death pressed hard. For all these needs, peasants and townspeople called upon a battery of wonder-workers, from cunning men, soothsayers, and witches to saints. Just as the peasant saint became an object of veneration that cut across class lines, so the saintly town worker might well become the patron of the entire commune, of patrician and poor alike.

Among those resorting to the supernatural, class differences were thus a matter of degree, not of kind. The culture of the poor gave greater play to the supernatural aspects of saintliness, but the saint's role as miracle-worker on earth and intercessor after death was compelling for all classes. The lesser prominence of supernatural activity among saints of upper-class backgrounds suggests not that miracles and visions were unimportant among those classes, but that highborn saints had alternative paths to recognition. Royalty itself carried a presumption of divine election, and, to state the matter plainly, a prelate was much more likely to be venerated after death than a parish priest. Canonization required cult; cult depended upon visibility; and visibility came with social position.

The popular idea of sanctity closely linked the possession of supernatural powers with the practice of austerity. In a crude equation, the holy person gave up worldly attachments in return for divine gifts. In the more sophisticated view of the hagiographer, God preferred to reveal his will through vessels purified by asceticism and immune to the temptations of the flesh. To the penitential ascetic, supernatural power was an unlooked-for gift, unexpected and sometimes embarrassing. The self-denying penitent, motivated by a sense of unworthiness and a need to expiate sin, strove to discipline the will and the body against pride and temptation. The sense of guilt might be highly personal and naively explicit, as when Elena di Udine chastised every member of her body in turn as she recalled the offense of each one. Teresa of Avila's guilt was also very personal, but it stemmed from a refined and philosophical sense of human imperfection and the soul's travail in seeking God. Guilt could also involve preoccupation with the sins of the church, Christendom, or all mankind: Catherine of

Table 11
Asceticism by Family Status

Activity	Royalty	Titled Nobles	Untitled Nobles	Good Family	Urban patrician	Other Urban	Peasantry	Unknown
Extended periods of reclusion								
Central to reputation (34)[a]	4.8[b]	1.8	3.2	3.2	3.3	5.3	7.9	3.4
Important in reputation (82)	2.4	8.0	13.5	6.2	13.3	11.6	8.8	6.9
Flagellation (94)	14.3	9.7	14.1	6.7	13.3	14.7	10.5	0
Other extreme austerities (185)	23.8	25.7	25.6	11.8	22.5	28.4	24.6	3.4
Fortitude in illness (47)	7.1	7.1	3.8	2.6	6.7	12.6	4.4	0
Extreme humility (235)	23.8	31.0	28.2	18.5	37.5	31.5	28.1	10.3
Death owing to austerities (75)	21.4	9.7	5.1	7.7	12.5	10.5	4.4	6.9
Extreme dedication to poverty (77)	9.5	10.6	10.3	9.2	8.3	9.5	6.1	3.4
Total number of cases	42	113	156	195	120	95	114	29

Note: "Good family" includes the "probably well-off" category of table 9; "other urban" combines the "other burghers," "urban poor," and "probably urban" categories of table 9; "peasantry" includes the "probably poor" category of table 9.

[a] Number of cases.

[b] Figures are percentages of saints from each class that are known for each activity.

Siena practiced austerity to atone not only for her sin but for the evil of her times. Disciplined and tempered by her penitential exercises, she spent her remarkable energy and concentration in working to reform the papacy.

Given the close connection between penitential practices and the experience of supernatural power, it is not surprising that the frequency of ascetic practices also varied from class to class. However, while we concluded that the essential distinction with regard to supernatural power was the division between rich and poor, between those who held worldly power and those who did not, asceticism was more emphatically an expression of the urban classes. Again, this was a matter of degree; penitence, self-denial, and the cultivation of humility were practiced by almost all saints; but the pattern of such activities was nowhere so central as it was among saints from towns and cities. The figures in table 11 are more consistently high for urban shopkeepers, artisans, and laborers than for urban patricians, but all urban holy men and women surpassed nonurban saints in their reputation as penitents and ascetics.

The heroic era of the urban penitent saint was the thirteenth century, the century of Francis of Assisi and the mendicant movement of which he was the supreme expression. Just as Francis rejected everything about his bourgeois past, so mendicancy sought to reverse the moral effects of commercial expansion and exploitation, to turn the church away from preoccupation with worldly power and society back to apostolic poverty and humility. The center of religious as well as social innovation was the town, where the clash between new practices and old values was sharpest. Procedures and organization of expressions of penance and expiation by the laity would find well-articulated forms beginning in the thirteenth century, whereas the full development of a value system supportive of commercial practices would not come for another two centuries.[19] In the meantime, the town's chief response to the divergence between behavior and values was to pay homage to tradition while fostering innovation.

The saint was an admirable instrument for this new civic need. The town required holy patrons to endow its origins and history with religious legitimacy; it needed intercessors to plead for its usurious and worldly citizens; most of all, it needed in its midst saintly penitents who by the completeness of their self-abnegation compensated for the pride and greed of their profane compatriots. Saints were surrogate expiators for members of communities who had too little time and inclination to pursue spiritual perfection for themselves. Saints performed an indispensable social service, easing the anxiety that stemmed from conflicts between religious values and material interests, serving as agents of change in the social as well as the spiritual world. Ironically, saints were called upon to protect and even promote trends inimicable to their own ideas of holiness, yet believers continued to count upon their generosity and their benevolence, and the saints did not disappoint them.

While saintly innovators and expiators continued to serve the faithful of the fourteenth century, popular movements such as the Beguines and Flagellants also provided vehicles for the expiation of an increasingly private and personal burden of guilt. Whereas the typical thirteenth-century burgher was likely to be comforted by the knowledge that saintly intercessors as well as priestly mediators would adequately represent him before the bar of divine judgment, his fourteenth-century descendants were much more sensitive about personal responsibility for their moral condition and therefore more likely to join a Flagellant procession, endow a chapel, or provide in their wills for restitution of usurious profits.

The plague of the mid-fourteenth century intensified personal struggles of conscience. Whether the Black Death, which first swept across Europe in 1348, was more lethal in towns than in the countryside is a contested point among historical demographers. Contemporary accounts suggest that it was, or at least that it was felt more horribly in the towns, where the stench of death drifted between close-packed houses and corpses were piled high in the narrow streets.[20] The Black Death was understood as God's judgment upon a community unmindful of its Christian duties. All could see that the plague did not strike everyone equally. Why were some spared? To the fourteenth-century mentality this could not happen at random; everything was part of a divine plan. The explanation of personal tragedy had to lie in personal sin, and the remedy for sin was individual penitence and expiation. The community continued to call upon its favorite saints for protection, but individual believers also sought to forestall divine punishment by putting their own consciences in order. Thus in times of crisis the Florentines carried their special protector, the image of the Madonna of Impruneta, into the city so she might shed her grace upon its walls and streets, and in 1399 the Prato merchant Francesco Datini joined the great penitential procession of the Bianchi to expiate his private guilt.[21]

Just as the town was the locus of heroic asceticism, so it was the most suitable environment for the practice of saintly charity. Towns pioneered in establishing hospitals and hospices for the poor and sick, the widow and orphan. The plight of widows may have been rather more severe in the town, where poor women without husbands found it difficult to earn a living, whereas in the countryside women might continue to hold some claim over their meager property or find work during busy times of planting and harvesting.[22] Not surprisingly, then, town saints were prominent in nurturing activities. Royal saints were also outstanding for their charity, particularly for helping the poor.

On the other hand, class differences were substantial only when charity was the principal feature of the saint's life (table 12). Stories in which charity was routine or conventional were told of saints of every class with the same approximate frequency. As with asceticism, a modicum of charity was expected of every pious Christian, but where charity was a central feature of the holy life it was most likely to be in the story of a town saint.

With temporal power and evangelical activity—the two remaining features of our five-sided paradigm of sainthood—class distinctions emphatically assert themselves. Saints of the upper classes dominated both these areas (see table 13). The reason for this bias we have already discussed: the secular power of the church itself and its close involvement with temporal authorities, the access of the elite to literacy and especially to higher education. Given these conditions, perhaps the only surprise is that saints from modest or lower-class origins appear at all as temporal power holders and great evangelists. Good birth increased the chances that a holy person would attain fame as a counselor to kings or princes or as a great preacher or missionary, but peasants and town workers were not absolutely barred from such positions. A good example is the late-fifteenth-century prophet Francesco di Paola, son of poor Calabrian villagers, whose reputation for sanctity gave him the ear of French kings. In the late tenth century, Pedro de Mezonzo, a servant from Galicia, was able to get a liberal education and became bishop of Compostela and an advisor of Spanish royalty. At about the same time, far to the north, Willigis of Schönigen, the son of a wheelwright, showed remarkable aptitude for learning as a boy and rose to become an imperial counselor and archbishop of Mainz. Willigis adopted a wheel as his coat of arms to remind everyone, not least himself, of his humble origins. In all these examples the poor boy's opportunity to learn to read and write, as in the case of Francesco di Paola, or to secure a higher education, as in the cases of Pedro de Mezonzo and Willigis, were undoubtedly the keys that opened the doors normally closed to their class.

Measured against the ideal of a loving community of believers united in Christ, the medieval church was a failure. The unedifying details of its involvement in the world as a landlord and power broker, its support for social inequities, its participation in the exploitation of the poor, shocked reformers who recalled the teachings of Christ its founder. Social prejudice even helped decide who would be venerated as a saint, both by determining the chances of living a saintly life and by influencing the perception of the faithful and recognition by the hierarchy. One of the principal avenues to veneration was high clerical status, and such positions generally went to members of the upper classes. Another route was prominence in the regular clergy, where mendicants as well as Benedictines favored high social status in their choice of leaders.

Table 12

Charitable Activity by Family Status

Activity	Royalty	Titled Nobles	Untitled Nobles	Good Family	Urban Patrician	Other Urban	Peasantry	Unknown
Helping the sick								
Central to reputation (108)[a]	9.5[b]	16.8	10.3	11.8	15.8	16.8·	9.6	0
Important to reputation (101)	9.5	10.6	14.7	10.3	13.3	10.5	12.3	6.9
Mentioned or implied (358)	42.9	43.4	41.7	44.1	42.5	42.1	34.2	37.9
Aiding the poor								
Central to reputation (73)	19.0	12.4	7.7	6.2	6.7	9.5	8.8	0
Important to reputation (126)	21.4	16.8	16.7	8.7	21.7	11.6	14.0	6.9
Mentioned or implied (400)	33.3	43.4	51.3	49.7	49.2	51.6	36.0	37.9
Spiritual and moral counseling (151)	0	15.0	17.3	7.4	24.2	21.1	17.5	13.8
Peacemaking (78)	16.7	8.0	11.5	5.6	11.7	7.4	9.6	3.4
Aiding pilgrims, widows, captives, etc. (176)	28.6	24.8	19.9	16.4	21.7	22.1	2.1	6.9
Total number of cases	42	113	156	195	120	95	114	29

[a] Number of cases.
[b] Figures are percentages of saints from each class that are known for each activity.

Table 13
Evangelical Activity and Temporal Power by Family Status

Activity	Royalty	Titled Nobles	Untitled Nobles	Good Family	Urban Patrician	Other Urban	Peasantry	Unknown
Preaching (193)[a]	0[b]	17.7	33.3	23.1	23.3	21.1	16.7	31.0
Missionary work (225)	23.8	16.8	21.2	41.5	19.2	23.2	20.2	48.3
Church reform (167)	14.3	24.8	30.8	15.4	16.7	20.0	13.2	3.4
Public reform (71)	9.5	12.4	9.0	8.7	9.2	5.3	5.3	0
Founded an order (57)	4.8	9.7	10.9	3.6	8.3	3.2	6.1	0
High temporal office or influence (94)	57.1	16.8	8.3	6.7	9.2	8.4	4.4	3.4
Considerable temporal influence (130)	2.4	12.4	22.4	14.4	15.0	21.1	11.4	3.4
Popes, cardinals, high church advisors (124)	21.4	19.5	18.9	14.4	13.3	12.6	4.4	10.3
Bishops, heads of monasteries (260)	7.1	33.6	41.7	26.7	36.7	27.4	24.6	13.8
Total number of cases	42	113	156	195	120	95	114	29

[a] Number of cases
[b] Figures are percentages of saints from each class that are known for each activity.

When veneration more often was accorded to nonclerics, in the thirteenth and especially in the fourteenth centuries, lay saints were usually urban patricians. The dramatic change in life that we have called conversion and that so riveted the admiration of the faithful was an upper-class phenomenon. Although Jesus had called the poor and humble blessed, and though medieval Christian thinkers declared poverty a holy state, few were the saints who embodied this value by virtue of their humble birth. The poor lived the material circumstances of the *vita apostolica* by necessity, not choice. But the whole point of conversion, as it was understood in the Middle Ages, was shedding worldly riches and power and, as Francis—a rich man's son—put it, marrying Lady Poverty. The medieval act of conversion was thus a religious mode that mirrored the elitist values of society. Jesus, himself a man of the people, had called unto himself poor fishermen; but the dominant conversion image that took root in medieval Christendom was that of a prince or a merchant who renounced his patrimony. Only voluntary poverty was holy; at most, the poverty of the peasant or town worker could inspire compassion. It followed that a poor peasant who aspired to holiness had no clear model for conversion. Nor was a poor peasant likely to capture the attention of the faithful, for whom the dramatic renunciation of great wealth or power was a favorite sign of holiness.

For all we have just said about the importance of class in determining sainthood, we must immediately add that social distinctions were never absolute—never as great, for example, as the distinction of gender. In the next chapter we shall suggest the existence of a male type of saint and a second type that we shall call androgynous rather than female. But we firmly reject the possibility of constructing an upper-class, lower-class, urban, or rural "type" of saint. Not only do the results of statistical analyses indicate considerable fluidity across class lines (see the discussion of discriminate function analysis in the Appendix on Method), but the sources convey forcefully the impression that sainthood was an aspect of medieval Christianity that attenuated class barriers rather than reinforced them. Even at the two ends of the social scale, royalty and peasantry, where class distinctions were important in the perception of sanctity, the distinctions were limited. The image of a royal saint retained the flavor and trappings of class, but even among royalty gender counted for more; the queen who became a saint was very different from the saintly king. Generally she was perceived as an ascetic who rejected all the vanities of her social position and as a nurturer of the poor and sick. Almost invariably she was perceived to be a vigorous defender of the faith and a powerful dispenser of justice. A peasant's lowly condition was also an important part of the perception of the faithful, but again distinctions of gender bifurcated the image. Peasant women were most often young maidenly visionaries, while peasant men were usually older wonder-workers. The holy life of the royal princess was closer to that of the saintly peasant girl than to that of the saintly men of her own class.

The importance of gender distinction was not the only factor that rendered class less significant. More positively, saintly activity cut across class lines in many ways. In the pursuit of holiness, rich and poor were comrades in the battle against the devil, the heretic, and the infidel. The struggle for chastity tormented pious youths of all social strata. Barriers that normally confined the poor to their place and station could more easily be transcended by those doing God's work. A reputation for prophecy or divinely infused wisdom was a passport through the gates of cities and an entrée into princely courts as well as a magnet that drew the great of the world to the hermit's cell. The poor pilgrim who had been to Jerusalem, Rome, or Compostela was an object of awe and authority to contemporaries who had never gone beyond the nearest market town. Holiness was a bridge between classes and estates. The poor hermit might enter the court of the prince; the prince might take up the life of a poor hermit.

In the monastery, class distinctions were less sharply defined than in the world, and if the abbot was likely to be of noble origin, as a monk he had taken on the style of what was referred to quite accurately as a "common life." Religious dress was an expression of equality as well as of humility, its rough cloth marked by no symbols of knightly pride or aristocratic birth, while distinctions of speech, gesture, and diet, the instantly recognizable marks of class, disappeared in the ideal uniformity envisioned in Benedict's rule. The even more drastically egalitarian style of the mendicants further dissolved class distinctions. Chaucer's fat monk, who wore gowns of softest cloth, kept sleek palfreys in his stable, and dined on choice meats and fine wine, was a fictional reproach, as the saint was a living one, to violators of the monastic ideal.

Medieval society was built upon class, and the church reflected social distinctions in its structure as well as in its hierarchical vision of world order. This was the world of sin, of accommodating to the imperfections of temporal existence in the long interlude between the Incarnation and the Second Coming. But medieval Christianity projected another world, one that did not have to await the millennium to begin the pursuit of holiness. Its inhabitants were good monks, penitent hermits, pastoral bishops. In the late Middle Ages they made room for the merchant who gave up his usurious profits, the judge who refused bribes, the wife who practiced mental prayer, the peasant who shared his mite; and in the Counter Reformation they were joined by mystics, church reformers, and a new army of martyrs. This was the world of the saints, where perfection was possible for those who sought it and from which weaker mortals could gain solace and hope.[23]

Classification of Family Status

Rather than select one or another competing classification system or a priori impose a modern theoretical system upon our material, we have taken our social categories from distinctions made in the saints' vitae themselves. Our category "royalty" presents little difficulty, although, to be sure, the term was equivocal in Scandinavia and there are some problems having to do with Irish kings. Titled nobility also present relatively minor problems. Here we have been rigid, including in this category only those for whom the sources provide an explicit title such as duke or count.

Our category "untitled nobles" is more ambiguous. Hagiographers loved to bestow the term "noble" upon the families of their heroes. Sometimes they clearly meant the word as a moral adjective to describe pious parents who were zealous in performing their Christian duties. In other cases they used the word as a courtesy noun because high status seemed to them to enhance the stature of their saints. We have resisted such inflation of honors by searching for other clues before allowing that a saint was noble instead of "good family." For example, we classified as "untitled noble" a woman who married into a titled family or a man described not only as of noble family but also as a knight, and we assumed that a person of "noble" birth who entered the clergy by accepting a bishopric was indeed "noble." Determining who was noble bedevils the modern historian for the very good reason that contemporaries themselves were confused. Legal definitions came late and were incomplete; moreover, they varied enormously from one place and time to another. Intermarriage blurred social boundaries, and life-style often counted for more than heredity. For all these reasons, the distinction between "untitled nobles" and our next category, "good family," is approximate.

The term "good family" was another of the hagiographer's favorites, used to describe a respected and established family, usually but not invariably landed. In this category we have included such designations as "honorable family," "gentry," "of good birth," and "well-to-do" whenever these terms were not accompanied by other qualifying terms indicating a more explicit social status. Without a doubt some of the families we have classifed as "untitled nobles" might instead be categorized as "good family," since we cannot be sure we have always detected the exaggeration of the sources. Vice versa, a few saints we have designated as "good family" may have been lesser nobles; but this does not affect our analysis in a significant way, since trends and patterns among lesser nobles are so similar to those among saints of good family.

Our next category, "urban elites," includes town patricians, bankers and merchants, most government officials, judges, lawyers, and professors. A few of these were nobles, and many held property in the countryside, but because of our interest in the urban-rural distinction we have given primacy to their town connection where this seemed justifiable. For example, many of the patricians of the Italian communes were members of old noble families, and many others intermarried with nobility; but those whose lives and careers were intertwined with the town we have placed in the category "urban elite." The designation "urban middle class" includes those shopkeepers, tradesmen, master craftsmen, and artisans who were not members of the urban patriciate but who clearly were better situated than persons in our next category, "urban workers," which includes journeymen, day laborers, servants, and a very few poor folk who from related evidence in the text we judge to have been townspeople. "Peasants," our next category, includes farm laborers, both serf and free. Finally, since many biographers introduce the saint in adulthood, referring only implicitly to his or her family background, we have four residual categories: "probably upper," "probably poor," "probably urban," and "no information."

8 ⊕ *Men and Women*

The ideal type we discussed in answering the question "Who was a saint?" might well have been separated into males and females, for nothing so clearly divided the ranks of the saints as gender. Our analysis of conversion showed that the path to the holy life was markedly different for girls and for boys. This divergence widened rather than narrowed as aspiring boys and girls became holy men and women. Moreover, cultic veneration, even as it began during the saint's lifetime and as it flourished at the tomb and in the memory of believers, continued to be sex-differentiated. Men and women did different things in their holy lives, and different values were placed on what they did, both by the faithful and by the church. As we shall show, women were more rigidly confined to a particular type of holiness than were men. Typologies are necessarily abstract, but in the case of male and female saints there is a close correspondence between concrete detail and the typological construct.

Overall, 17.5 percent (151 of 864) of the saints in our sample were women, a little more than one female to every five males. But in the eleventh century only one in twelve saints was a woman (11 of 128), a proportion that rose in the twelfth century only to 11.8 percent (18 of 153). The era of the female saint began in the thirteenth century, when the percentage of women nearly doubled to 22.6 percent (36 of 159), and continued into the fourteenth (25 of 107, or 23.4 percent) and through the fifteenth century, when 23 of 83 saints (27.7 percent) were female. This increase is even more impressive when we consider that the total number of saints in our sample declined from 153 in the twelfth century to 83 in the fifteenth. In short, the proportion of women in the ranks of new saints continued to increase even during a time of overall downturn. In the sixteenth century the total number of saints turned slightly upward; but the percentage of women dropped sharply, from 27.7 percent to 18.1 (21 of 116), and in the seventeenth century women slipped still further, to 14.4 percent (17 of 118). Corresponding to this pattern, there also emerged in the thirteenth century what we shall refer to as an "androgynous" type, which then declined in the sixteenth; but before we examine either of these trends we need to present a few more details. In table 14 we have classified men and women saints according to their social class, as measured by the saint's family status. (For a discussion of the family status categories see the final section of chap. 7, p. 218.) Next, table 15 sets forth the occupations of the saints at the time they began to be recognized widely for their special holiness.

If the preference for male saints in the eleventh and twelfth centuries suggests a deep-seated prejudice in medieval society, it also shows a society that more often than not looked to its designated leaders for its spiritual heroes. In the period of Cluny, the Crusades, and the Investiture Controversy, the skilled administrator—the bishop who assiduously devoted himself to his flock, the archbishop who fought for the liberties of the church, the earnest reformer of a simoniacal clergy or of errant monastic houses— these were the religious models of clergy and laity alike. The causes of the church still seemed holy and were able to capture the popular imagination. The issue for which the martyred Becket died may have been a matter of high state politics, but the laity who gathered at his tomb to witness his miracles regarded him as a fallen hero in a struggle that touched their lives as well. At Cologne, Augsburg, Gubbio, and numerous other cities and towns the great bishop who preached the gospel, visited the sick, practiced celibacy, and insisted that his priests do likewise was promoted for ven-

Table 14
Family Status by Gender

Family Status	Number of Females	Number of Males	Percentage Female
Royalty	19	23	45.2
Titled nobles	31	82	27.4
Untitled nobles	23	133	14.7
Good family/gentry/rich	13	76	14.6
Urban patrician/professional	21	99	17.5
Artisans/small shopkeepers	3	18	14.3
Urban poor	4	21	16.0
Peasant	13	34	27.7
Probably well-off	7	99	6.6
Probably poor	9	58	13.4
Probably urban	8	41	16.3
Nothing known	0	29	0.0

Table 15
Occupational Category by Gender

Occupation	Number of Females	Number of Males	Percentage Female
Popes	0	10	0.0
Cardinals	0	12	0.0
Archbishops	0	37	0.0
Bishops	0	84	0.0
Abbots, abbesses, priors, prioresses	24	136	15.0
Monks, nuns	24	47	33.8
Canons regular	2	15	11.8
Friars	0	42	0.0
Secular priests	0	100	0.0
Lay brothers, lay sisters, tertiaries	21	28	42.9
Royalty	15	14	51.7
Titled nobles	8	9	47.1
Untitled nobles, courtiers	6	8	42.9
Professionals	0	62	0.0
Military officers	0	21	0.0
Merchants/bankers	0	9	0.0
Shopkeepers/artisans	0	10	0.0
Peasants	3	13	18.8
Housewives/matrons	26	0	100.0
Youths	20	19	51.3
Marginal persons	2	37	5.1

eration by his cathedral clergy, but his cult found a ready response among the laity. Whereas Becket's cult was unusual in its widespread appeal, the feast day celebrations of most saintly bishops expressed a more local chauvinism, the burgeoning pride of the city.[1] The relics of great bishops and other local religious heroes made sacred the space within the town's walls, legitimized its contests against communal neighbors and encroaching princes, both temporal and ecclesiastical, protected it in times of sickness and famine. Insofar as such exalted status was reached only by holy bishops and other clerics, it was the exclusive preserve of men.

During the same centuries royalty also gave a presumption of holiness. An aura of divinity surrounded the king as well as the saintly prelate, and kings who won fame for their special piety were obvious candidates for veneration, the intensity of which was enhanced by their awesome power to do justice and practice mercy as well as by their healing touch. Sanctity was readily attributed to queens too, especially to those who remained humble, pious, and charitable in the midst of worldly distractions and temptations. Wherever emerging royal authority engaged in contests against local feudal magnates or took up arms against the infidel Moslem, holy queens as well as kings arose to call forth the admiration and veneration of their subjects. In Hungary, Iberia, France, and, to a lesser degree, the German empire, cults of royal saints of both sexes helped to mold the Christian faithful into a body politic.[2]

The third major avenue to sanctity in the eleventh and twelfth centuries was Benedictine monasticism, since the sixth century the virtually universal form of the cenobitic life in the West. However much reformers railed at the worldliness of the monks—at their corrupting wealth and simoniacal involvement in temporal affairs, at their greater concern for the profits of their manors than for their own souls— the penitent who sought a life of prayer and contemplation or the weary prince who yearned for spiritual respite from the burdens of power found it in these same Benedictine houses. Besides, the eleventh century was a time of reforming excitement among the Benedictines. It had begun in the late tenth century at the monastery of Cluny in Burgundy, and in the next decades Cluniac reform spread over much of Western Europe.[3] In the twelfth century the white-robed monks of Cîteaux brought a new vigor to the Benedictine rule and produced Christendom's greatest monkish saint after Benedict himself, Bernard of Clairvaux. Combining contemplative genius with vigorous public activity as an adviser to popes and kings, Bernard had an enormous impact upon his own time; and as a writer of devotional works he was a major influence on piety for centuries to come.[4] He was not unique. Although they are less well known, Hugh of Cluny, Pietro di Cava, Peter Damian, Guillaume le Grand, and Etienne de Liège, among others, achieved great reputations in their lifetimes as exemplars of the best in Benedictine piety.

Among Benedictines, however, very few women were celebrated as saintly. Of the 134 Benedictine saints in our sample, 106 died in the eleventh and twelfth centuries, and of this latter figure only 11 percent were women. Whether contemplatives or reformers, Benedictine women were not often venerated as saints. Powerful and holy abbesses there were aplenty, but in the ranks of sainthood they were overshadowed by their male counterparts.

It has been alleged that in the heyday of feudalism in the central Middle Ages medieval women enjoyed a far more important and powerful place than they came to have in late medieval or Renaissance bourgeois society. Noblewomen inherited property and exercised feudal dominion, while near the bottom of the social scale poor women in manor and village worked alongside their men and shared in making decisions about the family economy.[5] Whatever the accuracy of this picture—for which documentation, particularly for lower-class women, is difficult to come by—it does not apply to sainthood or, we would suggest, to religious life more generally. Eleventh- and twelfth-century European Christendom was a man's world.

Moreover, the argument that the position of women deteriorated in the transition from a feudal to an urban commercial society does not hold for religious history. Among saints, at least, the reverse was true. Beginning in the thirteenth century, possibly as early as the twelfth, there were not only more female saints but more women pioneering new forms of piety. The rise of the mendicant orders, Franciscans, Dominicans, Carmelites, and others, which directed religious enthusiasm away from the cloister and took it out into the streets, appealed to women as well as to men. Less often were young girls dumped into a convent by fathers who were not able to marry them off, and more often did inspired girls such as Bona of Pisa and Sperandea of Gubbio struggle against their families to fulfill visionary aspirations. Among the heroes of the new orders women were prominent; of the 212 mendicant order saints in our sample, 50 were female (23.5 percent).

Moreover, the class base from which saints were drawn expanded dramatically. Whereas a female saint of the eleventh or twelfth century was likely to be a queen, a princess, or a highborn noble, the chance that she came from the middle or lower classes increased in the thirteenth century. Mendicants were somewhat more open than Benedictines to novices who brought into the order no other endowment than their enthusiasm. But a widening of class base was true of all female saints, not only mendicants, suggesting that mendicancy was only one reflection of deeper social change. The broadening social base of sainthood indicates that more women were finding opportunities for religious expression. And with more saintly models for women to choose from, more women were attracted to the religious life. Such expansion must have been especially important for middle- and lower-class women, who could only have regarded the queenly and noble saints of earlier centuries as from a world apart, to be venerated, perhaps, but never imitated.[6]

The rise in the number of female saints by no means implies that they achieved numerical dominance, or even equality with males; more than three of every four thirteenth-century saints were men. The widening class base affected men too, as did the shift of religious leadership from Benedictine monasticism to mendicancy. Franciscans and Dominicans were closer to the social changes of the thirteenth and fourteenth centuries and thus much more in tune with the religious needs of middle- and lower-class townspeople. The statistics presented on class and occupation are but one reflection—a very important one, since saints served as models of piety—of the growth of lay religious enthusiasm. As in earlier centuries, the focal point for the veneration of a saint was a community, which might be as large as a nation or even all Christendom, but much more often was a town or a monastery. In the eleventh and twelfth centuries the community hero was most likely to be a bishop or a Benedictine abbot—in either case, an upper-class male. Beginning in the thirteenth century, however, and continuing into the fifteenth, the town's favorite new saint was less likely to be a high prelate than a tertiary, a mendicant, or a saintly lay person. While the faithful still chose more often than not to venerate a man, they were now much more likely to pay that honor to a woman. And chances were now better than ever that new male and female saints came from the middle or lower classes.

The pattern established in the thirteenth century—greater numbers of female saints, widening of the class base for both males and females, and more saints from Italy—continued with some important variations for the next two centuries. In the sixteenth century, however, a major change occurred. The proportion of male saints rose not to the level of the twelfth century, but much higher than it had been in the intervening three hundred years. Concomitant with this change there was again a narrowing of the class base and a shift in the geographical pattern of saints' birthplaces. All three of these changes were related, but for the time being we will concentrate on the first, the decline of new cults of women.

Two great sixteenth century movements provide the context: the Reformation and the overseas expansion of European nations. Whatever the place it gave to women within its own ranks, and this is highly controversial, the Protestant Reformation had the indirect effect of curtailing the role of women as leaders of Catholic piety. The Catholic Reformation, both in the way it responded to the Protestant challenge and in the way it pursued its inherent reform goals, affected women in several respects. The most far-reaching of these was the reaffirmation of hierarchical, that is to say, of male, authority. The Catholic Reformation was above all else a reformation of the episcopacy, a rededication of the bishop to the care of souls, the nurturing of his flock, the reforming of his clergy, and the monitoring of correct doctrine. The archetype of the Catholic Reformation prelate was Carlo Borromeo, the bishop of Milan, canonized in 1610 just twenty-six years after his death. Borromeo's official recognition rested less on an outpouring of veneration from the rank and file of the faithful than on the initiative of the hierarchy, who had some difficulty finding evidence of his miraculous intercession or other supernatural graces. Borromeo was a model Catholic Reformation prelate, not a popular hero.[7]

Even the upsurge of new religious orders emphasized authority, hierarchy, and distance from the laity. The Society of Jesus established in 1540 found strength in its rigorous—we may say elitist—training and in its special oath of obedience to the pope. Some mendicant orders sought to adjust—the Capuchins were reformed Franciscans, for example—but even their reforms leaned heavily to discipline and conformity.[8] Nor were the mendicants the central force in piety that they had been in earlier times. If the Catholic Reformation recalled the church to the founder's admonition to "feed my sheep," it interpreted that duty by establishing a patron-client relationship rather than a brotherhood in the body of Christ. The key to reassertion of clerical authority was a theological doctrine, the role of the sacraments in the process of justification and salvation. Catholicism responded to the Protestant challenge by emphasizing more emphatically than ever before the centrality of the sacraments, and therefore the indispensable mediating role of the priest. The Mass was reaffirmed as a sacrifice that could be perfomed only by an ordained priest who, at the altar and with his back to the congregation, presided over the miracle of transubstantiation. Whereas in the rest of Christendom the equality of the community of believers came to be symbolized by the sharing of the Lord's Supper, in Catholicism the priest first drank from the cup, then bestowed the wafer on passive communicants. To be sure, this had been Catholic practice for centuries; but in the preceding period lay piety had encroached upon the priestly function and in some cases questioned it outright. Now, challenged by new churches and sects that asserted the priesthood of all believers, Reformation Catholicism rejected all such experiments with religious democracy and reaffirmed the most extreme version of clerical authority and practice.[9]

These reforms were inherently if not consciously unfavorable to women: barred from ordination, women were excluded from the clergy and, to the degree that the clergy and religion became synonymous, were excluded from important aspects of Catholic Reformation piety as well. A Teresa of Avila or a Caterina de' Ricci was still a possibility, but when women attempted to go beyond the tightly restricted sphere allotted to them they encountered serious obstacles. Only the most extraordinary of their gender chose to fight against such obstacles. Most probably never thought of doing so.

More difficult to assess than institutional bias is the question of changing cultural attitudes toward women. However, we suggest that the church's new emphasis on male leadership both reflected and promoted sexual prejudice. The decided increase in hagiographic stories of holy men assaulted by lewd women is telling. In an era when the virtue of celibacy was being asserted over the family values of the fourteenth and fifteenth centuries, clerical misogyny was again elevated to a model virtue. Philip Neri's declaration that he had attained so perfect a state of purity that he cared for a woman no more than for a stone goes beyond the trite chastity story to the very essence of male attitudes in the sixteenth century. Gone from sixteenth- and seventeenth-century hagiographic accounts is the sympathy toward marriage and family that made earlier accounts of struggle so poignant and so ambivalent. Moreover, women seem to have internalized the denigration of their sex's spirituality. Absent from most of the accounts of female saints who lived in this era is the phenomenon of spiritual marriage. During the Catholic Reformation Christ's female companions were more likely to be his handmaidens than his brides. Again, Teresa of Avila is an exception that supports the rule; she attained the mystical phenomenon of spiritual marriage at the advanced age of forty-two, and then only after enormous spiritual suffering.

More blatantly hostile to women than these trends, but perhaps related to them, were the witch hunts that swept across sixteenth-century Europe. Ideologically prepared for in such patently women-hating works as Kramer and Sprenger's *Witches' Hammer* of 1484, and undoubtedly stimulated by terrifying recurrences of plague and warfare, the hysterical conviction that women had a peculiar affinity for devil worship broke upon Europe just as the Reformation began to be "haunted by a sense of the devil," in Norman O. Brown's phrase. That the obsession with witchcraft was as endemic in Protestant regions as in Catholic areas suggests that misogyny was not solely the result of the bias of a celibate male clergy but was deeply rooted in European sexual attitudes, reasserting itself when, as in eras of plague, war, and religious turmoil, Satan appeared to be stalking the earth.[10]

Then, too, the Catholic Reformation brought changes in the church's tasks that were unfavorable to women's participation. Once more missionaries were being recruited to carry the gospel to unbelievers, both to Protestant heretics and schismatics in Europe and to the natives encountered by the Portuguese and Spanish fleets in Asia and the New World. English Catholic exiles prepared themselves on the Continent to bring spiritual comfort and the Blessed Sacrament back to their coreligionists at home. Apostles to the heretic and the heathen faced arduous journeys and great personal danger in order to preach and baptize, while the English apostles risked certain torture and death. In this time especially, the world of the missionary was a man's world, if anything more dangerous than during the thirteenth-century wave of overseas evangelism. In a later era Catholic as well as Protestant foreign missions, particularly their nurturing and educational aspects, would be opened to women, but in this earlier heroic age they were confined to men—the "stronger sex" and the one from which priests were ordained to baptize and to celebrate Mass.

The holy lives of men and women varied significantly. As we have just seen, two of the major elements of saintly reputations, that is, worldly power and evangelical activity, were exclusive to men. But in themselves the achievements of the prince, the bishop, or the missionary did not lead to cultic veneration except when they were combined with evidence of

supernatural power and heroic virtue, and it is in respect to these phenomena that gender differentiation needs to be examined and explained.

Supernatural power, the principal evidence of divine election, manifested
itself in many ways. The birth of a future saint was frequently heralded
by celestial signs, and divine intervention continued to mark out God's
agents throughout their lives and after their deaths. From the age of six
or seven holy children received visions that inspired and instructed them
in their holy courses. Visions might be prophetic, but divine prophecy
came through other channels as well. Often it was linked with the gift of
clairvoyance. The power to exorcise demons sent by the devil to test the
holy adolescent or to torment an unhappy housewife also was regarded
as a divine gift. Of the several manifestations of supernatural power, the
most compelling was miracle, the all-powerful bond between saints and
their devotees, whether in life or in death. (See figs. 29, 30, and 31.)

In the lives of female saints supernatural power in its various forms was
almost twice as prominent as in the lives of males. (See table 16 for specific
figures, and recall that the yardstick against which to evaluate these percentages is 17.5 percent, the proportion of women in the entire sample.)
Women were the victims of social prejudices that disqualified them from
most alternative avenues of recognition, made them a caste apart, and put
them almost entirely at the mercy and the arbitrary pleasure of men. In all
centuries they had less worldly power than men—much less. It has been
suggested that lower-class, middle-aged women were the special targets
of witchcraft accusations because they represented the failed conscience
of late medieval society. Denying them charity, the community then suspected these women of covenanting with the devil to take their revenge.
Thus they became scapegoats for whatever local tragedy might arise.[11] We
would make a somewhat different argument, converting it from the passive
to the active, so to speak, by suggesting that in the Middle Ages powerless
people of whatever condition were especially likely to resort to magic,
sorcery, and miracle, and that the social powerlessness of women helps
explain the frequency of supernatural activity in their lives. Although our
concern is with saints, not witches, the similarities between them arose
from the common plight of women. Women were socially vulnerable, they
were regarded as physically and morally inferior, and they internalized the
culture's misogyny. Presented with a limited set of options, they were more
likely than men to turn to the supernatural to work some particular effect.
If they were successful, their neighbors were quick to suspect them of
witchcraft or, much less often, to venerate them as saints.

While men too worked miracles, other supernatural powers—visions,
signs, prophecies, and struggles with demons—pervaded the lives of female saints in a way not true of males. All four of these phenomena are

Table 16
Supernatural Power by Gender

Major Activity	Number of Females	Number of Males	Percentage Female
Mystic contemplation	76	112	40.4
Visionary experiences	54	67	44.6
Struggles with demons	25	44	36.2
Famous prophecies	29	53	35.4
Miracle-working	23	80	22.3
Supernatural signs	41	38	51.9
Intercessions	87	373	18.9
Wonder-working relics	25	67	27.2

distinguished from miracle-working by their essentially private and passive character. Miraculous healing, the commonest form of miracle-working, necessarily involved a public, whereas visions, celestial apparitions and dialogues, prophetic voices, signs, and demonic visitations usually were experienced in the solitude of a recluse's cell or a young girl's bedchamber. Supernatural communications were highly individual exchanges between a subject and a divine (or a demonic) agent. That they were so much more prominent in the lives of female saints was in part a consequence of the church's definition of sex roles: women might not express their spiritual impulses by pursuing clerical careers or, for the most part, by engaging in such active pursuits as missionary work or preaching. The approved outlets for pious women were two: nurturing the sick and cultivating the life of the spirit. Apart from the hospice, the theater of their activity had to be the cloister or the contemplative's cell.

While ecclesiastical and social regulations explain a great deal about the directions of female religiousness, they do not explain everything. They do not explain why seven-year-old girls experienced visions while seven-year-old boys did not, why adolescent girls longed to take Christ as their bridegroom, why married women were so much more frequently harassed by demons than were their husbands. The holy woman reacted not only to ecclesiastical barriers but also to society's more subtle yet pervasive definition of womanhood. The girl's vision was a weapon she used in her struggle against the destiny her parents were shaping for her: the young maiden's choice of Christ as her bridegroom relieved her of the burden of taking a worldly husband; the matron's demonic assaults were the products of guilt and depression arising from a life imposed upon her and from which she longed to escape. While women's supernatural experiences tended to be more private and personal than men's, holy women often lived active public lives as spiritual counselors, peacemakers, and healers. They did so in spite of great obstacles, for in religion as in other walks of

Fig. 29. (opposite, top) The parents of Vincent Ferrer are told of the sanctity of their unborn child. Naples, Church of St. Peter Martyr. Altarpiece by Colantonio. Photograph courtesy of Ministero Beni Culturali e Ambientali: Istituto Centrale per il Catalogo e la Documentazione. Number E56973.

Fig. 30. (opposite, bottom) Lorenzo Giustiniani appears to be giving communion to a nun one place while he says mass in another. Haarlem, Frau von Pannivity Collection. Predella on canvas by Francesco Morone, Cycle ex Bennebroeck. Photograph courtesy of Fototeca Berenson.

Fig. 31. Francesca Romana (de' Ponziani) is given the Christ child to hold as she kneels before the Virgin Mary. Unknown painter from the School of the Marches, fifteenth century. Photograph courtesy of the Metropolitan Museum of Art, Robert Lehman Collection, 1975.

life women were discouraged from aspiring to autonomous, much less public, roles. A reading of hundreds of accounts of male saints' lives renders again and again a picture of the faithful beating a path to the door of the hermit's cell, swarming to touch the bishop's robe, flocking to hear a holy preacher. For saintly women an equally vivid but sharply contrasting picture emerges: they gave unasked advice; they sought out the poor and the sick; if they preached at all, it was only to a very few who would listen. A woman claiming divine inspiration was immediately subject to special supervision, a male confessor assigned to review her every manifestation; and a woman whose religious impulses led her into the streets became fair game for every form of ridicule and even violence. Women who aspired to roles normally reserved for men had to have a powerful self-discipline as well as a mighty inspiration. The self-mastery that came with contemplation and the sense of power that resulted from triumph over demonic temptations armored the determined woman against the world's indifference or hostility. Supernatural experience was a seal of authenticity reassuring her that God was with her, a badge of authority to present to a skeptical male world.

Saints of either sex who did not stay in the cloister to perfect their own souls by contemplation and penance might go out into the world to serve Christ through charity. The holy man or woman who selflessly ministered to the sick or labored to make peace between mortal enemies won the awe and gratitude of the faithful. Table 17 sets forth some figures from our sample on the importance and the range of good works in the lives of male and female saints.

When we recall that the percentage of saints who were women was 17.5,

Table 17
Charitable Activity by Gender

Activity	Number of Females	Number of Males	Percentage Female
Helping the sick			
Central to reputation	27	81	25.0
Important to reputation	21	80	20.8
Mentioned or implied	50	308	14.0
Aiding the poor			
Central to reputation	16	57	21.9
Important in reputation	31	95	24.6
Mentioned or implied	64	336	16.0
Ransoming prisoners	3	12	20.0
Assisting pilgrims	8	17	32.0
Helping widows and children	9	20	31.0
Spiritual and moral counseling	36	115	23.8
Peacemaking	6	72	7.7

we can see that, statistically, women appear in disproportionately high numbers among the great healer and helper saints. Given the sex stereotyping of religious roles, this is no more than we might expect, since nurturing was one of the activities regarded as suitable to women. On the other hand, some women did not accept the limitations of being solely nurses and nurturers, but won enough respect and authority to intervene in the moral and spiritual life of the community as counselors and, occasionally, even as peacemakers. The delimitations of religious roles according to gender worked only in one direction, however. Holy men felt little hesitation about taking on nurturing activities. The good bishop or the zealous missionary might also be a great healer or dedicate himself to helping widows and the poor.

A more pronounced gender distinction is observable in our fifth and final component of saintly reputation, penitential asceticism. As with good works, neither ecclesiastical nor social barriers blocked members of either sex who were inspired to penitence and austerity. Penitence played an important part in the lives of most saints. But humility, expiation of guilt, ritual prayer, and self-mortification admitted of degrees, and to a degree these activities were more dominant in the lives of women than of men. The difficulties of attempting to measure objectively such qualitative activities are self-evident, but the lives do record concrete details that allow us to make some estimate of the importance of ascetic practices in holy reputations. For example, the life of Herman the Cripple, who was perceived by his contemporaries as holy because he bore his paralysis with heroic fortitude, was almost totally dominated by the theme of penitential asceticism. In other lives, such as those of Francis of Assisi and Catherine of Siena, the theme is important, but not exclusively so. In still others, for example, Carlo Borromeo and Vincent de Paul, penitence is a relatively minor theme overshadowed by others. Table 18 provides figures showing variations in the penitential themes of saints' vitae in our sample that include only cases in which such activities were the principle or a very important feature.

Measured against the proportion of women in the total sample, the prominence of penitential activities in the biographies of female saints is striking. The direction of the evidence is unambiguous; it is easy to distinguish between those lives in which penitence and ascetic practice were paramount and those in which these themes merely contributed to a saintly reputation that rested primarily on other factors. We include humility and poverty because they so often appear as means of expiating pride and avarice—in other words, they appear as part of a penitential impulse whose motivation is self-abasement. The career of Juan de Dios illustrates the point. After learning of the death of his father, he turned to a life of penance

Table 18
Asceticism by Gender

Activity	Number of Females	Number of Males	Percentage Female
Extended periods of reclusion			
Central to reputation	10	24	29.4
Important to reputation	14	68	17.0
Flagellation	27	67	28.7
Other extreme austerities	53	132	28.6
Fortitude in illness	25	22	53.2
Extreme humility	55	180	23.4
Death owing to austerities	20	56	23.3
Extreme dedication to poverty	18	59	23.4

that led him into ever more strenuous efforts to find true poverty and humility. Moved by the preaching of Juan de Avila, he begged for divine mercy, throwing himself on the ground, pulling out the hairs of his head, beard, and eyebrows, stripping himself of clothes and shoes, declaring that he wanted to follow the naked Christ through the streets of Granada. So great was his drive to self-abasement that he chose to appear crazy so that people would heap still more abuse upon him.

Even if we were to leave out humility, poverty, or for that matter any single theme, the results would be unchanged; women would still stand out as penitents and ascetics. Penitence and austerity were forms of religious expression easily accessible to women who aspired to holiness. They were among the regular features of the cloistered life, and they reinforced rather than challenged the medieval view of what was appropriate to the female sex. Vanity, lust, and frivolity were regarded as the besetting sins of femininity; they could best be expiated by practices that banished pride, chastised the flesh, and disciplined the spirit.

In girls the penitential impulse appeared early and invariably was associated with the rejection of sexuality, expressed in a vow of chastity. Girls whipped and starved their bodies, tormented themselves with hair shirts and chain girdles, gave their pretty garments to the poor and put on plain clothes or rags, refused to ornament their faces and bodies, occasionally even disfigured themselves. Those holy young women who were forced by their parents (usually their fathers) to break their vows and surrender their virginity to unwelcome husbands shouldered a burden of guilt that no amount of expiation could completely remove. If they did give themselves to the pleasures of marriage, they came to repent and to treat their bodies as reservoirs of sin. Even those who resisted the pressure to marry were much more likely than celibate men to suffer demonic attacks and to endure punishing illness. Indeed, such illness was a prominent feature of female holiness, the one category of activity in which women were not merely statistically overrepresented but constituted an absolute majority. (It bears repeating that table 18 includes only those cases in which the activity or theme was central in the perception of the saintly life.) Consider that of 151 female saints fully 25, or one in six, suffered debilitating illness for much of their lives after conversion, while of 713 males saints only 22 were chronically ill.

Two illustrative cases come from Italy and France. Maria Maddalena de' Pazzi, the sixteenth-century Florentine visionary, fell ill when she was seventeen, immediately after completing her novitiate, and thereafter illness, which sometimes displayed the symptoms of what today would be diagnosed as anorexia, was seldom absent in a lifetime filled with ecstasies and demonic temptations. The seventeenth-century French mystic Marguerite-Marie Alacoque was paralyzed for four years and was cured only after a special vow to the Blessed Virgin. Thereupon she dedicated herself to the pursuit of holiness, a quest that led her to fight temptations by binding her body with ropes and chains, scourging her flesh, and humbling herself by sucking the pus from the sore of a sick person. Marguerite-Marie's highest aspiration was to have the image of the Savior's passion imprinted upon her.

The hagiographic accounts appear to show that women adopted society's view that they were both morally and spiritually the weaker sex. They might marry or remain virgin; in either case they saw themselves as especially prone by nature to the lusts and vanities of the flesh. In her autobiography Teresa of Avila chastised herself for sins of worldliness and vanity that the reader is scarcely able to detect. The remarkable story of this powerful woman is permeated with her sense of her own weakness. She achieved heights of spirituality but felt herself a backslider; again and again she had to be converted to piety.

While all saints fought against sin to achieve holiness, the pattern of struggle was noticeably different for men and for women. Men may have been slower to recognize a call to the holy life, but once called they progressed steadily to ever higher plateaus of heroic virtue. Women were inspired earlier, but their quest for spiritual perfection was less regular. Not only did they encounter obstacles in the form of angry parents and a distrusting world, but they were more likely to judge themselves harshly, to condemn their own backsliding as due to the frailty they shared with all the daughters of Eve.

These contrasting paths to spiritual perfection suggest a still more fundamental difference in the way medieval society perceived the moral nature of men and women. In the vitae of male saints the occasion of sin most often was a response to an external stimulus, the surrender to an evil force or agent that came from outside the sinner himself. The young man dedicated to chastity had less to fear from his inherent carnality than from the temptations of the devil and lewd women. Doctrinal error in men was likely to be explained as a result of pernicious outside influence. Even a knight's sin of pride was an external condition or status he could shed like his armor (St. Martin's sharing his cloak with a beggar comes to mind as the paradigmatic story), leaving his nature inviolate.

By contrast, in the lives of female saints sin usually appeared to arise from the depths of woman herself. The devil was not so much a foreign enemy assaulting the ramparts of godly virtue as a domestic parasite boring from within, feeding upon the weakness of his female host. While male saints often were gifted with a special form of clairvoyance that enabled them to sniff out the faintest odor of sin in their fellows, it was woman's part to root out the evil within herself rather than to act as champion of morality and censor of the hidden sins of others. In the world of the spirit as in the world of the flesh, men and women were different and unequal.[12]

If the moral nature of men and women differed, can it be said that there existed a male and a female *type* of saint? The question can only be answered after first considering the relation between the perception of sainthood and the shifting concerns of the Christian community during the centuries of our study. It can hardly have been an accident that in the eleventh and twelfth centuries—when the church was rallying its spiritual and material forces for the Crusades and the clerical hierarchy was ascending to new heights of autonomy and power in Europe—its saints were primarily men of power and action, whose spirituality was less a matter of reflection than of external zeal. In the thirteenth century, and more especially in the fourteenth and fifteenth centuries, when Christian society was deeply troubled and divided, first by heresies and then by corruption and schism among its own leadership, when the faithful were more concerned with the salvation of their own souls than with carrying the Christian message to new frontiers, men and women who came to be honored as saints were known primarily for extreme penance, asceticism, and supernatural experiences. Saints of the sixteenth and seventeenth centuries, the age of Catholic Reformation and overseas expansion, were honored as great reforming bishops, missionaries, and martyrs, and, less frequently, as mystics who combined ecstatic experience with service to the church militant.

From what we have already said it should be clear that those virtues and achievements that were honored in the earlier centuries were more likely to be displayed by men than by women, whereas both sexes might display the saintly ideals of the thirteenth and especially the fourteenth and fifteenth centuries. In the Counter Reformation men again would begin to be more strongly represented in the ranks of sainthood. This suggests that

Table 19
Correlation Coefficients Indicating Relationships among
Components of Saintly Reputation by Gender

	Female				
	Supernatural Power	Asceticism	Charitable Activity	Temporal Power	Evangelical Activity
Supernatural power	—	.60	.47	.12	.18
Asceticism	.60	—	.50	.10	.05
Charitable activity	.47	.50	—	.23	.25
Temporal power	.12	.10	.23	—	.25
Evangelical activity	.18	.05	.25	.25	—

	Male				
	Supernatural Power	Asceticism	Charitable Activity	Temporal Power	Evangelical Activity
Supernatural power	—	.63	.35	.03	.27
Asceticism	.63	—	.44	.04	.10
Charitable activity	.35	.44	—	.19	.33
Temporal power	.03	.04	.19	—	.37
Evangelical activity	.27	.10	.33	.37	—

there was indeed a "masculine type" of saint—holder of temporal or ec- clesiastical power, missionary to the heathen and fiery preacher of the word, champion of public morality, heroic defender of his virtue—a par- adigm reflecting both societal values and church regulations. But was there a "feminine" type of saint? The virtues of penitential asceticism, private prayer, mystical communion with the Godhead, and charity often were found in male saints as well as in females. The most widely venerated saints, both in their own lifetimes and after death, were of the latter type, which might more accurately be termed "androgynous" than female.

The close links between asceticism, charity, and supernatural power, and their clear distinction from temporal power and evangelical activity, may be seen in the correlation matrices in table 19. Consistently, for men as for women, asceticism and supernatural power went hand in hand. The mag- nitude of the difference in correlation coefficients for male and female saints is small. This suggests that the relationship between asceticism and super- natural power was similar for both sexes (.60 and .63) even though, as shown in tables 16 and 18, the separate components arose far more fre- quently in female lives than in the lives of men. Multiple classification analysis (see the Appendix on Method) reveals that higher supernatural activity and asceticism scores (41.26 for women versus 30.02 for men on supernatural activity and 35.97 versus 26.67 on asceticism) for women are substantially independent of the effects of quality of reputation, extent of cult, and type of canonization (38.34 versus 30.65 and 33.19 versus 27.26, respectively).

The holy person upon whom God bestowed the power to do his work had first to cleanse the body of all impurity, the mind of all worldly desire. The linkage between asceticism and supernatural power has a long history in Christian thought. In the twelfth century the Cathar, or Albigensian, heresy reasserted the notion that divine grace could be held only in vessels purified of all material contamination. The theologically sophisticated hagiographer reflected a less extreme but more universal Catholic position: while God might work in any way he chose, he usually bestowed his favor on those who purified themselves of earthly desires, chastised their flesh, and humbled their spirits.

In this matter of the connection between asceticism and supernatural power, theology and popular belief reinforced each other. The multitudes who appeared at the tomb to watch for miracles had little familiarity with theology; they came because they believed that a holy penitent might now be placed to intercede for them with God. They made a connection between the overcoming of worldliness and the possession of supernatural power that owed less to theology and philosophy than to the human urge to transcend the limits of the body. The many who would not or could not aspire to such spiritual achievement stood in awe and in need of those who did. So central to the idea of saintliness was the connection between supernatural power and asceticism that, in the many cases where more was known about miraculous intercessions at a tomb than about the life of the holy person who was believed to inhabit it, the biographical details invented to fill the void usually took the form of a model ascetic life.

Hagiography was a meeting place for myth and experience, for learned and popular culture. What counted above all else to the faithful was miraculous intercession, and this power the popular mind ascribed far more readily to the holy ascetic than to the powerful prelate. The ascetic saint, male or female, embodied not the church militant or the God of judgment and power but Mother Church, the forgiveness of sin, divine providence and bounty, the equality of all believers.

Conclusion
New Directions

We divided this book into two parts to emphasize the two worlds of sainthood. First we observed men and women reaching out toward spiritual perfection; then we saw believers seeking advantage from the merits of the saints. This division reflects a paradox. The holy man or woman strains to transcend material existence and to attain a direct personal relationship to divinity. The saint is one who takes literally the invitation to follow Christ and to seek perfection. Saints were dutiful sons and daughters of Mother Church, at times even her saviors, but their spiritual hunger could not be satiated by the everyday nourishment offered by the sacraments, the routine of the monastery, or the ministrations of the priests. Saintly piety was personal, direct, unworldly, and extraordinary.

The cult of the saint was something else again; in a sense it was everything that the saint was not. Originally intended to honor the martyred heroes of the church's persecution by the Roman state, saints' cults continued to edify the faithful with Christian ideals. But already in the age of the martyrs, veneration was mixed with supplication, and the spiritual power of the saints came to be manifested in their material remains. In popular piety the very meaning of the saint's life was turned upside down: the physical remains of those who had transcended material existence were collected as talismans against the vicissitudes of worldly life. Where saints had regarded their bodies as reservoirs of sin and mortal enemies of the spirit, their remains were treated as vessels of miracle. The saint who had spent a lifetime resisting the importunities of the world became a dispenser of worldly favors. Serafina of San Gimignano, whose life demonstrated that illness was an occasion for spiritual growth, became a protector against disease; the ascetic Francesco di Paola became the provider of good harvests; Rita di Cascia, whose life was a model of passive acceptance of God's will, became the saint who provides the impossible. Saints whose lives were dedicated to the peace of Christian love found themselves carried into battle on the standards of communes and nations, their very names forming the battle cry of their devotees.

Besides the inversion from spiritual to material values, cultic veneration transformed spiritual geometry. Whereas the saint, through mystical union or some other form of direct spiritual communication, had experienced God's immediacy, a believer who prayed to a saint for intercession with God practiced a form of religion whose underlying premise was God's remoteness from or inaccessibility to the ordinary sinner. Whereas the saint's life demonstrated the highly personal nature of piety and the demands made upon individual religious conscience, the cult was a collective enterprise in which the community joined in supplication and celebration of a holy person who consented to share hard-won spiritual graces with ordinary sinners. Thus cultic piety was collective, vicarious, material, and pragmatic.

The relationship between the saint's life and the saint's cult, however paradoxical it might seem from a modern perspective, was in the medieval view perfectly coherent. This view was of a hierarchy in which God occupied the pinnacle and the ordinary sinner the base. Exemplified in religious literature and illustration, symbolized in the very shapes of churches, the spiritual hierarchy of medieval Catholicism made room for every degree of religious expression from the frankest invocation of divine help for the satisfaction of material needs to the perfection of the spirit purged of worldly affections. Saints were those rare individuals who, through an indivisible combination of election and religious merit, had gained a place near the divine presence. Their importance in this hierarchy stemmed not only from their having attained a position close to God, but also from the fact of their origins: having lived mortal lives, they understood and sympathized with human needs and imperfections in a way not to be expected of the Godhead. They were fathomable whereas God was not. Even Christ, the god-man, was more awesome and remote, despite medieval efforts to humanize him as the universal babe and the suffering martyr. Closest to the faithful were the saints, who had walked their streets and shared their bread. The saint partook of both the humanity of the many and the perfection of the One and thus satisfied the diadic logic of the medieval mind.

Medieval thinking encompassed the paradox of the saints, and the culture took enrichment from both the saint's life and the saint's cult. Even as they stressed the old values of Christ and the gospels, individual saints fostered and protected new forms of piety, and in so doing they fed the living river of Catholicism. Even as they exploited the saints' generosity for their own mundane ends, cultic venerators imbibed the spiritual lessons of their heroes. Yet this harmony of saint's life and cult was fragile: the first implied a piety of strenuous personal conscience and individual responsibility, of self-abnegation and world renunciation; the second, a piety that submerged individual responsibility into the community and sought not to overcome worldly needs but to satisfy them.

Protestant doctrine exposed the paradox and rejected the logic that contained it, placing the burden of saintly individualism upon every believer. But before we consider this outcome and the Catholic response to it, we wish to review briefly what saints' lives tell us about the religious and social history of Europe from the eleventh century on, at the same time pointing out some limitations of our study and some implications for future work.

In part 1 we looked at the vitae of saints, accounts constructed out of the legends and beliefs of the faithful, hagiographic conventions interwoven with the kernels of fact frequently recounted by the saints themselves or by their confessors, colleagues, and contemporary devotees. From these we drew a variety of inferences about medieval society, especially regarding life and personality development. We found that medieval people recognized childhood as a stage of life, that parents loved their children as children, and that they were perplexed when children set their innocent hearts upon a course of religious asceticism that seemed inconsistent with the normal behavior of their peers. While parents often ascribed divine qualities to a young son and encouraged his angelic ways, they were less likely to sympathize with a seven-year-old daughter's vow of virginity or to countenance her ventures into self-flagellation and other physical austerities. However much men and women looked to the saints in their own religious devotions, the extreme courses that led to sanctity were alien to them, too extreme to be practiced under their own roofs, especially by their own children, for whose well-being and future worldly success they were actively concerned.

A glimpse into the atypical childhood of the future saint helps us understand some of the norms of medieval child-rearing. The frequent appearance of the conventionalized "old child" in eleventh-century vitae suggests that normal childhood was regarded as a stage when frivolity, mischief, and sexual experimentation were the rule. The seven-year-old girl's vow of virginity, a commonplace of thirteenth- and fourteenth-century hagiography, we took not as a meaningless convention but as a hint that sexual awareness was seen to come early to medieval girls and probably did. Girls were slated for marriage long before puberty, and this practice brought with it the possibility that they might just as precociously revolt against their assigned role as wife and mother. Some accounts suggest that the future saint's mother shared vicariously in the girl's rebellion, but most admit of no such inference. In the case of girls even more than boys, parents clung to the notion that what had been good for them was good for their children. Seldom do the accounts, however, suggest that medieval parents were indifferent to their children or that they failed to comprehend that children had special attributes and needs. Nicholas the Pilgrim's vicious mother, an unusual and undoubtedly embellished example of parental cruelty, was an object lesson to other mothers. Conversely, the story of Peter Celestine and his mother warned the faithful that maternal protectiveness could be carried too far.

Attitudes toward childhood were, of course, not constant over these seven centuries, and within this long period childhood had its own history. The eleventh century and the first part of the twelfth appear to have been a time when parental goals and childhood aspirations were generally in harmony. Life choices were few, for rich as for poor. Of these, the religious path was respectable and well marked, leading to the priesthood, monastery, or convent. Beginning in the late twelfth century, however, childhood religious aspirations more often came into conflict with parental wishes. The very intensity of such conflicts showed not only that a great deal of domestic emotion was involved, but also that there was much at stake. Thomas Aquinas's mother made it plain that the Dominicans, one of the newer orders dedicated to mendicancy and poverty, were beneath the dignity of her noble family. Pietro Geremia's father, good Sicilian that he was, intended his son to be a lawyer, a profession only recently come into its own with the expansion of urban society. Like Thomas, Pietro was inflamed by the Dominican call to spiritual arms, and, like Thomas, Pietro won his first battle, which was with his family, his father realizing that he must either acquiesce in the boy's choice or lose him altogether. Even in a family of more than twenty children such as the Benincasas of Siena, love between parents and children and among brothers and sisters was powerful and determinative. Catherine of Siena's bizarre actions alternately angered and frightened her parents, who might make her their maidservant or patiently bring her soup in her illness, but who never turned their backs on her. For her part, Catherine might withdraw into her oratory, but she always included her family in her prayers.

The thirteenth century initiated a period in which the family was especially likely to be the theater both of spiritual growth and of conflict. The expansion of worldly options attractive to parents and of religious alternatives appealing to children multiplied occasions for tension and disagreement. If saints' vitae tell us only about those families where children were the winners, they also shed light on the ties of affection that must have bound other families as well. In threatening to repudiate their parents, saints held the weapon to which their fathers and mothers ultimately yielded.

From the second quarter of the sixteenth century to the end of the seventeenth, childhood appears less prominently as a decisive period in saints' lives. With some notable exceptions, such as Louis of Gonzaga and Rose of Lima, the religious impulse tends to appear later, and childhood loses its interest for hagiographers and, perhaps, for believers as well. Protestant theology did not find the notion of childhood holiness congenial, and Catholic religious thought, with its renewed emphasis upon both individual religious responsibility and sacerdotal leadership, may also have militated against the notion of the holy child. If it can be said that for several centuries before the Reformation childhood flourished under the loving admiration of adults, it may also be that the sixteenth-century religious upheaval, with its renewed consciousness of original sin and its insistence upon mature religious choice, was a time when the life stage of childhood receded from prominence in society's attention. The evidence of hagiographic literature suggests this, but obviously much more research into other kinds of sources is needed before we can know. Some contrary evidence exists. In *Luther's House of Learning* Gerald Strauss finds appreciation and affection for children in Lutheran treatises and visitation records.[1]

Perhaps different kinds of material and other Christian viewpoints would tell a different story. Even with respect to saints' vitae there is much more to be done. While we have opted for a collective approach, we are aware that studies of individual cases can be rewarding, and we hope that such studies will be the more fruitful when placed against the collective patterns we have traced.

In studying the phenomenon of religious conversion we found that in the medieval period adolescence too was seen as a distinct life stage with a history of its own. More than an arbitrary number of years between puberty and marriage, it was seen as a time when young men and women made choices about their future that were more reflective and conscious than those of childhood but that were still short of irrevocable—with one exception. That exception was chastity, and it held particular force for young women, for whom virginity was a spiritual state whose abandonment closed the principal path to holiness. The vitae suggest that adolescent religiousness attained a new intensity at about the same time as the religiousness of children—that is, in the thirteenth century—and, for related reasons, at the same time as the rise of mendicancy, with its appeal to youth, and the proliferation of worldly opportunities that appealed to parents. Adolescent conversion, however, involved rather different family dynamics from conversion in childhood. In childhood conversion the mother loomed larger, either as antagonist or as supporter; in adolescent conversion the father played the more prominent role, especially in opposition to daughters who embraced poverty and chose virginity over marriage, and to sons who rejected education and worldly careers. Whereas children more often responded to visions and other supernatural phenomena in the inception of their religious careers, adolescents were more likely to respond to the evangelical preacher, the literary model of a saint's life, or a personal crisis. The distinction is one of degree: rejection of sexuality was a factor in the religious choice of some girl saints, and divine signs played a role in many adolescent conversions, but saints' biographers appear to have recognized that children were less fully aware of the implications of their religious choice than were adolescents. However, whereas childhood fades as a significant stage of sanctity in the sixteenth century, adolescence does not. On the contrary, adolescence, as the onset of maturity and the quest for identity, becomes the crucial period of development with the Reformation. Here too further research is necessary. When did childhood end and adolescence begin? When, and with what rites of passage, did youth become man or woman? How did adolescence as a life stage vary by class and by region? Was the Reformation, as has been alleged for various radical movements, a movement by youth? Our examination of hagiographic literature suggests a firmer delineation of adolescence than some scholars have allowed, but it by no means provides definitive answers to all these questions.[2]

The conversions of adult saints brought into sharp relief the medieval propensity for dramatic reversals. What we have called the medieval logic of inversion is obvious in cases where prostitutes became recluses or princes became hermits. The pattern of the conversion drama was one not of struggle, climax, and denouement, but of climax alone, since divine inspiration was instantaneous and total. Medieval psychology assumed that the mature personality was a fixed quality no longer capable of the growth and development that characterized childhood and adolescence. The drama of sudden conversion, however pleasing aesthetically and intellectually in an aristocratic culture in which style took precedence over substance, proved less meaningful in accounts from the thirteenth, fourteenth, and fifteenth centuries. Where riches were accumulated by patient calculation and industry rather than by luck or birth, where family ties had more to do with affection than power, dramatic renunciations were only the beginning of a protracted struggle to overcome both worldly ties and the pangs of guilt they induced. We cannot be sure that affective family ties were weaker in the eleventh and twelfth centuries, but beginning with the thirteenth century the accounts become especially rich in the details of family life, and by the time of Colombini's biographer a positive ethos of family life is apparent.

These same centuries saw a rise in the number of female saints; their conversions too departed from the earlier scenario of sudden reversal or inversion. Indeed, the increasing number of female saints who had been married and borne children suggests that respect for marriage and family was coming to offer a modest alternative to the stark requirement of celibacy and virginity. Thus, saints' vitae, like so many other historical sources, demonstrate the capacity of late medieval culture to contain contrasting ideas; the aristocratic model of noblesse oblige coexisted, even interacted with, the pragmatic bourgeois ethos of work and family. The first persisted long after it had ceased to be a central motif or a major determinant of behavior, the second was practiced long before it achieved its preeminence in modern society.

The prominence of family ties wanes in sixteenth-century hagiographic accounts. For the English martyrs, the zealous missionaries, and the energetic prelates of the Catholic Reformation, the context of conversion was the university, not the home, the public arena of religious controversy, not the family, while the saints' formative struggles were with conscience, not with parents or spouses. Reformation Catholicism demanded personal responsibility for religious choice even as it emphasized the saving mission of the church militant as against the ties of family affection. In a larger perspective the sixteenth century was—as many historians have demonstrated—an era of aristocratic resurgence, and the traditional values of honor and courage are clearly manifested in the vitae of English recusants and Spanish Jesuits. Even the bourgeois Thomas More, whose family sentiment occupies an important place in his biographical tradition, seems to have had few problems of conscience in placing his allegiance to the Roman church above the importunities of his wife that he save himself by subscribing to the Act of Supremacy.

Conversion stories, whether in childhood, adolescence, or adulthood, suggest that the time from the end of the twelfth century to the early sixteenth century formed a coherent period in the history of the family. More than in either the two centuries preceding or the two following, this was a time when affective family ties were positively affirmed, when the idea of the family as a unit of love relationships emerged as an object of reflection in both religious and secular literature. Appreciation of childhood and adolescence was an integral part of this heightened family consciousness, along with a growing sensitivity to the psychology of these two life stages. This is a different picture of the history of the family from that offered in the work of Ariès, Stone, Lebrun, Shorter, Poster, and others who maintain that the affective family emerged in eighteenth-century Europe.[3] Our data strongly suggest that the affective family was not unknown in medieval society, that it began to come into its own in the thirteenth century, flourished in practice and theory in the fifteenth, and declined from the mid-sixteenth century through the late seventeenth. It follows that what Stone and others discover in the eighteenth century is not the first appearance of the affective family and the idea of childhood but a *re*appearance.

This is more than a semantic quibble: our evidence suggests that in some areas of Europe, not coincidentaily those areas Wallerstein terms "semiperipheral," which we may note were also centers of Catholic Reformation strength, the decline of the affective family was far less precipitous than in Wallerstein's "core areas," which were mainly Protestant.[4] A study of saints' lives can only suggest the problem: Why did the growth of bourgeois life give rise to an affective family in the thirteenth, fourteenth, and fifteenth centuries, and then, in just those areas where it consolidated, undergo a subsequent decline? Why, in the eighteenth century, did it again nurture the growth of the affective family? We think the answer lies in the process of interaction between aristocratic and bourgeois values that coexisted fitfully until the sixteenth- and seventeenth-century revolution in religion, economy, and politics. We are the first to acknowledge that this is purely a hypothesis, to be tested by resorting to many other kinds of materials, but our study does suggest that in the final analysis religious factors will have reclaimed some of the ground that has been too readily given up to neo-Marxists and quasi-Freudians.

Whatever the circumstances of conversion, the saint's concern was with spiritual perfection, whether through ecstatic union, self-abnegation, charitable service, or militant propagation of the faith. No matter how much saints might labor in the world, their attention was fixed beyond it and their lives were models of the successful transcendence of normal earthly needs. In this, as we have pointed out, they could not have been more at odds with their devotees, the great majority of whom regarded saints primarily as intercessors. In the eleventh century saints were predominantly power holders—kings, princes, great prelates, and leaders of the monastic orders. They were upper-class males, and they were distributed fairly equally across all parts of Christian Europe. Royalty was believed to possess sacerdotal as well as temporal power, and prelates exercised sway over the bodies as well as the souls of their flocks. The prince who exercised power in this world, it was believed, was likely to do so in the next. All power came from God, and few saw any distinction between its temporal and its spiritual manifestations. Sanctity was power, and power was holy.

By the twelfth century this simple equation of power and sanctity was coming under the criticism of church reformers and popular leaders alike. A new dedication to the life of Christ and the *vita apostolica,* with their implications for moral purpose and spiritual perfection, created a ferment that took a variety of forms, from the struggle against feudal control of the church to the heresies of Peter Waldo and the Cathars. The great model of twelfth-century saintliness was Bernard of Clairvaux, monastic reformer, preacher of crusade, powerful counselor to kings and popes, defender of orthodoxy against the newfangled rationalist notions of Abelard, and censor of excessive preoccupation with material beauty in churches. Bernard was first and last a monk and stood for the traditional ascendancy of monastic culture in medieval society. At the same time he left a literature of religious devotion that earned him a place as one of the builders of the popular and lay piety of the future. In the thirteenth century this current came into its own, finding acceptable expression in mendicancy and confraternities. The model saint of the thirteenth century was, of course, Francis of Assisi, who in contrast to Bernard sought to make the gospel accessible to every believer. Francis brought his quest for Christlike humility out into the streets, where by embracing Lady Poverty he sought to combine ascetic self-abnegation with a life of Christian charity. Whereas the faithful of earlier generations had tended to associate holiness with visible power, thirteenth-century believers found sanctity among the lowliest, those who not only gave up worldly status to follow the apostolic way, but did it in the public world rather than in the cloister. The preponderance of saints of this period came from the mendicant orders that, in propagandizing their own heroes, made asceticism a public and social virtue. The social attributes of saints underwent a radical transformation. The prelate gave way to the mendicant tertiary as a spiritual hero; the awesome king to his ascetic consort; the feudal magnate to the urban worker. Whereas saints had formerly come from every part of Europe, they now were overwhelmingly Italian. Women were objects of veneration as never before: The occasional saintly abbess of the eleventh and twelfth centuries was now joined by the pious widow, the repentant matron, and the guilt-ridden girl. Gender came to count for little and class distinction for even less in the cult of sanctity.

These social changes were accompanied by changes in the fabric of piety. With the waning of domination by prelates and nobles, sainthood came increasingly to represent a piety of personal commitment. Private self-denial and public charity replaced the institutionalized discipline and formalized almsgiving of the monastic rule. Private conscience became the central theme of the quest for holiness, and saints' vitae are enriched with the details of inner discourse. Reflection on personal unworthiness, the immensity of the distance from God, the spiritual hunger for union, and the temptations of worldly pleasures, often in the form of demonic assaults, made up the material of piety in the new hagiography that began to appear in the late twelfth century, became dominant in the thirteenth, and grew still more widespread in the fourteenth and fifteenth.

Certainly the terrors of the Black Death led people to venerate saintly intercessors and to take them as models not only in such practices as penitential flagellation and ritual prayer, but also in the examination of conscience and the acceptance of personal responsibility for the state of their souls. But the Black Death merely heightened a set of trends that had begun considerably earlier and that went much deeper than could be accounted for by the impact of a natural catastrophe. Catholic piety had long since begun to emerge from the confines of the monastery; lay people sought to participate more directly in communing with divinity in everything from the salvation of their souls to the consolation of their hearts, the well-being of their bodies, and the prosperity of their enterprises. Without denying that priests were indispensable, lay people became increasingly impatient with and critical of clerical leadership. The deplorable record of the ecclesiastical establishment should not obscure the fact that these same centuries saw a deepening and spreading of lay piety that is abundantly evident in the lives of the era's saints and in their cults.

But the legacy of sainthood was ambiguous. The saint's life was a lesson in the achievement of holiness through intense self-abnegation for the love of God, of the sacrifice of self in the service of God's creatures. It sought no other reward than nearness to the Creator; it regarded earthly life as a prison and the body as a punishment. Illness was a divine gift and martyrdom the crowning glory. Acknowledging the authority of the church militant, saints nonetheless took upon themselves the personal burden of Christ: to follow him was to imitate him in their own lives. No one could carry the cross for them.

These goals were honored in the lay piety of the Middle Ages and pursued by many who nonetheless fell far short of saintliness. Unquestionably, devotional literature and practice increasingly stressed the personal responsibility of the individual believer. It is worth reminding ourselves that Thomas à Kempis's *Imitation of Christ* was one of the most widely read books of the fifteenth century. The saints' lives themselves were a powerful medium for disseminating these aspirations. But they were also, in the very nature of the phenomenon of cult, a seductive invitation to vicarious piety. The ordinary believer had no hope of achieving the spiritual perfection of a saint, could hardly expect to understand illness as a divine gift or gnawing hunger as an opportunity for spiritual growth. Indeed, the very retelling of the saint's story placed the life in an aura of divinity that was unapproachable for the rank and file. The athlete of Christ had been marked out by divine choice as a child, perhaps even before birth. The stern lesson of the saint's life combined with belief in divine election to convince ordinary devotees of the existence of a spiritual hierarchy in which they themselves occupied a humble position. A few were inspired to imitate the strenuous life of the saints; the many, resigned to their human frailty, asked only for favor.

The saintly treasury of merits reinforced the notion of a vicarious grace; sinners need not imitate Christ, only repent for having failed to do so. The saints had earned enough for all. Even more pervasive was the idea that the saint provided material benefits. Theologians might insist that the saints merely interceded with God for the suppliant, possessing only the power of an influential mediator; but practice by clerics as well as by the laity overrode theological doctrine and turned the saint into a direct dispenser and worker of miracles. When even bones, blood, and bits of clothing were advertised as having supernatural power, the difference between devotion and magic was obscured. When saints and their relics were assumed to work miracles, the distinction between worship and veneration was obliterated. If the life of the saint was the antithesis of vicarious religion, the cult of saints was its most fertile medium.

With the sixteenth century the dualism of Catholic religiousness, with its double message of individual responsibility and vicarious merit, most strikingly evidenced in the phenomenon of sainthood, became the chief issue of the Reformation. Luther's attack on indulgences opened the whole question of Everyman's responsibility for salvation. Protestants condemned the notion of spiritual hierarchy and also a religion of utilitarian motives. Luther, Calvin, and the other reformers had before them the legacy of the saints' lives. They concluded that saints were those who lived in God's grace, but God's grace being a free gift of faith, saints were the community of the faithful. Neither the prelate nor the king nor even the strenuous athlete of Christ was any more likely to possess God's spiritual gifts than the lowliest sinner. All lived in hope that their faith was true. Christians should act like Christ to their neighbors, but no one could redeem or intercede for another.

Catholic reformers also had before them the legacy of the saints. They drew a different conclusion. Since Christians cooperated with divine grace in attaining a state of sanctity, saints were the visible leaders of a community hierarchy ordered according to spiritual achievement. All Christians were part of the body of Christ and were deeply involved in each other's spiritual and physical well-being. As consolation for their low place in the hierarchy, faithful Catholics knew that their spiritual betters would not forget them. The medieval dualism of individual responsibility and vicarious piety, of saints' lives and saints' cults, continues in modern Catholicism, a dualism that is comforting for some, archaic for others.

Here again we reach a conclusion that is also a point of departure. To understand more fully the perception of sanctity and the role of cult, and how these changed from medieval times to our own, we would need to extend our study regionally and locally, combining the archival methods of the historian with the field research of the anthropologist.[5] Such a study would embrace the whole range of supernatural forces of a given locale, including not only its favored saints, but its other wonder-working heroes and its ritual practices. A series of such studies would make more concrete the connections between the two worlds of sainthood that we have taken as our theme.

Appendix on Sources

The following list contains the names of the 864 "saints" included in the statistical analyses for our study. To eliminate any ambiguities about particular saints we also provide date of death and calendar date. Finally, the list indicates the principal sources we used in coding data about the saints' lives and cults. Source type provides a general indication of the nature of available sources for each case. Codes are defined below. Frequently cited texts are designated by an alphabetic abbreviation, while those consulted primarily for a particular case are numbered. Full references for both abbreviated and numbered items will be found in the list of biographical materials beginning on page 271.

Source Type

A = Surviving biographies by contemporaries
B = Surviving notices by contemporaries
C = Contemporary documentation or other information
D = Biography or other information from about twenty-five years after saint's death
E = Information about one century after death
F = Information about two centuries after death
G = Information about three centuries after death
H = Information about four centuries after death
I = Information about five centuries after death
J = Information about six centuries after death
K = Information about seven centuries after death
L = Information about eight centuries after death

M = Information about nine centuries after death
O = Information very weak, even legendary
P = Contemporary notices plus a later biography
Q = Information forged

Name	Date of Death	Calendar Date	Source Type	Source
Adalgott	1031	1026	B	Acta SS. (Novembris I)
Adalgott	1160	1003	B	BSS I
Adamo di Fermo	1212	0516	O	Acta SS.
Adam of Loccum	1210	1222	A	BSS I
Adelaide of Bellich	1015	0205	A	Acta SS.
Adelberto di Cassoria	1065	1123	C	ASB
Adelelmus	1097	0130	D	Acta SS.
Adeline	c 1125	1020	C	Acta SS.
Adelinus	1152	0427	C	Acta SS.
Aderald	c 1004	1020	A	Acta SS.
Adolf	1222	0214	B	Acta SS.
Aelfheâh	1012	0419	D	Acta SS.
Aelfric	1005	0806	O	Acta SS. (Praetermissi)
Agatha Hildegard	1024	0205	B	Acta SS.
Agathange (François Noury)	1638	0807	C	42, 54
Agnese da Sarsina	c 1105	0904	G	MAC III
Agnese di Montepulciano	1317	0420	D	Acta SS.
Agostino Cennini	1420	0831	B	BSS X
Agostino di Biella	1493	0724	B	BSS I
Agostino Novello	1309	0519	A	Acta SS.
Alain de la Roche	1475	0908	B	QE I
Alban Roe	1642	0121	C	19
Albert	1192	1121	A	MGH Sc XXV
Albertino da Montone	1294	0831	C	Acta SS.
Alberto di Bergamo	1279	0314	C	Acta SS. (Maii II)
Alberto di Montecorvino	1127	0405	H	Acta SS.
Alberto di Pontida	1095	0905	P	Acta SS.
Alberto di Siena	c 1181	0707	E	Acta SS. (Februarii II) BSS I
Alberto di Trapani	1307	0807	E	AB XVII (1898)
Albert of Jerusalem	1214	0925	A	Acta SS. (Aprilis I)
Alberto Pandoni	1274	0814	B	Acta SS.
Alberto Quadrelli da Rivalta	1179	0704	I	Acta SS.
Albert the Great	1280	1115	B	BSS I
Aldebrando	1219	0501	A	Acta SS.
Alessandro Sauli	1592	1011	A	Acta SS.
Alessio Falconeri	1310	0212	A	75

Aleth	1105	0404	B	MPL 185
Alex Rawlins and companion	1595	0407	C	POL
Alferio	1050	0412	E	Acta SS.
Alfonso Rodriguez	1617	1030	A	Acta SS.
Alix Le Clerc	1622	0109	C	86
Allucio	1134	1023	C	Acta SS.
Alonso de Orozco	1591	0919	A	BSS IX
Alpais	1211	1103	A	Acta SS.
Altmann	1091	0808	A	MGH Sc XII
Amadeus of Portugal	1482	0810	A	Acta SS.
Amadeus IX	1472	0330	P	Acta SS.
Amata	c 1236	0609	C	33
Ambrogio Sansedoni	1286	0320	B	Acta SS.
Ambrose Barlow	1641	0910	C	19
Amico	c 1045	1102	D	Acta SS.
Amnichad	1043	0130	O	Acta SS.
Ana de S. Bartolomé	1626	0607	A	BSS I
Anafrid of Utrecht	1010	0511	C	Acta SS.
Andrea Avellino	1608	1110	A	Acta SS.
André Abellon	1450	0518	P	BSS I
Andrea Caccioli da Spello	1254	0603	A	Acta SS.
Andrea Corsini	1373	0130	D	Acta SS.
Andrea da Montereale	1480	0412	E	Acta SS.
Andrea dei Conti di Segni	1302	0217	C	Acta SS. (Praetermissi)
Andrea di Strumi	1097	0310	C	Acta SS.
Andrea Dotti	1315	0903	C	BSS IV
Andrea Franchi	1401	0530	P	BSS V
Andrea Gregoda Peschiera	1485	0119	B	Acta SS. (Maii IV)
Andres Hibernon	1602	0418	C	72
Andrew Bobola	1657	0521	C	BSS I
Andrew of Antioch	1360	1130	O	49
Andrew of Chios	1465	0529	A	Acta SS.
Andrew of Rinn	1462	0712	C	Acta SS.
Ange del Pas	1596	0823	A	Acta SS. (Praetermissi)
Angela di Foligno	1309	0228	A	Acta SS. (Ianuarii I)
Angela Merici	1540	0531	C	BSS I
Angela of Bohemia	1243	0706	G	Acta SS.
Angelina dei Conti di Marsciano	1435	0721	F	BSS I
Angelo da Sansepolcro	1306	0215	O	BSS I
Angelo di Acquapagana	1313	0819	G	Acta SS. (Praetermissi)
Angelo di Furcio	1327	0206	P	Acta SS.
Angelo di Sicilia	1220	0505	O	Acta SS.
Angelo Mazzinghi	1438	0818	G	BSS IX
Anne Line	1601	0227	C	MMP

Anselmo	1086	0318	A	Acta SS.
Anselm of Canterbury	1109	0421	A	Acta SS.
Ansuerus and companions	1066	0717	A	Acta SS.
Anthelme	1178	0626	A	Acta SS.
Anthony of Padua	1231	0613	A	Acta SS.
Anthony the Pilgrim	1267	0201	C	Acta SS.
Antonino Pierozzi	1459	0510	A	Acta SS.
Antonio da S. Germano Vercellese	1459	0728	C	BSS II
Antonio di Amandola	1350	0128	B	BSS II
Antonio di Monticiano	1311	0427	A	Acta SS.
Antonio Fatati	1484	0119	C	BSS V
Antonio Grassi	1671	1213	A	BSS VII
Antonio Maria Zaccaria	1539	0705	C	BSS II
Antonio Pavo	1374	0409	B	Acta SS.
Antonio Rossi di Sulmona	15th c	1115	F	Acta SS.
Arcangelo Canetulo	1513	0416	A	Acta SS. (Octobris XIII)
Arcangelo da Calatafimi	1460	0730	E	AB XLV (1927)
Arialdo Alciati	c 1066	0627	A	Acta SS.
Arnolf	1087	0815	A	Acta SS.
Arnoul	c 1075	0919	F	Acta SS.
Attila	c 1009	1005	B	Acta SS.
Atto	c 1153	0522	G	Acta SS.
Augustine Gazotich	1323	0803	P	Acta SS
Austinde	1068	0925	C	Acta SS.
Avertinus of Luigné	1189	0505	B	Acta SS., 33
Barduccio	1331	0704	B	Acta SS.
Bartolo da S. Gimignano	1300	1214	E	BSS II
Bartolomeo di Cevere	1466	0422	B	Acta SS.
Bartolomeo di Foresto	1489	0823	P	Acta SS.
Bartolomeo di Grottaferrata	1050	1111	O	MPL 127
Bartolomeo di Vicenza	1271	1023	P	Acta SS. (Iulii I)
Bartolomeo Fanti	1495	1205	B	BSS V
Battista Spagnoli	1516	0320	B	BSS XI
Beatrice de Lens	c 1217	0119	O	Acta SS. (Praetermissi)
Beatrice de Silva Meneses	1490	0818	C	1
Beatrice d'Este	1226	0510	A	18
Beatrice d'Este	1262	0118	O	Acta SS. (Praetermissi)
Benedetto	1100	0217	B	88
Benedetto da Arezzo	1281	0303	D	Acta SS. (Augusti VI)
Benedetto da Urbino	1625	0430	C	BSS II
Benedict the Moor	1589	0404	C	Acta SS. (Praetermissi)
Benedict XI	1304	0707	A	Acta SS. (Praetermissi)
Bénézet	1184	0414	A	Acta SS.
Benincasa da Montepulciano	1426	0511	F	BSS II
Benigno Visdomini	1236	0717	E	Acta SS.

Benno of Hildesheim	1105	0616	O	Acta SS.
Benno of Osnabrück	1088	0722	A	MGH Sc XXX Pt II
Bentivoglio de Bonis da San Severino	1232	1226	O	BSS II
Benvenuta Bojani	1292	1030	A	Acta SS.
Benvenuto di Gubbio	1232	0627	B	Acta SS. (Septembris V)
Berardo	1130	1103	A	Acta SS.
Berardo di Carbio and companions	1220	0116	P	Acta SS.
Berardo di Pagliara	1123	1219	B	BSS II
Berengar	1108	1029	B	MGH Sc XV
Berengar de Peralta	1256	1002	G	Acta SS.
Berengar de St. Papoul	1093	0526	A	Acta SS.
Bernardo Calvò	1243	1024	C	Acta SS.
Bernard de Abbeville	1117	0414	A	Acta SS.
Bernard de Aosta	1081	0528	F	BSS II
Bernardino da Siena	1444	0520	A	Acta SS.
Bernardino Realino	1616	0703	C	Acta SS. (Praetermissi)
Bernardo da Corleone	1667	0119	A	BSS III
Bernardo da Offida	1694	0826	C	BSS III
Bernard of Clairvaux	1153	0820	A	MGH Sc XXVI Acta SS.
Bernard the Penitent	1182	0419	A	Acta SS.
Bernerius	12th c	1120	E	Acta SS.
Bernold	1054	1125	K	BSS III
Bernwald of Hildesheim	1022	1120	A	MGH Sc IV
Berthold	1142	0727	D	Acta SS.
Berthold	1195	0329	O	Acta SS.
Bertrand	1125	1116	A	Acta SS.
Bona of Pisa	1208	0529	A	Acta SS.
Bonaventura di Forlì	1491	0331	B	BSS III
Bonaventure	1274	0714	B	Acta SS.
Bonavita	1375	0301	B	Acta SS.
Boniface	1260	0219	B	Acta SS.
Bonifacio di Savoia	1270	0714	B	Acta SS. (Praetermissi)
Bonne d'Armagnac	1457	1016	F	36
Bononio	1026	0830	A	Acta SS.
Boris	1015	0724	B	VS
Botwid	1100	0728	D	Acta SS.
Bridget of Sweden	1373	1008	A	Acta SS.
Brihtwold	1045	0122	B	ASB
Bruno di Segni	1123	0718	A	Acta SS.
Bruno of Cologne	1101	1006	P	Acta SS.
Bruno of Ottobeuren	11th c	1224	O	BSS III
Bruno of Querfurt and companions	1009	0619	P	MGH Sc XXX Pt II
Burchard	1022	0304	J	VS

Burchard	1164	0419	C	BSS III
Caietano di Tiene	1547	0807	D	Acta SS.
Camilla Battista da Verano	1527	0607	A	Acta SS. (Maii VII)
Camillo de Lellis	1614	0718	A	BSS III
Caradoc	1124	0414	C	BSS III
Carlo Borromeo	1584	1104	A	51
Carlo da Sezze	1670	0119	A	BSS III
Casilda of Toledo	c 1107	0409	G	Acta SS.
Casimir of Poland	1484	0304	D	Acta SS.
Castora Gabrielli	1391	0614	F	Acta SS.
Caterina de' Ricci	1590	0313	A	85
Caterina di Pallanza	1478	0406	B	Acta SS.
Caterina Tomàs	1574	0405	B	BSS III
Catherine of Bologna	1463	0309	D	Acta SS.
Catherine of Genoa	1510	0915	A	Acta SS.
Catherine of Siena	1380	0430	A	Acta SS.
Catherine of Sweden	1381	0324	P	Acta SS.
Cecilia	1290	0609	B	33
Celsus	1129	0407	B	Acta SS.
Ceslaus of Krakow	1242	0717	P	Acta SS.
Charles de Blois	1364	0929	B	BSS III
Chiara di Montefalco	1308	0817	P	Acta SS.
Chiarito di Firenze	1352	0515	G	Acta SS.
Chremes	c 1116	0806	I	Acta SS.
Christina of Stommeln	1312	1106	A	Acta SS.
Christopher Bales	1590	0304	C	POL
Cicco di Pesaro	c 1350	1001	B	Acta SS.
Clare of Assisi	1253	0812	A	Acta SS.
Claude de la Colombière	1682	0215	A	BSS VII
Clemente da Osimo	1291	0408	E	Acta SS.
Clementia of Hohenberg	1176	0321	G	Acta SS.
Colette Boëllet	1447	0306	A	Acta SS.
Colman	1012	1013	A	Acta SS.
Conrad of Hain	1270	0601	K	Acta SS. (Praetermissi)
Conrad of Saxony	1288	0405	E	Acta SS. (Praetermissi)
Corrado Confalonieri	c 1354	0219	B	20, 82
Corrado d'Offida	c 1292	1214	P	AF III
Corrado Miliani	1289	0419	B	Acta SS.
Costanzo da Fabriano	1481	0225	C	Acta SS. (Praetermissi)
Cristobal	1490	0926	B	BSS IV
Cristoforo di Milano	1484	0301	B	BSS IV
Cunegund	c 1033	0303	P	Acta SS.
Cunegund of Poland	1292	0724	P	Acta SS.
Cuthbert Mayne	1577	1129	C	Camm II
Daniele and companions	1227	1013	C	BSS IV
David Gonson	1541	0712	C	BSS VII

David of Himmerod	1179	1211	B	102
David of Munktorp	c 1082	0715	O	SRS II
Davinus	1051	0603	D	Acta SS.
Desiderius	1194	0120	B	BSS IV
Diego de Alcala	c 1463	1113	E	BSS IV
Domenico Loricato	1060	1114	A	Acta SS.
Domingo	1300	0425	C	BSS IV
Domingo de la Calzada	1190	0512	G	Acta SS.
Domingo de Silos	1073	1220	A	53
Dominic de Guzmán	1221	0804	A	Acta SS.
Druthmar	1046	0215	B	Acta SS. (Augusti III)
Eberhard	1178	0417	C	Acta SS.
Eberhard of Nellenburg	1075	0326	B	BSS V
Edigna	1109	0226	J	Acta SS.
Edmund Arrowsmith	1628	0828	C	MMP
Edmund Campion	1581	1201	A	80
Edmund Catherick	1642	0413	C	MMP
Edmund of Abingdon	1240	1116	A	64
Edward Coleman	1678	0620	C	MMP
Edward Jones and companion	1590	0506	C	POL
Edward Oldcorne	1606	0407	C	MMP
Edward Stransham	1586	0121	C	MMP
Edward the Confessor	1066	1013	A	AB XLI (1923)
Edward Waterson	1593	0107	C	MMP
Egidio da Laurenzana	1518	0114	P	BSS IV
Egidio d'Assisi	1262	0423	A	AF III
Elena dall'Oglio a Bologna	1520	0923	A	Acta SS.
Elena di Udine	1458	0423	A	Acta SS.
Elena Enselmini di Padova	1231	1107	F	Acta SS.
Elizabeth of Hungary	1231	1119	A	MGH Sc XXV AB XXVII (1908)
Elizabeth of Roosendaël	c 1560	0104	O	Acta SS. (Praetermissi)
Elizabeth of Schönau	1164	0618	A	Acta SS.
Elspeth Achler von Reute	1420	1125	A	10
Elzéar de Saban	1323	0927	E	Acta SS.
Emma	1040	0419	B	Acta SS.
Engelbert	1225	1107	A	Acta SS.
Erlembaldo	1075	0627	G	Acta SS.
Ermengardus	1035	1103	C	Acta SS.
Esso	1130	1227	G	100
Ethelnoth	1038	1030	C	Acta SS.
Etienne de Chatillon	1208	0907	D	Acta SS.
Etienne de Liège	1059	0113	B	BSS XI
Eugene III	1153	0708	A	MGH Sc XX
Eustochio Calafato	1491	0216	A	Acta SS. (Praetermissi)

Eustochio di Padova	1469	0213	A	BSS V
Eve de Liège	1265	0314	C	Acta SS. (Aprilis I)
Everard Hanse	1581	0730	C	MMP
Eystein Erlendsson	1188	0126	B	BSS V
Falco di Palena	1130	0809	O	BSS V
Falcone	1146	0606	B	BSS V
Famian ofCologne	1150	0808	O	Acta SS.
Famianus	1150	0808	H	Acta SS.
Fastred	1163	0421	B	MPL 185
Fazio di Cremona	1272	0118	A	Acta SS.
Felice di Cantalicio	1587	0518	A	Acta SS.
Felix de Valois	1212	1120	Q	BSS V
Ferdinand III	1252	0530	A	Acta SS.
Fidel of Sigmaringen	1622	0424	C	BSS V
Filippa Mareri	1236	0216	E	27
Fleur de Beaulieu	1347	1005	A	AB LXIV (1946)
Folquet de Marseilles	1231	1225	C	BSS V
Francesca de' Ponziani	1440	0309	A	Acta SS.
Francesco Caracciolo	1608	0604	D	BSS V
Francesco Catalano	1306	1206	O	BSS III
Francesco da Calderola	1507	0928	O	Acta SS. (Octobris XI)
Francesco di Paola	1507	0402	P	Acta SS.
Francisco de Borja	1572	1010	A	BSS V
Francisco Solano	1610	0713	D	Acta SS.
Francis de Sales	1622	0129	A	26
Francis Dickenson	1590	0430	C	POL
Francis of Assisi	1226	1004	A	Acta SS.
Francis Xavier	1552	1203	A	77
François Page	1602	0420	C	POL
Fulbert	1029	0410	B	Acta SS. (Praetermissi) MPL
Fulcran de Lodève	1006	0213	P	Acta SS.
Fulk	1229	1026	P	Acta SS.
Gabriele Feretti	1456	1112	P	70 AFH IV, L, LI
Galdino	1176	0418	D	Acta SS.
Galgano Guidotti	1181	1205	F	6
Garcia	1073	0926	B	ASB
Gaspar de Bono	1604	0714	E	BSS III
Gaucher d'Aureil	1140	0409	D	Acta SS.
Gaudentius	c 1011	0105	B	Acta SS. (Praetermissi) BSS VI
Gautier de Bierbeck	c 1222	0122	A	Acta SS.
Gautier de Bruges	1307	0122	E	Acta SS.
Gautier de l'Estep	1070	0511	D	Acta SS.
Gebizo di Montecassino	1087	1021	D	Acta SS.
Gelasius	1174	0327	C	97, 31

Gentile da Matelica	c 1355	0905	D	BSS VI
Geoffroy	1138	1020	A	Acta SS. AB I (1882)
Geoffroy de Loudun	1255	0803	A	Acta SS.
George Gervase	1608	0411	C	POL
George Napier	1610	1109	C	MMP
Gerald	1109	1205	C	VS
Gerard	1029	1229	C	99
Gérard	1095	0405	E	Acta SS.
Gerardesca of Pisa	c 1269	0529	A	Acta SS.
Gerardo	1123	1030	A	Acta SS.
Gerardo Mecatti di Villamagna	1245	0523	G	Acta SS.
Gerardo Sagreda	1046	0909	D	Acta SS.
Géraud de Salles	1120	0420	F	Acta SS.
Géri	c 1270	0524	O	Acta SS.
Gerlac of Valkenberg	1170	0105	D	Acta SS.
Germain de Montfort	11th c	1029	D	Acta SS.
Germaine Cousin	1601	0615	C	BSS VI
Gerold of Cologne	1241	1007	O	Acta SS.
Gertrude	1297	0813	B	Acta SS.
Gertrude of Oosten	1358	0106	A	Acta SS.
Gertrude the Great	1302	1116	C	BSS VI 78
Gervin of Rheims	1075	0303	B	BSS VI
Gervin	1117	0417	P	Acta SS.
Gherardo	1119	1030	A	Acta SS.
Giacinta Marescotti	1640	0130	C	28
Giacomina di Settesoli	1239	1004	B	WAM I
Giacomo Benefatti	1332	1126	O	BSS II
Giacomo da Varazze	1298	0713	B	QE I
Giacomo della Marca	1476	1128	A	AFH XVII
Gil	1050	0901	O	Acta SS.
Gilbert	1245	0401	O	Acta SS.
Gilbert of Sempringham	1189	0216	A	Acta SS. (Februarii I)
Gilbert the Great	1167	1017	C	Acta SS. (Praetermissi) MPL
Gilles de Saumur	1266	0423	B	BSS IV
Giordano di Pisa	1311	0303	B	84
Giordano di Pulsano	1152	0905	O	Acta SS.
Giovanna di Reggio	1491	0709	P	Acta SS.
Giovanna Girlani	1495	0125	F	41
Giovanna Maria Bonomo	1670	0301	C	BSS III
Giovanna Soderini	1367	0901	B	Acta SS. (Octobris XII)
Giovanni Angelo Porro	1506	1024	P	Acta SS.
Giovanni Bono	1249	1023	P	Acta SS.
Giovanni Colombini	1367	0731	C	Acta SS.
Giovanni dalle Celle	1380	0310	B	Acta SS.

Giovanni da Matera	1139	0620	D	Acta SS.
Giovanni della Verna	1322	0813	A	Acta SS.
Giovanni di Cagli	1370	0421	B	Acta SS.
Giovanni di Lodi	c 1106	0907	A	Acta SS.
Giovanni di Montemarano	c 1094	0817	B	Acta SS.
Giovanni di Perugia	1231	0901	P	Acta SS. (Augusti VI)
Giovanni di Tossignano	1446	0724	A	Acta SS.
Giovanni di Vercelli	1283	1201	A	BSS VI
Giovanni Dominici	1419	0610	A	Acta SS.
Giovanni Giovenale Ancina	1604	0830	A	BSS I
Giovanni Grandenico	1003	1112	A	MGH Sc XV Pt II
Giovanni Gualberto	1073	0712	A	Acta SS. MGH Sc XXX Pt II
Giovanni Leonardi	1609	1009	C	BSS VI
Giovanni Rainuzzi	1330	0608	O	Acta SS.
Giovanni Terrestri	c 1127	0224	P	Acta SS.
Girolamo di Corsica	1479	1125	C	BSS VI
Girolamo di Vallombrosa	1135	0618	B	Acta SS.
Girolamo Miani	1537	0720	D	Acta SS.
Girolamo Ranuzzi	c 1467	1211	B	BSS XI
Giuliana di Busto Arsizio	1501	0814	A	Acta SS. (Octobris X)
Giuliana Falconeri	1341	0619	G	Acta SS.
Giuliano Cesarello	c 1350	0511	O	Acta SS.
Giuliano Maiali	1470	1004	C	VS
Giuseppe da Leonessa	1612	0204	C	BSS VI
Giuseppe di Cupertino	1663	0918	P	Acta SS.
Godefroy de Péronne	1147	0115	O	32
Godelieve	1070	0706	A	Acta SS.
Gonçalo de Amarante	1259	0116	A	Acta SS.
Gonçalo de Lagos	1422	1021	B	Acta SS.
Gonsalo Vas Lopes-Netto	1638	0807	C	42, 54
Goswin	1165	1009	A	Acta SS. MGH Sc XIV
Goswin de Boulancourt	1203	1027	C	Acta SS.
Gothalm	c 1020	0726	G	Acta SS.
Gothard of Hildesheim	1038	0604	A	MGH Sc XI
Grazia of Cataro	1508	1116	E	Acta SS.
Gregoria Barbarigo	1697	0617	C	BSS VII
Gregorio Celli	1343	0504	O	BSS III
Gregory VII	1085	0525	A	Acta SS.
Guala of Bergamo	1244	0903	F	Acta SS.
Gualterio	1224	0722	H	Acta SS.
Gualterio	c 1258	0802	C	Acta SS.
Gualterio	13th c	0604	F	Acta SS.
Guarino	1159	0206	C	Acta SS.
Guerric	1157	0819	B	MPL 182, 185
Guglielmo della Torre	1226	1021	C	Acta SS.

Guglielmo di Polizzi	1317	0416	G	Acta SS.
Guglielmo di Scicli	1404	0404	E	79
Guido	1045	1123	A	76
Guillaume	1131	0714	C	AOB VI
Guillaume de Brabant	1241	0210	A	Acta SS.
Guillaume de Dongelberg	c 1250	0524	B	Acta SS. (Praetermissi) BSS VII
Guillaume de Pontoise	1192	0510	B	Acta SS.
Guillaume de St. Bénigne	1031	0101	A	Acta SS.
Guillaume de Sauvigny	12th c	1020	B	Acta SS.
Guillaume de Toulouse	1369	0518	P	Acta SS.
Guillaume Firmatus	1090	0424	D	Acta SS.
Guillaume le Grand	1157	0210	O	Acta SS.
Guillaume Tempier	1195	0327	C	Acta SS.
Gurloes	1057	0825	O	BSS VII
Guy de Durnes	1157	0923	C	VS
Hanno of Cologne	1075	1204	D	MGH Sc XI
Haseka	1261	0126	F	Acta SS.
Hathebrand	1198	0730	P	Acta SS.
Hedwige of Bavaria	1243	1016	D	Acta SS.
Heimerad	1019	0628	E	MGH Sc X
Helen of Skövde	1160	0731	P	Acta SS.
Helinand	1237	0203	B	Acta SS. (Praetermissi) BSS IV
Henry	c 1055	0215	C	Acta SS.
Henry Morse	1645	0201	A	MMP
Henry of Hungary	1031	1104	E	Acta SS.
Henry Suso	1366	0302	A	11
Henry II	1024	0715	A	Acta SS. MGH Sc IV
Herbert Hoscam	1180	0820	C	Acta SS.
Heribert	1021	0316	A	Acta SS.
Herman of Heidelberg	1326	0903	C	BSS V
Herman the Cripple	1054	0925	C	MGH Sc V
Hervé de Ile-de-Chalonne	1119	0718	C	25
Hildegard of Bingen	1179	0917	A	Acta SS.
Honoré de Buzançais	1250	0109	G	BSS IX
Hosanna of Releza	1565	0427	A	BSS IX
Hroznata	1217	0719	A	Acta SS.
Hugh Green	1642	0819	A	68
Hugh of Cluny	1109	0429	A	Acta SS.
Hugh of Lincoln	1200	1117	A	2
Hugues de Glazinis	1250	1108	O	Acta SS. (Praetermissi)
Hugues de Grenoble	1132	0401	A	Acta SS.
Hugues de Marchiennes	1158	0611	A	69
Hugues de Montaigu	1136	0810	B	Acta SS.
Humbaud	1114	1020	B	Acta SS.

Iacopo da Cerqueto	1367	0417	O	Acta SS. (Praetermissi)
Iacopo di Padova	1322	0409	B	Acta SS.
Iazech	1257	0817	E	95
Ida de Louvain	1290	0413	P	Acta SS.
Ignatius Loyola	1556	0731	A	Acta SS.
Imelda Lambertini	1333	0513	C	Acta SS.
Inácio de Azevedo and thirty-nine companions	1570	0715	C	66
Iñigo	1057	0601	P	Acta SS.
Innocent V	1277	0622	A	BSS VII
Innocent XI	1689	0812	B	BSS VII
Ippolito Galantini	1619	0320	D	BSS V
Isabella of Portugal	1336	0708	A	Acta SS.
Isabelle of France	1270	0226	A	Acta SS.
Isaiah Boner	1471	0208	C	Acta SS.
Isarn	1408	0924	A	Acta SS.
Isidore the Farmer	1130	0515	F	Acta SS.
Ismidon	c 1095	1029	K	Acta SS.
Ismidon de Sassenage	1115	0928	B	Acta SS.
Jacques Salès and companion	1593	0207	D	BSS XI
Jadwiga of Poland	1399	0228	B	BSS IV
James Bell and companion	1584	0420	C	MMP
James Bird	1593	0325	C	POL
James Duckett	1602	0419	A	POL
James the Almsgiver	1304	0128	D	21
Jean	1146	0426	D	67
Jean de Gand	1439	0929	C	37
Jean Eudes	1680	0819	A	BSS VI
Jean François Régis	1640	0616	A	62
Jeanne de Lestonnac	1640	0202	C	BSS VI
Jeanne de Valois	1505	0204	P	Acta SS.
Jeanne Françoise Fremyot de Chantal	1641	0821	A	BSS VI
Jeanne Marie de Maillé	1414	1106	A	Acta SS. (Martii III)
Jermyn Gardiner	1544	0307	C	Camm I
Joan of Arc	1431	0530	C	81
Johannes Lobedaw	1264	1009	P	Acta SS.
John and companions	1342	0414	B	Acta SS.
John Almond	1612	1205	C	POL
John Amias and companion	1589	0316	C	POL
John Berchmans	1621	1126	A	AB XXXIV–XXXV (1915)
John Bodey	1583	1102	C	POL
John Boste and companions	1594	0724	C	MMP
John Cornelius and companions	1594	0704	C	POL

John Duckett	1644	0907	C	MMP
John Fisher	1535	0709	A	45 AB X (1891) XII (1893)
John Ireland	1544	0311	D	50
John Jones	1598	0712	C	MMP
John Lockwood	1642	0413	C	MMP
John Nepomucene	1383	0516	O	Acta SS.
John of Bridlington	1379	1021	A	AB LIII (1935)
John of Capistrano	1456	0328	A	Acta SS. (Octobris X)
John of Dukla	1484	0928	C	61
John of Kenty	1473	1020	F	Acta SS.
John of Matha	1213	0208	B	BSS VI
John of the Cross	1591	1124	A	38
John Ogilvie	1615	0310	C	LS
John Payne	1582	0402	C	Camm II
John Pibush	1601	0218	C	MMP
John Prandota	1266	0921	F	Acta SS.
John Rigby	1600	0621	A	MMP
John Roberts	1610	1210	C	POL
John Sarkander	1620	0317	A	BSS XI
John Slade	1583	1030	C	MMP
John Southworth	1654	0628	C	MMP
John Stone	1539	0512	D	Camm I
John Storey	1571	0601	C	Camm II
John the Good	12th c	0905	B	Acta SS. (Iunii IV)
John the Spaniard	1160	0625	A	Acta SS.
Joscius	1186	1130	C	Acta SS. AB XXI (1902), XXII (1903)
José Calasanto	1648	0827	A	BSS VI
Josefa	1696	0122	C	BSS VI
Josephat Kuncewicz	1623	1114	C	14
Juana de Aza	1190	0808	O	4
Juan Batista Garcias	1613	0214	C	BSS VI
Juan Cirita	1164	1223	B	MPL 188
Juan de Avila	1569	0510	A	55
Juan de Britto	1693	0204	A	BSS VI
Juan de Dios	1550	0308	D	Acta SS.
Juan de Montfort	1177	0524	O	5
Juan de Prado	1631	0524	C	BSS VI
Juan de Ribera	1611	0106	A	74
Juan de Sahagún	1479	0612	A	Acta SS.
Juan Grande	1600	0603	C	BSS VII
Juan Marcías	1645	0918	C	29
Jules Maunoir	1683	0128	C	LS
Julián de S. Augustin	1606	0408	C	WAM XXIV
Julian of Norwich	1423	0513	B	60

Jutta de Huy	1228	0113	A	Acta SS.
Jutta of Diessenberg	c 1136	1222	O	BSS VII
Jutta I of Fuchstadt	1250	1129	A	CC XI (1899)
Kennocha	1007	0313	O	Acta SS.
Ketillus	1150	0711	O	Acta SS.
Ketillus of Viborg	1151	0711	H	Acta SS. (Iulii III)
Knut	1086	0119	A	Acta SS.
Knut Lavard	1131	0107	A	Acta SS.
Ladislas of Gielnow	1505	0511	F	Acta SS.
Ladislas of Hungary	1095	0627	E	Acta SS.
Lanfranc	1089	0524	A	Acta SS.
Lanfranc of Pavia	1194	0623	A	Acta SS.
Lanzo	1100	0401	C	104
Lawrence O'Toole	1181	1114	E	AB XXXIII (1914)
Leon de St. Bertin	1163	0226	B	12
Leone II di Cava dei Tirreni	1295	0819	C	57
Leopold	1136	0115	P	83
Libentius	1013	0104	B	Acta SS.
Liberato da Loro Piceno	1258	0906	O	Acta SS. (Augusti V)
Lidano	1118	0702	F	Acta SS.
Lidwige of Schiedam	1433	0414	A	Acta SS.
Liébert	1076	0623	A	Acta SS.
Lorenzo da Brindisi	1619	0723	C	23
Lorenzo da Villamagna	1535	0606	O	BSS VIII
Lorenzo Giustiniani	1455	0905	A	Acta SS. (Ianuarii I)
Louise de Marillac	1660	0315	A	BSS VIII
Louis of Anjou	1297	0819	B	Acta SS.
Louis of Gonzaga	1591	0621	A	24
Louis IX	1270	0825	A	Acta SS.
Lucia Broccadeli	1544	1116	A	BSS III
Lucia da Caltagirone	1400	0926	A	Acta SS.
Ludan	1202	0212	O	Acta SS.
Ludolf	1250	0330	C	Acta SS.
Ludovica Albertoni	1533	0228	F	WAM XXVI
Ludovico Morbioli	1485	1116	A	Acta SS.
Ludwig of Thuringia	1227	0911	A	Acta SS.
Luigi Rabata	1490	0511	D	BSS X
Luis Bertran	1581	1009	A	Acta SS.
Maddalena Panatieri	1503	1013	D	BSS X
Mafalda	1257	0502	H	Acta SS. (Praetermissi)
Magnus of Orkney	1106	0416	E	Acta SS.
Malachy of Armagh	1148	1103	A	Acta SS.
Malrub	1040	0827	O	Acta SS.
Manez de Guzmán	c 1230	0730	B	VS
Marc Barkworth	1601	0227	C	POL
Marco de' Marconi	1510	0224	B	Acta SS. (Septembris VI Praetermissi)

Marco di Modena	1498	0924	B	Acta SS.
Margaret Clitherow	1586	0325	A	77
Margaret of Cortona	1297	0222	A	Acta SS.
Margaret of Hungary	1270	0126	B	Acta SS.
Margaret of Roskilde	1177	1025	B	Acta SS.
Margaret of Scotland	1093	0610	A	Acta SS.
Margaret Pole	1541	0528	C	Camm I
Margaret the Barefooted	1395	0827	B	Acta SS.
Margherita da Faenza	1330	0826	A	Acta SS.
Marguerite de Lorraine	1521	1102	D	56
Marguerite de Louvain	1225	0902	B	Acta SS.
Marguerite-Marie Alacoque	1690	1017	A	47
Maria Anna de Jesus	1624	0427	A	BSS VIII
Maria Anna de Jesus de Paredes y Flores	1645	0526	B	BSS VII
Maria de Alzira	1180	0601	I	Acta SS. (Augusti IV)
Maria de la Cabeza	12th c	0908	B	Acta SS.
Maria di Pisa	c 1200	1204	A	BSS VIII
Maria Maddalena de' Pazzi	1607	0529	A	Acta SS.
Maria Mancini	1431	0128	C	BSS VIII
Marie de l'Incarnation	1618	0418	A	VS
Marina Villarina	c 1300	0618	F	Acta SS.
Marino	1170	1215	B	BSS VIII
Mark Xineiemon	1622	0819	B	BSS VI
Martin Cid	1152	1008	B	Acta SS.
Martin de Soure	c 1156	0131	A	Acta SS.
Martin of Porres	1639	1105	A	Acta SS.
Martyrs, English Carthusian	1535	0511	C	AB XXII (1903) d. 1535 and 1537
Martyrs of Gorkum	1572	0709	A	Acta SS.
Martyrs of Japan, II	1617	0601	C	BSS VI
Martyrs of Kaschau	1619	0907	C	BSS III
Martyrs of London, 1582	1582	0528	C	Camm II MMP
Martyrs of London, 1588	1588	0828	B	MMP POL
Martyrs of London, 1591	1591	1210	A	POL
Martyrs of Nagasaki	1597	0205	C	Acta SS.
Martyrs of North America	1642	0926	C	BSS III, IV d. 1642–1650
Martyrs of Paraguay	1628	1117	C	LS
Martyrs of the Titus Oates Plot	1679	0620	C	MMP
Matilda	c 1200	0411	O	Acta SS. (Praetermissi)
Matilda of Spannheim	1154	0226	H	VS
Matteo di Masaccio	1320	0911	F	BSS IX
Matthew	1003	1112	B	MGH Sc XV
Maurice of Hungary	1336	0320	A	Acta SS.
Mechtild of Diessen	1160	0531	A	Acta SS.
Michael Gedroye	1485	0504	P	Acta SS.

Miguel de los Santos	1625	0410	E	91
Miles Gerard	1590	0430	C	POL
Milon	1070	0223	B	Acta SS.
Milon de Sélincourt	1158	0716	C	Acta SS. (Praetermissi)
Monaldo	1314	0315	B	Acta SS.
Morand	1115	0603	D	Acta SS.
Morico	1236	0330	B	Acta SS.
Nevelone da Faenza	1280	0813	D	Acta SS.
Niccolò Albergati	1443	0509	A	Acta SS.
Niccolò da Orvieto	1259	0128	O	Acta SS. (Praetermissi)
Niccolò Giustiniani	1180	1121	O	BSS VII
Nicholas Hermansson	1391	0724	D	93
Nicholas of Tolentino	1306	0910	A	Acta SS.
Nicholas Owen	1606	0312	A	POL
Nicholas Tavilić	1391	1205	B	52
Nicholas the Pilgrim	1094	0602	A	Acta SS.
Nicholas von Flüe	1487	0322	A	Acta SS.
Nicola da Forca Palena	1449	1001	G	Acta SS. (Septembris VIII)
Nicola da Montecorvino	1358	0404	B	AF III
Nicola Paglia	1255	0214	O	BSS X
Nicola Politi	1167	0817	P	Acta SS.
Nicolás Factor	1583	1214	D	73
Norbert of Xanten	1134	0606	A	MGH Sc XII
Obizio da Niardo	1204	0204	C	Acta SS.
Octavien	1132	0806	B	BSS IX
Odon	1113	0619	A	Acta SS. MGH XIV, XV
Oldegarius	1137	0306	P	Acta SS.
Oliver Plunket	1681	0711	D	MMP
Omobono di Cremona	1197	1113	C	BSS XI
Ordoño Didaz	1065	0223	B	BSS IX
Osanna Andreasi	1505	0620	A	Acta SS.
Osmond	1099	1204	C	22
Ottone	c 1120	0323	Q	Acta SS.
Otto of Bamberg	1139	0702	A	MGH Sc XII
Otto of Kappenberg	1171	0223	A	Acta SS. (Praetermissi) MGH Sc
Pacifico di Cerano	1482	0608	C	Acta SS.
Pagano di Lecco	1277	1226	B	90
Panacea	1383	0501	A	Acta SS.
Paola Gambara-Costa	1515	0131	C	BSS VI
Paolo Burali	1578	0617	A	BSS III
Pascual Baylon	1592	0517	A	Acta SS.
Paternus	1058	0410	C	Acta SS.
Pedro Armengol	1304	0427	O	Acta SS. (Septembris I)
Pedro Claver	1654	0909	D	BSS X

Pedro de Alcantara	1562	1019	D	Acta SS.
Pedro de Arbues	1485	0917	C	Acta SS.
Pedro de Dueñas	1397	0519	O	Acta SS. (Praetermissi)
				WAM I
Pedro de Mezonzo	1003	0910	C	Acta SS (Praetermissi)
Pedro Regalado	1456	0513	P	Acta SS. (Martii III)
Pellegrino	c 1250	0320	O	Acta SS.
Pellegrino Laziosi	1345	0501	E	Acta SS.
Peregrinus	c 1190	0426	P	Acta SS.
Peter Canisius	1595	0427	A	17, 15
Peter Celestine	1296	0519	A	Acta SS.
Peter Damian	1072	0223	A	Acta SS.
Peter Martyr of Verona	1252	0429	A	Acta SS.
Peter Nolasco	1258	0128	Q	Acta SS.
Peter of Tarentaise	1175	0508	A	Acta SS.
Peter of the Cross	1522	0706	O	Acta SS.
Peter Wright	1651	0519	C	MMP
Petronille	12th c	0713	B	Acta SS.
Petronille de Moncel	1355	0514	O	BSS X
Philip Benizi	1285	0823	P	Acta SS.
Philip Howard	1595	1019	C	LS
Philip Neri	1595	0526	A	Acta SS.
Philippa de Chantemilan	1451	1015	A	Acta SS.
Philippa de Gheldre	1547	0226	B	VS
Philip Powell	1646	0630	C	19
Pierre	1115	0404	B	Acta SS. (Praetermissi)
Pierre Berthelot	1638	1129	A	43
Pierre de Chavanon	1080	0911	D	Acta SS.
Pierre de Luxembourg	1387	0702	A	Acta SS.
Pierre Fourier	1640	1209	A	40
Pietro Acotanto	c 1180	0923	G	Acta SS.
Pietro Becheti	1221	0811	C	BSS VI
Pietro Capucci	1445	1021	B	BSS III
Pietro di Anagni	1105	0803	B	Acta SS.
Pietro di Cava	1123	0304	A	Acta SS.
Pietro di Gubbio	1287	0323	O	Acta SS.
Pietro di Sassoferrato	1231	0901	B	Acta SS. (Augusti VI)
Pietro Geremia	1452	0310	A	Acta SS.
Pietro Petroni	1361	0529	A	Acta SS.
Pietro Pettinaio	1289	1211	A	35
Pius V	1572	0505	A	Acta SS.
Placido di Rosi	1248	0612	A	Acta SS.
Poppo	1048	0125	A	Acta SS.
Procopius	1053	0704	A	Acta SS.
Radegunda	c 1152	0129	I	Acta SS.
Raimondo di Capua	1399	1005	C	Acta SS. (Praetermissi)

Raimondo di Palmerio	1200	0728	A	Acta SS.
Rainaldo di Ravenna	1321	0818	E	Acta SS.
Ralph Ashley	1606	0407	O	MMP
Ralph Corby	1644	0907	C	MMP
Raniero	1077	1230	C	BSS XI
Raymond de Barbastro	1126	0621	A	103
Raymond Lull	1315	0905	A	AB XLVIII (1930)
Raymond Nonnatus	1240	0831	G	Acta SS.
Raymond of Peñafort	1275	0123	P	Acta SS.
Rayner the Cloistered	c 1237	0411	P	Acta SS.
Regimbald	1039	1013	D	Acta SS. (Praetermissi)
Reginaldo Montemarti	1348	0409	B	MFP XX
Richard Gwyn	1584	1025	A	94
Richard Herst	1628	0829	C	MMP
Richard Langley	1586	1201	B	MMP
Richard Newport	1612	0530	C	19
Richard of Chichester	1253	0430	E	Acta SS.
Richard Rolle	1349	0929	C	3
Richard Whiting and companions	1539	1201	C	Camm I
Richildis	1100	0823	O	Acta SS.
Rita di Cascia	1456	0522	F	Acta SS.
Robert Anderton	1586	0426	B	POL
Robert Bellarmine	1621	0513	A	9, 16
Robert de Bruges	1157	0429	B	BSS XI
Robert de la Chaise-Dieu	1067	0417	A	Acta SS.
Robert de Molesme	1110	0429	E	Acta SS.
Roberto di Sulmo	1341	0718	A	Acta SS.
Robert of Newminster	1139	0607	E	Acta SS. AB LVI (1938)
Robert Southwell	1595	0221	C	POL
Robert Watkinson	1602	0420	C	POL
Robert Wilcox and companions	1588	1001	B	MMP
Roche	1327	0816	O	Acta SS.
Rodolfo Acquaviva and companions	1583	0727	C	BSS XI
Rodolfo di Gubbio	1064	1017	A	Acta SS.
Roger	1160	0101	A	Acta SS.
Roger Dickenson	1591	0707	C	POL
Roger the Strong	c 1367	0301	A	Acta SS.
Rolando de' Medici	1386	0915	A	Acta SS.
Romuald	1027	0207	A	Acta SS.
Rosalia	12th c	0904	H	Acta SS.
Roseline de Villeneuve	1329	0117	C	Acta SS. (Iunii II)
Rose of Lima	1617	0830	A	Acta SS.
Rose of Viterbo	1252	0904	P	Acta SS.

Rouph	1041	1031	K	Acta SS.
Rudolph	1287	0417	C	Acta SS.
Sadoc of Poland and companions	1260	0602	B	BSS XI 101
Salvador de Horta	1567	0318	P	Acta SS.
Sancho	1082	0315	B	BSS XI
Santuccia Terrebotti	1305	0321	C	Acta SS.
Sebastian of the Apparition	1600	0225	C	BSS XI
Sebastiano Maggi	1496	1216	C	34
Séhère	1128	0508	B	MGH Sc XII
Serafina	1253	0312	E	Acta SS.
Serafino di Montegranaro	1604	1017	D	Acta SS.
Serlo of Bayeux	1104	0303	B	96
Sigfrid	1045	0215	F	Acta SS.
Silvestro	1348	0609	A	Acta SS.
Silvestro Gozzalini	1267	1126	A	13.
Simeon	1016	0726	C	Acta SS.
Simeone di Treviri	1035	0601	A	Acta SS.
Simon de Crèpy	c 1080	0930	A	Acta SS.
Simon de Rojas	1624	0928	C	BSS XI
Simon de St. Bertin	1148	0204	B	Acta SS. (Praetermissi)
Simone da Todi	1322	0420	C	Acta SS.
Simone di Rimini	1319	1103	D	Acta SS.
Simon Stock	1265	0516	F	Acta SS.
Sperandea	1276	0911	P	Acta SS.
Stanislas Kostka	1568	1113	A	AB IX, XI, XIII–XVI (1890–1897)
Stanislas of Krakow	1079	0507	P	Acta SS.
Stefana Quinzani	1530	0102	C	BSS X
Stèphan	1242	0529	B	Acta SS.
Stephen of Grandmont	1124	0208	E	Acta SS.
Stephen of Hungary	1038	0902	A	Acta SS.
Sura of Dordrecht	11th c	0210	O	Acta SS.
Teobaldo Roggeri	1150	0601	P	Acta SS.
Teresa de Portugal	1250	0617	P	Acta SS.
Teresa of Avila	1582	1015	A	Acta SS.
Tesauro	1258	0912	C	VS
Thaddeus	1497	1025	O	LS
Theobaldus	1066	0630	A	Acta SS.
Thibaud de Le Dorat	1070	0127	A	Acta SS. (Novembris III)
Thibaut	1247	0727	A	CC XV (1903)
Thiemo	1102	0928	B	Acta SS. (Praetermissi)
Thomas Abel and companions	1540	0730	C	Camm I
Thomas à Kempis	1471	0805	A	98
Thomas Alfield	1585	0706	C	MMP

Thomas Aquinas	1274	0307	A	Acta SS.
Thomas Becket	1070	1229	A	87
Thomas Garnet	1608	0623	C	POL
Thomas Hemerford	1584	0212	C	MMP
Thomas Holland	1642	1212	A	POL
Thomas Maxfield	1616	0701	A	MMP
Thomas More	1535	0709	A	89, 92
Thomas of Cantilupe	1282	1003	C	Acta SS.
Thomas of Ely	1257	1019	A	Acta SS.
Thomas of Walden	1430	1102	C	BSS XII
Thomas Plumtree	1570	0204	C	Camm II
Thomas Reynolds	1642	0121	C	POL
Thomas Sherwood	1578	0207	A	Camm II POL
Thomas Somers	1610	1210	C	POL
Thomas Tunstal	1616	0713	C	19
Thomas Welbourn	1605	0801	O	MMP
Thomas Woodhouse	1573	0619	C	Camm II 46
Thorlak Thorkellson	1193	1227	A	63
Thorphin	1284	0108	H	Acta SS.
Tomàs de Villanueva	1555	0922	A	Acta SS.
Tomàs Rodriguez	1638	1129	B	BSS IV
Tommaso di Orvieto	c 1343	0623	B	48
Tommaso di Tolentino	1321	0409	B	Acta SS.
Torello	1282	0316	A	Acta SS.
Toubio Alfonso de Mogrovejo	1606	0427	C	58
Tregidia	c 1030	1122	H	BSS XII
Ubaldo Adimari	1315	0409	C	BSS I
Ubaldo di Gubbio	1160	0516	A	Acta SS.
Ugolina di Vercelli	1300	0808	C	7
Ugolino di Gualdo	1260	0101	O	BSS XII
Ulrich of Zell	1093	0714	A	MGH Sc XII
Umile da Bisignano	1637	1127	C	BSS XII
Umiliana Cerchi	1246	0519	A	Acta SS.
Umiltà	1310	0522	A	Acta SS.
Urban II	1099	0729	A	BSS XII
Ursulina di Parma	1410	0407	D	Acta SS.
Ventura da Spello	c 1258	0503	O	Acta SS.
Venturino di Bergamo	1346	0328	A	30
Victor III	1087	0916	A	Acta SS. MGH Sc VII
Villana Botti	1360	0228	C	Acta SS.
Villano	1240	0506	B	Acta SS.
Vincent de Paul	1660	0719	A	BSS XII
Vincent Ferrer	1419	0405	D	Acta SS.
Vincent Kadlubek	1223	0308	B	Acta SS. (Praetermissi)
Vincenzo di l'Aquila	1504	0813	P	BSS XII

Vital de Savigny	1122	0916	A	Acta SS. (Ianuarii I) AB I (1882)
Vittoria Maria Fornari-Stratta	1617	0912	A	BSS V
Vivaldo	1300	0501	O	Acta SS.
Vladimir of Kiev	1015	0715	A	VS
Volkuin of Sittenbach	1154	0918	E	71
Wallenbert	1141	1231	C	8
Walstan of Bawburgh	1016	0530	A	59
Waltmann	1138	0411	C	Acta SS. (Iunii I)
Walto	1156	1227	O	BSS II ("Baltone")
Wilfrida	c 1000	0909	E	Acta SS.
William Andleby and companions	1597	0704	C	MMP
William Browne	1605	0801	C	44
William Freeman	1595	0813	C	MMP
William Harrington	1594	0218	C	LS
William Hart	1583	0315	C	Camm II
William Lacey	1582	0822	C	Camm II
William Maroden	1586	0425	B	POL
William of Montevergine	1142	0625	A	Acta SS.
William of Rochester	1201	0523	A	Acta SS.
William of Roschild	1203	0406	A	Acta SS.
William of St. Brieuc	1234	0729	A	Acta SS.
William of York	1154	0608	B	Acta SS.
William Pattinson	1592	0122	C	POL
William Richardson	1603	0217	O	LS
William Scott	1612	0530	C	19
William Ward	1641	0726	C	POL
Willigis	1011	0223	B	MGH Sc XV Pt I
Wirnto	1127	1029	E	MGH Sc XV Pt II
Wizelin	1154	1212	A	MGH Sc XXI
Wolfhard	1127	0430	D	Acta SS.
Wolfhelm	1091	0422	A	MGH Sc XII
Wulfstan	1095	0119	A	Acta SS.
Yves Helory	1303	0519	A	Acta SS.

Biographical Materials

AB   *Analecta Bollandiana.* Brussels, 1882 sgg.
Acta SS.   *Acta Sanctorum.* Brussels and others, 1643 sgg.
AF   *Analecta Franciscana.*
AFH   *Archivum Franciscanum Historicum.*
AOB   Mabillon, J. *Annales Ordinis S. Benedicti.* Paris, 1703–39.
ASB   Mabillon, J. *Acta Sanctorum Ordinis Sancti Benedicti.* Paris, 1668–1701.

BSS   *Bibliotheca Sanctorum.* Rome, 1961.
Camm   Camm, Bede. *Lives of the English Martyrs.* London, 1914.
CC   *Cistercienser Chronik.*
LS   Thurston, Herbert, and Attwater, Donald, eds. *Butler's Lives of the Saints.* New York, 1963.
MAC   Mittarelli, Giovanni Benedetto. *Annales Camaldulenses.* Venice, 1758.
MFP   *Monumenta Ordinis Fratrum Praedicatorum Historica.*
MGH Sc   Pertz, G.H., et al., eds. *Monumenta Germaniae Historica, Scriptores.* Hanover and Berlin, 1826 sgg.
MMP   Challoner, Richard. *Memoires of Missionary Priests.* London, 1741, edited London, 1924 by J. H. Pollen.
MPL   Migne, J. P., ed. *Patrologia Latina.* Paris, 1844–64.
POL   Burton, E. H., and Pollen, J. H. *Lives of the English Martyrs.* 2d ser. London, 1914.
QE   Quétif, J., and Echard, J. *Scriptores Ordinis Praedicatorum recensiti.* Paris, 1719–21.
SRS   *Scriptores Rerum Suecicarum Medii Aevi.* Upsala, 1838.
VS   *Vies des saints et des bienheureux.* Paris, 1935–56.
WAM   Wadding, L., et al. *Annales Minorum,* 3d ser. Quaracchi, 1931 sgg.

1. *Acta Ordinis Fratrum Minorum,* 93, fasc. 1–2. Rome, 1974.
2. Adam of Eynsham. *Magna Vita Sancti Hugonis,* 2 vols., ed. D. Douie and H. Farmer. London, 1961.
3. Allen, Hope E. *Writings Ascribed to Richard Rolle Hermit of Hampole and Materials for His Biography.* New York, 1927.
4. *Annalium Ordinis Praedicatorum,* vol. 1. Rome, 1756.
5. Aranda, Antonio de. *Verdadura informacion dela tierra sancta segun,* folio 109. Toledo, 1550.
6. Arbesmann, R. "The Three Earliest Vitae of St. Galganus." In *Didascaliae: Studies in Honour of Anselm M. Albareda,* presented by a group of American scholars, New York, 1961.
7. Arnoldi, Domenico. *L'eremita di Biliemme.* Vercelli, 1909.
8. Backmund, Norbert. *Monasticon Praemonstratense,* vol. 2. Strasbourg, 1952.
9. Bartoli, Danillo. *Della vita di Roberto Cardinal Bellarmino.* Rome, 1678.
10. Bihlmeyer, Karl. "Die Schwäbische Mystikerin Elsbeth Achler von Reute (†1420) und die Überlieferung iher Vita." *Festgabe Phillipp Strauch,* ed Georg Baesecke und Ferdinand Joseph Schneide, 88–109. Halle a.d. Saale, 1932. Reprinted Tübingen 1973.
11. Bihlmeyer, Karl. *Heinrich Seuse, Deutsche Schriften.* Stuttgart, 1907.

12. *Biographie nationale* Académie Royale des Sciences, des Lettres et des Beaux-Arts de Belgique. Brussels, 1866 ff., vol. 11.
13. Bolzonetti, Amadeo. *Il monte Fano e un grande anacoreta.* Rome, 1906.
14. Boresky, Theodosia. *Life of St. Josephat Martyr of the Union.* New York, 1955.
15. Braunsberger, Otto, ed. *Petrus Canisius, Epistolae et Acta.* 8 vols. Freiburg. 1896–1923.
16. Brodrick, James. *Robert Bellarmine: Saint and Scholar.* London, 1961.
17. Brodrick, James. *Saint Peter Canisius.* Chicago, 1962.
18. Brunacci, G., ed. *Della B. Beatrice D'Este vita antichissima.* Padua, 1767.
19. Camm, Bede. *Nine Martyr Monks.* London, 1931.
20. Campi, Pietromaria. *Vita di S. Corrado Eremita.* Piacenza, 1614.
21. Canuti, Fiorenzo, ed. *Documenti per la vita e per il culto del B. Giacomo Villa di Città della Pieve.* Perugia, 1952.
22. Capgrave [John?]. "De Sancto Osmundo," in *Nova Legenda Anglie,* ed. Carl Horstman, vol. 2. Oxford, 1801.
23. Carmignano, Arturo da. *San Lorenzo da Brindisi.* 4 vols. Padua, 1960–63.
24. Cepari, Virgilio. *Vita del Beato Luigi Gonzaga della Compania di Gesu.* Piacenza, 1630.
25. Chamard, François. *Les vies des saints personnages d'Anjou,* vol. 2. Paris 1863.
26. Chantal, Jeanne Françoise. *St. Francis de Sales: A Testimony by St. Chantal.* London, 1967.
27. Chiappini, A. "S. Filippa Mareri e il suo monastero di Borgo S. Pietro de Molito nel Cicolano." *Miscellanea Francescana* 22 (1922):65–119.
28. Chiappini, A. "S. Hycinthae Mariscotti Vita." *Annales Minorum* 28 (1941):604–46.
29. Cipolletti, Tommaso. *Vida del b. Fr. Juan Masias.* Rome, 1837.
30. Clementi, Giuseppe. *Un santo patriota. Il b. Venturino da Bergamo dell' Ordine de' Praedicatori.* Rome, 1909.
31. Colgan, John. *Acta Sanctorum Hiberniae.* Dublin, 1948.
32. Corblet, J. *Hagiographie du diocèse d'Amiens,* vol. 2. Paris, 1869.
33. Cormier, H. M. *La b. Diana d'Andali et les bb. Cecile et Aimée.* Rome, 1892.
34. Creytens, R. "Les vicaires généraux de la Congrégation O.P. de Lombardie." *Archivum Fratrum Praedicatorum* 32 (1962):244–46.
35. Cristofani, F. "Memorie del B. P. Pettignaio." *Miscellanea Francescana* 5 (1890):34–35.
36. Daval, Guy. *La Bienheureuse Bonne d'Armagnac.* Paris, 1912.
37. DeBuck, Victor. "Le Bienheureux Jean de Gand." In *Revue belge et étrangère,* vol. 13. Gand, 1862.
38. DeJesus, Crisógono. *The Life of St. John of the Cross.* London, 1958.
39. DeMontault, X. Barbier. *Oeuvres completes.* Vol. 10, Rome 6. Hagiographie, pt. 2. Poitiers, 1895.

40. Derréal, H. *Une grande figure lorraine du xviie siècle, saint Pierre Fourrier, humaniste et épistolier.* Paris, 1942.
41. Donesmondi, Ippolito. *Dell'historia ecclesiastica di Mantova.* Mantova, 1616.
42. *Etudes Franciscaines* 11 (1904):621–29.
43. Famiglia, S. "Recherches sur le b. Denis de la Nativité." *Etudes Carmélitanes,* 3 (1913):215–27, 387–97.
44. Foley, Henry. *Records of the English Province of the Society of Jesus,* vol. 3 London, 1878.
45. Gairdner, James, ed. *Letters and Papers, Foreign and Domestic of the Reign of Henry VIII,* vol. 8. London, 1885.
46. Garnet, Henry. "Relation of Sufferings and Death of Mr. Thomas Woodhouse." In Henry Foley, *Records of the English Province of the Society of Jesus,* vol. 7 pt. 2. London. 1883.
47. Gauthey, Léon, ed. *Vie et ouvres del bienheureuse Marguerite Marie Alacoque.* 3 vols. Paris, 1915.
48. Giani, Archangelo. *Annalium Sacri Ordinis Fratrum Servorum,* vol. 1. Lucae, 1719.
49. Giaveno, Gallizia di. *Atti de' santi che fiorirono ne' dominii della casa di Savoia,* vol. 5. Turin, 1757.
50. Gillow, Joseph. *A Literary and Biographical History; or, Bibliographical Dictionary of the English Catholics,* vol. 3. London, 1887.
51. Giussano, Giovanni Pietro. *De Vita et Rebus Gestis Sancti Caroli Borromei.* Milan, 1751; reprint of 1610 ed.
52. Golubovich, Girolamo. *Biblioteca bio-bibliografica della Terra Santa e dell'Oriente Francescano,* vol. 5. Quaracchi, 1927.
53. Gomes, Ambrosio. *El moysen segundo nuevo redentor de España Santo Domingo Manso.* Madrid, 1653.
54. Goyau, Georges. *La France missionaire dans les cinq parties du monde,* vol. 1. Paris, 1948.
55. Granada, Luis de. *Vidas del Padre Juan de Avila.* Barcelona, 1964.
56. Guérin, René. *La bienheureuse Marguerite de Lorraine.* Paris, 1921.
57. Guillaume, Paul. *Essai historique sur l'Abbaye de Cava.* Cava dei Tirreni, 1877.
58. Irigoyen, Carlos Garcia. *Santo Toribio,* vol. 3. Lima, 1907.
59. James, M. R. "Lives of St. Walstan." *Norfolk Archaeological Society* 19 (1917):238–67.
60. Julian of Norwich. *Revelations of Divine Love,* ed. Clifton Walders. Baltimore, 1966.
61. Komorowski, J. "Memoriale Ordinis Fratrum Minorum." *Monumenta Poloniae Historica* 5 (1888):246–49.
62. LaBrüe, Claude. *La vie du reverend P. Jean François Régis S.J.* Liège, 1654.

63. Langebek, Jacob, ed. *Scriptores Rerum Danicarum,* vol. 4. Nendeln, Liechtenstein; 1969 reprint.
64. Lawrence, Clifford H. *St. Edmund of Abingdon.* Oxford, 1960.
65. Lecina, M. *Monumenta Xaveriana.* 2 vols. Madrid, 1899–1900.
66. Lucchesini, C. *Narrazione della vita del v.p.I. d'Azevedo e della morte del medesimo e di 39 altri d.C.d.G.* Rome, 1702.
67. Manrique, Angelo. *Cisterciensium, Seu Verius Ecclesiasticorum Annalium a Condito Cistercio.* 4 vols. Anisson, 1642–59; reprinted Westmead, 1970.
68. Marsys, F de. *Histoire de la persécution présente des catholiques en Angleterre.* N.p., 1646.
69. Martène, E., and Durand, U., eds. "Vita Hugonis Abbatis Marchianensis." In *Thesaurus Novus Anecdotorum,* vol. 3. Paris, 1717.
70. Melchiorri, Stanislao. *Leggenda del Beato Gabriele de' Ferretti di Ancona.* Ancona, 1844.
71. "Miracula Sancti Volquini." In *Die Zisterzienser des nordöstlichen Deutschlands,* ed. Franz Winter, vol. 1. Neudruck der Ausgabe Gotha, 1868.
72. Mondina, Vincenzo. *Vita del beato Andrea Ibernon.* Rome, 1791.
73. Moreno, C. *Libro de la vida y obras maravillosas del siervo de Dios y bienaventurado P. Fray N.F.* Barcelona, 1618.
74. Moreno, J. G. "San Juan de Ribera y Sevilla." *Archivio Hispalense,* 32 (1960):9–19.
75. Morini, Augustino, ed. *Monumenta ordinis servorum Sanctae Mariae.* Brussels, 1897.
76. Muratori, Ludovico Antonio, ed. *Rerum Italicarum Scriptores,* vol. 2, pt. 2. Milan, 1726.
77. Mush, John. "The Life of Margaret Clitherow." In *Troubles of Our Catholic Forefathers Related by Themselves,* ed. John Morris, 3:331–440. London, 1877.
78. Oliver, Michael. *St. Gertrude the Great.* Dublin, 1930.
79. Parisi, Giovanni. *Il Beato Guglielmo da Scicli.* Turin, 1958.
80. Parsons, Robert. *A True Report of the Death and Matyrdom of M. Campion.* 1581.
81. Pernoud, Régine. *The Retrial of Joan of Arc.* New York, 1955.
82. Pitré, Giuseppe. *Biblioteca delle tradizioni popolari siciliane: Spettacoli e feste popolari siciliane,* vol. 12. Palermo, 1881.
83. Poltzmann, Balthasar. *Compendium Vitae Miraculorum S. Leopoldi.* Klosterneuberg, 1591.
84. Razzi, Girolamo. *Vite de santi e beati Toscani.* 2 vols. Florence, 1593.
85. Razzi, Serafino. *La vita della reverenda serva di Dio la Madre Suor Caterina de Ricci.* Lucca, 1594.
86. Renard, Edmond. *La Mère Alix Le Clercq.* Paris, 1935.

87. Robertson, J. C., and Sheppard, J. B., eds. *Materials for the History of Thomas Becket.* 7 vols. London, 1875–85.
88. Rodgers, Robert H., ed. *Petri Diaconi: Ortus et Vita Iustorum Genobii Casinenis.* Berkeley, 1972.
89. Roper, William. *The Lyfe of Sir Thomas More, Knighte,* ed. James M. Clive. New York, 1950.
90. Salaniaco, Stephanus de, and Guidonis, Bernardus. "De Quatuor in Quibus Deus Praedicatorum Ordinem Insignivit." *Monumenta Ordinis Fratrum Praedicatorum Historica,* vol. 22. Paris, 1949.
91. San Diego, Luis de. *Compendio de la vida de S. Miguel de los Santos.* Madrid, 1782.
92. Stapleton, Thomas. *Life and Illustrious Martyrdom of Sir Thomas More,* ed. E. E. Reynolds. New York, 1966.
93. Schück, Henrik, ed. "De Vita Sancti Nicholai." In *Antiquarisk Tidskrift för Sverige,* vol. 5. 1895.
94. Simpson, Richard. "A True Report of the Life and Martyrdom of Mr. R. White, Schoolmaster." *Rambler,* 3d ser., 3:233–48, 366–88.
95. Stanislas of Krakow. "De Vita et Miraculis S. Jacchonis." In *Monumenta Poloniae Historica,* vol. 4. 1884.
96. Stephen, Leslie, et al. *Dictionary of National Biography,* s.v. "Serlo of Bayeux." Reprinted Oxford, 1973, 17:1193
97. Stuart, James. *Historical Memoires of the City of Armagh.* Dublin, 1900; new edition by A. Coleman.
98. Thomas à Kempis. "Chronica Montis Sanctae Agnetis." In *Opera Omnia,* ed. Michael Pohle, vol. 7. Freiburg, 1922.
99. Toustain, D., and Tassin, D. *Histoire de l'Abbaïe de Saint-Vandrille.* Abbaye de Saint-Wandrille, 1936.
100. Trithemius, Joannis of Spannheim. *Annalium Hirsaugiensium.* 2 vols. S. Gall, 1690.
101. "Un catalogue d'écrivains et deux catalogues de Martyrs Dominicains." *Archivum Fratrum Praedicatorum* 12 (1942):288–97.
102. "Vita B. Davidis Monachi Hemmenrodensis." *Analecta Sacri Ordinis Cisterciensis* 11 (1955):27–44.
103. "Vita Sancti Raimundi." In *Viaje literario a las Iglesias de España,* ed. James Villanueva, vol. 15. Madrid, 1802–52.
104. William of Malmesbury. *Chronicle of the Kings of England,* ed. J. A. Giles. London, 1847.

Appendix on Method

Selection of the Sample

There is no "official" list of saints, nor, at least until the sixteenth century, was there a meaningful distinction between *sanctus* and *beatus*. More troublesome perhaps is that none of the various compilations of materials on saints or lists of saints gives a clear and coherent set of criteria for including one or another individual who may have been venerated at some time. Virtually all lists include those who received papal canonizations, but for most of the period of our study such saints constitute only a small fraction of the total number venerated in an order, a town, or a diocese. We are dealing here not with the occasional papal decision to drop from the ranks of saints an individual who turns out never to have existed (such as the recent case of Christopher) but, rather, with the literally thousands of names that appear in martyrologies, iconographical records, and hagiographical surveys. None of these compilations is complete, and, whatever the possible value of ultimately compiling a "correct'," list, such an endeavor would not necessarily serve the historian of popular religion.

The most thorough effort to compile a "correct" list, at least for the thirteenth century, was made by the historian Michael Goodich for his quantitative study "The Dimensions of Thirteenth Century Sainthood" (Ph.D. diss., Columbia University, 1972). Goodich listed holy people "who clearly became the objects of a cult within fifty years of their deaths" as attested to by "at least two independent contemporary sources" (p. 374). But, as his brief examples indicate, Goodich cannot consistently establish the *independence* of the sources. Moreover, by excluding persons whose historicity he doubts, Goodich falls into the logical trap of seeming to assert

277

the *historical* accuracy of the material he does include. Our concern is with perception. Whereas Goodich dropped Ventura da Spello because he is thought to have died either in the twelfth or the thirteenth century, we note the vagueness or ambiguity of that perception but do not therefore exclude Ventura. Finally, Goodich's exclusion of those whose cults did not find documentation until more than fifty years after their death, although reasonable for the more limited time frame he chose, would eliminate an important dimension of changes in popular piety over the much longer period of our study.

Instead of engaging in what we are convinced would be a futile effort to compile a "correct and complete" list of saints, we chose a "good" list, that of Pierre Delooz. This French sociologist in turn relied primarily on Baudot's *Les vies des saints*, a thirteen-volume twentieth-century account. Delooz was especially interested in the canonization process, how it shifted from episcopal to papal control and how official standards for judging a person worthy of veneration changed over time. Our interests were very different—unofficial criteria, popular piety, social history—and therefore we specifically chose Delooz's list because its criteria for inclusion were independent of our interests. Nevertheless, in drawing our sample we gave due attention to the canonization process by including all saints in Delooz's first category, those who received papal canonizations, either directly in the period before Urban VIII's decrees or in an equipollent canonization thereafter. We also included all saints in Delooz's third category, those whose canonizations were prepared by the Congregation of Rites, as well as the holy people of his fourth group, those who have been beatified officially. People in group four who were officially canonized as well as beatified are listed by Delooz in both categories three and four, but for obvious reasons we count them only once in our tables. This leaves the 1,188 saints in Delooz's second category, holy people who were "canonized" locally by a bishop, popular will, or monastic tradition. Of these we took a 50 percent sample, simply choosing every other name on the list. Thus our tables include all the "official" saints and blesseds, the major ones who are recognized widely in Christendom and in papal pronouncements, and half of the less official saints in Delooz's list; these in turn represent some unknown fraction of the unknown total number of holy men and women who at one time or another may have been venerated. While here in the text we refer to numbers of saints, it would be more precise, but hopelessly awkward in style, to refer to "object or objects of veneration" because in the tables we count groups of martyrs or other grouped saints only once for each group. Thus, the seven founders of the Servite order count as one, not seven, of our total of 864 cases, as do the 205 martyrs of Japan beatified by Pius IX in 1867.

In sum, we make no claim that our sample is random in a technical statistical sense. Since no one agrees even on the "population-at-risk," such a sample would be impossible. Rather, we have included all the major cases and a large enough number of others to be reasonably confident about our statistical findings. Nevertheless, we are most confident about the numerical findings when they corroborate literary sources or other forms of evidence. Readers who interpret our numbers as orders of magnitude rather than precise quantities will be following our intent.

Relationship of the Sample to "Sainthood"

Although we would not assert that the 864 cases in our sample represent a precise cross section of the total population of saints, we are able to reach certain statistically based conclusions about the sample that should aid the reader in assessing the significance of findings presented in the text. Three distinct yet related pieces of information are central to this effort.

First, the extent of each saint's cult tells us something about the saint's importance or "weight" relative to the other 863 cases. From a lengthy categorization scheme we ultimately settled upon four basic ordinal categories for extent of cult: international or strong national; patrons, whether of cities, job categories, or conditions, or of other phenomena such as harvest yields, childbirth, or travel; primarily in a religious order; and local. Although we made due note of any church pronouncements about where a saint might be officially venerated, our primary concern was with popular religious expression, and we recorded extent of cult at its zenith.

Second, the quality of each saint's reputation suggested ways to estimate the relative importance of one saint as against another. We drew distinctions among saints who achieved wide popularity and fame in their lifetimes, those whose reputations rested primarily upon their martyrdom, those whose canonizations involved very well organized pressure upon the church by religious or secular groups, those known primarily because of their association or friendship with a more prominent saint, and finally a residual group comprising those who fit none of the preceding categories.

Third, the specific types of canonization—papal, local, Congregation of Rites, beatification only, and popular—allowed us to assess generally the impact of changing official criteria upon the composition of the roll of saints and specifically the consequences of our decision to use a 50 percent sample of Delooz's second group (local and popular canonization) of saints.

Categorizations by extent of cult and quality of reputation are not without their ambiguities, although the statistics that follow suggest that the overall classification scheme is historically useful. We would not go beyond this statement, however, to assert that a precise "weight" of importance could meaningfully be assigned to each individual saint. Is Francis of Assisi ten, one hundred, one thousand, or one million times more important than Herman the Cripple when we turn to using perceptions of sanctity as an index of changes in popular piety? And would such a weighting factor change over time and across different geographic areas? We believe that any individual weighting system would be more misleading than not, and for that reason we have opted for a group approach leading to "lower-bound" estimates.

In the various tables in the text each saint is counted equally and arranged according to the categories being analyzed, without regard to his or her "importance." We count one for extreme asceticism for Francis of Assisi and one for Herman the Cripple, so that what we conclude statistically about popular ideas concerning the virtue of asceticism rests as much on Herman as it does on Francis. Now, if the many Hermans represent a different direction in piety than the rare or even unique Francis, the numerical results may become quite misleading. In rather traditional and commonsense fashion we have checked each table to be sure that conclusions about the individuals it refers to, if studied as individuals and with appropriate consideration of their relative importance, would be similar. Still, such a procedure is necessarily impressionistic and cannot lead to verification of precise numerical results, for example the finding in table 1 that saints called to the holy life in childhood were twice as likely (score of 200) as all saints to be known for deep mystical contemplation. It bears repeating that we intend the score of 200 to be understood as an order of magnitude rather than as an exact description.

Moreover, it is a lower-bound estimate; *any* reasonable scheme for weighting the relative importance of each saint would produce a result at least this great and probably greater. However, any of several equally reasonable weighting schemes would yield varying results, all above 200 but possibly quite different from each other. We set forth conclusions about trends and directions in popular piety, but we do not claim to be providing exact measures of the strengths of these trends. Indeed, the numbers given are *minimum* estimates.

Evidence to support the statement that we are providing lower-bound estimates is summarized in table Al. The most "important" saints—those with the most extensive cults, those who were most beloved in their own times, those canonized by the direct authority of Rome—score higher on *all* categories of activity than do less prominent saints.

Comparison of these results with the multivariate analyses in tables 1 through 5 and with the data that follow in this appendix shows that the tendency of major saints to score high in all categories of activity is consistent for various age cohorts, for both genders, and across divisions of time, place, and class.

Table A1
Components of Saintly Reputation by "Importance" of Saint: Category Means

	Supernatural Power	Charitable Activity	Asceticism	Temporal Power	Evangelical Activity
Type of Canonization eta	.35	.32	.32	.34	.37
Papal $N = 110$	48.71	41.49	37.16	39.96	36.74
Local $N = 129$	29.95	33.49	23.92	27.50	25.42
Congregation of rites $N = 97$	46.65	54.35	41.77	20.48	43.24
Beatified $N = 336$	26.50	32.14	25.27	14.11	25.68
Popular $N = 192$	25.97	25.09	24.66	20.70	22.61
Reputation eta	.45	.34	.43	.38	.32
Not exceptional $N = 305$	34.70	34.70	29.76	19.84	24.06
By association $N = 116$	30.15	35.45	31.06	23.86	34.25
Through promotion $N = 60$	34.00	32.92	31.17	20.77	29.87
Martyrdom $N = 159$	10.18	18.48	11.35	5.81	21.38
Wide popularity $N = 224$	44.19	45.38	36.15	34.18	35.65
Extent of cult eta	.33	.26	.25	.28	.31
National and international $N = 147$	42.87	42.98	32.91	34.31	36.09
Patrons $N = 148$	40.00	42.14	31.83	24.37	27.45
In an order $N = 287$	33.07	34.80	30.84	20.99	31.87
Local $N = 282$	21.02	25.65	21.46	14.08	21.17

Recording of the Data

Like most historians, we read the sources and took down information on note cards (note sheets to be more precise). In addition, we coded in more structured form a series of variables—some hard, some impressionistic. Even the "hard" data on saints is often "soft," and no one will be surprised to learn that in many cases we had to approximate a date of birth or judge whether a saint's family was noble not only in spirit but also legally (see chap. 7). The relatively hard variables used in our study are:

Source of the data—a vita by a contemporary, other contemporary documentation, a later biography, forgery, or whatever
Gender
Year of birth—often a rough estimate
Year of death—usually quite accurate
Liturgical calendar date
Place of birth
Type of canonization
Year of canonization, if any
Year of beatification, if any

Extent of the saint's cult—all of Christendom, patron of a city, mainly in an order, local, and so forth

Time when veneration began—during the lifetime, at the tomb, or how long after death

Order—the order, if any, with which the saint was principally associated

Siblings—number mentioned

Marriage—whether the saint ever married

Children—saint's children, if any

Principal walk of life before, or at the time of, beginning a life of special holiness, being martyred, or venerated

Social status of the saint's family of birth

Age at first influences or tendencies to a holy life

Cause of death

We also used a set of somewhat more impressionistic variables to record what saints' lives told about how these men and women came to the holy life, about what they did during their lifetimes, and about what most attracted the faithful to venerate them. Some of this information was straightforward, such as whether the saint was an abbess or a peacemaker, but other data clearly reflect subjective evaluations on our part. We ranked on ordinal scales from one to eight the importance of influences such as contact with another saint, maternal pleading, or visionary experiences in calling the saint to a life of extraordinary holiness. Similarly, we used ordinal scales to record the *centrality* to a saint's reputation of activities such as miracle-working or extreme austerity and phenomena such as celestial signs or wonder-working relics. (As teachers, we do something analogous all the time when we read students' essays and term papers and assign them grades of A, B, C, and so on. We have not always graded with uniform and unassailable accuracy, but for the most part we think our students have gotten about what they deserved. So also with the saints, except that we read each case independently, and from separate sources wherever possible, and then compared and ajudicated our results.) Between a score of one and two we would draw no great distinction—indeed, in most of our tables "ones" and "twos" are combined under the label "very important"—but between a one, a five, and an eight we record differences of obvious magnitude even if, like most historians, we are more comfortable conveying these differences in the text with words like "very," "somewhat," and "slight." The ordinally ranked variables are as follows (an asterisk denotes bivariate—that is, yes or no—coding):

Moral quality of the saint's life before turning to special holiness

Initial attitude of the saint's family toward his or her religious career

Saint's religious influence upon his or her family

Influence of the father in the saint's early life

Influence of the mother in the saint's early life

Influence of brothers and sisters in the saint's early life
Religious influence of a friend
Religious influence of a spouse
Religious influence of another saint
Influence of visions and dreams in turning to the holy life
Influence of worldly crisis in turning to the holy life
Influence of travel and pilgrimage in turning to the holy life
* Other influences: reading, early religious education, illness, reaction
   to secular involvement, other relatives, liberal education, a doctorate
   in law or theology, response to preaching, to a religious rite, or to
   someone's martyrdom
Centrality of a struggle to preserve chastity
Dedication to helping the sick
Dedication to helping the poor
* Other forms of charitable activity or help: relief of Christian prisoners
   of infidels, aiding pilgrims, visiting prisoners, restoration of crops,
   opposition to the slave trade, aid to children, to widows, to pros-
   titutes, to Jews, to Slavs, to travelers, hiding fugitive priests, sacrifice
   to avoid bloodshed, aid in battle, peacemaking, promoting learning,
   or being an especially charitable bishop or king
Centrality of reclusion or hermitage
Practice of flagellation
Extreme self-mortification and austerity
Fortitude in illness
Mystical contemplation and prayer
Visionary experiences
Humility
Demonic struggle, exorcism
Pilgrimage
Preaching
Apostle to heretics, infidels, and heathens
Reform activity
Prophecy and clairvoyance
Founding an order, a monastery, a church, or an observance
Religious writings
Influence or position in the temporal order
Influence or position in the ecclesiastical order
Reputation dependent upon association with important friends or pro-
   motion by influential persons or groups
Supernatural signs (other than visions)
Miracle-working during lifetime
Intercession or signs of sanctity after death
Importance of wonder-working relics
Poverty
Perception by others in the lifetime
* Devotional cults or religious practices promoted by the saint: eremitical
   life, cenobitic life, Marian devotion, Jesus, penitential prayer, litur-

gical reforms, Eucharist, religious arts, hagiolatry, relics, the Passion, the Trinity, the Sacred Heart, Bible study, processions and public displays, communing with nature and with animals

Statistical Profiles

Tables 1–5 consist of indexes of representativeness calculated as follows:

index $= [(a/A)/(b/B)]100$ where:
a = number of saints in the category listed for the group specified
b = number of saints in the group specified
A = number of saints in the category listed for the entire sample
B = number of saints in the entire sample.

Thus, for example:$[(25/151)/(128/864)]100 = 112$; that is 25 child saints in the eleventh century divided by 151 child saints overall equals 16.6 percent; 128 saints overall in the eleventh century divided by 864 saints in the entire sample equals 14.8 percent; 16.6 divided by 14.8 equals 1.12 and multiplied by 100 equals 112, the first entry in table 1. An index number of 100 means that saints in the group specified (children, those who struggled with chastity, and so forth) appear as frequently in the category shown (fifteenth century, female, and so forth) as is true for the sample as a whole. Numbers under 100 indicate increasing absence from a particular category, whereas numbers above 100 reflect more than the expected random frequency in the category. In short, the index is a ratio of observed to expected frequency, as in the usual chi-square calculation; 200 indicates twice the expected frequency, and 50 indicates half the expected frequency.

The Five Components of Sanctity

In the multivariate segments of tables in part 1 and in part 2 we refer frequently to the five principal components of a reputation for holiness: supernatural power, asceticism, charitable activity, the exercise of temporal and ecclesiastical power, and evangelical activity. Although we would give primacy to the structural formulation set forth in chapter 5, we also considered these five components as statistical constructs involving combinations of the variables used in coding our sample. To construct interval-type scales appropriate for correlation, regression, and factor analysis, we converted our impressionistic ordinal scales (one to eight) according to their frequency distributions. For example, for the variable dealing with prayer and mystic contemplation, the conversion was as shown in table A2. Thus the original scale, from 1 for a saint known primarily as a mystic, through 5 for someone who was known for deep and regular prayer but who was not a mystic, through 7 for a cleric whose biography makes no

Table A2
Transformed Values for Coding of Saints' Activities: Prayer

Ordinal Scale Value	Absolute Frequency of Cases	Cumulative % of Total Cases	Transformed Value
1	104	12.0	88
2	84	21.8	78
3	141	38.1	62
4	31	41.7	58
5	121	55.7	44
6	19	57.9	42
7	329	95.9	4
8	35	100.0	0

specific mention of prayer and contemplation (for surely he prayed on occasion) and 8 for a lay person about whom there is no reference to prayer, was transformed to reflect frequency. The result in this instance is to minimize the distinction between an original scoring of 7 or 8, whereas, for example, the same technique for the variable "fortitude in illness" results in a transformation of one through eight respectively into 98, 97, 95, 88, 83, 72, 70, 0, and therefore a great distinction between any story that mentions illness (minimum score 70) and all others (score 0) and relatively little distinction among scores of one, two, and three (transformed into 98, 97, 95).

The transformed variables were then weighted and combined by summation to yield estimates of the five principal components of a reputation for holiness, as follows:

Supernatural power—mystic contemplation and prayer, visionary experiences, demonic struggle, prophecy and clairvoyance, miracle-working during life, supernatural signs, importance of relics, and intercession.

Asceticism—centrality of reclusion, practice of flagellation, extreme self-mortification and austerity, fortitude in illness, humility, poverty, and asceticism leading to death.

Charitable activity—helping the sick, helping the poor, and any of the other forms of charitable activity noted earlier except peacemaking.

Temporal and ecclesiastical power—peacemaking, public reform activity, and influence and position in the temporal and ecclesiastical orders.

Evangelical activity—preaching, apostle to heretics, ecclesiastical reform activity, founding an order, pilgrimage, religious writings, spiritual and moral counseling, and promotion of devotional cults or religious practices.

Table A3
Components of Saintly Reputation: Grand Means and Standard Deviations

Component	Mean	Standard Deviation
Supernatural power	31.98	25.52
Asceticism	28.29	19.54
Charitable activity	34.45	26.32
Temporal power	21.57	24.83
Evangelical activity	28.33	18.22

The choice of which variables to include in each of the five principal components was made on the basis of cross-tabulations of untransformed values, factor analysis of transformed values, and common sense. Each variable included in a given component has a higher correlation with that component (recalculated to exclude the variable being tested) than with any of the other components. To facilitate comparisons of scores on the five principal components, each was normalized into a zero to one hundred scale by dividing the raw totals by the appropriate maximum possible scores and multiplying by one hundred. Means and standard deviations for the total sample of 864 cases are shown in table A3.

Analysis of Variance

Analysis of variance was done for each of the five principal components with the results shown in table A4. The standard F test for significance of main effects yields significance levels of .01 or better for all entries except charitable activity by gender (.037) and by century of death (.076).

Discriminant Function Analysis

We used discriminant function analysis extensively because it is generally held to be a technique appropriate for imperfect interval scale measurements and even for nominal or bivariate distributions. It has been used effectively, for example, by Heyck and Klecka (*Journal of Interdisciplinary History*, winter 1973) on roll call votes. (See their article for a good nontechnical explanation of this technique.) In general, results obtained from analysis of variance are congruent with those from discriminant function analysis, which gives us some confidence that we have been reasonably successful in overcoming problems of measurement. The results below were obtained without a Bayesian adjustment for number of cases in various groups. (A Bayesian adjustment raises the number of correct classifications but unfortunately discriminant functions are more ambiguous than without the adjustment.)

Table A4
Analysis of Variance: Category Means

	Supernatural Power	Asceticism	Charitable Activity	Temporal Power	Evangelical Activity
Gender eta	.17	.18	.09	.16	.17
Female	41.27	35.98	39.58	13.14	21.68
Male	30.02	26.67	33.37	23.37	29.75
Place eta	.34	.33	.22	.17	.21
Italy	37.74	32.98	38.51	23.50	29.21
Iberia	42.21	35.07	40.95	22.03	35.34
France	33.74	29.25	37.38	25.51	32.16
Northern Europe	29.92	26.81	30.93	22.85	25.56
England	14.68	15.24	23.77	12.32	22.57
Class eta	.35	.32	.27	.23	.20
Royalty	32.72	31.41	41.33	34.67	22.74
Titled nobility	36.04	31.12	40.07	26.23	31.20
Untitled nobility	35.39	31.77	35.64	26.84	31.97
Gentry	13.52	16.49	27.42	9.98	24.78
Good family	35.35	30.03	37.50	20.31	35.04
Urban patrician	35.29	33.48	41.49	25.85	31.68
Urban middle and poor	48.73	41.88	44.75	21.23	31.58
Peasantry	53.60	36.07	44.81	16.49	28.64
Other and unknown	24.69	22.32	26.43	16.95	24.70
Century of death eta	.20	.14	.11	.32	.13
Eleventh	31.57	25.24	31.04	31.51	27.22
Twelfth	30.15	26.07	31.42	29.60	26.01
Thirteenth	38.41	31.03	35.07	23.91	28.27
Fourteenth	34.85	31.65	35.40	13.37	24.99
Fifteenth	38.40	31.93	37.35	25.62	31.28
Sixteenth	25.95	25.31	33.55	12.61	29.65
Seventeenth	25.00	28.18	39.30	10.70	32.34

The discriminant function analysis of gender (table A5) yields coefficients showing the obvious fact that women were excluded by the church from most avenues of its evangelical work (− .69), and also a significant difference in the importance to holy reputation of supernatural power (.40) and asceticism (.46). The classification results reveal that one-third of the female saints (fifty in absolute number) do not fit the typical pattern for women, whereas for males 70 percent are correctly classified.

The centrality of supernatural power and asceticism is also clear with regard to geographical differences (table A6). Function one isolates English saints by scoring for what they were *not* (since this group includes large

Table A5
Discriminant Function Analysis: Gender

Component	Univariate F Ratio	Coefficient for Function
Supernatural power	24.85	.40
Asceticism	29.15	.46
Charitable activity	6.97	.20
Temporal power	21.63	− .32
Evangelical activity	25.13	− .69
Canonical correlation		.32

Gender	Centroid for Function	% Correctly Classified
Female	.74	67
Male	− .15	70

Table A6
Discriminant Function Analysis: Place

Component	Univariate F Ratio	Coefficients for Function One	Two
Supernatural power	28.32	− .47	− .05
Asceticism	27.10	− .52	.35
Charitable activity	11.05	− .09	− .15
Temporal power	6.74	− .30	.71
Evangelical activity	9.91	− .05	− 1.01
Canonical correlation		.40	.15

Place	Centroids for Functions One	Two	% Correctly Classified
Italy	− .29	.06	22
Iberia	− .45	− .32	45
France	− .13	− .11	11
Northern Europe	.09	.19	16
England	.88	− .08	73

numbers of martyrs, the results are self-evident). Thus the Italian group acts in a statistical sense as a norm against which saints from elsewhere are evaluated. Function two locates the Iberian type as an extreme variant of the Italian norm and, in an opposite direction from English saints, scores heavily on evangelical activity and power holding. These coefficients reflect the ascendancy of the Jesuits and Iberia's role in the Catholic Reformation. The classification results express the homogeneity of the English group, a distinctive Iberian component, a more heterogeneous Italian set, and ambiguous constructs for Northern Europe and France. Eliminating martyrs (results not shown) retains the Italians as a norm and results in a sharp bifurcation of Iberian from both English and northern saints, with France still ambiguous.

Results of the analysis of class (with or without the gentry category which consists mostly of English martyrs) show (table A7) that the opposite ends of the social spectrum, kings and peasants, are alike in prominence of supernatural power relative to all classes. (The apparent contradiction between this result and the analysis of variance, where royalty scores low, occurs because the discriminant function picks up royalty with very high supernatural power scores and misclassifies the remainder, a result of bifurcation within the class of royalty.) Although function one suggests that this prominent role of supernatural power extends also to the urban middle and poor strata, the coefficients and centroids on function two not only discriminate between urban and rural poor but separate sharply the power-holding healer-king or ascetic queen from the peasant (a wonder-worker, perhaps a preacher, but not a ruler and not ascetic.) Homogeneous types (with the obvious exception of the Gentry martyrs), at least according to the classification results, exist only for a portion of the royalty and for the poor, especially for poor peasants.

Finally, the analysis of century of death (table A8) shows a different pattern. Whereas supernatural power and, to a lesser extent, asceticism loom large in distinguishing saints of different genders, places, and classes, it is worldly position—power holding—that most clearly delineates change over time. The powerful bishop or temporal ruler of the eleventh and twelfth centuries is replaced in the sixteenth and seventeenth centuries by the martyr who sacrifices his life in the contest between faith and state. Within the long period of our study, the fourteenth century, certainly a dismal period for the church, stands out as a time when the wonder-working ascetic (see coefficient and centroids for function two) emerged most clearly in the ranks of saints, a long moment of popular piety extending back to the thirteenth and forward to the fifteenth century and clearly distinct from what came before and after.

Table A7
Discriminant Function Analysis: Class

Component	Univariate F Ratio	Coefficients for Functions		
		One	Two	Three
Supernatural power	11.16	−.71	−.61	.22
Asceticism	6.28	−.38	.44	−.35
Charitable activity	2.87	−.13	.17	.39
Temporal power	4.33	−.33	.97	−.15
Evangelical activity	2.32	.31	−.59	−.88
Canonical correlation		.37	.28	.17

Class	Centroids for Functions			% Correctly Classified
	One	Two	Three	
Royalty	−.18	.74	.32	48
Titled nobles	−.01	.05	−.03	3
Untitled nobles	.02	.05	−.15	9
Gentry	1.12	−.21	.24	76
Good family	.19	−.32	−.20	19
Urban patrician	−.03	.10	−.07	6
Urban middle and poor	−.57	−.18	.02	33
Peasantry	−.57	−.54	.30	51

Table A8
Discriminant Function Analysis: Century of Death

Component	Univariate F Ratio	Coefficients for Functions		
		One	Two	Three
Supernatural power	5.65	−.51	.76	.20
Asceticism	2.86	.06	.36	−.04
Charitable activity	1.59	.37	−.12	.11
Temporal power	16.53	−.99	−.34	.16
Evangelical activity	2.54	.62	−.25	.81
Canonical correlation		.42	.19	.11

Century	Centroids for Functions			% Correctly Classified
	One	Two	Three	
Eleventh	−.15	−.18	.00	32
Twelfth	−.43	−.16	−.07	16
Thirteenth	−.21	.21	.06	7
Fourteenth	.20	.31	−.18	35
Fifteenth	−.15	.15	.21	8
Sixteenth	.52	−.12	−.05	32
Seventeenth	.80	−.13	.07	43

Notes

Introduction

1. For a good brief review of hagiographic scholarship see Sofia Boesch Gajano's introduction to her edited volume *Agiografia altomedioevale* (Bologna, 1976), 7–48. There is an excellent bibliography, 261–300.

2. *Acta Sanctorum Quotquot Toto Orbe Coluntur Vel a Catholicis Scriptoribus Celebrantur, Quae ab Antiquis Monumentis Latinis Aliarumque Gentium Collegit Digressit Notis Illustravit J. Bollandus . . . Operam et Studium Contulit G. Henschenius*, 58 vols. (Antwerp, 1643–1867); 2d ed., ed. Jean Carnandet, 69 vols. (Paris, 1863 ff.). Among the many works of Delehaye see especially *Les légendes hagiographiques*, 4th ed. (Brussels, 1955); Engl. transl., *The Legends of the Saints*, by Donald Attwater (London, 1962); *Cinq leçons sur la méthode hagiographique* (Brussels, 1934); *L'oeuvre des Bollandistes à travers trois siècles, 1615–1915*, 2d ed. (Brussels, 1959); see also M. D. Knowles, "Great Historical Enterprises. I. The Bollandists," *Transactions of the Royal Historical Society*, 5th ser., 8 (1958): 147–166.

3. Charles W. Jones, *Saint Nicholas of Myra, Bari, and Manhattan: Biography of a Legend* (Chicago, 1978).

4. John M. Mecklin, *The Passing of the Saint: A Study of a Culture Type* (Chicago, 1941).

5. Ludwig Hertling, "Der Mittelalterliche Heiligentypus nach den Tugendkatalogen," *Zeitschrift für Aszese und Mystik* 8 (1933): 260–268.

6. Ptirim A. Sorokin, *Altruistic Love: A Study of American "Good Neighbors" and Christian Saints* (Boston, 1950; Kraus Reprint, New York, 1969). For further elaboration of the theoretical basis of his investigation see Ptirim A. Sorokin, ed., *Explorations in Altruistic Love and Behavior* (Boston, 1950), 3–73.

7. Herbert S. Thurston, ed. *The Lives of the Saints by Alban Butler*, vols. 1–12 (London, 1926).

8. Katherine George and Charles H. George, "Roman Catholic Sainthood and Social Status: A Statistical and Analytical Study," *Journal of Religion* 35 (1955): 85–98.

9. Michael E. Goodich, "The Dimensions of Thirteenth Century Sainthood" (Ph.D. diss., Columbia University, 1972).

10. Frantisek Graus, *Volk, Herrscher und Heiliger im Reich der Merowinger* (Prague, 1965); Joseph-Claude Poulin, *L'ideal de sainteté dans l'Aquitaine carolingienne d'après les sources hagiographiques (750–950)* (Quebec, 1975); Simone Roisin; *L'Hagiographie cistercienne dans le diocèse de Liège au xiiie siècle* (Louvain, 1947). An important new study, which arrived after this book was already in press, is André Vauchez, *La sainteté en occident aux derniers siècles du Moyen Age: D'aprè les procès de canonisation et les documents hagiographiques.* Bibliothèque des Ecoles Françaises d'Athènes et de Rome 241 (Rome, 1981).

11. Romeo De Maio, "L'idéale eroico nei processi di Canonizzazione della Controriforma," *Ricerche di Storia Sociale e Religiosa* 2 (1972): 139–60; reprinted in De Maio, *Riforme e miti nella Chiesa del Cinquecento* (Naples, 1973), 257–278.

12. Pierre Delooz, "Pour une étude sociologique de la sainteté canonisée dans l'église Catholique," *Archives de Sociologie des Religions* 13 (1962): 17–43, and his *Sociologie et canonisations* (Liège, 1969).

13. Peter Brown makes a similar point for an earlier period: "If, as Ortega y Gasset once wrote, 'The virtues which count most for us are those we do not possess,' then the cult of saints from the fourth century onwards made plain the virtues which late-Roman men lacked and wished for most" (*The Cult of Saints: Its Rise and Function in Latin Christianity* [Chicago, 1981], p. 93).

14. "The *Miles Literatus* in Twelfth- and Thirteenth-Century England: How Rare a Phenomenon?" *American Historical Review* 83 (1978): 930.

15. Lionel Rothkrug, "Popular Religion and Holy Shrines: Their Influence on the Origins of the German Reformation and Their Role in German Cultural Development," in *Religion and the People 1000–1700,* ed. James Obelkevich (Chapel Hill, 1979), 20–86, and his *Religious Practices and Collective Perceptions: Hidden Homologies in the Renaissance and Reformation* (*Historical Reflections,* suppl. 7.1, 1980), especially chaps. 3–5.

16. Jean Delumeau, *Catholicism between Luther and Voltaire: a New View of the Counter-Reformation* (London, 1977), esp. 26–29.

17. Obelkevich, *Religion and the People,* 5; Delumeau, *Catholicism between Luther and Voltaire,* 186.

18. Mikhail Bakhtin, *Rabelais and His World,* trans. Helene Iswolsky (Cambridge, 1968).

19. This point is well made by Roisin, *L'hagiographie cistercienne,* especially 276–78.

20. A good example of careful use of hagiographical material as well as other sources to make some inferences about medieval families is Mary M. McLaughlin, "Survivors and Surrogates: Children and Parents from the Ninth to the Thirteenth Centuries," in *The History of Childhood,* ed. Lloyd de Mause (New York, 1974), 182–228.

1 Children

1. The fullest presentation of the view we are questioning is found in Philippe Ariès, *Centuries of Childhood: A Social History of Family Life* (New York, 1962 translation by Robert Baldick), especially 33 ff., 44, 50, 61, 71, and 128; see p. 125 for a partial concession by Ariès that saints' vitae do not support his general contention that medieval people had no concept of childhood. Also see Andreas Flitner and Walter Hornstein, "Kindheit und Jugendalter in geschichtlicher Betrachtung," *Zeitschrift für Pädagogie,* 10, no. 4 (1964): 311–39.

2. On some of the problems of interpreting saints' childhoods see Michael Goodich, "Childhood and Adolescence among the Thirteenth Century Saints," *History*

of Childhood Quarterly: Journal of Psychohistory 1, no. 2 (1973): 286–87; Dorothy Abrahamse, "Images of Childhood in Early Byzantine Hagiography," *Journal of Psychohistory*, 2, no. 4 (1979): 497–98.

On the idea of childhood in the Middle Ages see Luke Demaitre, "The Idea of Childhood and Child Care in Medical Writings of the Middle Ages," *Journal of Psychohistory* 4 (1977): 461–90; James Bruce Ross, "The Middle-Class Child in Urban Italy, Fourteenth to Early Sixteenth Century," in *The History of Childhood*, ed. Lloyd de Mause (New York, 1974), 183–228; McLaughlin, "Survivors and Surrogates," 182–228; Michael Goodich, "Bartholomaeus Anglicus on Child-Rearing," *History of Childhood Quarterly: Journal of Psychohistory* 3 (1975): 75–84; Ilene H. Forsyth, "Children in Early Medieval Art: Ninth through Twelfth Centuries," *Journal of Psychohistory* 4 (1976): 31–78.

3. Louis Henry, *Anciennes familles génévoises: Etude démographique, xvie–xxe siècle* (Paris, 1956), 81–87, is the classic study. For a good bibliography including studies based on the family reconstitution method that allows such estimates, see Charles Tilly, ed., *Historical Studies of Changing Fertility* (Princeton, 1978), 355–80.

4. Léon Chertok, *Motherhood and Personality* (London, 1969), especially 140–62; for a critical assessment of male-dominated literature on this point see Ann Oakley, *Women Confined: Towards a Sociology of Childbirth* (New York, 1980), 277–91.

5. A frequent association is between breast-feeding and fertility, although this may take strange turns, as in the Sicilian rough wisdom that says nuns make the best cheeses (a food that enhances virility) because no one has ever suckled from them. See Rudolph Bell, *Fate and Honor, Family and Village* (Chicago, 1979), 249, and Ernesto de Martino, *Sud e magia* (Milan, 1959), 41–48. On the anxieties attendant upon nursing medieval infants see McLaughlin, "Survivors and Surrogates," 115–17. On nursing of middle-class Italian children, see Ross, "Middle-Class Child in Urban Italy," 184–96.

6. For the documentation of Rose of Lima, see De Maio, "L'ideale eroico," 260 n.6.

7. On the cult of relics, see Hippolyte Delehaye, *Sanctus essai sur le culte des saints dans l'antiquité* (Brussels, 1927), 196–207. Two recent treatments of the importance of relics in the Middle Ages are Patrick J. Geary, *Furta Sacra: Thefts of Relics in the Central Middle Ages* (Princeton, 1978); and Nicole Hermann-Mascard, *Les reliques des saints: Formation coutumière d'un droit* (Paris, 1975); also, Jonathan Sumption, *Pilgrimage: An Image of Medieval Religion* (London, 1975), chap. 2.

8. For an excellent case study of alleged Jewish ritual murder see Gavin I. Langmuir, "The Knight's Tale of Young Hugh of Lincoln," *Speculum* 47, no. 3 (1972): 459–482.

9. For the theory that infanticide in medieval England was due to destructive urges on the part of the mother see Barbara A. Kellum, "Infanticide in England in the Later Middle Ages," *History of Childhood Quarterly: Journal of Psychohistory*, 1, no. 3 (1974): 381–82. For examples of maternal affection in saints' vitae of the early Middle Ages see McLaughlin, "Survivors and Surrogates," 123–28.

10. Richard C. Trexler, "Ritual in Florence: Adolescence and Salvation in the Renaissance," in *The Pursuit of Holiness in Late Medieval and Renaissance Religion: Papers from the University of Michigan Conference Studies in Medieval and Reformation Thought*, ed. Charles Trinkaus and Heiko A. Oberman, 10:200–264 (Leiden, 1974).

11. The choice of death over sexual sinning was a topos employed to demonstrate the chastity of adults as well as the innocence of children. It was, for example, told of King Louis VIII of France. His barons placed a young woman in his bed, but, though copulation would have cured him, Louis sent her away with a marriage

dowry, preferring to die rather than to sin. The source of the story is William of Puy-Laurent, *Recueil des historiens des Gauls et de la France*, ed. Martin Bouquet et al., 25 vols. (Paris, 1738–1904), 19:27. Cited in Andrew W. Lewis, *Royal Succession in Capetian France: Studies on Familial Order and the State* (Cambridge, Mass., 1981), 45 and n. 369.

12. For some references to the old child see Goodich, "Childhood and Adolescence," 287–88.

13. For the development of Christian doctrine with specific reference to the problems of sin and grace see J. Daniélou, *Message évangélique et culture hellénistique au iie et iiie siècles* (Tournai, 1961). St. Augustine was a major influence on medieval ideas of grace. He dealt with it in many places; see especially *Admonition and Grace (De correptione et gratia)*, trans. John Courtney Murray in *Writings of Saint Augustine*, vol. 4, *The Fathers of the Church* (New York, 1947), 239–305.

14. Augustine's own view is summed up in the famous passage in his *Confessions:* "Thus the innocence of children is in the helplessness of their bodies rather than in any quality in their minds." *The Confessions*, trans. F. J. Sheed (New York, 1943), 10. Not all Protestant reformers were so consistent. Luther took a relatively benign view of childhood innocence; see Gerald Strauss, *Luther's House of Learning: Indoctrination of the Young in the German Reformation* (Baltimore, 1978), 85–107. English Puritans were more pessimistic; see Lawrence Stone, *The Family, Sex and Marriage in England, 1500–1800* (London, 1977), 174–78.

15. On popular and lay piety in the Middle Ages see Etienne Delaruelle, *La pietà populaire au Moyen Age* (Turin, 1975). On the rise of the *vita apostolica* in the twelfth century and its relation to lay as well as monastic and clerical spirituality see M.-D. Chenu, *La théologie au douzième siècle*, 3d ed. (Paris, 1976), 224–51. An important recent treatment of medieval religion is Lester Little, *Religious Poverty and the Profit Economy in Medieval England* (Ithaca, 1978).

16. For a good brief introduction to the rise of the Italian communes, see Daniel Waley, *The Italian City-Republics* (New York, 1969).

17. See especially Colin Morris, *The Discovery of the Individual, 1050–1200* (London, 1972); P. Dronke, *Poetic Individuality in the Middle Ages* (Oxford, 1970); Robert W. Hanning, *The Individual in Twelfth Century Romance* (New Haven and London, 1977).

18. *Sacra Rituum Congregatio: Index ac Status Causarum Beatificationis Servorum Dei et Canonizationis Beatorum* (Vatican City, 1962).

19. Ilza Veith, *Hysteria: The History of a Disease* (Chicago, 1965), 55–73.

20. We are guided here by the reasoned approach of Judith M. Bardwick, *Psychology of Women: A Study of Bio-Cultural Conflicts* (New York, 1971), and the essays collected in Jean B. Miller, *Psychoanalysis and Women* (Baltimore, 1973). Useful despite its stridency is Juliet Mitchell, *Psychoanalysis and Feminism* (New York, 1974).

21. On medieval carnival behavior see Peter Burke, *Popular Culture in Early Modern Europe* (London, 1978), chap. 7; Bakhtin, *Rabelais and His World*, especially 7–17, 196–277; Natalie Z. Davis, *Society and Culture in Early Modern France* (Stanford, 1975).

22. On parturition see Jacques Guillemean, *Childbirth; or, The Happy Deliverie of Women* (London, 1612; reprinted New York, 1972).

23. On childhood and adolescent conversion in the thirteenth century see Goodich, "Childhood and Adolescence."

24. John G. Cawelti, *Apostles of the Self-Made Man* (Chicago, 1965), 101–23.

25. Ariès, *Centuries of Childhood*, 39, 61, 403; Lawrence Stone, *Family, Sex and Marriage*, 221–69, 655–58; François Lebrun, *Les hommes et la mort en Anjou aux 17e et 18e siècles* (Paris, 1971), 430.

26. James B. Given notes the particular horror that was attached to the killing

of children in the Middle Ages, and states that, in one Scottish chronicler at least, the horror of the (alleged) killing of a Christian child by Jews was associated with the horror caused by the killing of a child by his parent. He concludes that, "children seem to have been highly valued in the Middle Ages." *Society and Homicide in Thirteenth Century England* (Stanford, 1977), 60–62.

2 Adolescents

1. Lina Eckenstein, *Women under Monasticism: Chapters on Saint-Lore and Convent Life Between* A.D. *500 and* A.D. *1500* (Cambridge, 1896); Eileen E. Power, *Medieval English Nunneries c. 1275 to 1535* (Cambridge, 1922).

2. For a brief treatment of the German church in the Middle Ages see David Knowles and Dmitri Obolensky, *The Middle Ages*, vol. 2 of *The Christian Centuries* (New York, 1968), 43–49; More extensive: Albert Hauck, *Kirchengeschichte Deutschlands*, 5 vols., 2d ed. (Leipzig, 1912–22); on the organization of the medieval church in general see Gabriel Le Bras, *Institutions ecclésiastiques de la Chrétienté médievale*, bk. 1; A. Fliche and V. Martin, *Histoire de L'Eglise*, vol. 12, especially 149–70.

3. On medieval schooling see, among others, *La scuola nell'Occidente latino dell'Alto Medioevo* (Settimane di Studio del Centro Italiano di Studi sull'Alto Medioevo 19), 15–21 April 1971, 2 vols. (Spoleto, 1972); Rudolf Limmer, *Bildungszustände und Bildungsideen des 13. Jahrhunderts* (Munich, 1970); Josiah C. Russell, "The Early Schools of Oxford and Cambridge," in *Twelfth Century Studies*, 167–80 (New York, 1978).

4. Other literary genres seem to have preceded hagiography in this development. For some examples see Hanning, *Individual in Twelfth Century Romance*, 17–52.

5. On the concept of the marital debt (based on 1 Corinthians 7) see John T. Noonan, Jr., *Contraception: A History of Its Treatment by the Catholic Theologians and Canonists* (Cambridge, Mass., 1965), 284–86.

6. Here the conjunction between hagiographic and popular ideas is especially close. See Philippe Ariès, *L'homme devant la mort* (Paris, 1977), 99–112; also see Stone, *Family, Sex and Marriage*, 208–15.

7. H. Newton Malony, ed., *Current Perspectives in the Psychology of Religion* (Grand Rapids, Mich., 1977), 238–35, reveals that even recent work has not moved very far from Freud's formulation on this point.

8. According to the Decretals of Pope Gregory IX, promulgated in 1234 (a compilation by Raymond of Peñafort of the canons promulgated since the twelfth-century *Decretum* of Gratian), a daughter under twelve years of age placed in a monastery by her parents cannot return to the world if she willingly takes the veil after reaching the age of twelve (book 3, title 31, section 12). In general, profession of monastic vows made before the fourteenth year is not binding (ibid., section 8). See R. S. Mylne, *The Canon Law* (London, 1912), 64.

9. Edwin Starbuck, *The Psychology of Religion: An Empirical Study of the Growth of Religious Consciousness* (New York, 1911), especially 49–57 and 101–17.

10. On charismatic call and response see Werner Stark, *The Sociology of Religion: A Study of Christendom* (New York, 1970), 4:36–74; also see George Shepperson, "The Comparative Study of Millenarian Movements," in *Millennial Dreams in Action*, ed. Sylvia L. Thrupp, 44–52 (New York, 1970).

11. R. F. Bennett, *The Early Dominicans* (Cambridge, 1937); William A. Hinnebusch, *The History of the Dominican Order*, 2 vols. (New York, 1973); H. Holzapfel, *History of the Franciscan Order*, trans. A. Tibesar (Teutopolis, Ill., 1948).

12. For a good overview and bibliography, Léopold Genicot, *Le xiiie siècle européen* (Paris, 1968).

13. On confraternities and lay piety see Gérard G. Meersseman, *Ordo fraternitatis: Confraternite e pietà dei laici nel medioevo*, 3 vols. (Rome, 1977); on the Beguines see Ernest McDonnell, *The Beguines and Beghards in Medieval Culture with Special Emphasis on the Belgian Scene* (New Brunswick, N.J., 1954).

14. Fundamental is Herbert Grundmann, *Religiöse Bewegungen im Mittelalter: Untersuchungen über der geschichtlichen Zusammenhänge zwischen der Ketzerei, den Bettelorden und der religiosen Frauenbewegungen im 12. und 13. Jahrhundert und über die geschichtlicher Grundlagen der deutschen Mystik*, 2d ed. (Hildesheim, 1961).

15. On Luther's theology see, among many studies, Paul Althaus, *The Theology of Martin Luther*, trans. R. C.. Schultz (Philadelphia, 1966); on Luther and Staupitz see Ernst Wolf, *Staupitz und Luther* (Leipzig, 1927); Reinhold Weier, *Das Theologieverständniss Martin Luthers* (Paderborn, 1976), 214–17.

16. H. O. Evennett, *The Spirit of the Counter-Reformation*, ed. John Bossy (Cambridge, 1968); Pierre Janelle, *The Catholic Reformation* (Milwaukee, 1949).

17. On Nicholas the Pilgrim see Eric W. Kemp, *Canonization and Authority in the Western Church* (London, 1948), 67–68.

18. On the universality of the wicked stepmother theme see Bruno Bettelheim, *The Uses of Enchantment: The Meaning and Importance of Fairy Tales* (New York, 1977), 66–73.

19. Still useful for the vivid quality of its portrayal is William S. Davis, *Life on a Medieval Barony* (New York, 1923), especially 253–74.

20. Dante Alighieri, *La Commedia, Inferno*, canto 3, lines 58–60, from Edizione Nazionale, Giorgio Petrocchi ed. (Verona, 1966).

21. For views on adolescence that we are calling into question here see Ariès, *Centuries of Childhood*, 19 ff., 239, 261–62, 268; Stone, *Family, Sex and Marriage*, 512, correctly disparages the myth that the troubled adolescent is a nineteenth-century phenomenon, but the evidence he presents reaches back only to the seventeenth century, and he limits his discussion to problems of sexuality.

22. For general developments see Charles Homer Haskins, *The Renaissance of the Twelfth Century* (Cambridge, Mass., 1971); Hastings Rashdall, *The Universities of Europe in the Middle Ages*, ed. F. M. Powicke and A. B. Emden, 3 vols. (Oxford, 1936); Richard W. Southern, *The Making of the Middle Ages* (New Haven, 1961). On the development of guilds, see Emile Coornaert, *Les corporations en France avant 1789*, 2d ed. (Paris, 1968).

23. On the Goliardic poets, see Helen J. Waddell, *The Wandering Scholars* (New York, 1932).

24. William H. Woodward, *Studies in Education during the Age of the Renaissance, 1400–1600* (New York, 1967).

25. On towns and opportunity see Henri Pirenne, *Medieval Cities: Their Origins and the Revival of Trade*, trans. F. V. Halsey (Princeton, 1925); Waley, *Italian City-Republics*; Robert S. Lopez, *The Birth of Europe* (New York, 1967), especially part 3. On the legal profession as a locus of opportunity from the end of the twelfth century see Lauro Martines, *Lawyers and Statecraft in Renaissance Florence* (Princeton, 1968), especially chap. 3.

26. For an overview of the history of Spain see Jaime Vicente Vives, *Approaches to the History of Spain*, trans. J. Connelly Ullman (Berkeley, 1967); for a brief survey, see Rafael Altamira, *A History of Spain*, trans. M. Lee (Toronto, 1949). The medieval and early modern periods are treated in detail in the monumental work by Ramon Menendez Pidal, *Historia de España*, 26 vols. (Madrid, 1935–68).

27. For a different view see Goodich, "Childhood and Adolescence."

3 Chastity

1. John Bugge, *Virginitas: An Essay in the History of a Medieval Ideal* (The Hague, 1975), especially 30–58. The classic, still indispensable work is, of course, Henry C. Lea, *The History of Sacerdotal Celibacy in the Christian Church*, 3d ed. (New York, 1907).

2. Bugge, *Virginitas*, 81.

3. On the marriage bond see Georges Duby, *Medieval Marriage: Two Models from Twelfth Century France*, trans. E. Forster (Baltimore and London, 1978), 3–11; Georges Duby and Jacques Le Goff, eds., *Famille et parenté dans l'occident médiéval: Actes du Colloque de Paris (6–8 Juin 1974)*, Collection de l'Ecole Française de Rome 30 (Rome, 1977); Marc Bloch, *Feudal Society*, (Chicago, 1961), 1:123–42.

4. Two of these practices, not unopposed by the church, were concubinage and repudiating barren wives (Duby, *Medieval Marriage*). Extramarital sexual activity was, of course, condemned by the church, but adultery was a legitimate ground for divorce available only to wronged husbands, not wives. Raoul Manselli, "Vie familiale et éthique sexuelle dans les pénitentiels," in *Famille et parenté dans l'occident médiéval: Actes du Colloque de Paris (6–8 Juin 1974) organisé par l'Ecole Pratique des Hautes Etudes (VIe Section) en collaboration avec le Collège de France et l'Ecole Française de Rome*, Collection de l'Ecole Française de Rome 30 (Rome, 1977), 363–78.

5. Frank Barlow, *Edward the Confessor* (Berkeley, 1970), 81–84, working from perhaps too "modern" a perspective, dismisses the whole story of Edward's presumed chastity, thereby, at least in our judgment, ignoring important evidence on the medieval mentality.

6. See Giuseppe Pitré, "Spettacoli e Feste," in *Biblioteca delle tradizioni popolari siciliane*, 12:200–204 (Palermo, 1881), for festivals in Corrado's honor and, more generally, Martino, *Sud e magia*, and Luigi M. Lombardi Satriani, *Menzogna e verità nella cultura contadina del sud* (Naples, 1974).

7. A famous and influential misogynist text was J. Sprenger and H. Kramer, *Malleus Maleficarum*, first published about 1484, but this was a restatement of older themes (trans. Montague Summers, New York, 1928).

8. On the association of the devil with witchcraft see, among others, Robert Mandrou, *Magistrats et sorciers en France au xviie siècle: Un analyse de psychologie historique* (Paris, 1968), 71–120; E. William Monter, *Witchcraft in France and Switzerland: The Borderlands during the Reformation* (Ithaca, 1976), 17–41; Jeffrey Burton Russell, *Witchcraft in the Middle Ages* (Ithaca, 1972).

9. For a brief Catholic discussion see "Concupiscence," *New Catholic Encyclopedia*, 16 vols. (New York, 1967–74) 4:121–24. For a discussion of Luther's conception of the term see Heinrich Boehmer, *Martin Luther: Road to Reformation*, trans. J. W. Doberstein and T. G. Tappert (Philadelphia, 1945), 128.

10. On the problems of twelfth-century monks studying classical literature see Jean Leclercq, *Monks and Love in Twelfth Century France: Psycho-Historical Essays* (Oxford, 1979), especially 62–82.

11. See especially two articles by Giles Constable, "The Popularity of Twelfth-Century Spiritual Writers in the Late Middle Ages," in *Renaissance Studies in Honor of Hans Baron*, ed. A. Molho and J. A. Tedeschi, 5–28, (Dekalb, Ill., 1971); "Twelfth-Century Spirituality and the Late Middle Ages," in *Medieval and Renaissance Studies*, ed. O. B. Hardison, Jr., 5 (1971): 27–60.

12. Andrew M. Greeley, *The Mary Myth: On the Femininity of God* (New York, 1977), 73–99; Marina Warner, *Alone of All Her Sex: The Myth and the Cult of the Virgin Mary* (London, 1976), 224–35, on the necessity of both the Virgin Mary and Mary Magdalene to accommodate this paradox.

13. Susan Brownmiller, *Against Our Will: Men, Women and Rape* (New York, 1975), 23–30, discusses the subject of rape briefly, but much more research needs to be done.

14. Duby, *Medieval Marriage*, 4–6.

15. Keith Thomas, *Religion and the Decline of Magic* (New York, 1971), 520, 568–69; Alan Macfarlane, *Witchcraft in Tudor and Stuart England: A Regional and Comparative Study* (New York, 1970), 147–57.

16. An excellent beginning at measuring some of the criminal dimensions of female victimization may be found in Barbara A. Hanawalt, *Crime and Conflict in English Communities 1300–1348* (Cambridge, Mass., 1979), 151–83.

17. For a brief introduction to Patristic misogyny see George H. Tavard, *Woman in Christian Tradition* (Notre Dame, 1973), 48–171. For a survey of misogynist vernacular literature in the Middle Ages see August Wulff, *Die frauenfeindlichen Dichtungen in den Romanischen Literaturen des Mittelalters bis zum Ende des XIII Jahrhunderts Romanische Arbeiten*, ed. Carl Voretzsch IV (Halle, 1914). A famous attack on women as unchaste, among other things, occurs, in The Romance of the Rose ("You riotous, filthy, vile, stinking bitch") lines 8687–9360, but recent critics tend to exculpate the author, Jean de Meun, arguing that he was ironically placing these misogynist ideas in the mouth of the Jaloux. See John Fleming, *The Roman de la Rose: A Study in Allegory and Iconography* (Princeton, 1969, 154–56. English translation cited: *The Romance of the Rose by Guillaume De Lorris and Jean De Meun*, trans. Charles Dahlberg (Princeton, 1971).

For medieval references to women as sexually dangerous see Phillippe Verdier, "Women in the Marginalia of Gothic Manuscripts and Related Works," in *The Role of Woman in the Middle Ages*, ed. Rosemarie Thee Morewedge, 145 n.7. This was by no means the only view of women in the Middle Ages, as Verdier's article and most of the others in this book demonstrate.

On the not inconsiderable property rights of medieval women see Jo Ann McNamara and Suzanne Wemple, "The Power of Woman through the Family in Medieval Europe, 500–1100," *Feminist Studies* 1 (1973): 126–41; David Herlihy, "Land, Family and Women in Continental Europe, 701–1200," *Tradition* 18 (1962): 89–113.

18. John F. Scott, *Internalization of Norms: A Sociological Theory of Moral Commitment* (Englewood Cliffs, N.J., 1971): 1–4.

4 Adults

1. Johan Huizinga, *The Waning of the Middle Ages* (London, 1924), 18.

2. Bakhtin, *Rabelais and His World*, especially 4–58.

3. For a valuable analysis of modes of perception of time and change see William J. Brandt, *The Shape of Medieval History* (New Haven, 1966). On changing views of time in the Renaissance see Agnes Heller, *Renaissance Man*, trans. R. E. Allen (London, 1978), 172–96.

4. On the Dominican recruitment of both youth and adults: "As master general, Jordan of Saxony deliberately set out to recruit students and teachers at the new universities of France, Italy, and England." John B. Freed, *The Friars and German Society in the Thirteenth Century*, (Cambridge, Mass., 1977) 124–25.

5. For the spread of the mendicants in southern France, *Les mendiants en pays d'Oc au xiii⁰ siècle*, Cahiers de Fanjeaux 8 (Toulouse, 1973). For an interesting reconstruction of the ideal of the *vita apostolica* as interpreted by popular preachers and their "folk listeners," see Christopher J. Kauffman, *Tamers of Death*, vol. 1, *The History of the Alexian Brothers from 1300 to 1789* (New York, 1976), 14–15.

6. Gerald R. Owst, *Preaching in Medieval England: An Introduction to Sermon Manuscripts of the Period c. 1350–1450* (Cambridge, 1926); J. W. Blench, *Preaching in England in the Late Fifteenth and Sixteenth Centuries: A Study of English Sermons 1450–c. 1600* (New York, 1964); Anscar Zawart, "The History of Franciscan Preaching and of Franciscan Preachers (1209–1927): A Bio-Bibliographical Study," *Franciscan Studies* 7 (1928): 241–596; Carlo Delcorno, *La predicazione nell'età comunale* (Florence, 1974).

7. For a vivid general introduction, see Barbara Tuchman, *A Distant Mirror: The Calamitous 14th Century* (New York, 1978), especially 24–48.

8. Etienne Delaruelle, "La spiritualité aux xive et xve siècles," *Cahiers d'Histoire Mondiale* 5 (1959): 59–70; idem, "L'influence de Saint François d'Assise sur la pieté populaire," *Comitato Internazionale di Scienze Storiche X Congresso Internazionale di Scienze Storiche*, Rome 4–11 September 1955, *Relazione* brief 3:449–66. For a good general account of the flowering and spread of more individual and affective piety in the thirteenth and fourteenth centuries, see Francis Oakley, *The Western Church in the Later Middle Ages* (Ithaca, 1979), chap. 2

9. Paul Oskar Kristeller, "Lay Religious Traditions and Florentine Platonism," in *Studies in Renaissance Thought and Letters*, 99–122 (Rome, 1956); Charles Trinkaus, *In Our Image and Likeness: Humanity and Divinity in Humanist Thought*, 2 vols. (London, 1970), especially vol. 1.

10. Victor Saxer, *Le dossier vézelien de Marie Madeleine: Invention et translation des reliques en 1265–1267* (Bruxelles, 1975), and idem, *Le culte de Marie Madeleine en Occident des origines à la fin du Moyen Age*, 2 vols. (Paris 1959).

11. On popular ideas about sanctity see chapter 5 below and Mecklin, *Passing of the Saint*, 17–30.

12. On the penitential system and indulgences, see Henry C. Lea, *A History of Auricular Confession and Indulgences in the Latin Church* (Philadelphia, 1896); Bernhard Poschmann, *Der Ablass im Licht der Bussgeschichte* (Bonn, 1948).

13. On papal revenues from pecuniary penances, see William E. Lunt, *Financial Relations of the Papacy with England*, vol. 1 (to 1327) (Cambridge, Mass., 1939), 525. On papal indulgences and remission of sin, see ibid., vol. 2 (1327–54) (Cambridge, Mass., 1962), 446–72.

14. Hans Conrad Peyer, *Stadt und Stadtpatron im mittelalterlichen Italien* (Zurich, 1955).

15. Indeed, Churchill could smile and Roosevelt fume about de Gaulle's "Joan of Arc complex." See Jacques de Launay, *De Gaulle and His France: A Psychopolitical and Historical Portrait*, trans. Dorothy Albertyn (New York), 87–134.

16. Jeremy Boissevain, *Saints and Fireworks: Religion and Politics in Rural Malta* (New York, 1965), 55–73.

17. On Lanfranc's controversy with Berengar see R. W. Southern, "Lanfranc of Bec and Berengar of Tours," in *Studies in Medieval History Presented to F. M. Powicke*, ed. R. W. Hunt et al., 27–48 (Oxford, 1948).

18. Georg Misch, *Geschichte der Autobiographie*, 4 vols. (Frankfurt, 1949–69), 4(2): 573–97; Walter Ullmann, *The Individual and Society in the Middle Ages* (Baltimore, 1966), especially 139–45.

19. Elizabeth McBrearty, who is preparing a doctoral dissertation on humanist hagiography at the University of Arizona, points out that the leper story is not included in the fifteenth-century version of the vita, but first appears in the seventeenth-century version by Rossi.

20. Max Weber, *The Protestant Ethic and the Spirit of Capitalism*, trans. Talcott Parsons (New York, 1958), n. 9, 193–94.

5 Who Was a Saint?

1. Delooz, *Sociologie et canonisations*, 105–7. See bibliography of treatises on canonization and their history in De Maio, *Riforme e miti*, 258–59 n.3.

2. St. Thomas Aquinas, *Summa Theologiae Secunda Secundae*. On the history of the virtues in general see Otto Zöckler, *Die Tugendlehre des Christentums* (Gütersloh, 1904).

3. Delooz, *Sociologie et canonisations*, 32. The question is dealt with by St. Thomas in his *Summa Theologiae Secunda Secundae*, question 63.

4. De Maio, *Riforme e miti*, 257–58.

5. See the account of the development of papal canonization in Edward W. Kemp, *Canonization and Authority in the Western Church* (Oxford, 1948).

6. See now Ronald C. Finucane, *Miracles and Pilgrims: Popular Beliefs in Medieval England* (London, 1977), especially 59–82.

7. Delehaye, *Legends of the Saints*, gives numerous examples of fortuitous coincidences that led to cults.

8. On so-called white magic see C. Grant Loomis, *White Magic: An Introduction to the Folklore of Christian Legend* (Cambridge, Mass., 1948).

9. On the theological distinction between *latria*, reverence or worship of God, and *dulia*, veneration or respect for persons, see St. Thomas Aquinas, *Summa Theologiae Secunda Secundae*, questions 84, 94, 103.

10. Thomas, *Religion and the Decline of Magic*, 237–44.

11. On the "great" themes of prophecy in the Middle Ages and the Renaissance see Marjorie Reeves, *The Influence of Prophecy in the Later Middle Ages: A study in Joachimism* (Oxford, 1969). See also Morton W. Bloomfield, "Recent Scholarship on Joachim of Fiore and His Influence," in *Prophecy and Millenarianism: Essays in Honour of Marjorie Reeves*, ed. Ann Williams, 21–52 (Harlow, Sussex, 1980).

12. Diana M. Webb, "Penitence and Peace-Making in City and Contado: The Bianchi of 1399," in *The Church in Town and Countryside* (papers read at the seventeenth summer and the eighteenth winter meeting of the Ecclesiastical History Society), ed. Derek Baker, Studies in Church History, no. 16, 243–56 (Oxford, 1979).

13. Loomis, *White Magic*, 104; De Martino, *Sud e magia*, 97–119; on Semitic origins of blood magic see R. Campbell Thompson, *Semitic Magic: Its Origins and Development* (New York, 1971 reprint of 1908 edition), 195–98.

14. "Quella che conta in un santo nell'epoca penitenziale è la sua capacità di farsi portatore di 'potenza' e di stabilire il contatto fra il sacro e l'uomo." Ida Magli, *Gli Uomini della Penitenza* (n.p., 1967), 129.

15. For a bibliography of mysticism in Christian Europe see Mary Ann Bowman, *Western Mysticism: A Guide to the Basic Works* (Chicago, 1978). On visionary experience in relation to mysticism, see Ernst Benz, *Die Vision Erfahrungsformen und Bilderwelt* (Stuttgart, 1969).

16. On athletic metaphors in Christian art see Colin Eisler, "The Athlete of Virtue: The Iconography of Asceticism," in *Essays in Honor of Erwin Panofsky*, 2 vols., ed. Millard Meiss, 1:82–97 (New York, 1961).

17. On cultic activity see Raoul Manselli, *La religion populaire au Moyen Age: Problèmes de méthode et d'histoire* (Montreal, 1975), chap. 2.

18. Pierre Doyère, "Erémètisme en Occident," *Dictionaire de spiritualité ascetique et mystique* 4 (1960): 953–82.

19. Edward Cuthbert Butler, *Benedictine Monachism: Studies in Benedictine Life and Rule*, 2d ed. (Cambridge, 1924), especially chaps. 4–8; Ursmer Berlière, *L'ascese bénédictine* (Paris, 1927).

20. On humility in the medieval contemplative life see for example, *The Steps of Humility by Bernard, Abbot of Clairvaux,* trans. George B. Burch (Cambridge, Mass.: 1942.

21. On flagellation and lay piety see John Henderson, "The Flagellant Movement and Flagellant Confraternities in Central Italy, 1260–1400," in *Religious Motivation: Biographical and Sociological Problems for the Church Historian* (papers read at the sixteenth summer meeting and seventeenth winter meeting of the Ecclesiastical History Society), ed. Derek Baker, Studies in Church History no. 15, 147–60 (Oxford, 1978).

22. The classic work is Marc Bloch, *The Royal Touch: Sacred Monarchy and Scrofula in England and France,* trans. J. E. Anderson (London, 1973).

23. Delooz, *Sociologie et canonisations.*

24. For an excellent, detailed account on the decline of saints' cults and on how saints "wear out" see William A. Christian, Jr., *Person and God in a Spanish Valley* (New York, 1972), 64–65, 88–93.

6 Place

1. For an introductory reevaluation of the myth of medieval social and cultural unity see Karl F. Morrison, *Europe's Middle Ages, 565–1500* (New York, 1970), especially 12–22. See also the brief but suggestive remarks on popular religion and the disunity of Western Christendom by Christopher Brooke, *Medieval Church and Society Collected Essays* (London, 1971), 139–61.

2. George and George, "Roman Catholic Sainthood and Social Status," 89–97.

3. Jacques Le Goff, "Ordres mendiants et urbanisation dans la France médiévale: Etat de l'enquête," *Annales: Economies, Sociétés, Civilisations* 25 (1970): 924–45.

4. On the most radical advocates of apostolic poverty see Decima L. Douie, *The Nature and the Effect of the Heresy of the Fraticelli* (Manchester, 1932). For a good recent overview see Oakley, *Western Church in the Later Middle Ages,* 178–203.

5. On mendicancy and popular piety, especially in the cities, see Freed, *Friars and German Society,* 5–17; Barbara H. Rosenwein and Lester K. Little, "Social Meaning in the Monastic and Mendicant Spiritualities," *Past and Present* 63 (1974): 20–32; Jacques Le Goff, "Apostolat mendiant et fait urbain dans la France médiévale: L'implantation des ordres mendiants; Programme questionnaire pour une enquête," *Annales* 25 (1968): 335–52; and idem, "Ordres mendiants et urbanisation dans la France médiévale"; Grundmann, *Religiöse Bewegungen.*

6. Guillaume Mollat demonstrated conclusively that the Avignon popes continued the trend toward papal centralization of church government; but their ability to intervene effectively in, much less to control, Italian affairs was another matter. See *The Popes at Avignon, 1305–1378,* trans. from the 9th French ed. by Janet Love (London, 1963).

7. E. Delaruelle, E.-R. Labande, and P. Ourliac, *L'église au temps du Grande Schisme et de la crise conciliare (1378–1449),* in *Histoire de l'église* ed. A. Fliche and V. Martin 14:1 (Paris, 1962). See also the valuable collection of studies, *Genèse et débuts du Grande Schisme d'Occident,* Avignon, 25–28 September 1978, Colloques Internationale du Centre de la Recherches Scientifique, no. 586 (Paris, 1980).

8. See, among many others, Gordon Leff, *Heresy in the Later Middle Ages,* 2 vols. (Manchester, 1967); Arno Borst, *Die Katharer* (Stuttgart, 1953); Herbert Grundmann, *Religiöse Bewegungen,* and idem, *Bibliographie zur Ketzergeschichte des Mittelalters, (1900–1966)* (Rome, 1967).

9. For one such survival in a fourteenth-century Pyrenees village, see Emanuel Le Roy Ladurie, *Montaillou: Village occitan de 1293–1324* (Paris, 1975), especially 535–39.

10. Marjorie Reeves, *The Influence of Prophecy in the Later Middle Ages: A Study in Joachimism* (Oxford, 1969), 145 ff., 322.

11. Douie, *Nature and Effect*, 20 and chap. 7.

12. Donald Weinstein, *Savonarola and Florence: Prophecy and Patriotism in the Renaissance* (Princeton, 1970), 43–46. The connection has not been established beyond question, however, as is pointed out by Roberto Rusconi, *L'Attesa della fine crisi della società, profezia ed apocalisse in Italia al tempo del grande scisma d'occidente (1378–1417)*, Instituto Storico Italiano per il Medio Evo Studi Storici, fasc. 115–18 (Rome, 1979), 40–41. Too exclusive an emphasis on the social radicalism of medieval apocalyptic ideas is maintained by Norman Cohn, *The Pursuit of the Millennium*, 2d ed., (New York, 1961). For a general study of worker and peasant revolts see Michel Mollat and Philippe Wolff, *The Popular Revolutions of the Later Middle Ages*, trans. A. L. Lytton-Sells (London, 1973).

13. On Venetian confraternities, flagellation, and civic ritual see Brian Pullan, *Rich and Poor in Renaissance Venice: The Social Institutions of a Catholic State, to 1620* (Cambridge, Mass., 1971), especially 34–40, 50–52. On civic and religious ritual, Richard Trexler, *Public Life in Renaissance Florence* (New York, 1980); Davis, *Society and Culture in Early Modern France*; Edward Muir, *Civic Ritual in Renaissance Venice* (Princeton, 1981).

14. On confraternities, see Meersseman, *Ordo fraternitatis*; J. Duhr, "La confrérie dans la vie de l'église," *Revue d'Histoire Ecclésiastique* 35 (1939): 437–78; on urban piety, and the burgeoning of popular piety in general, see the survey by François Vandenbroucke in J. Leclercq, F. Vandenbroucke, and L. Bouyer, *La spiritualité du Moyen Age: Histoire de la spiritualité chrétienne* (Aubier, 1961), 2:299–447. Engl. transl., *The Spirituality of the Middle Ages* (New York, 1968), 243–372.

15. As Jacques Chiffoleau put it, confraternities were under the control of the church but "reste cependant une affaire de laics." "Les confréries, la mort et la religion en Comtat Venaissin à la fin du Moyen Age," *Mélanges de l'Ecole Française de Rome Moyen Age Temps Modernes* 91 (1979): 785–825.

16. Le Roy Ladurie, *Montaillou*, 487–522; Robert Anderson, *Traditional Europe: A Study in Anthropology and History* (Belmont, Calif., 1971), 170; on the continuation of a distinct rural piety even to the recent past see Boissevain, *Saints and Fireworks*; and Christian, *Person and God in a Spanish Valley*.

17. Thus Enrico Scrovegni built the Arena Chapel and commissioned Giotto to decorate it with frescoes depicting the life of Christ to pacify the church's wrath against his usurious father Rinaldo, whom Dante placed in hell. S.v. "Scrovegni, Enrico," *Enciclopedia Italiana* (Rome, 1936), 35: 235. So also Cosimo de' Medici subsidized statues, shrines, and church buildings for "the settling of debts to the Supreme Creditor." E. H. Gombrich, "The Early Medici as Patrons of Art: A Survey of Primary Sources," in *Italian Renaissance Studies*, ed. E. F. Jacob, 282–85 (London, 1960). For a succinct but penetrating statement of the relation between Renaissance artistic patronage and the anxieties of Florentine businessmen see Gene Brucker, *Renaissance Florence* (New York, 1969), 107–9.

18. For Florence see Marvin B. Becker, *Florence in Transition*, 2 vols. (Baltimore, 1967, 1968), 1:211.

19. The relation between the twelfth-century "awakening" of subjective con-

science and the acceptance of new modes of association and levels of authority is lucidly expressed by Father M.-D. Chenu in his *L' éveil de la conscience dans la civilisation médiévale* (Montreal, 1969), "un idéal de fraternité, sociologiquement solidaire des émancipations économiques et politiques, impose un mode d'exercice nouveau aux relations d'autorité, non seulement dans les comportements mais bientôt dans les structures gouvernementales" (p. 27).

20. See the few but sensitively written pages in Bloch, *Feudal Society*, 1:81–87.

21. Brucker, *Renaissance Florence*, 32. On the interdependence of the Florentine guilds and the life of the commune, see Alfred Doren, *Das Florentiner Zunftwesen vom 14. bis zum 16. Jahrhundert*, Studien aus der Florentiner Wirtschaftsgeschichte, vol. 2 (Stuttgart, 1969).

22. Pullan, *Rich and Poor in Renaissance Venice*, 50–52.

23. "L'adaptation de l'examen de conscience, non seulement à la personnalité de chacun, mais aux divers états de vie et professions, représente un remarquable effort d'intériorisation, y compris dans la manière de juger les fonctions de la vie sociale, dans l'objectivité des relations humaines transformées par la société marchande nouvelle." Chenu, *L'eveil de la conscience*, 45. For a survey of the phases of development of conscience see Benjamin Nelson, "Self-Images and Systems of Spiritual Direction in the History of European Civilization," in *The Quest for Self-Control*, ed. Samuel Klausner, 49–69 (New York, 1965).

24. A succinct overview is provided by Harry A. Miskimin, *The Economy of Europe, 1300–1460* (Cambridge, 1975).

25. Still the most comprehensive survey is Aziz Suryal Atiya, *The Crusade in the Later Middle Ages* (London, 1938).

26. William McNeill, *Plagues and Peoples* (New York, 1976), 168–170.

27. Ecole Pratique des Hautes Etudes—VIe Section, *Villages désertes et histoire économique, xie-xviiie siècle* (Paris, 1965), 276–82. For a survey of the demographic impact of the Black Death see E. Carpentier, "Autour de la peste noire: Famines et epidémies dans l'histoire du xiv siècle," *Annales: Economies, Sociétés, Civilisations* 17 (1962): 1062–92.

28. Giovanni Boccaccio, *Decameron*, ed. Vittore Branca (Florence, 1976), Prima giornata-introduzione.

29. Millard Meiss, *Painting in Florence and Siena after the Black Death* (Princeton, 1951); Benjamin Kedar, *Merchants in Crisis: Genovese and Venetian Men of Affairs and the Fourteenth-Century Depression* (New Haven, 1976), especially 81–117.

30. See, for example, Thomas, *Religion and the Decline of Magic*, 86–88.

31. For a survey of European economic conditions in this period see *The Cambridge Economic History of Europe*, ed. J. H. Clapham, E. E. Power, et al., 7 vols. (Cambridge, 1966–78), especially 2:338–54, 3:206–29, 4:1–40. For a contemporary complaint against the *gente nuova* see William M. Bowsky, "The Impact of the Black Death upon Sienese Government and Society," *Speculum* 39 (1964): 29.

32. For an analysis of St. Bernardino's popular preaching style, see Carlo Delcorno, " 'L'ars praedicandi' di Bernardino da Siena," *Lettere Italiane* 32 (1980): 441–75.

33. Rusconi, *L'Attesa*, 219–33.

34. Weinstein, *Savonarola and Florence*, 138–84.

35. Howard Kaminsky, *The Hussite Revolution* (Berkeley, 1967).

36. For example, see the conclusion of the discussion of the victory of the papacy over the Conciliarists in Delaruelle, Labande, and Ourliac, *L'église au temps du Grande Schisme*, 291.

37. Waley, *Italian City-Republics*, 56–87.

38. Jacob Burckhardt, *The Civilization of the Renaissance in Italy* (New York, 1958 ed. of 1929 translation), 143.

39. The point has been made numerous times; among others, and very effectively, by Waley, *Italian City-Republics*.

40. For example, Craig B. Fischer, "The Pisan Clergy and an Awakening of Historical Interest in a Medieval Commune," *Studies in Medieval and Renaissance History* 3 (1966): 143–219.

41. See Franco Sacchetti's complaints about the proliferation of cults of local *beati* and their promotion to saintly status, not only in his native Florence but in other cities as well, in his letter of 1365 to Iacomo di Conte da Perugia in *Opere*, ed. Alberto Chiari, 2 vols. (Bari, 1958), 2:99–104.

42. Nelda Guglielmi, "Le groupe cathédral dans le paysage urbain en Italie (xiii–xve siècles)," *Journal of Medieval History* 6 (1980): 87–101.

43. Weinstein, *Savonarola and Florence*, 43–51.

44. The interaction of popular enthusiasm and national state formation may be seen in William C. Jordan, *Louis IX and the Challenge of the Crusade* (Princeton, 1979), 182–213.

45. A. N. Galpern, *The Religions of the People in Sixteenth-Century Champagne* (Cambridge, Mass., 1976), 43–51.

46. On Italy see Annabella Rossi, *Le feste dei poveri* (Bari, 1969), especially 145 ff., and on Iberia see José Deleito y Pinuela, *La vida religiosa española bajo el cuarto Felipe: Santos y pecadores* (Madrid, 1963), 14–17, 20–23, 138–41, 185–206, and A. H. de Oliveira Marques, *Daily Life in Portugal in the Late Middle Ages*, trans. S. S. Wyatt, (Madison, Wis., 1971), 212–28.

47. Fernand Braudel, *The Mediterranean and the Mediterranean World in the Age of Philip II*, trans. Sian Reynolds, (New York, 1972), 1:232, 234; B. H. Slicher Van Bath, *The Agrarian History of Western Europe*, A.D. *500–1850*, trans. Olive Ordish (London, 1963), 58, 244; Giacomo Devoto, *The Languages of Italy*, trans. V. Louise Katainen (Chicago, 1978), 8–15.

48. Braudel, *Mediterranean*, 453–59, on poverty, and Edward Fox, *History in Geographic Perspective: The Other France* (New York, 1971), on the commercial community.

49. Emilio Sereni, *Storia del paesaggio agrario italiano* (Bari, 1961), 212–14; Jane Schneider and Peter Schneider, *Culture and Political Economy in Western Sicily* (New York, 1976), 36–55; Edward E. Malefakis, *Agrarian Reform and Peasant Revolution in Spain: Origins of the Civil War* (New Haven, 1970), 50–59.

50. While contemporary rural Mediterranean fatalism and resort to magic have been intensely studied and commented upon in such recent works as de Martino, *Sud e magia*, and Bell, *Fate and Honor*, little comparative work has been attempted for either the modern or the medieval period. Unfortunately Braudel has little to say on the subject in his noted book *The Mediterranean*, and Keith Thomas concentrates mainly on the English evidence in his *Religion and the Decline of Magic*. We can only speculate about the north-south contrast, but we believe that further studies will show that its roots go far back, to the Middle Ages.

51. The classic humanist text is Erasmus's account of his visit to the shrine of Our Lady of Walsingham with John Colet, *Opera Omnia Desiderii Erasmi Roterdami*, 5 vols. in 9 parts (Amsterdam, 1969–79) (1972); 1.3, (1972): 470–94. English translation, "A Pilgrimage for Religion's Sake," in *The Colloquies of Erasmus*, trans. Craig R. Thompson, 2 vols. 1:287–312 (Chicago, 1964).

52. William J. Bouwsma, *Venice and the Defense of Republican Liberty: Renaissance*

Values in the Age of the Counter Reformation (Berkeley, Calif., 1968), especially 417 ff. on the Venetian interdict.

53. There were a few exceptions, such as the survival of St. George as patron of England, the cult of St. Nicholas (Santa Claus), and so forth. Burke, *Popular Culture*, 149.

54. For a suggestive and inevitably controversial thesis that explains the Reformation in Germany as largely due to the uneven distribution of saints' shrines between the northern and southern parts of the country, see Rothkrug, *Religious Practices and Collective Perceptions*, and his briefer treatment, "Popular Religion and Holy Shrines." On iconoclasm in the Netherlands see Phyllis Mack Crew, *Calvinist Preaching and Iconoclasm in the Netherlands, 1544–1569*, (Cambridge, 1978), 54.

55. On the "Spanish thesis" of Catholic revival and the limitations of this thesis, see Evennett, *Spirit of the Counter-Reformation*, 11–19.

56. Marvin R. O'Connell, *The Counter-Reformation, 1559–1610* (New York, 1974), 213.

57. For Venice see Paul F. Grendler, *The Roman Inquisition and the Venetian Press, 1540–1605* (Princeton, 1977), 232–33. The influx of Protestant books from the north was even more serious (ibid., 102–15). For Lucca see Marino Berengo, *Nobili e mercanti nella Lucca del Cinquecento* (Turin, 1965), 399–419.

58. On the revival of papal supremacy see Evennett, *Spirit of the Counter-Revolution*, 92–3. On the reform of bishops see Hubert Jedin, *A History of the Council of Trent*, trans. E. Graf., 2 vols. (London, 1957), 2:317–69.

7   Class

1. See, for example, Eric Hobsbawm, *Primitive Rebels: Studies in Archaic Forms of Social Movement in the 19th and 20th Centuries* (London, 1959), 57–73; Cohn, *Pursuit of the Millennium*, especially 29–36, 53–60, and 223–80. On "the democracy of hell" and its illustration, see Robert Hughes, *Heaven and Hell in Western Art* (New York, 1968), 14–16.

2. A useful schema of lower-class attitudes toward social injustice is provided by Peter Burke. He identifies five attitudes that tend to shade into each other: fatalist, moralist, traditionalist, radical, and millenarian (*Popular Culture*, 174–75).

3. St. Augustine, *The City of God* 15.1.

4. Among those who employed a tripartite hierarchical ordering were Thomas Aquinas, Peter of Auvergne, Ptolemy of Lucca, Egidius Romanus, and Marsilius of Padua. See Alan Gewirth's discussion in his edition of Marsilius of Padua, *The Defender of Peace*, 2 vols. (New York, 1951), 1:191. Giles Constable finds that the twelfth-century *dictatores* almost unanimously agreed on the division of society into upper, middle, and lower orders, mainly on the basis of dignity, power, and office, but not of wealth or clerical vis-à-vis lay status. "The Structure of Medieval Society According to the *Dictatores* of the Twelfth Century," in *Law, Church and Society: Essays in Honor of Stephan Kuttner*, ed. K. Pennington and R. Somerville (Philadelphia, 1977), 253–67.

5. See note 2, chap. 6.

6. *The Rule of Saint Benedict in Latin and English*, ed. and trans. Justin McCann (Westminster, Md., 1952), chap. 64.

7. Hastings Rashdall, *The Universities of Europe in the Middle Ages*, ed. F. M. Powicke and A. B. Emden, 3 vols. (Oxford, 1936), 1:344–50, 370–97.

8. Along related lines, William J. Brandt sees medieval clerical notions of personality as deriving from Augustinian realism. He contrasts this, however, with

aristocratic perceptions that regarded personality as susceptible to experience (*Shape of Medieval History*, 160–62).

9. Emmanuel Le Roy Ladurie, *Times of Feast, Times of Famine: A History of Climate since the Year 1000*, trans. Barbara Bray (New York, 1971); but also see book 11 of Augustine's Confessions.

10. Mark Poster, *Critical Theory of the Family* (New York, 1978), 178–90; Stone, *Family Sex and Marriage*, 9, 85–93, and the general argument and structure of chapters 4, 5, 7, 9 and part 5.

11. Goodich, "Childhood and Adolescence."

12. On the medieval hagiographers' practice of ennobling saints' families, see George and George, "Roman Catholic Sainthood and Social Status."

13. The argument that Christianity was "the myth all shared" is presented in Anderson, *Traditional Europe*, 153–63. We have no quarrel with this as such, but we will suggest that the ways different segments of the Christian community dealt with this common myth were partially determined by their diverse life situations.

14. Jerome Blum, *The End of the Old Order in Rural Europe* (Princeton, 1978), 29–79; Georges Duby, *L'économie rurale et la vie des compagnes dans l'occident médiéval*, 2 vols. (Paris, 1962).

15. As we said earlier, we believe that the circuits between elite and popular culture were multidirectional, neither exclusively from the elite to the multitude nor the reverse (see above, p. 12). Here we are emphasizing one channel of cultural flow, but not to the exclusion of others. For vertical models of cultural transmission see George M. Foster, "What Is a Peasant?" in *Peasant Society: A Reader*, ed. Jack M. Potter et al., 10–12 (Boston, 1967), and the partial critique of Anderson, *Traditional Europe*, 9–18. An approach more in keeping with our own may be found in Bakhtin, *Rabelais and His World*, 1–58, and Carlo Ginzburg, *I Benandanti: Stregoneria e culti agrari tra Cinquecento e Seicento* (Turin, 1966), vii–xv. On the whole question of cultural transmission see Burke, *Popular Culture*, 59–64, 91–115.

16. The Enlightenment, represented by David Hume and Edward Gibbon, was largely responsible for the idea that the Christian cult of saints represented the successful invasion of monotheistic Christianity by the polytheism of late antiquity's vulgar multitudes. For a recent thoughtful critique of this still-pervasive "two-tiered" model of early Christianity, see Peter Brown, *The Cult of the Saints: Its Rise and Function in Latin Christianity* (Chicago, 1981), 12–22. Brown's assertion that "late-antique Christianity, as it impinged on the outside world, was shrines and relics" (p. 12) is less true but not without point for Christianity in the Middle Ages as well.

17. The initiative of nobles and knights in promoting cults and shrines in Germany is stressed by Lionel Rothkrug in "Popular Religion and Holy Shrines: Their Influence on the Origins of the German Reformation and their Role in German Cultural Development," in Obelkevich, ed., *Religion and the People*, 27–31.

18. This is emphasized for the cities of the greater Mediterranean basin by Braudel, *Mediterranean*. See especially the section "The Indispensable Immigrant," 1:334–38, and 1:44–47.

19. This aspect of Max Weber's essay of 1904–5, namely that a capitalistic value system followed long after capitalist practices had become widespread in Europe, seems to be generally accepted, although other aspects of Weber's thesis such as the close connection between Calvinist "calling" and predestination and the spirit of capitalism have given rise to a small mountain of revisionist literature that we make no effort to cite here. But see Max Weber, *The Protestant Ethic and the Spirit*

of Capitalism, trans. Talcott Parsons (New York, 1958); R. H. Tawney, *Religion and the Rise of Capitalism* (New York, 1937); Robert W. Green, ed. *Protestantism and Capitalism* (Boston, 1959).

20. Carlo M. Cipolla, *Cristofano and the Plague: A Study in the History of Public Health in the Age of Galileo* (Berkeley, Calif., 1973), and idem, "Peste del 1630–31 nell'Empolese," *Archivio Storico Italiano* 136 (1978): 469–82; Braudel, *Mediterranean*, 1:332–34.

21. G. B. Casotti, *Memorie istoriche della miracolosa immagine di Santa Maria Vergine dell' Impruneta* (Florence, 1714); Iris Origo, *The Merchant of Prato*, 2d ed. (New York, 1963).

22. Still useful is Alice Clark, *Working Life of Women in the Seventeenth Century* (New York, 1920).

23. Saints, writes Alexander Murray, were classless; their appeal was universal, their essence a quality of "social amphibiousness." See chapter 16, entitled "The Saint: The Man without Social Class," in his *Reason and Society in the Middle Ages* (Oxford, 1978), 383–404.

8 Men and Women

1. On the celebration by medieval (c. 738–1340) cities of their saints and great bishops, with a list of sources, see J. K. Hyde, "Medieval Descriptions of Cities," *Bulletin of the John Rylands Library, Manchester* 48 (1966): 308–340; Peyer, *Stadt und Stadtpatron*.

2. On the cult of kings see Ernst H. Kantorowicz, *Laudes Regiae: A Study in Liturgical Acclamations and Mediaeval Ruler Worship*, University of California Publications in History, vol. 32 (Berkeley, 1946). A controversial work that regards the sacred powers of saintly kings in a universal perspective is A. M. Hocart, *Kingship* (Oxford, 1969).

3. Noreen Hunt, comp., *Cluniac Monasticism in the Central Middle Ages* (London, 1971).

4. See above, chapter 3, note 11.

5. David Herlihy, "The Natural History of Medieval Women," *Natural History* 57, no. 3 (1978): 56–67.

6. *Movimento religioso femminile e francescanesimo nel secolo xiii*, Atti della Societa Internazionale di Studi Francescani (Assisi, 1979). Michael Goodich, "The Contours of Female Piety in Later Medieval Hagiography," *Church History* 50 (1981): 20–32. For an extreme example, Stephen E. Wessley, "The Thirteenth Century Guglielmites: Salvation through Women," in *Medieval Women*, Studies in Church History, ed. Derek Baker 1:289–303 (Oxford, 1978).

7. De Maio, *Riforme e miti*, 24–25, 271–75.

8. Dom Cuthbert, *The Capuchins: A Contribution to the History of the Counter Reformation*, 2 vols. (London, 1929), 1:57–84; Delumeau, *Catholicism between Luther and Voltaire*, 34–40.

9. This seems to be the consensual view of scholars of various viewpoints, Catholic, Protestant, and secular alike, such as Jedin, Delumeau, Dickens, and Burke.

10. Norman O. Brown, *Life against Death: The Psychoanalytical Meaning of History* (Middletown, Conn., 1957), 210. See also Braudel's "The Devil seems to have been afoot in all the countries of Europe as the sixteenth century drew to a close, and even more in the first decades of the following century" (*Mediterranean* 1:38). Most recent studies of the European witchcraft obsession emphasize the prominence of women among the suspected and the accused. See for example, Macfarlane, *Witch-*

craft in Tudor and Stuart England; Norman Cohn, *Europe's Inner Demons* (New York, 1975); Julio Caro Baroja, *The World of Witches,* trans. O. N. V. Glendinning (Chicago, 1965).

11. Macfarlane, *Witchcraft in Tudor and Stuart England,* 152–54; Thomas, *Decline of Magic,* 552–64.

12. Some interesting parallel observations on male and female "disorderliness" are made by Natalie Z. Davis: "The defects of the males were thought to stem not so much from nature as from nurture: the ignorance in which they were reared, the brutish quality of life. . . . With the women disorderliness was founded in physiology" (*Society and Culture in Early Modern France,* 124).

Conclusion: New Directions

1. Strauss, *Luther's House of Learning,* 85–107.

2. For an excellent statement of the agenda that lies ahead see John R. Gillis, *Youth and History: Tradition and Change in European Age Relations, 1770–Present* (New York, 1974), 1–35; for earlier work also see the references in Creighton Gilbert, "When Did a Man in the Renaissance Grow Old?" *Studies in the Renaissance* 14 (1967): 7–32.

3. In addition to works already cited in our notes see Edward Shorter, *The Making of the Modern Family* (New York, 1975).

4. We find the treatment of religion in Immanuel Wallerstein, *The Modern World-System: Capitalist Agriculture and the Origins of the European World-Economy in the Sixteenth Century* (New York, 1974), to be suggestive but incomplete as, for example, the equation of religion and nationalism, pp. 206–8. In the second volume, *Mercantilism and the Consolidation of the European World-Economy, 1600–1750* (New York, 1980), Wallerstein almost completely ignores religious issues.

5. Two outstanding examples of the kind of work we have in mind here are Christian, *Person and God,* and Galpern, *Religions of the People in Sixteenth-Century Champagne.*

Index

For individual saints see also the alphabetical list in the Appendix on Sources. In the index the given name of the saint takes precedence.